ASIAN REVOLUTIONARY

The Life of Sen Katayama

Asian Revolutionary

THE LIFE OF SEN KATAYAMA

BY HYMAN KUBLIN

PRINCETON, NEW JERSEY

PRINCETON UNIVERSITY PRESS

1964

L.C. Card: 63-7156

Publication of this book
has been aided by the Ford Foundation Program
to support publication,
through university presses, of work in the
humanities and social sciences.

Printed in the United States of America by
Princeton University Press, Princeton, New Jersey

to Pearl

CONTENTS

Preface ix

Prologue 3

I. THE ANCESTRAL LINE 7

II. THE YOUTHFUL YEARS 15

III. LIFE IN TOKYO 33

IV. STRUGGLE IN AMERICA 47

V. COLLEGE DAYS IN IOWA 60

VI. ANDOVER AND YALE 75

VII. HOME-COMING 88

VIII. LABOR ORGANIZER 105

IX. SOCIALIST AGITATOR 129

X. PACIFISM AND WAR 157

XI. THE LONELY YEARS 184

XII. ONCE MORE AMERICA 213

XIII. THE END OF SOCIALISM 235

XIV. TOWARD BOLSHEVISM 261

XV. WITH THE COMMUNIST INTERNATIONAL 288

XVI. NO FURTHER ROADS 316

Epilogue 337

Selected Bibliography 341

Index 363

PREFACE

Sen Katayama is somewhat distinctive in the history of modern revolution. A rebel from his adolescent years, he devoted his entire adult life of almost half a century to social struggle. His career ultimately mirrored the entire spectrum of social-political radicalism in modern Japan. First upholding Christian Socialism, he gradually shifted his loyalties to Marxism and finally to revolutionary Communism.

Many notable achievements have been ascribed to Katayama. In his home land he is known as a pioneer in the social movement, a founder of professional social work, and a leader of the early trade-union movement. He is also remembered as the editor of Japan's first labor newspaper, as an organizer of his country's initial Social Democratic Party, as Japan's first Bolshevik, and as an active force in the creation of the Japan Communist Party. In the final years of his life he was a member of the Executive Committee and Praesidium of the Communist International.

No really satisfactory biography of Katayama has yet been written. The Japanese revolutionary was a wanderer. About two-thirds of his adult years were spent in the United States, Western Europe, Mexico, and Soviet Russia. To follow his trail during his periods of prominence and obscurity is a staggering and frequently frustrating task. And the prospect of a search for his voluminous writings and personal records, which are scattered about in the libraries, institutions, and private collections of three continents, has been enough to cool the ardor of his most devoted students and admirers.

Probably the most difficult problem in writing a biography of Katayama is to reconstruct the first thirty-five years of his life. Though he prepared an Autobiography covering the period from 1860 to about 1900, it is replete with inaccuracies and gaps. Most of his Japanese biographers have unfortunately been content not only to accept this lengthy document at its face value but also to desist from searching out necessary supplementary materials. This neglect is epitomized by the publication in Japan, on the occasion of the centennial of Katayama's birth, of a two-volume biography which omits the first half of his life!

In my own study of the "father of Asian Communism" I have attempted to give more than usual attention to Katayama's early years as well as to his later and more easily documented political career. This approach reflects not only my own scholarly scruples but my personal "philosophy" of the nature and purpose of biography. By its very etymology biography is the writing of the life of a human being. While due regard must be paid to the historical context in which the life of one's subject unfolds, there is always the danger of forgetting that the tree in the forest is nonetheless a tree.

A second characteristic, which doubtless distinguishes my account of Katayama from most, probably all, other biographical studies, particularly the Japanese and Russian, is that I have no political axe to grind. If I have exploded ideological myths and fabrications which are widely current, I have also sought to accord Katayama his meed of praise. His life, as I have sought to reconstruct it, was sufficiently extraordinary. As a subject of biography he holds, I believe, greater intrinsic interest as he was and not as his political eulogists would prefer him to have been.

A book which has taken so long to complete calls for extensive acknowledgements of assistance. If I do not explicitly express my thanks to all the friends who have helped me, there are, however, some indications of appreciation which I would like to record.

To my wife as well as to Michael and Barbara the name of Katayama has literally become a household word. Three pillars of patience and forbearance, they have heard every word of this book read aloud several times. Responding to a call over and above the requirements of family duty, their excellent suggestions pervade the entire volume.

Among Japanese friends it is with pleasure that I make known the long and steadfast help of Mr. Doi Takuji of Okayama City. Teacher, scholar, and editor, he assisted me in my research for many years. Despite his delicate health, he painstakingly searched for records of Katayama and his family. If much new data about the Japanese revolutionary's ancestors, family, and childhood years are embodied in this biography, the credit is largely his.

I remember also the many courtesies of other friends in Okayama City. Mr. Yoshii Sumi of the Japan-America Cultural Center generously shared with me his wonderfully rich knowledge of the history and lore of the Okayama area. No less memorable was the time passed with Mr. Tsunoda Hisatsune, "the youngest old man in Okayama," who guided me about on the trail of Katayama. And no scholar, and a stranger to boot, could not be touched by the warm hospitality of Katayama's descendants in Hadeki and thereabouts. They kindly permitted me to examine materials on Katayama from their own extensive but unpublished collections.

Of friends elsewhere in Japan I must single out for grateful mention Professor Irimajiri Yoshinaga of Waseda University, my "host associate" during a Fulbright year. At Waseda, too, Professor Toba Kin'ichiro and Professor Kobayashi Masayuki were ceaselessly on the alert for ways and means to advance my research. And Waseda will always enjoy a warm spot in my heart because of its unrivaled policy of international scholarly liaison fostered by President Ohama Nobuo, Dean Nakashima Shoshin, and Dr. Kitazawa Shinjirō, former Dean of the Graduate School of Commerce and currently President of Tokyo Keizai Daigaku.

Still other colleagues in Japan whose aid I valued are Professors Ōkōchi Kazuo and Ōuchi Tsutomu of Tokyo University; Professor Nakamura Kikuo and Mr. Nakamura Katsunori of Keio University; and Mr. Kanō Masamichi. Mr. Nishimura Iwao of the Fulbright Commission in Japan and Mr. Kajita Ichirō of the Exchange of Persons Branch of the American Embassy in Tokyo were also unfailingly solicitous of my many needs.

In the United States I am under heavy obligation to Professor G. L. Thornton, Registrar of Grinnell College. The search which he conducted at my request for records of Katayama not only brought to light much invaluable information but also spared me considerable labor and time. His constant concern to provide me with a full and accurate record I deem an act of rare professional courtesy.

At Brooklyn College I have over the years been strongly encouraged by many of my colleagues. I owe a double measure of thanks to Professor William R. Gaede, Dean of Faculty Emeritus, who was always ready to help a young scholar over the rough spots and to protect him against his own follies. Dr. Harry D. Gideonse, President of the College, Professor Walter S. Mais, Dean of Faculty, and Professor Rex Hopper, Chairman of the College Area Studies Committee, were invariably generous in their allocation of time and resources for my research.

Among scholars at various American universities it is a pleasure to acknowledge the assistance of Dr. Hugh Borton, now President of Haverford College; Professor Ardath Burks of Rutgers; Professor John K. Fairbank of Harvard; Professor Roger Hackett of Michigan; Professor John Hall of Yale; Professor Paul Langer of Southern California; Professor Edwin O. Reischauer of Harvard; and Professor Robert E. Ward of Michigan. Few scholars engaged in research on the Far East in this country have ever been able to escape obligation to Dr. Howard Linton, Director of the East Asian Library at Columbia. Though I troubled him too often, I presumed correctly that our friendship would stand the strain.

For several years my research assistant, Mr. Kil-young Zo, was a source of strength to me. My son Michael was of immense help in the checking of a bibliography that ever threatened to get out of hand. I am deeply appreciative of the assistance of Miss R. Miriam Brokaw and, especially, of Mrs. Polly Hanford of Princeton University Press who did wonders in transforming a bulky manuscript into a book.

The study of Katayama's life has necessitated considerable travel in the United States and Japan. For financial backing and other assistance I must express my heartfelt appreciation to the United States Fulbright Commission which enabled me to spend the academic year 1955-1956 in Japan; to the Carnegie Corporation of New York whose support of Area Studies at Brooklyn College benefited me in countless ways in the pursuit of my research; and to the Social Science Research Council and the American Council of Learned Societies for a grant-in-aid of Asian studies which permitted me to bring this biography to its conclusion.

My final but by no means least hearty profession of gratitude is for Mrs. Gilda Koeppel. From the beginning she not only "adopted" this book and typed the entire manuscript but also gave it the impress of her intelligence and precision. This published volume is my note of thanks to her.

My acknowledgement of the assistance of many institutions, organizations, and individuals should not be construed as involvement of them in responsibility for the facts and opinions presented in this book. If need be, no one but me should be called to account.

July 5, 1963
Brooklyn, New York

HYMAN KUBLIN

ASIAN REVOLUTIONARY

The Life of Sen Katayama

Sen Katayama as a Student
(Grinnell College Yearbook, 1892; courtesy
of Professor G. L. Thornton)

Sen Katayama in Moscow, September 1932
(courtesy of the Reverend Kiyota Jakutan)

PROLOGUE

OLD OKAYAMA

With far less poetic license Japan, the "Land of the Rising Sun," might well have been named Okayama, the "Land of Hills and Mountains." The name Okayama was, however, preempted by one of the southernmost prefectures of Honshu, the main island of the Japanese archipelago. Okayama owes its apt name, thus, not merely to its rugged terrain, which is far from unique in a country where peaks and people exist in superfluity, but also perhaps to oversight of the obvious by other inhabitants of the islands.

Though Japan is physically a land of mountains, the Japanese have culturally been a people of the plains. This has been the result not so much of deliberate choice as of stern necessity, for in the several thousand years that the islands have been inhabited, few real alternatives have been available. The true tragedy of Japan historically is not only that the seas have been so niggardly in surrendering a portion of their realm but also that the mountains have claimed more than their due. From the moment in ancient times when ancestors of the Japanese people introduced the cultivation of rice into the islands, the quest for and possession of level land which could be transformed into paddy field have continued inexorably to shape the history of their descendants. Restricted to flat terrain by the conditions demanded for the production of his staple foodstuff, the Japanese has learned to treasure the plain and to admire the mountain.[1]

Both archaeology and local traditions suggest that one of the first coastal plain areas to be settled and subjected to agricultural production by the ancient peoples of Japan was

[1] For a sensitive discussion of the pervasive influence of the mountains upon Japanese culture, note Donald Keene, *Living Japan; the Land, the People and Their Changing World*, Garden City, New York, 1959, pp. 11-12.

the low land pocket of eastern Okayama. Even today, more than twenty-six hundred legendary years after the event, the inhabitants of Okayama City and its vicinity point to the site where Jimmu, the mythical first Emperor, allegedly tarried during his epochal campaign of conquest from the south.[2] All Japanese school children soon learn, moreover, the ancient name of this area: Kibi no Kuni, or the "Land of Millet," cryptically hints that an early granary arose here, making possible the revolutionary transition from the older hunting and fishing economy.

At some time in the remote past, when opportunities for wresting a livelihood from the soil of the coastal regions had seemingly become marginal, many a desperate or adventurous peasant sought an escape by abandoning "civilization." In Okayama as elsewhere this often meant following the rivers westward into the rapidly rising mountain country of the interior. Here and there, scattered about on river banks and valley floors, small plots of land were to be found, capable at most of providing sustenance for isolated families and their few neighbors. These small and dispersed settlements, too insignificant ever to be graced with the designation *mura*, or "village," have nevertheless persisted through time.

Isolated as he was, the peasant of the Okayama highlands could never escape for long the troublesome touch of war and politics. The historical distinctions among tribal, imperial, and feudal government were lost upon the mountaineer, to whom administrative and military authority was neither good nor bad but rather endurable or intolerable. Government, however it may have been designated, meant to the peasant the deprivation of a greater or lesser portion of his meager crop and he was as stoically resigned to the advent of the tax-collector as he was to the coming of the winter snows. Even during the titanic struggles of the sixteenth

[2] Maruyama Yugehei, *Yuge-machi Shi*, Yuge-machi, Okayama, 1954, p. 10.

century, when the loose and sprawling feudal system was gradually reduced to a draconian order, the outlook of the peasant understandably did not change a whit.

About three and a half centuries ago the feudal lord, Tokugawa Ieyasu, founded the last of the great military dynasties of Japan. Noted less for his military skills than for his political and administrative genius, Ieyasu set himself the task of constructing a governmental system to perpetuate the hegemony of his house. How completely he succeeded is well attested by the fact that the Tokugawa Shogunate, founded in 1603, lasted for two hundred and sixty-five years. So securely did Ieyasu lay the foundations for the political control of Japan by his family and its feudal allies that for two and a half centuries no serious threat to Tokugawa rule was raised.

One of the most important projects undertaken by the Tokugawa Shoguns to ensure the maintenance of a stable political order was the reorganization of the fief system itself.[3] Determined to forestall the concentrations of feudal military and economic power, which alone could bring the Shogunate down in collapse, the earlier Tokugawa rulers regrouped and reduced the domains of friends and foes alike.

In what is today known as the prefecture of Okayama the Tokugawa Shogunate permitted three fiefs to exist.[4] Bizen and Bitchū lay along the lovely Inland Sea, embracing the agriculturally valuable lands as far westward as the mountain country of the interior. Beyond was landlocked but strategically vital Mimisaka, the pivot of rings of fiefs encircling the territories of politically unreliable feudal lords on the coasts to east and west. Only with the downfall of the Shogunate in

[3] A clear exposition of the Tokugawa social and political order will be found in Sir George B. Sansom, *Japan; a Short Cultural History*, New York, 1943, pp. 441ff. For the administrative system of the Shogunate, John Whitney Hall, *Tanuma Okitsugu, 1719-1788, Forerunner of Modern Japan*, Cambridge, Mass., 1955, ch. II, is particularly useful.

[4] See the map in Sanshō-dō Henshū-jo, *Nihon Rekishi Chizu*, Tokyo, 1939, pp. 38-39.

1868 and the consequent administrative reorganization launched by the new imperial government were these three fiefs integrated into the political unit since called Okayama.[5]

It is true that Okayama is young in name but it is also old in history. Its citizens are justly proud of the role their area has played in the affairs of their land from the earliest times to the present. Not the least important reason for their local pride is that Okayama has been the place of birth and the home country of many an eminent individual. It was in Okayama that Sen Katayama was born.

[5] The reorganization of the fiefs and the construction of Okayama Prefecture is clearly presented in Irimajiri Yoshinaga, *Meiji Ishin-shi Kenkyū no Hatten*, Tokyo, 1949, pp. 192-193. Note also Ardath W. Burks, "Administrative Transition from *Han* to *Ken:* the Example of Okayama," *Far Eastern Quarterly*, xv, No. 3 (May 1956), 371-382.

CHAPTER I

THE ANCESTRAL LINE

There are few towns in all Japan which can claim to be the birthplace of a revolutionary of international renown. Yet, with the exception of his direct descendants and family friends, it is doubtful that many of the inhabitants of the sprawling villages around old Hadeki in central Okayama are today more than vaguely familiar with the life and career of Sen Katayama.

Primarily responsible for the obscurity of Katayama in his childhood haunts is the very name by which he is known to social reformers and revolutionaries in many lands. Sen Katayama is not a sobriquet of the type adopted by Communist conspirators and underground agents of recent times; it is a name assumed when he was legally adopted at the age of nineteen by a friend of his family.[1] Shortly thereafter Katayama left his native Hadeki and Okayama, and what few memories of him lingered on were mainly associated with his childhood name.

Katayama was actually born a son of the Yabuki family on January 8, 1860.[2] Though the Yabuki was one of Hadeki's

[1] See p. 29.

[2] There has been a great deal of confusion concerning Katayama's date of birth. In his Introduction to Katayama's *The Labor Movement in Japan*, Chicago, 1918, p. 23, Louis Fraina gives this date as December 7, 1858; this is erroneous. In his *Jiden* (Autobiography), Tokyo, 1954, p. 9, Katayama states that he was born on the seventh day of the twelfth month of the sixth year of the Ansei Era (1859 in the Old Style calendar). The Chronology (*Nempu*) in this work notes, however, that his birth date is recorded in his domiciliary register as the third day of the twelfth month of the sixth year of the Ansei Era. But during his later years in the United States Katayama usually listed his birth date as January 8, 1860 (New Style), which corresponds to December 5, 1859 (Old Style). See, *inter alia*, Andover Theological Seminary, *General Catalogue of the Theological Seminary, Andover, Mass., 1808-1908*, Boston, 1909, p. 484.

Though the compilers of the Chronology in Katayama's *Jiden* have performed a valuable service in pointing out the discrepancy in the Old

oldest and most prominent families, its history and traditions had been blurred by the time of his birth. But according to a belief transmitted in his family for many generations, the Yabuki claimed descent from a retainer of a feudal lord who had founded Hadeki itself about the turn of the seventeenth century. This warrior, it was maintained, had abandoned the military in favor of a rustic life after his superior had been defeated in one of the great battles that foreshadowed the rise of the Tokugawa Shogunate.[3]

It was not until 1650, when the fief of which it was a part was redistributed, that the village of Hadeki was given its corporate name and status.[4] Its population, amounting to thirty households and one hundred and seventy inhabitants in 1689, did not change significantly during the remaining years of the Tokugawa period.[5] At the time of Katayama's birth there were still only thirty households in all Hadeki.

Girdled by rippling hills cut only by a pass through which a narrow road led to the town of Yuge a short distance away, Hadeki always reminded Katayama of the "bottom of a bowl." Save for an infrequent peddler, wandering Buddhist priest, or agent of the feudal government, strangers rarely appeared in the village. For the men of the community, trips into the world beyond the enclosing mountains, even to the castle town of Tsuyama ten miles away, were memorable occasions, and many a citizen of Hadeki never in his entire life traveled more than a day's journey from his home.

The Yabuki farm, which is still in existence and worked by a descendant of the family, hints at its extremely early establishment in the area. Squatting on the fringe of the

---

Style date of his birth, it should also be noted that the Chronology as a whole, which is based upon an uncritical and careless use of the *Jiden,* is incorrect in many places and should be used only with the utmost caution. The chronology reconstructed in this biography has been checked against numerous other source materials.

[3] *Jiden,* p. 15; and Maruyama Yugehei, *Yuge-machi Shi,* Yuge-machi, Okayama, 1954, p. 210.

[4] *ibid.,* p. 151.

[5] *ibid.,* p. 156.

valley, its proximity to the valuable level land used in the cultivation of rice and to the swift-running brook which bisects Hadeki attests to occupation of the locale when opportunity of choice prevailed. Behind the Yabuki homestead, which in Katayama's boyhood comprised an old thatch-roofed main house, fronted by a fairly large garden, and a somewhat smaller but newer outbuilding in which Katayama and his parents lived, undulating terraced strips followed the contour of the slopes almost to the crest of the range of hills separating Hadeki from the valley beyond. The homes of the later settlers are scattered among the paddy fields cut laboriously from the body of the hills.

Most of the valley in which Hadeki lies may be observed in a sweeping glance from the Yabuki farmyard. Slightly to the right, at a lower level than the old Yabuki home, and almost completely surrounded by the fields which cover the trough of the valley is a small grove of *yae-zakura,* or double-petaled cherry trees, whose sudden and ecstatic blooming in the early spring has annually enlivened with delicate tints of white and pink a landscape ordinarily dominated by the green and brown monotones of rice and pine. Several generations of the Yabuki family, including Katayama's mother and older brother,[6] are buried there, the graves marked by the typical weather-beaten, moss-covered stones that may still be seen in cemeteries throughout Japan.

The Yabuki during the eighteenth and early nineteenth centuries were obviously people of prominence and standing in tiny Hadeki. Surviving village records reveal that the elder members of the family frequently served as local headmen.[7] This most important position on the lowest level of officialdom was commonly held by peasants only slightly less poor than their fellow villagers. Among other functions of the headmen

[6] A monument in memory of Katayama was erected in front of this grove by his friends and admirers on the occasion of the centennial of his birth (Old Style). See above, n. 2.

[7] Maruyama, *op.cit.,* p. 210; see also Katayama, *Jiden,* p. 15.

was the preservation of the village records; in his later years Katayama recalled the numerous bundles of musty and dusty manuscripts stored for safekeeping in his childhood home.

One of the first known village headmen of Hadeki and the earliest ancestor of Katayama of whom there is record was Yabuki Kichizaemon.[8] Born in 1745 as perhaps the fifth or sixth generation of descendants in the Yabuki line, he died at about the age of eighty in 1825. His wife, whose name is unknown, was four years younger; she lived to an even more advanced age than her husband, succumbing in 1836. From the available evidence it would appear that the Yabuki were, if not particularly prolific in their progeny, unusually long-lived people. Among Katayama's ancestors and descendants an unusual number of septuagenarians and octogenarians may be noted.

Following Kichizaemon, the line of descent of the Yabuki is not clear for about fifty years. The next scion of whom there is record was a daughter, Noe. Since she was born in 1794, at a time when Kichizaemon and his wife were about forty-nine and forty-five years of age respectively, it is not unlikely that she was their granddaughter and not, as has been sometimes assumed, their daughter.[9] As the heir to the family

[8] The information on his forebears, which Katayama sets forth in his Autobiography, is frequently vague and erroneous and marked by numerous omissions. The genealogy of the Yabuki family, which appears in the following pages, has been reconstructed from data culled from gravestones extant in Hadeki, from entries in the village and Yabuki family records, and from funerary tablets still preserved in the Yabuki household. In piecing together the Yabuki family history, generous and invaluable assistance was provided over a period of several years by Mr. Doi Takuji of Okayama City, a long-time scholar of the history and anthropology of his prefecture. Grateful acknowledgement is also made of the help and cooperation of the descendants of the Katayama and Kiyota families still living in and about Hadeki. For a study of Katayama's family and ancestral village, see Sugiyama Sakae, "Kyōri ni okeru Katayama Sen Shi," *Meiji Bunka Kenkyū*, I (February 1934), pp. 132-134.

[9] This conclusion postulates the existence of a "lost generation" in the Yabuki line, namely the father and mother of Noe. Further research may establish whether she was the daughter or granddaughter of Kichizaemon.

name, perhaps because of the lack of a son, she was married, in keeping with an old Japanese custom, to an "adopted husband." The *yoshi,* or "adopted husband," was required to forsake his own family and name at the time of his marriage and, usually being selected from a family of inferior social and economic status and from the ranks of younger sons with uncertain futures, he was often accorded the treatment of a "poor relation" by his wife's family.

Noe's adopted husband, also named Kichizaemon, was born in 1794. He was Katayama's great-grandfather. Dying in 1876, his exceptional character clearly made a lasting impression upon Katayama, who through the years spoke and thought of his great-grandfather only in terms of love and awe. Not only his great-grandparents but his grandparents were alive and dwelling in the Yabuki home when Katayama was born. Evidently not being fond of his grandparents, Katayama rarely refers to them in his Autobiography. His grandfather Yoshisaburo, born in 1816, was the father of three children. His older daughter, Kichi, was born in 1838 to his first wife; she was Katayama's mother.[10] His younger daughter, Matsu, and his son, Mansaburō, born in 1852, were children of his second marriage. Mansaburō was thus a child of seven when his nephew Katayama was born.[11] The remaining youngster in the Yabuki home was Katayama's older brother Mokutarō who was born in 1856. When Katayama was a child, there were, consequently, four generations of the Yabuki residing in his home.

Far more obscure than his maternal ancestors, in fact completely unknown, are Katayama's paternal predecessors. His father's personal name was Kunizō, though he is also

[10] Katayama calls her Kichiyo, *Jiden,* p. 14, but the editors of the work note, also on p. 14, that her name is given in the village records simply as Kichi. The second daughter, Matsu, who was Katayama's aunt, was married at an early age and "lost" to the Yabuki family.

[11] See Doi Takuji, "Katayama Sen no Tegami," *Okayama Shunjū,* VII, no. 6 (July 20, 1957), 27, 4.

referred to as Kunihei in the village records at Hadeki.[12] His surname Koyō was derived from his family's village, located a few miles from Hadeki on the road to the castle town of Tsuyama. At the age of about fifteen Kunizō left Koyō-mura to marry the slightly younger Kichi and to take up his abode in the Yabuki home as a *yoshi.* That he was deemed acceptable to the socially proud Yabuki suggests that he was more than a mere peasant lad with an amiable disposition and a strong back.

Why the Yabuki thought it necessary to secure a *yoshi* for the daughter of the family may, in the absence of specific evidence, only be conjectured. It is clear that, until the birth of Mansaburō, Kichi and Matsu were the only children in the family; their marriage into other houses would obviously have posed the Yabuki elders with the serious problem of arranging for a suitable heir.[13] During the many years when he did not have a son who would ultimately carry on the family name and inherit the family property, it is most probable that Yoshisaburō had planned to adopt a husband for Kichi as soon as she was of marriageable age. And, though early marriages are not uncommon in peasant societies, that Kichi was wedded before she had reached her fifteenth year suggests the Yabuki concern, if not desperation, for a male heir.

From all indications Kichi and Kunizō were a happy and devoted couple. After several years of marriage they became the parents of two sons. The birth of Mokutarō in 1856 gladdened the hearts of the entire Yabuki family, even if it did complicate the problem of dividing the inheritance. Less than four years later the arrival of Sugatarō, the future Sen Katayama, was greeted, we are told, with deep disappoint-

[12] Though Katayama calls his father Kunizō, *Jiden,* p. 14, the editors of the *Jiden,* p. 14, indicate that the name Kunihei is entered in the village records.

[13] This conclusion assumes that Matsu may not have been much younger than Kichi.

ment by a family hoping for the birth of a daughter. Katayama's personality and the course of his life were influenced in countless ways because he was born an unwelcome second son. Though it is not necessary to accept seriously many of his later allegations of family favoritism toward the older Mansaburō and Mokutarō, since the play of a normal sibling rivalry may be assumed, it is indisputable that in fundamental family matters Katayama was not treated so generously as his brother and young uncle. Long after he had achieved adulthood and an unusually dispassionate understanding of himself, he always recalled that he had not been fairly dealt with in his youthful years.[14] If he retained a sentimental attachment for Hadeki, the village of his childhood, Katayama's memories of his Yabuki forebears were as often as not tinged with a sense of grievance.

Even more traumatic than the realization that he was an unwanted child was the "loss" of his father: Kunizō, tragically caught in a bitter family quarrel, was compelled to dissolve his marriage ties with Kichi. In his Autobiography Katayama states that his paternal grandfather appeared one day at the Yabuki home and, after a furious quarrel, ordered Kunizō to return to his family in Koyō-mura.[15] All the other details he records are probably irrelevant. Since Katayama himself was only a child at the time and could not have remembered the scene, his commentary is largely sentimental.[16] The true cause of the unfortunate affair will most likely never be entirely known.

[14] Even today many Japanese assume that a younger son will not be accorded the preferential treatment reserved for the heir to the family name. When I discussed the problem of Katayama's complaint with his relatives in September 1960, I was assured that Katayama had been dealt with no differently from most younger children.

[15] *Jiden*, p. 14.

[16] In the Chronology of the *Jiden*, p. 337, the separation of Kunizō and Kichi is dated 1861 when Katayama was three years old (Japanese Style). But since Katayama dates some of his recollections of his father to when he was about four, it would seem more likely that the enforced estrangement occurred about 1864.

The dissolution of the marriage of Katayama's parents may perhaps best be explained by the decisions reached by the Yabuki on the legal succession to the family name and the disposition of the ancestral property. Whatever promises may have been made at the time of Kunizō's adoption, it is possible that Yoshisaburō's misgivings increased as his own son grew older. Then came the crucial moment when it was finally decided to establish the legal succession in Mansaburō. Though the interests of Kichi and her older son, Mokutarō, but not of Katayama, were to some extent cared for in the division of the Yabuki patrimony, it is possible that the settlement, unsatisfactory to the Koyō, was responsible for arousing their wrath. Since no particular advantage had accrued to Kunizō, the Koyō family was probably left with no face-saving alternative but denouncement of the adoption agreement.

The tragic denouement of Kichi's marriage affected three lives in particular. Sugatarō, as a fatherless younger son denied a share of the family property, was to learn before he reached early manhood that his principal tie with the Yabuki line was only the fragile thread of a surname.[17] For Kichi the enforced separation from her husband meant the sudden termination of her youth and womanhood. Even had she so desired, it would have been extremely difficult for her family to arrange a new marriage. With the departure of Kunizō from Hadeki in 1864 Kichi thereafter lived only for the sake of her unfortunate children.[18]

[17] The few years spent in the Yabuki household were for Kunizō a sad interlude in a life which could, however, still be repaired. Following his return to his native village, he shaved his pate, donned the cowl of a Buddhist priest, and for the remaining years of his long life was known as Jakusen. His monastic order not being celibate, he married again. Jakusen's three sons and one daughter by his second wife were the half-brothers and sister of Sen Katayama. Several of their principal descendants, with family names of Kiyota and Mizuno respectively, are living today not far from Hadeki.

CHAPTER II

THE YOUTHFUL YEARS

Katayama grew into manhood during some of the most exciting and fateful years in the entire history of his country. Like most youngsters of his day he was oblivious to the import of the revolutionary events which were thrusting a simultaneously protesting and acquiescent Japan into a completely new historical era. But though he may have been unable to fathom the meaning of the epochal occurrences, nevertheless they formed the social matrix in which his subsequent life was molded. Had he been born but a single generation before, he would in all probability have lived out his allotted span totally undifferentiated from the vast and amorphous mass of peasants dwelling in the ten thousand and one villages of Japan. Coming into the world when he did, however, he was given the novel, if slender, opportunity to escape from the fetters which bound the peasantry of his native land to social anonymity and to become all that the name Sen Katayama has signified to his descendent countrymen.

The most significant change during Katayama's boyhood was the disintegration of the old social and political order. By the middle of the nineteenth century the inability of the peasants of Japan to fulfill the insatiable demands of their feudal masters had become unmistakably evident. Grave as the economic situation had been for years, however, it became politically explosive only when an increasingly large part of the dominant warrior class itself began to share the destitution which had become the normal lot of the great mass of the peasantry. To add to the political discomfort of the Shogunate, power-hungry feudal bureaucrats, leagued with economically ambitious members of the rural gentry, no longer hesitated to express their dissatisfaction and resentment over the patently outmoded laws of the land. When the disgruntled military élite of Tokugawa society started to turn against the social order that had been maintained for its own advantage, the remaining days of the Shogunate were numbered.

The peasants were ignorant of these events. Having troubles enough of their own, they had never concerned themselves with affairs of state. Politics was, even more than a neighbor's fields, an inviolable area into which peasants were careful not to trespass. When utter desperation drove them to stage uprisings, as happened frequently during the final century of Tokugawa rule, their aims were usually to secure measures of immediate relief and not to compel alteration of the established order. Thus both in fiefs like Mimisaka, where the administration of the local daimyo was reasonably moderate,[1] and in other feudal realms, where government was mercilessly oppressive, the peasants were by and large quiescent during the decline of the Shogunate. The principal symptom of widespread political and social unrest was the haphazard appearance in the villages of wandering *ronin* in search of employment, adventure, or a meal.

Katayama, who was not yet nine years old when the Tokugawa regime was finally overthrown, was understandably unconcerned with the news of social and military turbulence which was borne to Hadeki. In the same way that life in his village continued for some time to function in accordance with traditional and respected ways, his world remained bounded by the limited horizons of the child. What existed or occurred in the Yabuki household or in the cottages of his village was alone of any consequence and more than this he did not want or seek.

[1] Katayama himself has testified that the fief in which Hadeki was situated, being part of the Shogun's domain, was for all practical purposes self-governing. Tax assessments in his native village, he also states, were comparatively light. Katayama Sen, *Jiden*, Tokyo, 1954, pp. 10-11.

In every childish universe there is a lodestar; in Katayama's boyhood years it was his mother. Having in infancy been denied a father, he was drawn into an unusually close relationship with Kichi. It was she above all who molded his personality and shaped the man who was her son. When she, like all Japanese mothers, trussed her younger son upon her back and patiently bore him about like a king on his throne, she in essence tied him to her for the remaining years of his life. And when she fed, fondled, and generally cared for her child, lavishing upon him an extra measure of devotion in silent atonement for his fatherless plight, no one could thereafter aspire to challenge successfully her primacy of position in his scheme of love. The injunctions of Neo-Confucian moral codes, drummed incessantly into his ears during his youth, demanded priority of respect for the male head of the Yabuki family but they could really never contend against the pristine emotional attachment between Kichi and her son. In his adult years Katayama recalled vividly his fright, which at times approached sheer hysteria, whenever he was physically separated from Kichi for more than a brief spell.[2]

For about a decade after Katayama's birth there were no strong young men in the Yabuki household and a goodly part of the family work fell upon Kichi's shoulders. It was, accordingly, exceedingly difficult for her to pay undivided attention to her children. During the planting and harvest seasons, the particularly busy months of the year, Katayama was taken to the rice paddies where he was tended by Mansaburō and Mokutarō. At other times, when Kichi and her father alone had to look after the crops, he was left at home in the care of his grandmother and, after Mansaburō was married, of his aunt.[3] As a result, he gradually became aware of his excessive association with the women of his family. In the

[2] *ibid.*, p. 17.

[3] In speaking of his aunt, Katayama probably meant Matsu, Kichi's sister.

full maturity of adulthood he did not hesitate, in analyzing the development of his own personality, to point to the powerful feminine influences of his childhood. "Too often," he confessed, "I was in the company of women."[4]

The image of himself as a child, set down by Katayama in his Autobiography, is that of an excessively shy and timid boy. Dominated by so many older members of the family, he sought attention and comfort from the few sympathetic and indulgent women of the household. Overly anxious for assurance and solicitude, he was pathetically reluctant to chance rebuff and possible failure and turned, accordingly, in moments of need to the tried and reliable figures of the family. Ecstatically happy when he was surrounded by friendly and familiar faces, he actually quailed and trembled before the strange and unknown in people and experiences. Yearning for human companionship and longing to share in the activities of others, he nevertheless resigned himself at too early an age to inevitable rejection. He was a lonely child.

It is a revealing commentary upon the nature of his childhood years that Katayama later spoke about few people in terms of endearment. But being a kindly, warm-hearted, and even timorous person, he was averse to leveling sharp and explicit reproof against those he believed had wronged him. Still his terse characterizations and his very silence, particularly about his familial relations, testify more eloquently than verbal censure to his deeply felt sense of grievance and neglect. For his father he never displayed more than a polite but odd lack of curiosity.[5] And apart from his doughty but

[4] *Jiden,* p. 17. This state of affairs in his youth is in sharp contrast to his adult life when he doubtless suffered from a lack of female companionship.

[5] Katayama has stated that he acquired a dislike for Buddhist temples and priests at an early age. Though there were probably various reasons for this antipathy, it cannot but occur to students of his early life that he unconsciously associated Buddhist establishments with the father he resented. It was not until he was about "fifteen or sixteen years old," he recalled, that he visited his father for the first time after his departure from the Yabuki home. See *Jiden,* p. 14.

aged great-grandfather, toward whom his sentiments were those of respect and admiration rather than fondness and friendliness, he could discourse with touching affection only about his mother.

If Katayama was consciously aware of his lack of love for the members of the Yabuki family, he was also firmly convinced that he himself had no hold upon their hearts. "Only my mother," he recalled appreciatively but bitterly, "loved me."[6] But, though he strove to monopolize Kichi's affection, it is clear that he was constantly disturbed by the presence of another contender for his mother's love. Conventional as it is to idealize the pattern of family relations in Japan, the system being more often than not described from the vantage of philosophy and rarely of psychology, the fact remains that the Yabuki household was not free from domestic tensions and antagonisms. Between Katayama, on the one hand, and the slightly older Mokutarō and Mansaburō, on the other, there existed a constantly smoldering, and at times overt, rivalry. Katayama did not cease to voice one complaint after another of blatant favoritism toward the other boys of the family.

Katayama's childhood years were by no means an unbroken sequence of trials and problems. From a time probably earlier than he could remember he learned to love the cyclical unfolding of the seasons and to look forward with eagerness to the regularly varied offerings of a bountiful nature. The advent of spring was a particularly gay and festive occasion. Before the snows of winter, which had only a few short weeks earlier blanketed the land with an argent covering as far as the eye could see, had completely melted under the ever warmer sun, all the men, women, and children of the village turned out to share in the joy of preparing the fields for the crops which promised food for the coming year. And while the men, happy to unlimber their muscles after the

[6] *ibid.*, p. 17.

many months of winter idleness, guided the heavy-jointed ploughs drawn by patient and undersized oxen back and forth across the narrow paddy strips, the women nursed the baby rice plants in the shimmering seedbeds. When finally each clump and clod had been broken and the soil had been smoothed by harrow and invigorated by fertilizer, the sluices were opened to flood the paddy fields with life-giving water.

Once the earth had been readied, the fields became the domain of the women. With several households working cooperatively the young rice shoots were now carried from their seedbeds and planted in the rich and viscous muck in straight and even rows plotted with geometrical precision by marker lines. Not even the early spring water could chill the spirits of the peasant women to whom the ritualistic impregnation of the earth was pleasureful and sacred. And so with kimono skirts tucked into the sashes about their midriffs and with sleeves tied back to elbow-length, they advanced slowly and in unison through the paddy plots, all the while chanting melodies of the planting season older than the village itself as with firm and confident motion they thrust the seedlings into the soil. When the sowing of the rice was finally completed, the fortune and fate of the village were entrusted to the mighty and mysterious powers of nature and its *kami.*

With mingled feelings of satisfaction and regret the villagers brought to a close the spring ritual of the planting of the rice. During the following weeks and months the routine of labor on the tiny farms followed a methodical, if monotonous, course. While husbands kept a watchful eye upon the budding plants and carefully regulated the flow of nourishing water, the women and children regularly visited the fields to nip the nascent weeds which flourished in the rich paddy soil. And as the cool and refreshing breezes of the spring slowly disappeared, to be followed by the humid "plum-blossom" rains of June and the mellowing heat of the deep summer sun, the young boys like Katayama dutifully but fretfully continued to tend the fields where the once-green rice-plants had turned into a soft and golden tan. A growing season had come to an end; there now remained only the work of reaping the crop.

Like the opening of the planting season the harvesting of the crops was a gala event in which every member of the village households participated. After the ripe rice plants had been cut with sharp hand sickles and dried in sheaves upon the wooden trestles which meandered throughout the fields, the customary stillness of the countryside was soon broken by the rustling and whisking and pounding which signified to the ears of every farmer that the threshing and winnowing of the rice grain was under way. And, as in the earlier days of the spring, when the ground had been broken after its long winter rest, the mood of the peasants could be sensed in the songs whose lyrics revealed undertones of supplication and cajolery of the Shinto gods, the melodies of the fall harvest were marked by notes of praise and thanksgiving. In solemn gratitude the first fruits were offered on the altars of homes and shrines and served to family and friends joined together to celebrate the gift of the land.

For a young boy in a Japanese mountain village the fall season was especially welcome. With no regular chores to be performed in the fields and around the home, the slopes and woods extended a standing invitation to sport and frolic. Katayama always clearly recalled the occasional family picnics in the cool retreats in the hills around Hadeki and the exciting searches for flowers, mushrooms, and herbs to embellish both the home and the family table. But perhaps most memorable in a country boy's life was the sense of awe and literal rapture evoked by the magnificent *momiji* during the all too brief span of a month or so when the myriad leaves of the maple trees changed from day to day into resplendent splashes of red and yellow, orange and tan. Once having viewed the "changing of the colors" in the fall, every Japanese was thereafter a humble votary of nature and its powers.

When deciduous leaves started to flutter to the ground and the brisk breezes began to give way to lacerating winds, the mountain villagers grimly resigned themselves to the onset of winter. It was the season above all which lent itself to poetical description and nostalgic memory but not to actual living. For with the successive falls of the snow the familiar landmarks of mountain and valley were gradually obliterated and the scattered cottages became so many isolated islands in a boundless icy waste. No other period of the year has perhaps ever taxed so heavily the almost limitless capacity of the Japanese for sublimation of misery than the wintry season of the interior highlands.

Katayama was no stranger to the cycle of Japanese peasant life. Through the years from infancy until he was a young man he continuously absorbed the customs, ways, and attitudes of Hadeki's rural environment and inhabitants. So penetrating were the impressions of his youth that, while his thought and values were later altered by the influences of new experiences, his behavior, personality, and temperament were to prove resistant to change. To his dying day he was never able nor, for that matter, did he ever seek to forget that he had been born and raised a country boy. At any moment of his life, regardless of his immediate fortune, he was always ready to state with utter candor, "I am a simple and unsophisticated person. I was, you see, brought up as a peasant."[7]

Katayama might well have passed his entire life as an obscure peasant in one or another of the many hamlets in the mountains of Okayama. At the very moment, however, when he was enjoying his eighth birthday, a train of historical events, presenting him with opportunities for social advancement categorically withheld from antecedent generations of

[7] Note the comments in *Jiden*, p. 3.

his family and countrymen, was being set in full motion. On the evening of January 3, 1868, a small group of desperate daimyo and samurai, court nobles and Shogunal officials, were commencing negotiations in the Imperial Palace at Kyoto to determine the fate of the Tokugawa regime. Three days later, after persuasion, arguments, and threats had been exhausted, the war for the restoration of the Emperor as *de facto* sovereign of his realm opened. By the spring of 1868 the young Meiji Emperor, in possession of the military and civil powers usurped by warrior-dynasts almost seven centuries before, sat with dignity upon a throne he was to occupy for the next forty-five years. The Meiji period, the era of Japan's transition to a modern state and world power, had begun.

With the completion of the Meiji Restoration the small and tightly-knit clique of young samurai and court nobles, who had engineered the successful revolt against the Tokugawa Shogunate, was not long in formulating the basic policies of the new political order. To consolidate their power and to fulfill their personal ambitions, to protect the precarious independence of their country against potential imperialistic aggression, and to satisfy the demands of their nationalistic pride, the ruling oligarchy soon set its sights upon the political targets of centralization and modernization of the Meiji state and society. And no matter what differences they may otherwise have had, the leaders of the Meiji government devoted the remainder of their lives and careers to the task of bringing Japan apace of the great nations of the world.

In the thousands of towns and villages in Japan the direct impact of the Meiji reforms was not felt for many years. Katayama himself has testified that, apart from the radical transformation in the traditional land and tax system, life in Hadeki was scarcely modified from the pattern of Tokugawa days. It is nevertheless apparent that the early Meiji government, by striking down many of the feudal proscriptions, extended tremendously the range of opportunities and possibilities for alteration of customary modes of living.

Katayama, who was a boy at the time of the Meiji Restoration, discovered the momentous event only in the retrospect of his adult age. If the first year of the Meiji era remained indelibly fixed in his memory, it was not because of the transfer of the imperial capital from Kyoto to Tokyo but rather because of the death of his great-grandmother whom he had idolized since infancy. The years immediately before and after the overthrow of the Tokugawa Shogunate were also memorable for Katayama, since they marked the beginning of his quest for an education that was to be carried on intermittently for almost three decades. His mother's decision to send him to school was of inestimable consequence: by the time little more than half the Meiji period had run its course he, the scorned and fatherless youngster of the Yabuki family, had acquired the most advanced education ever known to a citizen of Hadeki.

Katayama's schooling began when he was "seven or eight years old." Since public education facilities were not introduced in Japan before the early Meiji period, it was necessary for Katayama to receive instruction from private tutors or to attend various *terakoya*, the Buddhist temple schools which were commonly available but not heavily attended in the rural areas of the country. The course of study was narrowly "classical," the children usually being taught the *i-ro-ha*, the native syllabary composed of forty-eight simple symbols, the far more intricate Chinese characters which were the essence of writing and literature, and the Confucian classics which were highly extolled during the Tokugawa era. It may in all fairness be said that in no other land have students been posed with so overwhelming an educational challenge as in China and its literary satellites, Japan and Korea.[8]

[8] On the Tokugawa educational system see Ronald S. Anderson, *Japan, Three Epochs of Modern Education*, Washington, D.C., 1959, pp. 2-4.

Katayama was not a gifted and energetic pupil. Like many children he was both bored and baffled by the complexities of Chinese characters and was ever on the alert for opportunities to shirk his lessons and to discover more interesting diversions. When he tired of practicing his calligraphy, as he quickly did, he turned his hand to sketching pictures, daydreaming, and listening to the shouts of children at play on the temple grounds. And no sooner had his teacher, usually a benign and patient Buddhist bonze, discontinued his lesson in order to perform a religious service in the neighborhood than Katayama had sought out a boyish acolyte or the temple caretaker with whom games could be played and tales exchanged. It is little wonder that his mother, disappointed with his progress, transferred him to several different schools within the space of a few years, apparently believing that it was the school and not the pupil that needed improvement.

Katayama's lackluster record in the *terakoya* around Hadeki may be attributed partly to the texts he was required to learn. The Chinese classics are difficult enough for intelligent adult minds; for children and adolescents to make their way through the Confucian writings unusual precocity and tenacity have ever been necessary. Reflecting upon Katayama's years in the *terakoya,* it cannot but occur to students of his life that he may have attempted, consciously or otherwise, to fail his lessons. Compelled to live away from home for days and weeks on end, he was lonely and depressed by the pervading silence and gloom of the isolated Buddhist temples and could scarcely wait for the infrequent vacation which permitted him to return to Hadeki and his mother. Katayama has suggested that *terakoya* life gave his personality a lasting stamp of melancholy and moodiness. Once he was home and in familiar surroundings again, he did not cease badgering his mother to withdraw him from school. Kichi, however, understanding that an education offered her younger son the only escape from a future life as a poverty-stricken, landless peasant, refused to listen to his pleas and sent him back to his Buddhist teachers with unfailing words of encouragement.

Katayama did not acquire his zest for education and knowledge until he was fourteen years old. In 1874, when a government-established primary school was opened nearby, the people of Hadeki were provided with concrete evidence that the new Meiji state was intent upon the alteration of the traditional order. None of the villagers had confidence in the new kind of school, and Katayama, who was held in no high esteem, was induced to enroll and thereby uphold the "face" of Hadeki. Though he attended the government primary school for only a few months, graduating in November 1874, Katayama was so enthusiastic about the new methods of instruction used by his teachers and so strongly impressed by the departures from the only curriculum he had ever known that education was thereafter one of the most powerful purposes of his life.[9]

Ironically enough, at the very time Katayama awakened to the delights of learning, he found it necessary to discontinue his schooling. The Yabuki family, which had for many generations been one of the better-to-do families in Hadeki, met hard and lean days. The once compact household began to disintegrate: as the older members of the family died, the younger scions lost no time in dividing the family patrimony. There was now no question of Katayama spending his days in the classrooms of country schools, for his strength was needed to till his mother's fields. With his dreams and hopes for a future different from that of his ancestors stifled, he had no alternative but to settle down to the life of a toiling peasant.

Until Katayama's fifteenth year, he had undertaken the

[9] I have a photographic copy of Katayama's certificate of graduation from this government primary school. Dated November 30, 1874 (New Style), it notes that Yabuki Sugatarō (Katayama) was at the time fourteen years and eleven months old.

chores on the family farm as a welcome diversion. Now he learned, as never before, what it meant to face the beginning of each day in the chill air of a mountain dawn, and to labor ceaselessly, body drenched with sweat, under the baking heat and glare of the overhead sun. And now as he worked with ox, plough, and mattock, his body not yet inured to the stabbing aches and pains and waves of fatigue, he recalled how he had but a short time before begged the Yabuki elders for the privilege of performing these laborious tasks. Having tasted, moreover, the less exacting way of the student, he fervently vowed to resume his education when an opportunity offered itself.

Refusal to resign himself to a life of toil and drudgery upon the land was unquestionably the most important decision made by Katayama during his adolescent years. He availed himself of every chance for self-study. In the evenings and during long periods of enforced idleness, he attempted as best he could to master the contents of what few books could be found in his home and in the village. What was important was not the knowledge he imbibed, for with the innumerable handicaps he faced he could really make little progress, but rather the fact that his hopes were kept alive. If he would not surrender to his frustration, neither would he permit himself to be discouraged by the derision of the villagers of Hadeki, to whom his aspirations for an education were deemed the unbecoming vanity and folly of a presumptuous country boy.

In the memories of a lifetime, events unfold fleetingly and impressionistically as in a moving picture. There are, however, a few distinct images which for all the passage of time remain clearly and vividly engraved upon the screen of the mind, fixed with all the sharpness and clarity of a photographic still. In Katayama's album of pictorial memories there was one incident in particular which was never to fade. No matter how distant in time the episode may have become, he could always see himself trudging along through a heavy winter snowfall, back bent under a heavy and bulky load of charcoal, with sweat and steam oozing from every pore of his aching body. Suddenly, as he was passing by a village school, the sounds of the classroom struck his ears and, when he stopped to listen, the scene was recorded by the camera of his mind. In that same instant when he felt the cutting pang of envy, he swore that no sacrifice would ever be too great to deter him from securing an education.[10]

Now that he was approaching manhood, Katayama grimly realized that he could no longer, if he were to escape a drab and unpromising fate, continue to dabble in his studies. He now lived only for those hours when the day's work had been done and he could turn uninterruptedly to his studies. Poring over the classics of Confucianism, absorbing with increasing satisfaction and appreciation the superbly beautiful Chinese characters, striving endlessly to perfect his calligraphy, and testing the art of Chinese and Japanese poetry, his steady progress was marked by a new and respectful attitude on the part of the once jeering villagers. No longer pitied for his junior and fatherless status, no longer mocked for his ambitions, Katayama was fast becoming the model and the pride of Hadeki.

Having acquired the rudiments of an education, Katayama was finally able at about the age of eighteen to take a major step in breaking away from a peasant's life. Knowing the Japanese syllabary, or *kana,* familiar with Chinese characters, and having some knowledge of the introductory works of Confucianism, he was successful in receiving an appointment as a teacher in the primary school at Yuge, a rather large town not far from Hadeki. His experience in his first teaching position as well as at the Uetsuki primary school, to which he transferred in the following year, convincingly demonstrated to him the inadequacies of his own training, however,

[10] *Jiden,* p. 70.

and he decided to undertake more formal and advanced studies. For the moment at least he was determined to pursue a career in primary school teaching.

Katayama's carefully considered plans for a teaching future were quickly threatened with disaster. Having reached the age of eighteen, he was, being a younger son and possessing no special claim for exemption, liable to conscription into the imperial military forces. Whether or not he would actually have been drafted into the new national army to serve for the two years required by the Conscription Law of 1872 is not known. Still, Yabuki Kichi, like many a peasant parent of the times, was not too happy about the opportunity extended to her robust son to become a successor to the vanishing samurai, and she hastened to take advantage of the loopholes in the military law. Since oldest sons and heirs of a family name were specifically excluded from the operation of the conscription regulations, she decided to arrange for her boy's adoption as the son of Katayama Ikutarō, a peasant of the nearby village of Shimo-Kamime. The arrangement was purely legal, for though Yabuki Sugatarō now officially became Sen Katayama, his relationships with his adopted father were nominal. By this action Katayama not only escaped induction into the army but also severed his legal connection with the family of his birth.

Having successfully circumvented military conscription, Katayama pushed forward with his preparations for further education. His coveted goal was admission to the Normal School, which had been established a few years before in Okayama City.[11] Entrance to the school, which boasted a modern curriculum and pedagogy, was by competitive examination in which hundreds of applicants from Okayama Prefecture participated. Again he concentrated upon his studies

[11] For the establishment and development of Okayama Normal School see Okayama-shi Kyōiku Iin-kai, *Okayama no Ayumi*, Okayama City, 1956, p. 227.

and, when announcement was made of the successful candidates, Katayama's name was near the top of the list.

Okayama City was only a long day's walk from Hadeki but, when Katayama arrived in the provincial capital in the early fall of 1880, it was as if he had stepped into a completely new world. Like most Japanese peasants, save perhaps the fortunate few who had undertaken a pilgrimage to a famous Shinto shrine or Buddhist center, he had probably never traveled more than ten miles distance from his ancestral home. Now he caught his first glimpse, in the forbidding castle of Okayama, in the magnificent *yashiki* of bygone daimyo, and in the lovely parks and gardens of the former feudal lords, of the might and splendor of the old Tokugawa order. Here, too, in Okayama City he viewed for the first time the physical evidences of Japan's new modern state and observed the strange "barbarians," from overseas, the Westerners who had settled in the city to preach the gospel of Christianity.[12]

For Katayama the Okayama Normal School was as refreshingly invigorating as the local primary school which had originally aroused his enthusiasm for education. Though the traditional curriculum of Chinese studies was not neglected, the government school also provided instruction in such modern subjects as arithmetic and geography, courses in which he was particularly interested. He was a superior student at the normal school, not because he was intellectually better endowed than his schoolmates but because he was more mature. It may be said, using modern pedagogical jargon, that he worked "to his maximum," pouring over his books, in defiance of the "lights-out" regulations of the school, until far into the night. On more than one occasion his routine of study, abetted perhaps by the inadequate fare served by the school, brought on attacks of fainting and "night-blindness,"

[12] One of the earliest Protestant missions in Japan was established in Okayama.

the first of the many student maladies from which he was to suffer.[13] But, though he was initially terrified by these ailments, he persisted in making draconian demands upon his body and mind.

At the Okayama Normal School Katayama was thrown in with a group of young men whose very presence signified that their ambitions transcended the ordinary and the traditional. Coming from the widely scattered towns and villages of south Japan, they were to receive and then to diffuse modern education in areas remote from the great political and cultural centers. Though few of these students became men of outstanding achievement, they constituted the pioneering younger generation and lower echelon of community leaders upon whose contributions the construction of a modern Japanese state and society depended.[14]

Whether it was as the result of a daring but idle pledge uttered in response to the challenge of a classmate, or the growing perception that the Okayama Normal School could never satisfy his academic yearnings, or a dawning fear that graduation would necessitate a return to a life both dull and tasteless, we shall never completely know. But it is certain that with each passing month in Okayama City Katayama became ever more restive and dubious about the worth of the ambition that had led him to leave home. By the time the school year had come to a close in the summer of 1881 he had decided to follow the lead of his bolder classmates and to transfer the site of his studies to the capital city of the land.

It is noteworthy that, in commenting upon his own nature, Katayama always felt constrained to insist that he was extremely shy, cautious, and patient. But it is clear from a consideration of his youthful years that he was unusually im-

[13] *Jiden,* p. 83.

[14] One of the most famous students of the Okayama school system was Kishi Nobusuke, Prime Minister of Japan from 1957-1960. See Dan Kurzman, *Kishi and Japan: The Search for the Sun,* New York, 1960, pp. 74-75.

pulsive, even if he acted upon his sudden inspirations only after the most careful deliberation. Thus, when he returned to Hadeki to announce his decision to go to Tokyo, the villagers were more astounded than surprised. They had long since learned to expect the unpredictable from Katayama.

CHAPTER III

LIFE IN TOKYO

In 1868, before the Imperial Restoration was completed, the capital of Japan was transferred from Kyoto, the home of emperors for more than a thousand years, to Edo in the east. Forthwith renamed Tokyo, the new seat of the central government exerted a magnetic attraction upon the people of the entire nation. For Tokyo, the "Eastern Capital," became the symbol not only of power and wealth but also of the new Japan itself.

During the centuries of Tokugawa rule a stream of people had flowed uninterruptedly toward the sprawling metropolis at the head of Edo Bay. Haughty feudal lords in magnificent array, galloping messengers from the castle towns, strutting *ronin* in their shabby attire, agents of the rice and money-exchange brokers of Osaka, merchants in search of business and a lark, mendicant priests of the far-flung Buddhist sects, artisans and peasants from remote cities and villages, all traveled the highways that terminated in the Shogun's capital. Castles, temples, and shrines—the monuments and vestiges of history, faith, and tradition—never failed to attract visitors and pilgrims to other parts of Japan, but Edo possessed an irresistible materialistic and sensual lure. Those in search of overpowering splendor were proverbially enjoined to "see Nikko and die" but many Japanese preferred to "see Edo and live."

With the overthrow of the Tokugawa the tide of travelers bound for Tokyo soon reached unprecedented proportions. As the new government pressed forward with its programs to create a modern centralized state, it simultaneously attacked the restrictive institutions and practices inherited from the defunct Shogunate. With the relaxation of the police controls and the elimination of the strategically established roadblocks and check-points, the Japanese were able as never before to roam about and see their own land. If many of them now flocked "up to the capital," it was not merely because the brothels and geisha houses, the theaters and fleshpots, beckoned. Perhaps more importantly, Tokyo, the new center of national life, offered seemingly boundless opportunities for the ambitious and the adventurous.

In the fall of 1881 Katayama joined the throng of young men thirsting for fame, fortune, or learning in the nation's capital. When he recounts in his Autobiography the circumstances which finally prompted him to leave home and family for the unknown world of Tokyo, Katayama dates the birth of the idea to his Okayama Normal School days.[1] There is no reason to dispute this assertion. But sensitively aware of his status as a younger and fatherless son and constantly stung by the taunts and jibes of the villagers of Hadeki, he understood at an even earlier time that his hope for the future lay only in a break with the past.[2]

Katayama's journey from Okayama to Tokyo was a memorable experience. Within the space of a few days he was, insofar as his exposure to transportation technology is concerned, literally catapulted through several centuries in time. Having made the trip from Hadeki to Okayama on foot, he boarded a small steamer on the Moji-Kobe run, his cheapest of fares providing an uncomfortable berth atop a pile of cargo on an open deck. After a day's stop-over in Kobe, where his first sight of a railroad train convinced him that the pictures he had seen in books had not been the product of an artist's fantasy, he continued his voyage to Tokyo by coastal steamer. Most exciting, however, was the short dash from Yokohama to Shimbashi Station in Tokyo on the first railway built in Japan.[3]

[1] Katayama Sen, *Jiden,* Tokyo, 1952, p. 83.
[2] *Jiden,* p. 84.
[3] Thomas C. Smith, *Political Change and Industrial Development in Japan,* Stanford, 1955, p. 43.

The harsh reality of Katayama's new life was not long in making its weight felt. With his money exhausted by his trip and with his living accommodations reduced to the level of the poorest of laborers, he simply could not afford the rich fare of learning. Board and room, room and board! They were to become the penalty and price of Katayama's existence. Here in Tokyo began his almost endless cycle of living in cheap boarding-houses and in bare and gloomy garrets. Here started that calendar of life with its months and years marked by dates of arrival and departure, by packing and unpacking, and by expressions of greeting and farewell. A transient in Tokyo and, later, in the world beyond, Katayama rarely had an address he could really call his own.

Elemental survival having a prior lien upon his time, Katayama accepted with alacrity the first job that came his way. When he went to work at the *Sekibun-sha,* a printing establishment in down-town Tokyo, he was initiated into the life of the proletarian. Being a novice at the printing craft and with only his tractability and industriousness to commend him, Katayama was both apprentice and worker. He was first assigned to help in the operation of a press, a relatively simple kind of work once he discovered how to fuse his personality with that of the machine. From the moment he sensed its full range of power and rhythm and learned the predictability of its behavior, he became an experienced hand. Thereafter he was submerged in the stream of sheer mechanical motion.[4]

After a brief stint as a press-man apprentice, Katayama became an assistant to the type-setters, the aristocrats of the shop. But regardless of the nature of the work he did while

[4] Many biographers date the beginning of Katayama's "proletarian" life from this time. See, *inter alia,* Nozaka Sanzō, "Katayama Sen," in Yasuda Tokutarō and others, *Hikari wo Ageta Hitobito,* Tokyo, 1956, p. 51; Louis Fraina in his Introduction to Sen Katayama, *The Labor Movement in Japan,* Chicago, 1918, p. 23; and Arakawa Jitsuzō, *Katayama Sen; Sekai ni okeru Kare ga Chii to Taiken,* Tokyo, 1930, p. 92.

in the employ of the *Sekibun-sha,* Katayama never complained. At this time and throughout his long life he invariably revealed docile acceptance of the exacting demands of physical toil. No matter how menial the task, no matter how small the return, Katayama never disappointed an employer. But it is not enough to adduce in explanation of his attitude toward work that he was conscientious and industrious. Perhaps of greater importance was the fact that he never considered his job of the moment as more than a necessary means to a desired end. Drudgery was for Katayama the steppingstone to a more satisfying life.

When his yesterdays started to become indistinguishable from his tomorrows, Katayama knew that the time had come to leave the printing trade. With his monthly wages of four *yen* fifty *sen* exactly equal to his bill for room and board and enjoying but two days rest a month, he had neither time nor money for a life outside his room and shop. The longer he worked at the *Sekibun-sha,* he knew, the more difficult it would be to make a break. It had not been with the intention of learning a trade or of earning a bare living that he had come to Tokyo.

During the early months of 1882, in the "dead of winter," Katayama took a half step toward the realization of his ambitions.[5] Upon the recommendation of a young student living in the same lodging house, he entered the *Oka Juku,* a small preparatory school located in a wing of the mansion of the former feudal lord of Sendai. Although the move did not solve all of Katayama's immediate problems, it did provide a number of advantages. Since the total expense for room, board, and tuition was smaller than his monthly bill at the lodging house, the transfer resulted in a small but vital measure of financial relief. Of far greater consequence, however, was the opportunity to continue his often-interrupted studies.

[5] *Jiden,* p. 96.

The *Oka Juku* was typical of the educational institutions which flourished in Tokyo after the Meiji Restoration. Success of the elaborate modernization projects of the central government was manifestly contingent upon its ability to recruit properly educated and trained personnel. In Japan itself a small number of academies and schools of higher learning was gradually established by the government. Though the need for men educated in modern ways and techniques was critical and education was oriented accordingly, there was no thought of destroying the Japanese culture and heritage. A qualification for admission to many of the new government schools and an essential for a civil service, military or legal career was, consequently, knowledge of the Chinese language and the Confucian classics.[6] To meet the demands of the thousands of aspirants, who correctly perceived in a degree from a government school the key to rapid advancement in political, business, and national life, preparatory schools, like the *Oka Juku,* specializing in instruction in the Chinese classics, were founded.

For several months after he entered the *Oka Juku* Katayama kept his job at the *Sekibun-sha,* for he had no other means to support himself. Only on rare occasions was he able to attend the lectures given by the academy's master. To learn the daily lessons he had to rely on self-study and discussions with his fellow students at the end of long and hard days of work. His indomitable determination to secure an education was, however, more than a match for the adverse conditions with which he had to contend. Stealing precious moments for study during the day and poring over his books deep into the night, while confronted simultaneously with hunger, privation, and discomfort, became a routine of learning during the greater part of his life.

The year he spent at the *Oka Juku* was for Katayama edu-

[6] *ibid.*, p. 97. For Confucianism in general during this period see Warren W. Smith Jr., *Confucianism in Modern Japan,* Tokyo, 1959, ch. II.

cationally useful but otherwise aimless. After a few months he fortunately obtained the position of school servant and, with his minimal keep assured by the discharge of a few nominal duties, he gave up his job at the *Sekibun-sha.* For the first time since his arrival in Tokyo he now had the opportunity to devote himself to his studies without major distraction and before long became the favorite of his teacher, Oka Shikamon. Accompanying him on his lecture tours and serving him as student assistant, Katayama gained a deeper understanding of the works of Confucius which he had studied almost continuously from his early school days.

Oka Shikamon, a distinguished and widely admired scholar, was also responsible for arousing within the young Katayama an awareness of the history of his own times. During Katayama's stay in the school Oka was engaged in the writing of a history of the Imperial Restoration, his pronounced royalist sentiments and his somewhat romantic outlook being transmitted to his pupils.[7] Katayama, as Oka's student assistant, was profoundly affected by his teacher's political ideas. Apart from acquiring his first systematic, if partisan, interpretation of the Meiji Restoration, his enchantment with tales of samurai daring and heroism evoked hitherto untapped emotions of patriotism and nationalism. Many years were to pass before his essentially idealistic and sentimental view of the Imperial Restoration crumbled before a mounting political disillusionment.

Grateful as he was for the attention he received at the *Oka Juku,* Katayama finally decided to embark upon a new educational course. In the early spring of 1883 he entered the *Kodama-sha,* a private preparatory school for naval service aspirants, where an opening for a school servant had become available.[8] There is no reason to assume that he

[7] Matsumoto Jin, *Meiji Taishō Showa Jiyū-jin no Hatten,* 2 vols., Osaka, 1946, p. 195. The sketch of Katayama's life and career in this work is incredibly inaccurate. See I, pp. 194-198.

[8] *Jiden,* p. 105.

seriously contemplated pursuing a naval career. It is rather likely that, much as he enjoyed his studies, he was becoming increasingly dubious about his prospects of earning a respectable livelihood as a teacher of the Confucian classics. He could not, moreover, remain oblivious to the fact that, insofar as most of his classmates were concerned, attendance at the *Oka Juku* was primarily a steppingstone to study elsewhere of the modern branches of knowledge and to ultimate government service. Katayama finally decided to leave his Chinese studies behind.

Only a brief stay at the *Kodama-sha* was enough to convince Katayama that he had made a grave error in entering the school. He had apparently no difficulty in coping with the technical curriculum, which consisted largely of mathematics but, by his own admission, the intricacies of drafting left him frustrated and baffled. It was not, however, merely the sense of academic defeat which shortly induced him to leave the school. At the *Kodama-sha* Katayama quickly discovered almost insuperable barriers between himself and his schoolmates. He was presumably becoming accustomed to being older by increasing spans of years than his fellow students. But at the *Kodama-sha* it was impossible to escape the difference in social background and in professional ambition of a country boy from Okayama, on the one hand, and of sons of conservative southern samurai, on the other. The many youngsters from Satsuma knew exactly why they were at the *Kodama-sha.* For them the challenges of modern Japan were relatively simple, for their fathers with their proud and martial traditions had long since taught them to regard the imperial navy as a sacred trust. But Katayama's future was not so clear-cut and for him attendance at the *Kodama-sha* could only be a point of departure from the uncertain to the unknown.

It was perhaps while he was at the *Kodama-sha* that Katayama read a book whose influence upon his thought he always stressed. In 1883 *Keikoku Bidan* (Tales of Statesmanship) by Yano Fumio was published, immediately becoming one of the best sellers of the day. Of dubious literary merit, its historical significance is unquestioned. The setting of *Keikoku Bidan* was the struggle of ancient Thebes against the tyrannical domination of Sparta. Yano, the author, with no pretense to subtlety, and with no fine regard for the historical facts, used the heroic adventures of Epaminondas, the famed Theban general, as a foil to attack the clan oligarchy in Japan and to advance his own political ideals. Possessing a moral familiar to the Japanese and enlivened by tales of intrigue and war not unlike those of the *kabuki* theater and the medieval romances, *Keikoku Bidan,* with its novel background and its presentation of peculiar but exciting ideas, made a powerful impact upon its readers.[9]

Yano's novel is one of the very few books mentioned by name in Katayama's Autobiography. Even late in life he was able to recall sitting up through the night to complete the absorbing reading which broadened and deepened his political and historical vistas. Until his encounter with *Keikoku Bidan* Katayama's educational development had, with the exception of his forays into the Confucian classics and the history of his own country, not advanced beyond the abecedarian point. *Keikoku Bidan* was, however, to introduce him to antiquities other than the Chinese and Indian and to philosophical and humanistic areas beyond the Confucian.

Fatefully, the nudge Katayama received from Yano was shortly followed by several intellectual jolts which were to tear him further loose from his somewhat conventional Confucian moorings. But before the unfolding of the event, which altered the course of his subsequent life, a lull occurred.

[9] For a further discussion of *Keikoku Bidan* see Horace Z. Feldman, "The Meiji Political Novel; a Brief Survey," *Far Eastern Quarterly,* IX, no. 3 (May 1950), pp. 247-248, 254. Yano, it might be noted, was also the author of *Shin-Shakai* (The New Society), published in 1901. This was one of the first Utopian books written in modern Japan.

Leaving the *Kodama-sha* and returning to the *Oka Juku,* Katayama resumed his study of the Chinese classics, doubtless the only area in which he possessed a moderately advanced learning.

His renewed life at the *Oka Juku* filled Katayama with a deep contentment. Not only did he hold his teacher, Oka, in high esteem but he established his circle of intimate acquaintances from among the students at the academy. Many of the friendships that Katayama formed in Oka's school were lifelong and, though classmates and teachers followed widely divergent paths in their later years, the camaraderie established at this time lost little of its strength and sentiment.

Perhaps the most fateful friendship struck up by Katayama at the *Oka Juku* was with Iwasaki Seishichi. The warm and enduring relationship between these two men of such contrasting background, diverse interests, and disparate careers is one of the most amazing tales of modern Japan. Seishichi, born in 1864, was Katayama's junior by almost five years. He was the nephew of Iwasaki Yatarō, an ex-samurai, whose meteoric rise in the business world was the marvel of the early Meiji period. Though Yatarō died in 1885, the shipping empire which he forged by a combination of shrewdness and ruthlessness was pyramided in the following years into the Mitsubishi holding company, one of the "Big Four" of the financial oligarchies, or *zaibatsu,* of modern Japan.[10] As a member of the Iwasaki family, Seishichi obviously had no need to worry about his future.

The hold which Katayama held on Iwasaki Seishichi was magnetic.[11] Despite many suppositions to the contrary, it certainly did not stem from the claim of a perpetually penniless suppliant upon the largesse of an overly rich patron. Nor

[10] E. Herbert Norman, *Japan's Emergence as a Modern State,* New York, 1946, pp. 129-130.

[11] Note the comments by H. Vere Redman, "Sen Katayama," *Contemporary Japan,* II, no. 4 (March 1934), pp. 669-671.

did Katayama's relationship with Iwasaki derive from the pity and condescension of a wealthy man who bore his good fortune with an uneasy conscience. These explanations are untenable not because of their apparency but because they ignore a similar attraction which Katayama exerted upon his innumerable friends.

The key to Katayama's character and the source of his power of attraction for men was his fresh and genuine simplicity. Warm, kind, and incapable of malice in either thought or behavior, he never lost the open-eyed and open-hearted goodness of unspoiled youth. He could never take himself seriously as a person, and the demonstrations of loyalty and devotion of his friends, which often bordered on veneration, aroused in Katayama neither gratitude nor conceit but rather an innocent puzzlement. Amused when others were annoyed and blessed with a boundless but gentle sense of humor, he was ever ready to enjoy a chuckle at his own expense.

In his own eyes Katayama saw himself as an easygoing and carefree person. Though he admitted unhesitatingly, but with a disarming candor, to a streak of irresponsibility, he was seriously contrite only when the consequences of his behavior impinged upon the sensitivities and welfare of his fellow men. And, yet, he was singularly indifferent to the powerful, if commonplace, drives and ambitions which were the very *raison d'être* of other people. He could never convince himself that the vanities of mankind were more than passing delusions and aberrations; in heart and mind he was a rock-ribbed idealist and humanist with a stubborn and unshakable faith in individual and social perfectibility. Whether he was a Christian, a Socialist, or a Communist, Katayama was never able to discard completely the value system and view of man inculcated by Confucianism.

It would be too much to imply that to his Confucian-minded friends Katayama epitomized the ideal of the *ch'un tzu,* or "true gentleman." It would also be an exaggeration to maintain that he personified the Christlike character to his brethren in the community of Christianity. Still, it is noteworthy that when, in his ceaseless search for a faith based upon a goodness of and for men, he moved on to more materialistic creeds, he rarely failed to symbolize the ideal of the devout. To Christians he was thus a "pillar of the Church"; to Socialists, the "true internationalist"; and to Communists, the "real proletarian."

The conclusion is ineluctable that Katayama possessed an unusual power to move men. With no hint of pretentiousness or guile he influenced people not so much by cajolery and reproof as by the silent and disturbing force of personal example.

Manifestly, one as ingenuous as Katayama had to be safeguarded, directly and indirectly, against the consequences of his own naïveté. And, fortunately for Katayama, there were usually candidates for the role of self-appointed guardian. Whether he was the frightened and insecure *Suga-chan* of his childhood seeking the comforting caresses and assurances of womenfolk, or the struggling student working his way through school who touched the hearts of sympathetic and warm-hearted teachers and parents, or the *O-jii-san* (Granddad) of his later years, a protecting hand would sooner or later appear. But no one was ever able to challenge Iwasaki Seishichi's primacy of claim to this unenviable responsibility.

When Katayama returned to the *Oka Juku* after leaving the *Kodama-sha,* Iwasaki was no longer a student at the academy. Planning to go to the United States to continue his education, he had entered Keio University. Founded by Fukuzawa Yukichi, it was then as it is now, one of the foremost institutions of higher learning in Japan.[12] It was not Iwasaki alone who

[12] For a recent appreciation of Fukuzawa see Nakamura Kikuo, *Kindai Nihon to Fukuzawa Yukichi,* Tokyo, 1953, pp. 3ff. See also Fukuzawa Yukichi, *The Autobiography of Fukuzawa Yukichi,* trans. Kiyooka Eiichi, Tokyo, 1947, ch. XI.

benefited from his studies at Keio University. As he was exposed to new areas of knowledge and as his range of academic interests was gradually extended, he shared his enthusiasms with his close friend. Thus, though Katayama had on occasion heard English spoken by Christian missionaries in both Okayama City and Tokyo, his own circumscribed orbit of study had precluded more than passive attention. But, as Iwasaki began to learn English in anticipation of his journey to the United States, he awakened in Katayama an awareness of the language and a curiosity about the country where it was spoken.

At Keio University it was impossible for any student to avoid immersion in the swirling intellectual and political currents which swept early Meiji Japan. Since the conclusion of the ill-fated Satsuma Rebellion of 1877, political agitation had continued to spread throughout the country as ambitious politicians sought to force an entry into a government monopolized by the several feudal clans that had overthrown the old Tokugawa regime. To secure a respite from the embarrassing accusations of the political "liberals" led by Okuma Shigenobu and Itagaki Taisuke, the harassed oligarchs arranged in 1881 for the promulgation of an imperial edict.[13] Calling upon the critics of the government to cease and desist, the Emperor handed down his epochal pledge to introduce parliamentary rule at the termination of a nine-year preparatory period. The publication of the Emperor's rescript was then followed by the appointment of a "safe" government commission to cope with the constitutional requirements of the situation. At Keio University, the faculty and student body, being politically informed, were active in debating pertinent issues and problems.

As a consequence of his close acquaintance with Iwasaki,

[13] An excellent discussion of this problem is Joyce C. Lebra, "Ōkuma Shigenobu and the 1881 Political Crisis," *Journal of Asian Studies*, XVIII, no. 4 (August 1959), pp. 475-487.

Katayama became more directly concerned with the vital political affairs of his time. But despite his love for discussion and argument, his attention was still directed primarily toward his classical studies. The new politics and philosophies did, nevertheless, provide topics for endless and inconclusive exchanges which were further whetted by the controversial ideas expressed in the lectures and forums which were fast becoming the vogue in Tokyo. And, since police regulations forbade the presence of students at political gatherings, both Iwasaki and Katayama engaged in an occasional adventure by attending meetings in disguise.[14]

Before Katayama became deeply involved in his newly discovered political interests, a favorable turn in his personal affairs induced him to leave Tokyo. At the end of the summer of 1883 word was received at the *Oka Juku* that a school at Fujioka, a provincial town to the northwest of Tokyo, needed a teacher of Chinese studies. Delighted to be recommended by Oka himself, Katayama left Tokyo to try his hand at teaching.

The year he spent at Fujioka was a pleasant, if inconsequential, interlude for Katayama. In his employer, Mori Ōson, as in Oka Shikamon, he found a scholar worthy of his personal and intellectual respect. Teaching Confucian studies to the youngsters of an area where the restless and culturally subversive tides of the modern age had not yet penetrated was, moreover, a satisfying experience. But for an ambitious young man like Katayama, who had already known the excitement of city life, the mountain retreat of Fujioka could not offer a career. But his affection for and loyalty to Mori Ōson deterred an early departure by Katayama.

Some months after he had started teaching at Fujioka, perhaps in the spring of 1884, Katayama became seriously ill. Though he was otherwise endowed with good health, time and again he paid the price for his many privations and

[14] These regulations remained in effect for many years.

overexertions. Many of the ailments from which he suffered, temporarily or chronically, were probably of malnutritional origin,[15] but their effect was to erase the youthful and vibrant look from his face. He himself has stated that at the age of twenty-four he looked like a man of fifty.

When Iwasaki came to visit his friend in Fujioka, he was shocked by Katayama's aged and emaciated face. The news that he brought of his impending departure for the United States served, however, to rouse the spirits of both young men. Anxious to see Iwasaki off at Yokohama, Katayama left Fujioka in the summer of 1884, almost a year after his arrival.

Katayama always remembered Iwasaki's departure for the United States. It was unquestionably an impulsive resolution he made in the excitement and emotion of Iwasaki's sailing but, when years later he recalled his meeting with his friend and benefactor aboard the ship that was to carry him across the Pacific, Katayama could not forget his promise. "I, too," he had blurted out, oblivious to his penniless condition and in total disregard of the realities of the moment, "I, too, shall go to America."[16]

[15] As early as his Okayama Normal School days he had been afflicted with vertigo, and not long after his arrival in Tokyo he contracted the haemorrhoids which caused him constant agony during the remaining years of his life. At Fujioka he was smitten with what was apparently an acute case of pyorrhea which necessitated his hospitalization for several months. Katayama's description of his symptoms will be found in *Jiden,* pp. 114-115. The diagnosis of pyorrhea has been suggested by several medical acquaintances of the author.

[16] *ibid.,* p. 121.

CHAPTER IV

STRUGGLE IN AMERICA

In the spring of 1868, at the very moment when the Tokugawa Shogunate was collapsing, the Meiji Emperor issued his famed Charter Oath. Sounding the keynote of one of the longest and most illustrious imperial reigns in Japanese history, this proclamation ended the shogunal feudal order. Noteworthy was the Emperor's exhortation to his subjects to seek knowledge and wisdom throughout the world. With a few rapid strokes of the brush the antiquated Tokugawa proscriptions against foreign travel were in effect expunged from the laws of the realm.

Although the early Meiji government could encourage travel abroad, it was not easy to overcome the insular outlook instilled by two centuries of national isolation. Few Japanese had legally or clandestinely visited the West after the arrival of Commodore Perry in 1853; not many more seized the opportunity to leave the country once the seclusion laws were abolished. A journey to the United States or Europe entailed a drastic psychological adjustment and a financial outlay far beyond the resources of most Japanese. For about fifteen years after the promulgation of the Charter Oath, accordingly, Japanese who traveled to foreign lands were usually state officials or young men dispatched to study in Western schools at government expense.

When Katayama resolved to follow his friend Iwasaki to America, he made a daring decision. Without official patronage, ignorant of conditions in the United States, and unconversant with the English language, he could not count upon the assistance of his countrymen who had preceded and who would follow him. From 1861 through 1880 little more than three hundred and fifty Japanese made the trip to the

United States.[1] The flow of Japanese across the Pacific, however, increased slightly during the following decade, when restrictions against the emigration of laborers were removed by the Meiji government. But, though more than two thousand Japanese entered the United States between 1881 and 1890, many returned to their homeland after only a brief stay; the remainder were scattered about America from the west to the east coast.[2]

In determining the origin of Katayama's decision to migrate to America too much may be made of his impulsive statement at the time of Iwasaki's departure from Yokohama. His words at the time should properly be considered the birth of an idea rather than the formulation of an intention. Once the ship with Iwasaki aboard had raised anchor, the futility of his ambition must have become painfully evident to Katayama. Practically penniless and with an unpromising future, he did not even dare to share his hopes with his most intimate friends.

Doubtless of paramount importance in inspiring Katayama to make the bold leap from silent hope to positive action was a letter he received from Iwasaki in the fall of 1884. Writing from Yale University, Katayama's friend assured him that in the United States poverty was no barrier to a higher education.[3] The idea, practically unheard of in Japan, that it was possible to "work one's way through college" was literally breathtaking. From Iwasaki's letter Katayama acquired, thus, his first glimmer of the meaning of the United States as a land of opportunity and was stimulated into appropriate action.

Katayama himself was surprised at the ease with which his plans progressed. His poverty had taken on a new and far less oppressive aspect; it was no longer an insuperable

[1] Yamato Ichihashi, *Japanese in the United States*, Stanford, 1932, p. 54.

[2] *ibid.*, p. 54.

[3] Katayama Sen, *Jiden*, Tokyo, 1954, p. 124.

obstacle. Like any commodity it could now be given a fixed monetary value—in his case, the cost of a third-class steamship ticket to San Francisco. By mobilizing his own sparse resources and by importuning the reluctant elder Iwasaki, who feared that Katayama would continue his dependence upon Seishichi in America, the minimum funds for the journey were accumulated. After he acquired a second-hand Western-style suit and a cheap trunk to hold his few books and papers, Katayama sailed from Yokohama on November 26, 1884. When he stepped ashore at San Francisco, dirty, bedraggled, and friendless, he had in his pocket exactly one Mexican silver dollar, worth sixty cents in American money.[4]

During his first year in the United States life for Katayama was an unbroken sequence of discouragements and disappointments but never of disillusionment. Drifting about, at times a mere vagabond, in a strange and unfamiliar world he endured hunger, privation, toil, and humiliation; yet he kept his belief that sooner or later he would secure an education and return to Japan with profit from his adventure.

Katayama's most pressing need in San Francisco was employment. Not only did he have to support himself but he was also determined to put aside some savings toward the day when his American schooling would begin. At first he secured odd jobs with the help of Japanese and American acquaintances at the local Methodist Episcopal Chinese Mission but, after a few trying months, he gradually learned to fend for himself. Because of his lack of a vocational skill and a knowledge of basic English, however, Katayama found it impossible during his entire stay in the San Francisco area to find other than menial work, usually as handy-man, cook, waiter, or housekeeper in hotels, schools, restaurants, and saloons. Such drudgery kept him so busy from early morning to late at night that, having inadequate time for study, he

[4] *ibid.*, p. 135. Probably no Japanese biographer of Katayama has ever failed to mention this fact.

kept on the move constantly, hoping to discover a job that would answer his needs. His many employers were reluctant to see him quit for, whatever work he undertook, Katayama performed industriously and conscientiously. He was obviously worth the fifteen or twenty dollars a month which were his customary wages.

In his Autobiography Katayama has graphically described the type of work he did at this time. While working at a private school at San Raphael, says Katayama, "I made the preparations for breakfast every morning, cleaned up the school building, made the fires (it being winter), then made the beds of the students and other people in the school, returned to serve breakfast, after this washed the dishes, then cleaned the rooms, and washed laundry. Occasionally there was a general house-cleaning and I had to wash the windows. By the end of the day I had not had one single minute of rest."[5] But, despite the heavy demands of his daily work, when night had fallen and he had retired wearily to his room, Katayama immediately opened his *National Readers*. No stranger to study under the most adverse conditions, he inched his way patiently into the maze of the English language. For all his efforts, however, knowledge of English came very slowly.

As a result of the many jobs he held around San Francisco, Katayama gradually developed the skill which enabled him on many subsequent occasions to earn a livelihood. He always recalled with a chuckle how he learned to cook, his teachers being patient ladies of the house and his own fertile imagination. In time he not only became adept at the culinary arts but he also achieved a modest fame amongst his friends for his excellence as a baker.[6]

After a year and more of a knockabout existence, Katayama secured a position in an Alameda household. For perhaps the

[5] *ibid.*, p. 137.
[6] Watanabe Haruo, *Katayama Sen to Tomo ni*, Tokyo, 1955, p. 33.

first time since his arrival in the United States he was truly happy. His employers were genial people who were tolerant of his unfamiliarity with American customs and language, and neither overworked him nor monopolized his entire time. During this period of his life in California he attended an evening English class at the Chinese Mission; his teachers there, an aged Mr. Hoyt and his spinster daughter, exercised a tremendous influence upon the course of his future education. At this time, too, Katayama was converted to Christianity.

Exactly how and why Katayama embraced Christianity is not known. His first exposure to the religion occurred, he has testified, during his school days in Okayama City where a Protestant mission had been established.[7] Apart from a passing curiosity in the strange ways of the foreign missionaries, however, he evinced no interest in their doctrines. Later, perhaps in 1883 and 1884, when he was in Tokyo, he occasionally attended the public lectures of Japanese Christian pioneers in the company of friends. Though deeply moved by their spirit and zeal, he was not, he stated, "excited to the extent of entering the gates of Christianity."[8] It is possible that, had Katayama not gone to the United States, he would not have been converted to a faith alien to his ancestors.

Despite the tremendous importance of the event in his life, Katayama never spoke at any great length about the circumstances of his conversion. In his Autobiography, written years after he had abandoned Christianity, he did present an extremely terse account. "It would have been but natural," he wrote, "for me to have joined the Presbyterian Church but I rather preferred the Congregational. It had many schools, and numerous scholars were members of this denomination. Through the kindness of Kanda Saichirō I thus entered the

[7] Morito Tatsuo, *Nihon ni okeru Kirisuto-kyō to Shakai Shugi Undō*, Tokyo, 1950, pp. 105-106.
[8] *Jiden*, p. 124.

First Congregational Church of Alameda."[9] In this enigmatic fashion Katayama disposed of the decision which altered his entire life.

Failing any explicit explanation, the reasons for Katayama's acceptance of Christianity may only be conjectured. The vital step was most likely prompted by his pathetic loneliness during his first year in the United States. Living in a world of his own thoughts and unable to communicate with his fellow human beings, save on the most elementary matters, and starved for attention and companionship, it was perhaps inevitable that he respond gratefully to kindness and sympathy. In Alameda he apparently found the human and social warmth he craved in his employers who, like many an American family of the late nineteenth century with "heathen" Chinese and Japanese household help, rose to the spiritual challenge. Unable to engage in the work of saving souls in far-off lands, such Americans carried on missionary activity in their own homes.

In addition to the persuasions of his employers, Katayama was also subjected to the urgings of his English teachers at the Chinese Mission. Mr. Hoyt, who was in retirement, had been a professor at the Presbyterian-founded Maryville College in Tennessee. To him and his daughter who was, as Katayama said, "kind to Japanese," he owed his interest in the Presbyterian establishment. But, when he finally decided to join a church, Katayama chose the Congregational because of the recommendation of his Christian countryman, Kanda Saichirō, because of his personal preference, and because of the richer opportunities for a higher education available in the Congregational schools.

Katayama's exposition of his attitude toward the Christianity he had made his faith is of more than usual interest. "I was neither ardent nor apathetic toward my new religion," he wrote. "Later, when I studied at the Andover Theological

[9] *ibid.*, p. 144.

Seminary, I read and reread my copy of the Bible until it was in shreds. My feelings toward Christ did not, however, undergo any change. I doubt that from the beginning I believed in His divinity; but from the life of Christ I did derive great inspiration and strength."[10] Considering his religious behavior during his Christian years, there is no reason to dispute this contention and to dismiss it as the apology of an apostate.

Katayama's adoption of Christianity led before long to a decision he was both hesitant and eager to make. In January 1887, he realized that, being twenty-seven years of age, he could no longer delay his quest for an American education. Having saved about five hundred dollars, and assured of a job serving the meals of the headmaster and his family, Katayama made arrangements to enter the Hopkins Academy.

Situated in Oakland across the bay from San Francisco, the Hopkins Academy had been founded in 1871. Affiliated with the Congregational Church, it was designed to train students either for advanced ministerial work or for entrance into the well-known universities in the East. The objective of the school, proudly but somewhat grimly set down in its bulletin, was "to promote high scholarship, practical knowledge, and Christian character."[11] Through the intercession of friends in San Francisco Katayama was permitted to attend classes at the beginning of the second, or spring, term. And no sooner had he begun his studies than his newly adopted ideal of brotherly love was sorely tested. The year he spent at the Hopkins Academy proved to be one of the unhappiest periods in his entire life but Katayama, determined and stubborn, refused for some time to admit that he had made a grave mistake in entering the school.

At the root of Katayama's problems at the Hopkins Academy was the harsh fact that he was too advanced in years

[10] *ibid.*, p. 144.

[11] Hopkins Academy, *Catalogue of Hopkins Academy, Oakland, Cal. [sic], 1882-1883*. No place of publication but probably San Francisco, [1882?], p. 13.

for a setting that was more properly that of a schoolboy. He was neither academically equipped for the program of studies offered at the academy nor psychologically prepared to cope with classmates whose robust behavior and flighty interests marked them for what they undeniably were, namely, normal American adolescents. Thus, though his chores were not time-consuming and he was able to devote many hours to study, the severely demanding curriculum warped his entire routine of life at the school. Starting his classes in the middle of the school year and handicapped by his inadequate knowledge of English, he could hardly be expected, save by stealing every free moment for study, to meet the challenge of so staggering an array of courses as Greek, Latin, English rhetoric, and grammar.[12] By almost superhuman application he was, extraordinary as it may seem, successful in passing all his courses but, unfortunately, at a cost in misery he was never to forget.

When Katayama entered the Hopkins Academy, he was a fullgrown man with a seriousness of purpose and a dedication to learning totally beyond the comprehension of the fun-loving youngsters in his classes. Rejected by them and being a mysterious foreigner as well, Katayama was teased mercilessly and made the butt of incessant childish tricks. Finally, in December 1887, unable to endure the torment, he withdrew from the Hopkins Academy in anger and anguish.[13] The extent of his exasperation is perhaps most succinctly

[12] Hopkins Academy, *Catalogue of Hopkins Academy, Oakland, Alameda County, California for the Year Ending May, 1892.* San Francisco, [1891?], *passim.* In the catalogue for 1887-1888, Katayama is listed as a student for the year 1886-1887. *Catalogue of Hopkins Academy, Oakland, Cal., 1887-1888*, San Francisco, 1888, p. 7.

[13] The entries in the Chronology of the *Jiden* for 1885, 1886, and 1887 are completely erroneous; there is no entry for 1888. *Jiden,* p. 340. Katayama himself states that he entered Hopkins Academy in January, 1887, *Jiden*, p. 144. The date actually given in all editions of the Autobiography is Meiji 30 (1897) which is obviously an error for Meiji 20 (1887). He also indicates quite clearly that he withdrew in December of the same year. *Jiden*, p. 146.

revealed by his refusal, rare for a Japanese, to pay a farewell visit to the school when he shortly thereafter departed from San Francisco.

After discussing his problems with the elderly Mr. Hoyt, Katayama decided to resume his studies at a school in the East. It is not surprising that he was persuaded to apply for admission to Maryville College, the Presbyterian institution where Hoyt himself had taught. Working for several months to earn his traveling expenses, Katayama left San Francisco in the early months of 1888. The school year had long been under way when Katayama arrived in the rustic college town of Maryville in the Great Smoky Mountains. Unable to meet the basic academic requirements for admission to the college, he was placed in the senior class of the attached preparatory school, which did not differ significantly from the Hopkins Academy in its purpose and curriculum.[14] And once again, because of a lack of an adequate alternative rather than because of particular aim or interest, he selected the classical course with its emphasis upon archaic languages, ancient history, English rhetoric, and mathematics. By the end of the summer of 1888 he was, in recognition of his achievements, permitted to matriculate as a freshman in the college, where he remained for the following year.[15]

[14] Samuel T. Wilson, *Chronicles of Maryville College: a Story of Altruism,* Maryville, Tennessee, 1935, *passim.*

[15] There is no doubt from Katayama's account of his journey from San Francisco to Maryville that it was made during the height of winter. *Jiden,* pp. 147-148. He also states that the school year was under way when he arrived in Tennessee and that he was not admitted to the college but rather entered the senior year of the attached preparatory school. *Jiden,* p. 149.

According to the records and catalogues of Maryville College, Katayama "entered the Middle Class of the Preparatory Department . . . in 1887 and was enrolled for two years, 1887-1888 and 1888-1889. He took what was called the Classical Course." Information provided by Miss Vickie Samburg, Secretary to the President, Maryville College, in letter to author, July 30, 1957. Though there is a discrepancy of one semester, it is likely that Katayama was correct in stating that he began in the second term of the academic year 1887-1888 as a

Attendance at Maryville College was in many ways a welcome change for Katayama. As the only Japanese the college community and the townspeople had ever seen, he was at first looked upon as an ethnological showpiece and subjected to volleys of polite but inane questions about the customs and habits of his countrymen. But once he had succeeded in assuring curious but lamentably uninformed interrogators that Japan was not peopled by cannibalistic savages but enjoyed a civilization of considerable age and complexity, he was accorded a friendly and hospitable reception.

Katayama was greatly relieved to be spared the numerous annoyances he had suffered at the hands of the juvenile pupils at the Hopkins Academy, who had generally come from urban middle-class homes. At Maryville the students were not only older and more mature but many had, like Katayama, to divide their time between study and work. Coming from a peasant household and being familiar with the problems and routine of farm life, Katayama did not find it difficult to establish friendships with the boys of the college, most of whom resided in the surrounding mountain communities.

While he lived in the border state of Tennessee, America's tragically complicated racial problem was thrust directly upon Katayama's attention. Before coming to the United States he had, like most Japanese, probably not even been aware of the existence of the issue. It is most likely that he first witnessed racial discrimination, American-style, in California where, apart from a small Negro population, large numbers of Chinese immigrants were to be found. Nativist antagonism against the Chinese was common throughout the American West during these years and, although Japanese *per se* were still too few to be singled out for racial bias,

student in the senior class. It would otherwise be difficult to explain his admission as a freshman in the College in the fall of 1888.

there is little doubt that many of them were the objects of discriminatory acts by Americans unable to distinguish among Orientals. In his Autobiography, however, Katayama entered no complaint on these grounds.

Though in his later years Katayama freely expressed his strong condemnation of prejudicial practices against Negroes in the United States, it is difficult to trace the evolution of his views on racial discrimination. At Maryville, where bias was rife, Katayama himself was subjected to no personal embarrassments. But, his own experience apart, he was highly critical of the treatment of Negroes in Maryville. Despite the college's practice of admitting Negroes, there were, Katayama recalled, only a few colored students actually in attendance during his own stay and he concluded, doubtless unfairly, that Maryville adhered only to the letter but not to the spirit of the educational policy demanded by its financial supporters in the North.[16] In addition to his criticism of the alleged policy of the school, Katayama also inveighed against the shameful treatment of Negroes in the town of Maryville itself.

The validity of his accusations aside, Katayama's views on the racial problem in the United States, as set forth in his Autobiography, were probably of an *ex post facto* nature, revealing convictions reached only after long ideological searching and political growth. There is, to be sure, no reason to discount an early distaste and, perhaps, disgust on his part with Southern racial bias. It is, on the other hand, impossible to demonstrate, either from his personal experience or from his social and political beliefs of the time, that he was unusually perturbed by the racial problem during his Maryville days.

With the opening of the school year in the fall of 1888 Katayama was not the sole Japanese in attendance at Maryville College. At his urging Ken Takahashi, a countryman

[16] *Jiden,* p. 152.

whom he had met at Hopkins Academy, had left California and entered Maryville in the same class as Katayama. Despite the similarity in their needs and ambitions, the two penurious students from Japan presented a fascinating study in contrasts. Katayama, who was five years older, was shy, grave, and plodding; Takahashi was quick, ebullient, and daring. Being a natural leader with almost superhuman drives, Takahashi became a local legend and tradition even before his graduation from the school in 1892.

The enterprise which enshrined Takahashi in the history of Maryville College was as magnificent in its conception as it was amazing in its execution. Lastingly appreciative for the educational benefits he had received at the denominational college, he deferred his return to Japan after his graduation. Organizing a fund-raising campaign, he then toured the United States soliciting contributions for the erection of a YMCA building on the Maryville campus. He then remained at the college for several years to help the student body construct the edifice. When Takahashi finally went home to Japan, he entered the field of Christian social work, ultimately becoming the Secretary of the YMCA in the Kanda section of Tokyo. He died in 1905 at the untimely age of forty.[17]

Unlike Takahashi, who developed a passionate and exuberant devotion to Maryville, Katayama saw his initial enthusiasm gradually give way to deep disappointment. A constant source of worry was his difficulty in finding sufficient employment, without which he could not maintain himself at the college. Suffice it to say that after working and studying in Maryville for almost a year and a half the proverbially frugal Katayama, who had learned to perform miracles with both Japanese and American money, was unable to save a single penny. At the end of his freshman year at Maryville he

[17] See Wilson, *op.cit.*, pp. 154-158 and *Jiden*, p. 152. Though his personal name was Kinta, he was known at Maryville as Ken.

reluctantly concluded that his college education would have to be pursued elsewhere, and made arrangements to transfer to Grinnell College in Iowa, one of the oldest and finest institutions of higher learning in the American Mid-West.

During his stay in the United States, his joys had been few and far between but, when he departed from Maryville, Katayama had, thanks to a gift from a Japanese acquaintance at Yale, exactly five dollars in his pocket. To others this may well have seemed a pittance; to Katayama it meant that he had exactly five dollars more than when he had first arrived in Tennessee.

CHAPTER V
COLLEGE DAYS IN IOWA

Sen Katayama was in the true sense of the term an elemental being. If first things came first with him, it was because of habituated necessity rather than deliberate conviction. From the time he left his home in Okayama and for many years thereafter, accordingly, his daily thoughts were rarely far removed from plans to fulfill his primary needs of food, clothing, and shelter.

Like many a chronically poor young man, Katayama was not averse to indulging in an occasional luxury. Nor was his infrequent spending for other than the bare necessities of life always devoted to cultural and intellectual enrichment. In his Tokyo days he had not frowned upon excursions to brothels and, before coming to the United States, when he took a teetotaling pledge, he had needed little encouragement to exhibit his capacity to consume great quantities of *sake,* the sweet Japanese rice-wine.[1] He always enjoyed, moreover, animated and festive gatherings, which being so uncommon in his customary routine of life, lingered on in his memory for months and years. But unfortunately he had rarely, if ever, been tempted by his ego or curiosity to patronize a photographer's studio to have his picture taken.

Pictures of Katayama as well as descriptions of him during his youth and early manhood years apparently do not exist. The earliest available photograph of Katayama is perhaps the portrait which appears in the class book of Grinnell College for the year 1892.[2] By collating the facial features in this

[1] Katayama Sen, *Jiden,* Tokyo, 1954, pp. 112-113. When he left Japan for the United States, however, he became a teetotaler. *ibid.,* 129. See also Oka Shigeki, "Katayama Sen to Amerika," *Kaizō,* XXXII, no. 8 (July 1951), p. 77.

[2] A copy of this photograph has been made available to me through the kindness of Dr. G. L. Thornton, Registrar of Grinnell College. This earliest known photograph of Katayama was later published on

picture with other physical characteristics revealed in the fairly numerous photographs taken during the last half of his life a fairly detailed description of Katayama may be reconstructed.[3]

By any standard, either Japanese or Western, Katayama was not a particularly handsome man. Short in stature—he was no more than 5′ 2″ or 3″ tall—he was slightly built, weighing perhaps 115 or 120 pounds, though in his later years he tended to be somewhat paunchy. Like his great-grandfather he carried himself severely erect and only during the final months of his long life did his back reveal the stoop of age. His arms were generously but trimly muscled from considerable physical labor, while his disproportionately large hands and heavy knuckles attested to more than ordinary strength. And in commenting upon his bodily assets Katayama invariably singled out his legs, which were firm and sturdy from inveterate walking, the only sport he was ever able to afford.

Katayama's head was oval-shaped, overly large perhaps for a man of his size and, when he was seated, he seemed much taller and heavier than he actually was. His hair was thick, straight, and jet black. In later life, however, streaks of grey appeared and, though his hair-line receded slightly at the temples, his hair remained full and rich almost to the day of his death.[4] During his stay in the United States and after his

the front cover of *Commons,* II, no. 8 (December 1897). A reproduction of this picture will be found in the frontispiece of the first volume of Kishimoto Eitarō, Watanabe Haruo, and Koyama Hirotake, *Katayama Sen,* 2 vols., Tokyo, 1959. It is dated 1884, "about the time of his first visit to the United States." The basis for this dating is not given.

[3] The most complete collection of photographs of Katayama will be found in *Katayama Sen: Seitan Hyakunen wo Kinen shite, Zen'ei* (Special Issue), no. 161 (November, 1959).

[4] For several photographs of Katayama during the last few years of his life see especially Shakai Keizai Rōdō Kenkyū-jo, *Katayama Senshū: Nihon ni okeru Kaikyū Tōsō,* Tokyo, 1940, frontispiece and plate facing p. 122. In the former plate one of the two photographs is of Katayama and his younger daughter Chiyo.

return to Japan he affected a cropped mustache which made him look older than his age. When he was close to sixty, he removed it.

In his class picture at Grinnell all lines and wrinkles have been eliminated from Katayama's face. Still, it is apparent that he had broad and heavy features which became almost leonine with the advance of age. His almond-shaped eyes were strongly accentuated by the absence of a nasal bridge and by the bushy inverted crescents of his eyebrows. The prominence of his nose was further emphasized by full nostrils and flaring alae. But his most striking feature was his mouth. A narrow upper lip, curving downward at the outer edges, and a conspicuously pouting lower and thicker twin, suggested not merely inurement to privation and suffering but also his stubbornness and resolution. The rounded contour of his face was broken by a strongly molded but dimple-softened chin. His many friends always commented upon his warm and disarming smile.

Katayama's face became more interesting and assumed a more distinctive cast as he grew older. As a young man in the prime of his life he would not have been distinguished in a passing crowd. It was only when he passed the half-century mark, at which time the lines and angles of his physiognomy were perceptibly sharpened, that his face acquired unmistakable individuality.[5] No photographer or painter but only a sculptor working in clay or stone could then adequately preserve Katayama's appearance and personality for posterity.

However he may have looked when he was rested and well fed, Katayama probably aroused more pity than admiration when he arrived in the neatly laid-out prairie town of

[5] Note especially the frontispiece in Nihon Kyōsan-tō Tōshi Shiryō Iin-kai, *Katayama Sen Senshū*, Tokyo, 1949, I. Subsequent volumes have apparently not been published. This photograph of Katayama was taken at the time he entered prison in Japan in 1912. He was then fifty-two years old.

Grinnell, Iowa, in the summer of 1889. It need hardly be said that he did not have enough money in his pocket to buy a loaf of bread when he reached his destination. He immediately called at the home of Professor Leonard Parker. It was he who had during a visit to Maryville encouraged Katayama to transfer to the Midwestern college. Katayama could not have had a better mentor. At the time of Katayama's visit Parker had completed almost a half century of service devoted to public school and higher education. In 1889, when Katayama became his protégé, Professor Parker was still actively engaged in teaching and, even after his retirement, he continued his scholarly writing almost to the day of his death at the age of eighty-six.[6]

Since Katayama arrived in Grinnell several months before the opening of the fall term and had no means of support, Professor Parker found a job for him on a farm outside the town.[7] His chores were light, requiring mainly the care of several horses and cows. At the beginning of the school year in September, however, Katayama was given employment in the home of H. H. Robbins, who was the Secretary to and a member of the Board of Trustees of the College. Katayama, by this time greatly experienced in light housekeeping, was not hard put to please his hosts and continued to live in the Robbins' household during the greater part of his stay in Grinnell.[8] He apparently received his room but not his board for his services.

[6] For a good sketch of his life and career see Jacob A. Swisher, *Leonard Fletcher Parker,* Iowa City, 1927. That Katayama transferred to Grinnell because of Professor Parker's influence is indicated in Sen Katayama, "Why We Are Coming to America," *News Letter* [Iowa College], XVII, no. 3 (October 12, 1889), p. 30.

[7] There is a considerable amount of literature dealing with the founding and history of Grinnell College. In addition to the biography of Professor Parker, cited above, Truman O. Douglass, *The Pilgrims of Iowa,* Boston, 1911, and *Grinnell College Bulletin: Catalogue Number* LVI, no. 1 (February 1959) 23ff. will be found particularly useful.

[8] Katayama in his Autobiography speaks with great warmth and feeling about Robbins and his wife. See especially the incident recounted in *Jiden,* p. 166.

It was not long before Katayama was invited to explain to the college community why Japanese students came to the United States. "What purpose have we in coming to America?" he rhetorically asked in the college newspaper. "Is it to make money? Or is it to see and enjoy America? No, we come neither to make money as do all Chinese and Hungarians, nor to see and enjoy pleasure. Far be this from us, for our country is in its most important and its busiest day of revolution both in political and religious affairs, and has need of every patriot. We come to this country for the purpose of gaining true knowledge of higher civilization, both to educate and to cultivate our minds for the future use of, in the service of our native land."[9] During the three years he was at Grinnell Katayama left no doubt in the minds of his fellow students that he was interested in "true knowledge."

Of the three concentrations of study at Grinnell, Katayama finally settled upon the literary. He had no taste for the physical sciences nor did a specialization in philosophy greatly interest him. During the freshman year all students in the college were required to undertake a common program of studies consisting of such courses as English, history, economics, and physical geography. The sophomore and junior years were then used for concentrated study in a major field; Katayama followed a regimen of Greek and Latin language and literature. The senior year was devoted to capstone courses in the student's special field as well as to several free electives.[10] Completion of this program of studies won for Katayama an A.B. degree in 1892.[11]

[9] Sen Katayama, "Why We Are Coming to America," p. 31.

[10] According to a letter from G. L. Thornton to me (June 3, 1959), Katayama matriculated as a classics major. But the *Unit* [Iowa College], I, no. 6 (November 29, 1890), p. 85, lists him as a literary major, the other two concentrations being classical and scientific. It is possible Katayama changed his field of specialization after entering Grinnell.

[11] There is a great deal of confusion about Katayama's official status at Grinnell. From a study of the various extant records the following conclusions seem likely. Admitted to the College in 1889, he was ap-

Of all the subjects which he studied in schools in the United States Katayama's favorite was Greek. It was not that he had any special liking for the language. It would seem rather that an almost fortuitous choice of schools had necessitated the study of Greek and, in response, he had devoted an extra measure of time to its mastery. As opposed to their language of expression, he was favorably impressed by the ideas of Plato, Aristotle, and Socrates, so much so that for years thereafter his own writings were enriched by allusions to the philosophy and literature of Greek antiquity.[12] Latin was, however, a burden. Caesar's works were, he ultimately concluded, well worth the tremendous effort of translation and study but Cicero and Vergil did not appeal to him. His grades were, on the whole, excellent, and what few setbacks he encountered were in Latin and "rhetoricals."[13]

Katayama acquired little intellectual depth during his years at Grinnell College; his areas of study were too diffuse. When it was too late to remedy the neglect, he lamented his failure to study the physical sciences. With the passage of time he also rued his lack of formal training in modern languages, his only experience at Grinnell being his few courses in German. As for history and the social sciences, he expressed regret that his studies had not advanced beyond the standard survey courses.[14] All in all, Katayama finally decided, what-

---

parently given credit for a year's attendance at Maryville. Beginning at Grinnell as a sophomore, he thus became a member of the Class of 1892. *Jiden,* pp. 158-159, is far from clear, while the entry in the Chronology, p. 341, is in error. The transcript of Katayama's courses and grades provided me by Dr. Thornton covers only the years from 1889 to 1892. Numerous references to Katayama in the publications of Grinnell, moreover, refer to Katayama as a member of the Class of 1892.

[12] Note the very first page of his Autobiography (*Jiden,* p. 3).

[13] Despite his lack of enthusiasm for Cicero, Katayama was rated highly in his Latin course. As for his other work, an "examination of his grades reveals that he got mostly A's and B's with an occasional C." Thornton to author, October 22, 1959.

[14] He atoned for this neglect, for his M.A. degree, awarded by Grinnell in 1896, was in the field of history.

ever other benefits he may have derived, his education at Grinnell College had been somewhat aimless and largely wasted for purposes of equipping him to earn a living.

Though he may have had second thoughts about the worth of his educational experience at Grinnell after he returned to Japan, Katayama was always happy to have lived in the small college town in Iowa. For the first time since his arrival in the United States he did not find himself constantly harassed by the demands of daily living. His housekeeping chores in the Robbins' home were quickly reduced to a manageable routine, leaving him ample time for study and for social and collegiate activities. Doing odd jobs about town, working during summer vacations, and receiving for some time a stipend of twenty-five dollars a month from his old friend, Iwasaki, who had completed his studies at Yale and returned to Japan, he was able to meet his expenses for living and education.

At school in Iowa Katayama was no ordinary "college boy," for he was almost twice as old as many of the students. It was only to be expected, in view of his age, that he devote his spare hours largely to serious social and cultural purposes. In Iowa he became a regular churchgoer for the first time since he had been converted to Christianity. Attending the local Congregational Church, he enjoyed the moments given to religious devotions. Rather than mere solace he now derived pleasure from his faith and by engaging actively in the community works and programs of his church he acquired an increasingly deep understanding of Christianity as a social as well as a religious force. His faith, he now began to realize, necessitated more than a single-minded dedication of the individual to his own spiritual salvation.

At Grinnell Katayama became an habitué of the library. During his entire previous education, both in Japan and in the United States, his studies had been generally restricted to the mastery of what were essentially textbooks. It is doubtful that he had, prior to his matriculation at Grinnell, a broad knowledge of books or even of the basic literature of the subjects he studied intensively. In Iowa, however, he discovered the values and pleasures of a library. He shrewdly learned also that a systematic exploitation of information readily at hand in books and periodicals promised a fairly assured way of earning a living. Becoming deeply involved in religious and political journalism after his return to Japan, Katayama, it may be concluded, ultimately applied his discovery to considerable practical advantage.

Katayama's extracurricular reading at Grinnell embraced several types of literature. Since the beginning of his schooling in Tokyo some years before, he had perused a novel only at intermittent moments. Considering the many demands upon his time, the enjoyment of literature was a luxury he believed he could not afford. But when Mrs. Parker, the wife of his mentor, pointed out that attention to the acknowledged masters of English prose would contribute immensely to the improvement of his knowledge of the English language, he undertook to read the works of George Eliot and Charles Dickens.[15] It was not long, however, before he abandoned this venture as a waste of time and his acquaintance with English as well as other literature thereafter remained sparse and spotty.

Of somewhat greater interest to Katayama were the increasingly numerous articles concerned with Japanese affairs published in the leading American literary and political journals. In the course of his wanderings about the United States he had not been able, or even attempted, to keep abreast of the epochal events and revolutionary changes occurring in his native land. For long periods of time he had probably been more inadequately informed about contemporary Japanese affairs than many curious Americans. But by 1889, when he acquired both the free time and language

[15] *Jiden*, p. 175.

ability to scan the standard periodicals, an episode of momentous importance took place in Japan which instantly attracted his attention.

On February 11, 1889, after some eight years of preparation, the Meiji Emperor presented his forty million subjects with a constitution. Inasmuch as this momentous document had been drawn up under the supervision of Count Itō Hirobumi, who reflected the political views of the conservative leaders around the throne, it was devoted more to the protection of the powers of the state than to the extension of basic rights to the citizenry of Japan. With its lack of provision for ministerial responsibility and with its safeguards against effective budgetary control by the national Diet, the Meiji Constitution, which endured until 1947, erected a liberal façade for oligarchical state power.

The years from 1889 to 1894 were also marked by the rise of a nationalistic agitation in Japan, in which domestic political differences were, on the whole, blurred. The objective of the nationalistic movement was revision of the so-called "unequal treaties" with the Western powers. Concluded during the closing years of the Tokugawa regime, these agreements perpetuated the extraterritorial privileges of foreign nations and limited the tariff autonomy of Japan. A few weeks after Katayama matriculated at Grinnell Japan's opportunistic politicians were given sober warning that no settlement with the Western powers which fell short of complete restoration of the nation's sovereign rights would be acceptable to militant nationalists. When the ambitious Count Okuma undertook negotiations with Great Britain providing for extensive but not full modification of the "unequal treaties," he was badly wounded by the bomb of a "patriotic" would-be assassin. Thereafter, until complete treaty revision was at last attained on the eve of the war with China, no political chieftain in Japan dared to compromise on the question of the sovereign powers of the land.

News about the exciting developments in his homeland was easily available to Katayama in the American press. Nevertheless, he was not at the time nor for some years to come politically minded. However radically his views may have later changed, he was not perturbed during his years at Grinnell by the disappointing denouement of the "liberal" and "democratic" movements for the establishment of constitutional, parliamentary government in Japan. Nor was he greatly disturbed by the implications of an unrestrained nationalistic agitation which threatened to blunt the good sense of Japanese leaders of all political camps. On the contrary, he continued to hold fast in his faith in the Japanese imperial monarchy, with all its extraordinary powers, and to share in the nationalist sentiments which were current among his countrymen.

If his years at Maryville and Grinnell were preparatory for Katayama's future career, they were, above all, noteworthy for the stirring of his social consciousness. During his long quest for an education he had been concerned almost exclusively with the ultimate symbols of social and economic success. His ambitions were, however, hoist with the petard of his college education. For it was while he was in Iowa that he caught the first vague glimpses of the life he was to lead after his return to his home in the East.

In his Autobiography Katayama has stated that he became a socialist when he was a student at Grinnell.[16] Though this claim has been accepted and repeated endlessly by his many admirers and biographers, there is no reason to take his assertion without qualification. It is not enough to aver that he became a socialist during his undergraduate years in college. What is infinitely more important, in view of the numerous socialist movements flourishing in the United States in the late nineteenth century, is determination of the socialist influences to which he was exposed and the type of socialism

[16] *ibid.*, p. 176.

toward which he leaned. Considered from these perspectives, it becomes clear that Katayama's first halting steps in the direction of a socialist faith were but a further evolution of his Christian creed.

Katayama himself has acknowledged the heavy socialistic influence of Richard T. Ely. While teaching at the Johns Hopkins University during the eighties, Professor Ely had launched his crusade to awaken the social conscience of the American public and to arouse public concern for the many social problems being bred by the dynamic expansion of industrial capitalism. Several of his articles were discovered by Katayama in the well-known magazine *Outlook* when he was at Maryville.[17] Not only was his interest permanently stimulated but for several years thereafter he was a faithful reader of Ely's writings. The extent of his admiration may be gauged from the fact that, when Ely's book *The Social Aspects of Christianity* was published in 1889, Katayama purchased a number of copies for distribution to his friends.

Though Ely was more familiar than most Americans of the times with the various European socialist movements, especially in Germany and France, he was neither intellectually sympathetic nor politically partisan toward them. Laudable as he deemed their millenarian goals, he refused to accept their peculiar ideas on leadership, methods, and organization for social change. To Ely the uplifting of man and the improvement of his conditions of life were a logical conclusion of the teachings of Christianity, a moral imperative and not an inevitable consequence in the evolution of social and economic systems. Swayed primarily by the particulars of American life, he believed that the road to a happier future for mankind lay in the fulfillment of Christian duty and in the implementation of Christian ethics rather than in the relentless unfolding of class struggle. If Ely thus was instrumental in advancing Katayama's social thought, it was by

[17] *ibid.*, p. 175.

the successful transmission of the social gospel of American Protestant Christianity.

Katayama's acceptance of the "social aspects of Christianity" required no radical intellectual shift nor sharp break with prior beliefs. An ethical command for social action aimed at the betterment of man was in consonance with the Confucian foundations of an educational experience which stretched back to his early childhood years. What is puzzling, however, is the second major influence upon the development of his socialist thought. From the moment he read a sketch of Ferdinand Lassalle in the *Atlantic Monthly* of May 1888, Katayama was captivated by the founder of the German social democratic movement.[18]

No student of the stormy years of modern socialism can fail to understand Katayama's fascination with Ferdinand Lassalle.[19] Though he died tragically in 1864 at the age of thirty-nine, Lassalle succeeded in laying the foundations for the most impressive European socialist movement before World War I. Being neither a wild-eyed Utopian nor a frenzied conspirator, he sought to integrate into an ideological creed the nationalistic emotions and the demand for social improvement of Germany's rapidly rising industrial working class. A man of tremendous intellect, an oratorical spellbinder, and a consummate political strategist, he was both respected and feared by his chosen antagonists. At the time of his death from a duelling wound, Lassalle was busily attempting to establish a political alliance between his socialist worker supporters and the conservative followers of the Junker Bismarck with the hope of checking and perhaps of destroying the powerful and ambitious capitalist class. This

[18] D. O. Kellogg, "Ferdinand Lassalle, the Socialist," *Atlantic Monthly*, LXI, no. 4 (April 1888), pp. 483-496.

[19] It is not unlikely that Lassalle appealed more to Katayama's romanticism than to his intellect. Many other pioneers in the Japanese social movement were also to be attracted to the German socialist, whose long fight on behalf of justice for the famous Countess von Hatzfeld was a never failing source of inspiration.

grand and daring design never ceased thereafter to intrigue the leaders and manipulators of the German workers.

Lassalle's socialism doubtless excited the interest of Katayama for the very reasons it repelled many other European socialists. The program of the German social democratic movement was determined in large measure by the unique personality of Lassalle himself as well as by the peculiar social and political conditions in the regime dominated by Bismarck. But, to Katayama and other Japanese of the late nineteenth century the similarities in the problems, trends, and ambitions of Germany and Japan were too suggestive to be ignored. In both nations numerous autonomous states and baronies had been welded into imperial regimes at about the same time under the leadership of paternalistic and autocratic oligarchs. Furthermore, both Germany and Japan, as late arrivals in a burgeoning new world order, were simultaneously engaged in drives for primacy in their respective political orbits and, despite their aspirations for social and economic change, were not minded to jettison their historical legacies and cultures. It was not difficult, consequently, for Katayama to think that the formula for a social democratic movement in Germany which was apparently solicitous of the interests of both state and people, might well be applied with some prospect of success in his own land.

For all his lively interest, however, Katayama could not accept Lassallian socialism completely. Influenced by the Christian social gospel, he could not before the passage of considerable time uphold the doctrine of the class struggle or the materialistic interpretation of history which Lassalle had borrowed from Karl Marx and his predecessors in social theory. Nor with his belief in the Christian brotherhood of man could he be swayed by the proletarian partisanship of Lassallian social democracy or by the advocacy of the trade-union rather than the church as the driving force for social justice. Still, Katayama probably learned from Lassalle his first lessons in the relationships between social movements and political action. For the while, however, he preferred to invest his hope in a crusading church rather than in a militant political party based on trade-union organizations.

It is characteristic of Katayama that, despite the amazing advances of the German social democratic movement, he maintained a stubborn fidelity in Christian socialism. At this juncture in his life, as at so many other times when he arrived at ideological crossroads, he refused to be deflected from a course to which he had committed himself. Apart from his wary regard for philosophy and theory, born of his own educational experience, he distrusted his ability to cope with abstract subtleties. His faiths, adopted only after deep and protracted deliberation, always enmeshed his mind and emotions so thoroughly that it was with a sense of guilt and apostasy that he could even bring himself to consider their abandonment. Only after much mental wrestling did he ever bring himself to forswear a creed or a cause.

Katayama's growing involvement in the social gospel and socialism soon influenced a decision necessitated by his graduation from Grinnell College. He had originally planned to return to Japan as soon as he received his degree, to pursue there whatever employment opportunities his American education opened to him. But in the spring of 1892, shortly before commencement, he was informed in a letter from Hadeki that his mother had died. It was a grievous blow to Katayama who had not seen Kichi since he had left his native village almost thirteen years before. His mind was soon made up. There being no pressing need to return home, he determined to continue his studies for the master's degree. He was to become thereby one of the first Japanese students to engage in graduate studies in the United States.

Exactly how Katayama made his choice of a graduate institution is not known but he was probably inspired by the oldest tradition of Grinnell College itself.[20] In any event, he applied for admission to the famed Andover Theological Seminary in Massachusetts as a candidate for the master's degree in history. Officially the degree was to be conferred *pro merito* by Grinnell College upon his satisfactory completion of a program of advanced study in the liberal arts. For a nonresident student, such as he was to be, a minimum of two years of graduate work was required.[21]

In the summer of 1892 Katayama bade farewell to his friends in Iowa and once again embarked upon his travels for an education, which apparently now had purpose if not necessarily the promise of an end.

[20] Every student presumably was familiar with the history of the "Iowa Band" from Andover.

[21] G. L. Thornton to author, October 22, 1959.

CHAPTER VI

ANDOVER AND YALE

Northfield, a quiet, little town in northern Massachusetts, was the birthplace and lifelong home of Dwight Lyman Moody, the famous lay evangelist of the post-Civil War era. Katayama worked here during the summers of 1891, 1892, and 1895.[1]

Moody, a revivalist zealot advocating Christianity in action, was also a restless innovator of religious and educational projects. Founding the Northfield Seminary for Young Ladies in 1879, Moody two years later set up a separate institution nearby, the Mount Hermon School for boys. In the following years the two campuses were the sites of many of his revivalist programs. When he inaugurated a series of summer religious conferences for college students in 1886, he succeeded in attracting young men and women from all over America to Northfield. The town's position as a major center of Protestant revivalism in the United States was soon confirmed.[2]

When in the spring of 1891 Katayama was invited to attend a student conclave at Northfield, he was faced with a dilemma. Toward the end of every school year his finances

[1] The Chronology in Katayama Sen, *Jiden,* Tokyo, 1954, pp. 340-341, notes for the year 1892 only the death of Katayama's mother, while the entry for 1893 refers inaccurately to his beginning his senior year at Grinnell. In *Jiden,* p. 197, however, Katayama says, "As soon as the graduation ceremony was over [in 1895], I left Yale on that very day and for the *third time* [italics mine] went to Northfield . . . . " For his stay in the New England town in the summer of 1891 see *Jiden,* pp. 166ff. His second visit to Northfield in the summer of 1892 is explicitly mentioned in *ibid.,* p. 174. During the summer of 1893 Katayama probably worked at Old Orchard Beach, Maine. See Arthur L. Weatherly, "Kingsley House, Tokyo, and Its Founder," *Commons,* II, no. 8 (December 1897), p. 1. He spent the summer of 1894 in England and Scotland.

[2] Herbert C. Parsons, *A Puritan Outpost; a History of the Town and People of Northfield, Massachusetts,* New York, 1937, pp. 367-369.

were always low. But assuming that he might not have another chance to participate in a revival, since he planned to return to Japan after his graduation from Grinnell in the following year, he threw prudence to the winds. Journeying to Northfield, he arrived with only a few dollars to spare.

Northfield made a vivid impression upon Katayama, so much so that, when he wrote in his later years about his college days in the United States, he looked back upon his life in the New England town with a rare warmth and tenderness.[3] During his stay in the summer of 1891 his spirits were uplifted by the inspirational program presented by Moody and his renowned coworker, Ira D. Sankey, but when the student gathering had come to an end, Katayama had neither the means to support himself nor to pay for the long trip back to Grinnell. After washing the school laundry with other needy students, he then secured employment as a pastry cook in the Hotel Northfield. Receiving forty-five dollars a month in wages as well as his room and board, he returned to Iowa at the end of the summer slightly more prosperous than when he had left.

Upon his graduation from Grinnell College in the spring of 1892 Katayama participated in the commencement ceremonies and festivities with a profound sense of satisfaction.[4] Few of his younger classmates could appreciate the pride with which he received his baccalaureate degree at the age of thirty-two and after seven years of unbroken sacrifice. Awarded a set of Goethe's complete works in recognition of his excellence in German, he could not but smile and recall his primary school days when his prize had been a pencil. If his happiness was tinged with a note of sadness, it was because his mother was no longer alive to share his triumph.

[3] *Jiden*, pp. 167ff. After the passage of many years Katayama's high regard for Moody waned. See his critical comments in *ibid.*, pp. 169-170.

[4] The entry in the Chronology of the *Jiden* for 1893 is incorrect. See above, n. 1.

Katayama did not tarry in Grinnell. With three more years of hard and concentrated study at Andover Theological Seminary ahead, he could not afford to remain idle for long. Once again he went to Northfield where he worked as a cook in the hotel for the next three months. Then, with the opening of the school year, he moved to the town of Andover about a hundred miles to the east. There he lived for almost two years.

Study at Andover had a very heavy influence upon Katayama's career and thought. Nevertheless, though he wrote at length in his Autobiography about his experiences at Maryville and Grinnell, he passed over his years at the seminary in almost complete silence.[5] Odd as it may seem, the reader of Katayama's life story becomes aware of his attendance at the theological school largely from parenthetical remarks and random allusions. His omission of reminiscences about his life at Andover may perhaps be due to the fact that his Autobiography was written some years after he had abandoned Christianity and turned to Marxist socialism.

Whatever second thoughts about his theological studies Katayama may have had at a later time, there is no question but that he considered himself fortunate to be admitted to Andover. One of the foremost seminaries in the United States, it had enjoyed an illustrious record since it was founded in 1807 by conservative New England Calvinists alarmed by the spread of free thought and liberal theology. The objective of the institution was to make "provision for increasing the number of learned and able Defenders of the gospel of Christ, as well as of orthodox, pious, and zealous Ministers of the New Testament."[6] By the closing years of the nineteenth

[5] *Jiden* skips the period from Katayama's graduation from Grinnell to the completion of his second year at Andover in the late spring of 1894. See *Jiden*, p. 176.

[6] "Constitution of the Theological Seminary, 1807," Andover Theological Seminary, *General Catalogue of the Theological Seminary, Andover, Mass., 1808-1908,* Boston, 1909, p. iv.

century about two thousand graduates had gone forth from Andover to "defend the gospel" in most of the states of the Union and to disseminate the spiritual message of their church among "benighted" peoples abroad. In Japan Andover Theological Seminary was well-known through the devoted work of such missionaries as Daniel C. Greene, Marquis L. Gordon, and Otis Cary, not to speak of Niijima Jō, the founder of Doshisha University in Kyoto.[7]

Katayama entered Andover in the class of 1895. Of the twenty-eight candidates for the ministry in this group, only eighteen completed their theological studies at the seminary. Sixteen of these graduates and five of the ten students classified in the alumni records as nongraduates were ultimately ordained, usually as Congregationalist and occasionally as Presbyterian or Unitarian ministers. Not all of Katayama's classmates pursued careers in the church, about one-third becoming teachers, lawyers, physicians, and scholars. In addition to the regular members of the class of 1895 one resident licentiate and one graduate student were enrolled.[8] All in all, Katayama's was a typical Andover class. He himself was never ordained; in the General Catalogue of the seminary he is described as a nongraduate, a teacher, a socialistic worker, and an editor.[9]

Katayama arrived at Andover during one of its most vibrant intellectual periods. Though the seminary had from its beginnings attempted to serve as a stronghold of conservative theology, it had, nevertheless, been compelled constantly to reappraise its position in keeping with the tides of social

[7] Niijima Jō studied in a "special course" in the Class of 1874. *ibid.*, p. 399.

[8] The graduate student was Hirotsu Tomonobu, a graduate of Doshisha College and Theological Seminary. After studying at Yale and Harvard Divinity School, he entered Andover. From 1899 to 1901 he directed Doshisha.

[9] *ibid.*, p. 484. Katayama's birth date is here given as January 8, 1860; the period of his attendance at Maryville as 1887-1888; and the date of his graduation from Grinnell as 1892.

change of nineteenth-century America. Having weathered the moral crisis raised by the issues of slavery and Civil War, it had been confronted by new dilemmas during the post-reconstruction era of booming industrialism. Initially the Andover theologians responded sluggishly to the challenges of capitalism but in 1884, when the *Andover Review* was founded as an organ of their ideas, they turned in earnest to the philosophical struggle. For almost five years the seminary's professors pursued hopefully and almost apologetically the optimistic theories of "progress" advanced by savants and churchmen in Europe and America but by 1889 disenchantment began to set in. Suspecting that prevailing industrial capitalism might not necessarily culminate in the fulfillment of the promise of the Kingdom of God, they now started to view the existing order more critically, even pessimistically, and to seek ways of coping with manifest social abuses.

Katayama's ministerial training at Andover was somewhat different from that of students who had attended the seminary but a few years earlier. Primary emphasis, to be sure, was still placed upon instruction in theology which was the *sine qua non* of the institution. Students continued to study sacred literature, sacred rhetoric, Hebrew, music, ecclesiastical history, foreign missions, homiletics, elocution, pastoral theology, and pastoral care. Prospective ministers were, moreover, still drilled in the Bible, particularly the New Testament; it is little wonder that Katayama never forgot that his copy was gradually reduced to shreds from constant use.[10] But at Andover a belief that the faith and moral worth of the individual, whether rich or poor, could not be realistically dissociated from societal conditions colored instruction as never before.

The formidable array of courses at Andover, taught by some of the most eminent Congregationalist theologians in

[10] *Jiden,* p. 144.

America, was more than enough to tax the capacities of the average student. Katayama's determination, his diligent study habits, and his improved facility in English, made learning a less exacting ordeal than it had been at Maryville and Grinnell. Yet Katayama was severely tried to hold the pace. Poring over his books far into the night, he also had to snatch a few extra hours of study here and there in order to keep up with his classmates. Arthur L. Weatherly, a fellow student at Grinnell and a close friend at Andover, said of Katayama that he had "never . . . known a man who obtained a complete college and professional training under such difficulties."[11]

No mere wish to secure the degree of bachelor of divinity will adequately explain Katayama's willingness to drive himself to the point of physical breakdown at Andover. It is obvious that, as opposed to the motives which had induced him to go to the United States, to Maryville, and to Iowa, namely, the desire for an "education," he now had a powerful sense of purpose. Grinnell had not made him, as he later claimed, a "socialist"; it had rather developed him into an ardent and crusading Christian. Filled with the spirit of brotherly love and pity for the poverty-stricken masses, he determined to devote his future to spiritual and social service.[12]

Once Katayama had set his heart upon a career in the church, the decision to matriculate at Andover was logical. As a confirmed Congregationalist he would hardly have looked elsewhere for the training he wanted. Whether or not he was stimulated by his study of theology is difficult to say but there is no gainsaying that his vision of a personally meaningful and socially useful life supported his morale for three years and enabled him to accept further privation without complaint. There was probably not a member of his class

[11] Weatherly, *loc.cit.*

[12] For Katayama's growth as a Christian see especially Morito Tatsuo, *Nihon ni okeru Kirisuto-kyō to Shakai Shugi Undō*, Tokyo, 1950, pp. 105-112.

with whom he did not share his noble dream. Weatherly has recalled Katayama's ambition "to go to Tokyo and to preach to the poor of that great city. His idea," he wrote, "was to live in their midst as one of them."[13] When he finally left the United States to return to Japan, his admiring classmates presented him with a gift of money to help him get started in his work.

Had Katayama entered Andover only a few years before, his training would have prepared him only for the conventional role of a pastor. But since 1889 the liberal theologian, Professor William Jewett Tucker, had undertaken to broaden the traditional curriculum. Unconvinced that the poor were alone responsible for their own misery and moral depravity, disillusioned with the philanthropic approach to the heart-rending problems of the working people of the cities, and conscience-stricken by the lack of social justice in the existing system of industrial capitalism, Tucker neatly summed up the quandary of his church:

"We say to those who are struggling at the bottom of society, who make up the great social residuum, 'Your only hope is in Christianity; all other remedies are a delusion.' And they not unnaturally or unjustly reply, 'That is what you have been saying for years, and here we are.'"[14] Tucker's gnawing doubts about the promise of capitalism were reflected in a personal conception of Social Christianity, a positive, if vaguely defined, effort to foster social equality and justice for the victims of capitalistic excesses and neglect.

Tucker's innovations at Andover were designed to familiarize future ministers with the living nature of the social problems weighing upon the working classes. "Most preachers," it was argued, "even those who have endured no little hardship, have become accustomed to a religion of prosperity.

[13] Weatherly, *op.cit.*, p. 2.

[14] Daniel Day Williams, *The Andover Liberals; a Study in American Theology*, New York, 1941, p. 141.

They have preached to prosperous people. They have tried to study their temptations, they have tried to teach them their duties."[15] With attention now directed to the plight of the poor, Tucker was instrumental in introducing into the curriculum a new course, Social Economics; it was a "radical departure in theological curricula at the time."[16]

Another major step to improve the sociological curriculum at Andover was also taken at Tucker's instigation. Alert to the possibilities of the university settlement house movement, started only a few years before in England, he encouraged one of his students, Robert Archey Woods, to investigate the program at firsthand.[17] Woods lived at Toynbee Hall in London in 1890 and upon his return to Andover lectured for the next five years on English Social Movements. His book on the subject, published in 1891, was for many years standard reading for clerical and lay social workers in the United States.

Woods's dedication to the university settlement idea was not limited to academic exposition. By October 1891, he had successfully persuaded Professor Tucker to establish a settlement house under the sponsorship of Andover. On New Year's Day of the following year the Andover House Association, headed by Tucker, opened Andover House in the South End district of Boston. Five years later the settlement was renamed the South End Settlement House. Though the aims of Andover House, which sought to improve moral behavior by improving social conditions, were nominally religious, the program was actually not distinguishable from secular social work.

Katayama was not unfamiliar with the activities of Andover House. His later work at the Kingsley Hall settlement in Tokyo, in fact, reveals an intimate knowledge of its organization, objectives, and program.[18] One may well assume that he

[15] *ibid.*, p. 140. [16] *ibid.*, p. 145. [17] *ibid.*, p. 150.
[18] For the objectives of the Kingsley Hall settlement house founded

not only followed Woods's efforts with close attention but that he himself spent some time at the settlement house in Boston's South End. The extent of his absorption in practical social work is well indicated by a major decision made in the spring of 1894, when he planned to spend the vacation period traveling in the British Isles with a junior classmate, Rollin Lynde Hartt. At the end of the spring term the two theological students sailed from Boston, landing a week later at Liverpool.[19]

Although he was interested in the many diversions tempting the tourist, Katayama's primary purpose in visiting England was to study social problems. A great part of his time, consequently, was spent roaming about English and, later, Scottish cities where he observed the slum areas. The stark poverty, disease, juvenile delinquency, alcoholism, and prostitution evident at every hand was a peerless textbook. Simultaneously he examined the various projects undertaken by public and private agencies for the improvement of social conditions. With his deepened understanding of the need for settlement houses and neighborhood associations, he observed all the more carefully the humanitarian programs being carried on by such worthy institutions as Toynbee Hall and Oxford House. Nor did he pass up an opportunity to attend a mass meeting held by the recently founded Salvation Army.

Favorably impressed as Katayama was by the efforts of enlightened social leaders in London, he was unstinting in his praise of the progressive social policies of the municipal

---

in Tokyo in the spring of 1897 see Katayama Sen and Nishikawa Kojirō, *Nihon no Rōdō Undō*, Tokyo, 1955, 184-185. The charter of Andover House will be found in "Social Christianity—The Andover House Association," *Andover Review*, XVII, no. 97 (January 1892), 87-88.

[19] The entry for 1894 in the Chronology of *Jiden*, which notes that Katayama took advantage of the school recess in the spring to travel in England, is apt to be misleading. *Jiden*, p. 176, indicates only that he *planned* the trip in the spring. It is most likely that he did not depart from Boston until about the beginning of the summer.

government of Glasgow. The Scottish city, he wrote in admiration, "had set an example for the world."

"Slums had been cleared away and municipal housing had been erected for the poor. The private supply of water had been abolished, the water works being owned by the city. With the reform of the sewage system, waste matter was converted into fertilizer. The refuse of the community was used as fuel for the production of electric power. The normal house-rent for workers was set at one-fifth the amount of their wages . . . And at just the time I arrived in Glasgow the local transit lines were being taken over from the private companies without compensation and being placed under municipal management."[20] It was here in Glasgow rather than in the classroom or library that Katayama acquired his ideas on the role and responsibilities of city government which were to underlie his later programs of "water and gas works" socialism.[21]

At the end of the summer Katayama returned to Boston. When he debarked, he had no more than ten dollars in his pocket. To make his situation even more serious, he had previously made arrangements to transfer from Andover to Yale Divinity School. Hoping to secure a loan, he called upon another Andover acquaintance, Carl Kelsey, who was then serving as prison chaplain at the Concord Reformatory School just outside Boston.[22] To his tremendous joy he was immediately greeted with the news that an article he had submitted to *Harper's Monthly* had been accepted with a payment of twenty-five dollars.[23]

[20] *Jiden*, p. 191.

[21] Note the discussion of Katayama's municipal socialism in Kishimoto Eitarō, *Nihon Rōdō Undō-shi*, Tokyo, 1953, pp. 34-36.

[22] Carl Kelsey, born in Grinnell, also graduated from Grinnell College in 1890, a year after Katayama had begun his studies in Iowa. After finishing his studies at Andover in 1895, he engaged in social work for a few years and then became a college teacher of sociology. His academic career was extremely distinguished.

[23] Both the *Katayama Sen Chosho Rombun Mokuroku* compiled by the

Katayama's first compensated writing, "The H'yakusho's Summer Pleasures," appeared in February 1895.[24] The strangest article he ever wrote, it is understandable only in the light of his thought and mood of the time. A rhapsodic essay in overly rich Victorian prose recounting the natural splendors and idyllic tranquillity of rural Japan, it reflected the author's almost unbearable nostalgia. Now informed that he had become an author, Katayama's delight was twofold: not only had he broken into a national publication but he was relieved, temporarily at least, of his financial distress. Little did he know that during the next forty years his literary and journalistic output would include more than forty books and monographs as well as over five hundred periodical and newspaper articles of varying length.[25]

In September 1894, Katayama moved to New Haven. Yale Divinity School provided the capstone of Katayama's educa-

---

Katayama Sen Zenshū Henshū Iin-kai, Tokyo, [1955?], p. 3, and the Chronology of the *Jiden*, p. 341, indicate that this article was published in the *Century Magazine* in 1894. The former states that the article was entitled "Social Problems," while the latter affirms that the piece is concerned with social problems studied by Katayama during his trip abroad. Presumably these listings and comments are based upon the account given by Katayama in the *Jiden*, p. 194, but it should be pointed out that no article by him appears in the journal cited for the year 1894. In his Autobiography he doubtless had in mind his essay, "The H'yakusho's Summer Pleasures," which was published in *Harper's Monthly*, a somewhat similar periodical, in February 1895. The statement that "social problems" is the theme of the article is probably sheer fancy. The erroneous dating of the article is possibly due to a mistake in the text of the *Jiden*, p. 194, where, in the comment that the article was "published several months before in the said journal," the reading should be "after" rather than "before."

[24] Three essays by Katayama had been published previously in the Grinnell College newspaper. See "Why We Are Coming to America," *News Letter* [Iowa College], XVII, no. 3 (October 12, 1889), 30-31; "The Origin of the Japanese," *News Letter*, XVII, no. 4 (October 26, 1889), 41-42; and "The Art of Japan," *News Letter* [Iowa College], XVII, no. 5 (November 9, 1889), 53. If one considers these amateurish pieces as "publications," his article in *Harper's* was not his first published writing.

[25] The incomplete *Katayama Sen Chosho Rombun Mokuroku* (Catalogue of the Books and Articles of Katayama Sen), cited above, lists some forty books and over five hundred thirty periodical pieces.

tion in the United States. He never regretted his transfer, for all his expectations were happily fulfilled in New Haven. In keeping with trends in the leading theological seminaries in the United States the curriculum at Yale was in process of expansion, more abundant opportunities being constantly offered for the study of social problems.[26] But, apart from his classwork, he steeped himself in reading, finding the library of the Divinity School more than adequate for his special interests. The climax of his concentrated study was his dissertation, "Urban Problems in Europe and America," on which he was to base several studies subsequently published in Japan.[27] Katayama unhesitatingly deemed his year of study at Yale the most fruitful of his entire college career.[28]

For all his pleasure at attending Yale, Katayama experienced deeper privation than he had ever known. "During the eight and a half years of my life as a college student," he stated, "my year at Yale probably caused me the greatest economic difficulties. . . . Work was very hard to find . . . For nine months I did not waste a cent. I often cooked my own food and secretly washed my own laundry."[29] Because of his circumstances he avoided participation in college recreational activities and, while starved for companionship, spent most of his time in his room. Were it not for a modest scholarship and an occasional "loan" from a friend, he might well have been compelled to interrupt his studies at the very moment his coveted Bachelor of Divinity degree was drawing into sight.

Katayama's last pleasant memory of Yale was his class dinner. Several days later he was off to New York for a well deserved vacation. Then, faced with the problem of returning to Japan, he went to Northfield where once again he

[26] See Roland H. Bainton, *Yale and the Ministry*, New York, 1957, *passim*.

[27] In Japanese works this dissertation is given the title *Ō-Bei no Tōshi Mondai*.

[28] *Jiden*, p. 195.

[29] *ibid.*, pp. 194-195.

worked in the hotel for the entire summer. Having earned enough money to pay for his trip home, he traveled to Amherst to wind up his affairs. Before leaving for the West Coast to board ship, he wrote to his dear friend at Grinnell, Professor Parker. "I intend to work in Japan quite hard," he stated, "just as I did in this country, and I feel I am prepared for the work now; the time is very encouraging now in Japan. Churches are striving to live and grow in spiritual and material life. Since the decision of the last meeting of Congal. [Congregational] churches in Japan the spirit of missionary enterprise has been quite alive, so that I shall have a quite good prospect in my work.

"I thank you dear Prof. for your kindness these last six years. I shall try to live and work in the spirit you have inspired me in the class room and through your thoughtful letters."[30]

Accompanied by Sugita Kinnosuke, who had studied at the Yale Law School, Katayama then set off across the American continent, bound for Japan.

[30] Katayama to Professor Leonard Parker, letter dated September 8, 1895, Amherst, Mass. Photostatic copy in possession of author.

CHAPTER VII

HOME-COMING

As he grew older, Sen Katayama suffered from a faulty memory. His years being full and varied, memorable events and impressions crowded in bewildering confusion upon one another, so much so that he was at times unable to recall the details of those unique and personal experiences which gave individuality to his life. If, however, there was an episode which remained indelibly impressed upon his memory, it was his return to Japan from the United States in 1895.

When Katayama and Sugita Kinnosuke boarded a Russian tramp steamer at Tacoma in October 1895, they stoically resigned themselves to the prospect of an unpleasant voyage. The most that could be said about each day spent at sea aboard the *Stratnievas*[1] was that it brought each passenger one day closer to home. Imagine then the fright which swept through the ship when on the eighth day the propeller tore loose from its shaft and sank to the bottom of the ocean. As the crippled ship drifted helplessly with the current, visions of inevitable death in the frozen wastes of the North Pacific began to haunt the more excitable and imaginative passengers. For more than two months the *Stratnievas* was buffeted by waves and storms in the North Pacific. When all aboard had just about given themselves up for lost, however, a ship hove into sight and took the disabled vessel in tow. It was Christmas when Katayama, disappointed, poorer, but happy to be alive, landed at Tacoma.[2] Several days later he embarked aboard the *Victoria* for Japan.

Home-coming in January 1896 was a never-to-be-forgotten

[1] In Katayama Sen, *Jiden*, Tokyo, 1954, p. 200, the name of this Russian ship is transliterated as *Sutoratenevwasu*. It may possibly be rendered as *Stratnievas*.

[2] *ibid.*, pp. 203-204.

event in Katayama's life. After the harrowing ordeal aboard the *Stratnievas,* the sight of the eastern shores of Tokyo Bay could not but evoke an unrestrained sigh of relief and joy. But behind the exhilaration of Katayama's home-coming lurked a shadow of uneasiness. Though the presence of his countrymen about him was a comforting reminder that he was home again, he sensed, nevertheless, that he had in many ways come to a land of strangers. Having lived for so long in America, where land, man, and culture were on a grand scale, it was some time before he was able to adjust to the Lilliputian proportions of Japan and the Japanese. And if he did not speak the language of his youth with the awkwardness of a tourist, thanks to constant practice aboard ship, yet the increasingly familiar sounds rolled off his tongue with a stiffness that made him feel far more self-conscious. In his room in a Tokyo lodging house he struggled with both amusement and embarrassment to recall the manner of summoning the chambermaid. No less difficult was the task of easing himself into the delicate web of behavior and custom in which he himself had once been a slender strand. Japanese indulgence for boorishness was, he recalled, reserved only for children, the senile, and Westerners.

Katayama was not long in discovering that Tokyo was as overpowering and impersonal as any great American city. Lonely and practically friendless, he realized with a shock that there were few acquaintances to whom he cared to communicate news of his return. After calling upon Iwasaki Seishichi, to whom he was so deeply indebted, and paying a visit to his old teacher Mori Ōson at Fujioka, his list of calls was exhausted with dismaying suddenness. In a somewhat frantic attempt to reestablish a link with his past, he decided to return to his native village and to visit his all but forgotten family.

When Katayama left Tokyo, in early February, nostalgia, that most Japanese of all emotions, welled up in him and overflowed. With a happiness that bordered on sadness he thought longingly and expectantly of his home in the "midst of the purple-robed, snow-tipped mountains, in the cozy, sheltered valley, where the rain falls softly and the winds are but breezes; where Nature's beauty is seldom storm-rent; where the brook runs murmuring beside [the] cottage, and then down among the magnolias and the live-oaks where the path goes on to the village."[3] In his desperate loneliness it did not matter to Katayama that this idyllic vision concealed the many heartaches of his childhood. With neither a family nor a dwelling he could call his own this was the way Katayama insisted upon remembering his home.

Hadeki and Yuge, which he had last seen fifteen years before, had changed but little during Katayama's long absence. The new and the young, however, seemed strange and all that had once impressed him as being old now appeared perceptibly older. It was easy, if disquieting, to count the toll of the years in the wrinkled faces and grizzled hair of the adults of his youth and in the backs of peasants bending and bent with advancing age and ceaseless toil. Apart from voices, what had changed least were the mountains and the valleys and the daily topics of conversation. These were as timeless and immutable as the Japanese village itself. It was to the village home he had so blithely departed, so sentimentally remembered, that Katayama now sought to return. But, after visiting with his brother and friends in Hadeki, paying his respects at his mother's grave, and calling upon his father in Tsuyama, he realized once and forever that he could not reconstruct a permanent link with his past. Within a few weeks Katayama was on his way back to Tokyo.

When he returned to Japan with degrees from Grinnell

[3] Katayama Sen, "The H'yakusho's Summer Pleasures," *Harper's Monthly*, xc, no. 537 (February 1895), 403. This was Katayama's first published piece.

College and Yale Divinity School, Katayama hoped to launch a career in the *Kumiai* (Congregational) Church. He naïvely assumed that his fervent faith and self-sacrificing zeal would suffice to open wide the doors of the Church in Japan. How often he had been told in the seminaries and congregations of the United States that in the "heathen" land of Japan there were countless souls to be saved. Had he not heard from many a returned missionary cries of frustration over the resistance of the Japanese to spiritual conversion? And had there not been questioned in the religious press the wisdom of a missionary policy which rested the burden of work in Japan upon the shoulders of foreign servants of the Church? But unfortunately for Katayama and his ambitions, Christianity in Japan had by the time of his return fallen upon lean days.[4]

Shortly after the Imperial Restoration prospects for missionary work in newly opened Japan had been greatly enlivened. To secure the sympathy of the Western powers for its program of modernization the Meiji government had quickly abolished the old proscriptions against Christianity, and had encouraged its dissemination. But as Christianity began to make inroads against the ancient faiths of Buddhism and Shinto, interested Japanese became aware that Western civilization was by no means as unitary as they had assumed. The introduction of Western science, the discovery of historical relativism, and exposure to Unitarian theological liberalism not only shook heavily belief in the indivisibility of Christianity and Western culture but, ironically, also strengthened the forces of political and religious opposition to Christianity within Japan.

Missionary Christianity might perhaps have weathered the storms of philosophical and theological criticism which arose

[4] See the view of Kozaki Hiromichi as quoted in Kishimoto Hideo, ed., *Japanese Religion in the Meiji Era*, trans. and adapted by John F. Howes, Tokyo, 1956, pp. 261-262. Note also Charles W. Iglehart, *A Century of Protestant Christianity in Japan*, Tokyo, 1959, pp. 91-92.

in Japan during the decade of the eighties. What was insurmountable were the tides of nationalism which swelled with every failure of the Meiji government to secure revision of the so-called unequal treaties with the Western powers.[5] In the resulting political reaction against the West the fate of the "Western religion" was settled for many years. "Probably no mission field in all the history of modern missions," it was officially reported shortly after the Sino-Japanese War, "has been the source of so much rejoicing, the center of such hopes and expectations, and the cause of such keen disappointment as has the Empire of Japan."[6] This bitter complaint did not, to be sure, propose the termination of missionary activity; it rather highlighted the need to rethink the methods and purposes of Protestant Christian work in Japan.

Having no immediate prospects for a position in the *Kumiai* Church and faced with the need to earn a living, Katayama decided in the spring to 1896 to try his hand at teaching.[7] Through the recommendation of Sugita Kinnosuke, who was a graduate of the institution, he was promised employment as an instructor in English at the Waseda Preparatory

[5] Winburn T. Thomas, *Protestant Beginnings in Japan; The First Three Decades, 1859-1889*, Tokyo, 1959, pp. 202-204.

[6] American Board of Commissioners for Foreign Missions, *Annual Survey of the Work of the American Board, 1897-1898*, Boston, 1898, pp. 11.

[7] In his Autobiography, p. 210, Katayama makes the following serious accusation, the significance of which has really not been adequately appreciated by his biographers: "During the spring and summer after my return to Japan . . . I tried to become a pastor [*semmon no bokushi*] or an evangelist but, the Doshisha clique dominating affairs, I could not work for the Congregationalist Church." What is implied here, it may be suggested, is that because Katayama had no association with the Japanese converts who controlled Doshisha University and wielded tremendous influence in the Congregationalist Church in Japan, he was refused ordination as a minister. He could, thus, labor thereafter only on the fringe of the Church as a lay worker. Had Katayama been ordained and been able to develop a more satisfying religious career, it is conceivable that he would not so easily have drifted toward secular radicalism in his later years.

School.[8] But though he had spent more than ten years in the United States and was the proud possessor of three American academic degrees, Katayama was really not fluent in the language.[9] While he did, to be sure, read English with no difficulty, his letters of the period, written to his friends in America, reveal that he had not mastered basic rhetoric and grammar.[10] With the passage of the years, moreover, infrequent use greatly reduced his facility in English. Yet, despite his limitations, there were probably few Japanese at the time as well qualified as Katayama to teach the language.

In the early days of the month of July, when the hot and humid summer settled upon Tokyo, Katayama left for a vacation at the small seaside resort of Hayama. In later years Katayama deemed his stay there one of the most delightful periods of his life. At Hayama he was able to live comfortably, if modestly, to find congenial companionship, and to delve deeply into his store of books which had recently arrived from the United States. Occasionally some of his friends, doubtless attracted by his rapturous letters, came to visit him, and the days and evenings were filled with discussions, hikes, and fishing trips.[11] While he was at Hayama Katayama also launched his writing career. His only previous attempts at serious writing had involved preparation of his graduation paper at Grinnell, his dissertation at Yale Divinity School,

[8] *Waseda Semmon Gakkō*, or Waseda Preparatory School, had no connection with the famous Waseda University.

[9] It is well known that Katayama received his A.B. degree from Grinnell and his D.B. degree from Yale Divinity School. A recent examination of his records at Grinnell reveals, however, that he was also granted the A.M. degree *in absentia* at the commencement ceremony in 1896. Presumably he applied for and received credit toward his master's degree for his non-theological studies at Andover and Yale. Letter of G. L. Thornton, Registrar of Grinnell College, to author, October 22, 1959.

[10] Katayama's two articles of this period, "The H'yakusho's Summer Pleasures," *op.cit.*, pp. 403-406, and "Labour Problem Old and New," *Far East*, II, no. 10 (October 1897), 477-490, do not accurately portray his English-language facility, for they were doubtless edited before publication.

[11] *Jiden*, p. 208.

and his literary piece in *Harper's Monthly.* From 1896 until his death in 1933, however, Katayama produced an unbroken stream of books, periodical articles, brochures, and newspaper pieces for publication not only in Japan but also in the United States, Mexico, England, France, Germany, Holland, Belgium, and Russia. So tremendous was his output of writing that to this day it has continued to defy complete and definitive bibliographical listing, though it must be observed that a very large part of the product of his brush and pen is mere polemical trivia.[12]

Katayama's venture into literary and journalistic activity was in some ways an odd decision. While he obviously believed that he had much of interest and value to communicate to his countrymen, he was nevertheless acutely aware that long disuse had deprived him of his once facile command of written Japanese. With the assistance of several ghost-writers, however, he undertook to produce two books. The first work was *Tetsudō Shinron* (An Essay on the Railroad Problem).[13] Written in a serious theoretical vein and advocating nationalization of Japan's railway lines, the book had only a limited sale and, apparently, no immediate influence upon official or public opinion. The second book, which did not appear until the following year, was *Eikoku Konnichi no Shakai* (English Society Today).[14] Based upon notes taken during his summer visit to Great Britain in 1894,

[12] The lengthiest, but still incomplete, listing of Katayama's writings is the *Katayama Sen Chosho Rombun Mokuroku* (Catalogue of the Books and Articles of Katayama Sen) compiled by the *Katayama Sen Zenshū Henshū Iin-kai* (Committee for the Collection of the Complete Works of Katayama Sen). See chapter VI, n. 23. A thirty-six page mimeographed brochure of folio size, it was issued in Tokyo, apparently for private circulation, in the winter of 1955-1956. There are various indications that the foreign-language listings are largely based, and without acknowledgement, upon Hyman Kublin, "A Bibliography of the Writings of Sen Katayama in Western Languages," *Far Eastern Quarterly*, XI, no. 1 (November 1951), 71-77, which is also incomplete.

[13] *Tetsudō Shinron* was published by the Hakubun-kan in 1896.

[14] *Eikoku Konnichi no Shakai* was brought out by the Keisui-sha in 1897.

the work was an undisguised potboiler, satisfying neither the Japanese appetite for travel literature nor Katayama's pressing need for funds. During the following months several studies on sociological and economic themes were also published in the widely read journal *Taiyō*, while his long biographical sketch of the German Socialist, Ferdinand Lassalle, appeared serially in the influential monthly of the *Kumiai* Church, the *Rikugo Zasshi.* These latter pieces provided the basis for a book on the life of Lassalle issued in 1897.[15]

In September Katayama eagerly began his English-language instruction at Waseda Preparatory School. Unfortunately the behavior of his students, who had unfeelingly taken the mark of their teacher, drove him to despair. When for the purposes of conversational practice he called for reports on social conditions in Tokyo, he listened in embarrassment to personal and uninhibited accounts of visits to the "red-light" districts or to geisha houses of questionable repute. In the primness of his adult years and with the stern morality of the Christian convert he preferred to forget his own excursions to houses of prostitution during his Tokyo school days. But even more shocking was his discovery that the amorous escapades of Waseda "Prep's" headmaster were the subject of common gossip among the students. It is improbable that Katayama, confronted with these aberrations from his personal moral standards, remained silent. His sermonic disapprobations must assuredly have singled him out as an insufferable bore and paved the way for his ultimate dismissal. Laid low by an attack of smallpox, which confined him to the hospital for many long weeks, Katayama was abruptly discharged in the late fall of 1896. Without the slightest regard for the demands of decency, he angrily

[15] *Rōdō-sha no Ryōyū; Razāru-den* (Lassalle; Friend of the Workers), Tokyo, Kingusurei-kan, 1897.

commented, "I was cast aside like a worn-out pair of straw sandals."[16]

For all his indignation at his treatment, it is rather unlikely that Katayama would have continued to serve as a teacher at Waseda Preparatory School. At the very time he was unhappy about conditions in the school, Katayama was visited by the Reverend Daniel C. Greene, who was in charge of the Congregational Mission in Japan. To his great delight he learned that the American Board had decided to establish a settlement house in Tokyo. Even more exciting to Katayama was the offer of the position of Director and a salary of twenty-five *yen* per month, a somewhat niggardly amount but really not ungenerous by the standards of the ever poorly paid callings of church and social work. That the proposition was accepted with alacrity attests to the self-sacrificing rather than self-seeking character of Katayama, for the most that could be said of social work in Japan, as in many other parts of the world of the time, was that it offered prospects for a career but not for a comfortable living.

On March 1, 1897, the new settlement house was opened in Kanda, a section of Tokyo largely inhabited by poor workers and perhaps even poorer university students. Kingsley Hall, named after the famous English Christian Socialist, may rightly claim to be the first settlement house established in Japan.[17] The new social center symbolized a modest but

[16] *Jiden*, p. 210. Katayama revealed the gravity of his illness in a letter to Professor Parker at Grinnell. "I got small pox," he wrote, "and been in the hospital for (?) weeks. I suffered great deal, but came out nicely so I am alright now but at one period of my illness I thought that I may never be of this world again, but God was with me as he is today and had been in the past. I am very much thankful that I am still alive. . . ." Katayama to Parker, Kanda, Tokyo, January 27, 1897. Photostatic copy of letter in possession of author.

[17] For the opening of Kingsley Hall see *Jiden*, pp. 211-212; Arthur L. Weatherly, "Kingsley Hall, Tokyo, and Its Founder," *Commons*, II, no. 8 (December 1897), 2-3; and Murai Tomoyoshi, "Japanese Settlements," *Commons*, I, no. 13 (April–May 1897), 1-2.

extremely important shift in Congregational missionary activity. Most denominational establishments in Japan were still primarily concerned with the saving of souls, and religious workers were dedicated to the objectives of spiritual conversion and Biblical instruction. This highest and most beneficent of aims could be, many servants of the Church continued to insist, the only justification and purpose of missionary endeavor.

Though religious orders and agencies had from the earliest years of the Meiji period founded hospitals, nurseries, kindergartens, and schools, the promotion of the social welfare of the Japanese had commonly been viewed as a useful means to a spiritual end. But however zealous missionaries may have presented their social and educational institutions to the public, there were not wanting sharp-eyed Japanese, both sympathetic converts and antagonistic non-Christians, who readily perceived their fundamental purpose. Thus, when the Reverend M. L. Gordon of the American Board in Kyoto opened the *Airin-sha* (House of Neighborly Love) shortly before the Sino-Japanese War, not all his friends accepted his claim that the institution was a bona-fide settlement house. "The distinctive feature of *Airin-sha*," a Japanese clergyman quickly pointed out, "is that it is missionary, and religious teaching is a large portion of its work. It is practically a household church, including Sunday school, Bible classes, etc."[18] Kingsley Hall did not completely ignore basic religious activities but its administration and program were more in line with the rising settlement-house movement in England and the United States.

The Constitution of Kingsley Hall was modeled on that of the already well-known South End Settlement House in Boston, where Katayama had worked for a brief period dur-

[18] "Social Settlements in Japan," *Outlook*, LVI, no. 9 (June 26, 1897), 511.

ing his Andover days.[19] The principal aim of Japan's pioneer settlement house was, he explained at the time of its opening, "to become a connecting link between the higher and lower classes of the country and . . . to impart scientific knowledge to young men."[20] It was the emphasis given to what in modern parlance is known as fundamental and adult education, to opportunities for intellectual advancement, and to moral improvement, with less stress upon formal religious exhortation, that especially distinguished Kingsley Hall's objectives. Financing of the admittedly ambitious venture in social work was made possible by a modest contribution from the American Board and by the organization of the Kingsley Hall Association with a dues-paying membership enlisted from sympathetic Japanese and foreigners.

For a short while after the opening of Kingsley Hall Katayama was assisted by Mrs. Daniel C. Greene and Miss Florence Denton of the American Board. Otherwise, activities and instruction rested heavily upon his own personal knowledge and interests. In addition to regular Bible classes, Sunday school, and other essential religious teaching, the settlement house hopefully offered "lectures on sociology, socialism, economics, and the German and English languages."[21] These subjects, with the exception of English-language instruction, being avant-garde, they failed to evoke any appreciable interest in the community. To Katayama's regret only a handful of the university students, who traditionally roomed in the cheap lodging houses of Kanda, were attracted by his lectures. As for the numerous common

[19] Weatherly, *op.cit.*, p. 2; Katayama Sen and Nishikawa Kōjirō, *Nihon no Rōdō Undō*, Tokyo, 1955, pp. 184-185, or Morito Tatsuo, *Nihon ni okeru Kirisuto-kyō to Shakai Shugi Undō*, Tokyo, 1950, pp. 108-109; and "Social Christianity—The Andover House Association," *Andover Review*, XVII, no. 97 (January 1892), 87-88.

[20] Katayama, as quoted in the *Asylum Record*, I, no. 4 (April–May 1897), 9.

[21] *ibid.*, p. 9.

laborers who lived in the area, the academic aspect of the program could not even arouse their curiosity.[22]

If workers could not be lured into Kingsley Hall to attend academic courses, the titles of which they literally did not understand, they responded with tremendous enthusiasm to a series of lectures devoted to the contemporary American scene. Presented by Katayama under the title *To-bei Annai* (Introducing the United States), these talks were based on the theme, "Go east, young man," and were designed to kindle an interest in immigration to America. Since no more than a few thousand Japanese, largely students and servants of the government, had as yet made the trip across the Pacific, the popular appeal of these lectures is understandable. And who better than Katayama, who had set out for the United States many years before utterly ignorant of its people, language, and customs, could better appreciate the dreams and fears of the unprivileged poor? Because of their instantaneous success his lectures on America not only had to be offered repeatedly but upon their publication the edition was sold out within a week. An alert Tokyo daily, moreover, quickly introduced a regular feature with the same title. In later years Katayama reverted to this popular topic, writing a book and several sequels as well as founding the magazine *To-bei Annai*.[23]

Particularly dear to Katayama was the hope of establishing a kindergarten at Kingsley Hall. The kindergarten as an experiment in early childhood education was not at the

[22] Yamakawa Hitoshi, one of the great leaders of the modern Japanese social movement, has recalled his first encounter with Katayama's name. While walking along the street in Tokyo shortly after the close of the Sino-Japanese War, he noticed a placard announcing a lecture by "Katayama Sen, Master of Arts." Puzzled at the time by the degree, he later scoffed at Katayama's "bourgeois pretensions." See Yamakawa Hitoshi, "Katayama Sen Shi no Omoidashi," *Kaizō*, xv, no. 12 (December 1933), 92.

[23] See Chapter xi. For the reminiscences of one of his students at Kingsley Hall see Miyakawa Torao, "Katayama Sen to Tobari Kogan," *Rekishi Hyōron*, no. 102 (February 1959), 66-68.

time completely unknown in Japan but Japanese, much like Western educational authorities, continued to vacillate in their attitudes and policies toward preschool education. At the very time Kingsley Hall was opened the entire problem was in process of review by the government. Not only did Katayama have difficulty in obtaining the required license but the construction and equipment of a kindergarten, which would fulfill the somewhat exacting requirements of the law, necessitated a financial outlay beyond the limited resources of the Kingsley Hall Association. Having no prospect of raising the required funds in Japan, Katayama addressed a desperate appeal to Arthur L. Weatherly, his old friend and classmate at Andover. This letter is of more than passing interest, for it poignantly reveals not only the great value which Katayama placed upon the establishment of the kindergarten but also the intensity of his religious fervor at the time. "I can only open my heart to you," he wrote, "and ask you for this [help] . . . I am, day and night, praying for the work to be done by the aid of our Master Jesus. You know," he reminded Weatherly, "I asked you Americans very little while I was in your country. If it was not for the mission work I would not appeal to you in this manner. I am sure that you will work for me and Japan."[24] So earnest a plea was understandably difficult to resist.

Weatherly's prompt response to the call for financial assistance evoked a heartfelt thanks from Katayama. "I shall try to make every cent count in building up the work for humanity," he wrote, "and shall spend it with greater care than if it were my own money."[25] To those who knew the perennially provident Katayama this pledge, so gratefully made, was an ironclad guarantee. And once the necessary funds were in hand and authorization had been received

[24] Letter from Katayama to Weatherly, September 1897, in Weatherly, *op.cit.*, p. 2.

[25] "Katayama's Thanks," *Commons*, III, no. 24 (April 1898), 5.

from the government, the Kingsley Hall kindergarten, one of the first early childhood centers to be operated under private auspices in Japan, met with conspicuous success. Filling an unmistakable need, especially of the numerous working mothers in Kanda, there was never any problem in filling the annual classes. One may easily appreciate Katayama's sense of jubilation and pride when he noted that during the years the kindergarten was maintained more than six hundred children were the recipients of its benefits.

After so many years of almost aimless and patient groping for a purpose in life Kingsley Hall, with its concrete achievements, was a vindication of Katayama's dreams. Having discovered a career which promised to satisfy his need to prove his worth to himself and to his fellow men, he proceeded to indulge in an orgy of creative work. Day after day he rushed exultantly from one responsibility to another, never too busy to accept new and demanding tasks. In addition to being Director of Kingsley Hall and participating vigorously in its growing program of activities, he permitted himself to be coopted as an all-round worker for the Unitarian Church. Here he taught Sunday school, assisted in the publication of and contributed articles to the monthly mission journal, the *Rikugo Zasshi,* and carried out whatever sundry tasks his superiors shunted his way. But rather than resent these supererogatory chores, Katayama accepted them with gratitude. In those days, he later confessed, "I was still a fervent Christian."[26] He was, in short, one of those typical individuals, essential to all organizations, who can always be relied upon to be unprotestingly exploited.

Amidst his endless routine of labor for Kingsley Hall and the church, Katayama also found time to continue his writing. The sheer volume of studies he succeeded in turning out

[26] *Jiden,* p. 212. See also Katayama Sen, "Waga Kuni Shōrai no Shūkyō," *Nihon Shūkyō,* II, no. 6 (December 20, 1896), 291-296.

during the year 1897 is amazing. Not a month passed without the appearance of a sober and thoughtful article in such highly esteemed journals as the *Rikugo Zasshi, Shakai Zasshi, Taiyō,* and *Kokumin no Tomo.* These pieces, less diffusive in their themes than his earlier studies, reveal, moreover, a constantly sharpening focus upon the problems of industrial-labor relations which more and more absorbed his thought and concern. Foreshadowing new directions in his social and intellectual effort, Katayama's writings of this period brought him to the direct and respectful attention of progressive political and educational leaders throughout Tokyo and Japan.

Katayama's sudden emergence to modest fame as a social and community leader was observed with deep satisfaction and unrestrained relief by his circle of old-time friends. Since he was at long last earning a secure living and enjoying, in addition, a respectable social standing, they now urged upon him an important decision he was obviously reluctant to make on his own initiative. Because of the very nature of his work, not to speak of his personal happiness, they insisted that it was neither proper nor wise that he continue to be a bachelor. For a Japanese male who was approaching his thirty-eighth birthday to be unmarried was unthinkable. But irrefutable as these arguments may have seemed to his well-wishers, there were, it may be surmised, less apparent but more profound reasons for his hesitation to assume the serious responsibilities of a wife and family.

During his early adult years and during his stay in the United States, marriage had been out of the question for Katayama. Pursuing his education unfalteringly and quite satisfied with only the basic necessities of life, he had had neither the inclination to maintain a household nor the prospect of supporting a spouse. But these considerations, obvious as they are, really throw no light upon his attitude toward marriage. His occasional views on the matter, expressed with a disarming naïveté, are not entirely convincing. Is it then too much to presume that he possessed a strong but unvocalized distaste for matrimony nurtured constantly by memory of the tragic experience of his own parents and, particularly, of his mother and her two sons? Is it not likely that he consciously but silently dreaded a repetition of a misfated marriage such as had caused so much pain and grief for his mother and father, for his brother and himself? In affairs of life and society Katayama was an incorrigible optimist, but a marital setback with its incalculable consequences was perhaps a risk he was hesitant to take.

Whatever Katayama's thoughts on marriage may have been, his apparent indifference and weak objections were no match for the persuasions of his friends. Once his consent had been received, his benefactor, Iwasaki, assumed forthwith the role of matchmaker. Not surprisingly, a wide search did not have to be made, for a suitable bride was found with transparent ease. Fude was the second daughter of the Yokodzuka family, whose home was in Mizushiro, a tiny village not far from Fujioka where Katayama had begun his teaching career many years before. With strongly molded features and a shy but winsome smile, she was a simple and unsophisticated girl in the full bloom of youth. Born on July 4, 1877, she was about half the age of her prospective husband. After the traditional introduction and necessary preliminaries had been completed, Sen and Fude were married on November 8, 1897.[27]

Marriages in Japan being customarily arranged by invited go-betweens, professional and otherwise, there was nothing unusual in the manner of Katayama's taking a wife. What was exceptional, however, was his overtly cavalier attitude and behavior, which was doubtless a cloak for his inner trepidations toward an event in life which his religious faith sternly enjoined was not to be flippantly approached.

[27] See the Chronology in *Jiden*, pp. 342-343.

In later years he himself was somewhat shamefacedly to recount the episode. "The arrangements having been made," Katayama recalled, "I went to Furukawa-machi and met my future wife. She provided me with a meal and, having partaken of her food, I went home. The day of the wedding arrived and I didn't quite know what to do. So," he continued, "I went to the barber and had my hair cut. That's all. Everything for the dinner that night was taken care of by my friend Iwasaki. How carefree can a person be?"[28] In a last and defiant gesture of independence Katayama, an uneasy bridegroom, thus drew down the curtain on his bachelor years.

With his marriage, Katayama enjoyed a family life for the first time since his Okayama years. Home now meant for him more than a mere address, a repository for his personal effects, and a place to eat his meals. He was truly happy with his young bride and his earlier fears and doubts about marital life now appeared to have been utterly groundless. And to add to his joy Fude bore him two children: Yasuko, a daughter, born on February 28, 1899, and, Kan'ichi, his son and heir, on May 19, 1901. This successor to the Katayama family name was unfortunately ill-fated; he succumbed to an attack of double pneumonia on July 18, 1922.[29]

Once he had accustomed himself to the pattern of domestic life, Katayama resumed his routine of activities at Kingsley Hall and at the Unitarian Church. And, as might perhaps have been expected, it was not long before his boundless energy impelled him to plunge into new and unprecedented social and community ventures. Modest and unpretentious as he may have been, Katayama nevertheless increasingly required a grand stage on which to perform his self-assigned act in life. Kingsley Hall was, after all, but another Hadeki, another academic institution, another point of departure into the beckoning unknown.

[28] *Jiden*, p. 211.

[29] Records of the Graves Registry Office, *Aoyama Reien* (Aoyama Cemetery), Tokyo.

CHAPTER VIII

LABOR ORGANIZER

In April 1897, Japanese factory workers, hurrying along in the chill morning air, were greeted by an unusual sight at the entrances to their places of employment. Two men, indifferent to the stir and comment their action aroused among passersby, were busily engaged in distributing copies of a slim pamphlet with polite exhortations that they be read with careful attention. Since it was not often that Japanese workers were offered something for nothing, they crowded about to share in the handout and large quantities of the brochure were quickly disposed of.

The pamphlet passed out to Japanese factory employees in the early spring of 1897 was entitled *Shokkō Shokun ni Yokosu* (A Summons to the Workers). Its author was Takano Fusatarō, a young but able journalist of the Yokohama *Advertiser*, an English-language daily catering to the needs of the small foreign community in Japan. The two distributors were Jō Tsunetarō, a cobbler by trade, and Sawada Hannosuke, a tailor. Though the appearance of the labor tract received at the time no widespread notice in Tokyo, the occasion became a red-letter day in the history of the Japanese labor movement. With its message aimed specifically at industrial workers, who were urged to organize in protection of their mutual interests, *Shokkō Shokun ni Yokosu* heralded the birth of trade-unionism in modern Japan.[1]

[1] The circumstances in which the labor pamphlet *Shokkō Shokun ni Yokosu* was prepared and distributed are discussed in Yokoyama Gennosuke, *Nihon no Shakai Undō*, reprinted in *Nihon no Kasō Shakai*, by the same author, Tokyo, 1955, pp. 314ff. See also Katayama Sen and Nishikawa Kōjirō, *Nihon no Rōdō Undō*, Tokyo, 1955, pp. 17ff. A pertinent commentary upon the authorship of the pamphlet will be found in Hyman Kublin, *Meiji Rōdō Undō-shi no Hito-koma; Takano Fusatarō no Shōgai to Shisō*, Tokyo, 1959, pp. 36-37. See also Hyman Kublin, "Takano Fusataro: a Study in Early Japanese Trades-Unionism," *American Philosophical Society, Proceedings*, CIII (August 15, 1959), p. 577.

The advent of would-be labor organizers and agitators upon the industrial-labor scene in Japan in the late nineteenth century was obviously a response to the economic transformations which had been occurring with mounting intensity since the closing years of the Tokugawa Shogunate. Though the feudal basis of Japanese life had, to be sure, been undergoing slow but constant modification during the several centuries of national isolation, it was really only with the Imperial Restoration in 1868 that a conscious and relatively systematic effort was launched to reshape the Japanese society and economy along modern lines. To foster the growth of a modern state it was taken as axiomatic by the Meiji oligarchs that industrialization had to be promoted as rapidly as possible. But, like many underdeveloped countries seeking to overcome their economic heritage, Japan was confronted with innumerable challenging problems. Of paramount importance were the lack of capital accumulation, managerial and technical skills, and entrepreneurial spirit. In the face of lethargic private initiative it was consequently necessary for the Meiji state itself to assume the role of leadership in programs to uplift the economy of the nation. As an inevitable result, the government for some years thereafter exercised a powerful, and at times inordinate, influence upon the nature and course of Japanese industrialization.

The industrial enterprises founded and nurtured under the auspices of the state in the early Meiji period were designed to further its immediate political interests. Determined to defend the new regime against actual internal threats and potential foreign enemies, government leaders lavished the meager resources of the nation upon the construction of heavy industries and communication facilities which strengthened the newly created national army and navy. The establishment of light consumer industries by private businessmen was also not neglected. By the generous allotment of direct and indirect subsidies, by the passage of beneficial legislation, and by a host of measures designed to encourage industrial activity, an attack was launched against the socio-economic system inherited from the preceding regime. Although the progress made by public and private entrepreneurs in the years before the Sino-Japanese War was impressive principally in comparison with the state of affairs prevailing during the late Tokugawa period, the foundations of an industrial capitalistic system were nevertheless firmly laid down.

This formative period in the history of modern Japan, embracing the years from 1868 to 1895, was perhaps more an era of adjustment to the pressures of a growing nation and of an expanding world than of actual physical achievement in the modernization of the country. Japan was, insofar as the dynamism of human affairs would permit, a vast social laboratory, in which endless experiments were undertaken to the end that the nation might as soon as possible become independent, rich, and powerful. In this welter of economic change, social flux, political struggle, and intellectual ferment workers first discovered or were apprised of their birthrights. For a decade and more before the Sino-Japanese War declassé agitators fulminated against the labor practices of the government and private business, while strikes occasionally broke out in widely dispersed factories because of dissatisfaction with wages and working conditions. But, as in other countries experiencing the first pangs of industrialism, the pioneer champions of labor's interests in Japan were all too often intellectuals who had awakened too soon and bewildered workers who opposed the very technological changes which could create a *raison d'être* for a labor movement. Because of their activities, however, an awareness that industrialization bred new and peculiar social problems was gradually aroused.

Numerous epochal effects upon the stimulation of the

Japanese labor movement have been ascribed to the Sino-Japanese War. Marxists have insisted that the conflict signalized the firm entrenchment of industrial capitalism in Japan. Few matters in Japanese social history demand more thorough restudy. Without discoursing upon the details of the problem, it may be suggested that what is essentially a question of history has too frequently been treated as an exercise in statistics, philosophy, or polemics. It is indisputably true that during the war with China the number of factories in Japan increased appreciably, that the amount of capital corporately subscribed rose considerably, and that the ranks of industrial workers multiplied slightly. But to infer from these data that industrial capitalism as a social and economic system had been solidly established in Japan is unwarranted.[2]

What is important for an understanding of the growth of industrial capitalism and of the unfolding of the labor movement in Japan is the relative rather than the absolute nature of the economic developments of the late nineteenth century. By the criteria that prevailed in the far more industrialized nations of the West, there did not exist in Japan the conditions ordinarily deemed necessary for the successful initiation of a labor movement. It is only fair to point out that Japanese intellectuals who sought to organize trade-unions in the aftermath of the Sino-Japanese War were acutely

[2] Japanese statistics for the Meiji period are not always adequate or complete. The following data, pertinent for the study of Japanese industrial capitalism, should, nevertheless, provide food for thought.

Year	*No. of Factories*	*Men*	*Women*	*Total*	*Population*
1896	7,640	173,614	261,218	434,832	———
1897	7,287	182,792	234,462	437,254	43,228,863
1898	7,085	177,632	234,573	412,205	43,763,855
1899	6,699	158,793	264,378	423,171	44,260,642
1900	7,284	164,712	257,307	422,019	44,815,980

For statistics on numbers of factories and factory workers, see *Japan Year Book*, 1907, Tokyo, 1908, p. 383; and for population figures, *Japan Year Book*, 1905, Tokyo, 1906, p. 14.

aware of the situation. Their actions were thus initially of an anticipatory character, motivated not only by a distaste for existing labor conditions but also, and perhaps more importantly, by a dread of what the future portended.[3] Unfortunately for Japan's pioneer trade-union leaders and the workers they hoped to lead, in preparing for a future day they could not rely upon the support of the armies of the proletariat yet to be.

It was under these circumstances that Takano Fusatarō, one of the outstanding trade-union organizers of the Meiji period, appeared on the labor stage. Born in Nagasaki in 1868, he had lived in Yokohama for several years before emigrating to the United States. In 1890 Takano joined with Jō Tsunetarō, Sawada Hannosuke, and a few other Japanese workers in San Francisco to establish a small study group named the *Shokkō Giyū-kai* (Friends of Labor). Planning to return to their homeland some day and noting the steady progress of industrialization in Japan, the members undertook to prepare themselves to assist their countrymen in coping with the industrial-labor problems that were certain to arise. During their years in the United States these aspiring trade-union organizers came under the strong influence of the American Federation of Labor and the trade-union philosophy of its president, Samuel Gompers.

Takano returned to Yokohama in 1896 and, while working as a reporter on the *Advertiser,* continued his studies of labor problems. As he had anticipated during his stay in the United States, bitter industrial-labor strife had set in at the close of the war with China. Manufacturers vied with one another for ever greater profits, displaying at the same time

[3] Some of the personal and psychological factors involved in the shaping of the attitudes of early Japanese radicals toward social problems are discussed in Hyman Kublin, "Left-Wing Leaders and Social Movements in Meiji Japan," an unpublished paper presented at the xxvth International Congress of Orientalists, Moscow, USSR, August 11, 1960.

a callous disregard for the welfare of their employees. At times, Japanese workers, disgruntled as much by the rise in the cost of living that had accompanied and followed the war as by the conditions of their employment, launched spontaneous strikes. But, save for an occasional note of warning and plea for corrective action in the "intellectual" press, the government and people were apathetic. The state was apparently far more concerned with the welfare of the country than with that of the populace, while a people still overwhelmingly agrarian in interest had too many troubles of its own to be disturbed by the misfortunes of others.

Well formed and clear as were his ideas upon industrial-labor relations in Japan, there is little evidence that Takano attempted to agitate on behalf of the workers during the first year after his return from the United States. Why this was so, in view of his strong beliefs, is difficult to explain. It may, however, be surmised that Takano hesitated to undertake alone the task of labor agitation and decided to await the return of other members of the *Shokkō Giyū-kai* from America. Not living in Tokyo or Osaka, the centers of the new and modern industries, not having any intimate acquaintance with progressive social leaders, and lacking the financial resources necessary to underwrite a campaign in the labor field, Takano may well have had no alternative but to bide his time. But when in late 1896 Jō Tsunetarō and Sawada Hannosuke returned to Tokyo, Takano soon embarked upon a new career.

During the next few months the *Shokkō Giyū-kai* was reconstituted. Presumably Takano, Jō, and Sawada debated for a brief while the course of action to be pursued. At issue was the question of deciding whether conditions in Japan were "ripe" for the promotion of a trade-union movement. Takano himself, it is known, had serious reservations about the wisdom of initiating agitation among the factory workers, believing that they were still too conservative and ill-informed to appreciate the need for organization. Since his stay in the United States he had been convinced that the first step in arousing the workers was the awakening of the "thinkers," the socially minded and intellectually enlightened leaders of the nation.[4] Jō and Sawada, on the other hand, held that conditions were timely for trade-union activity, and succeeded in persuading Takano to fire the opening salvo in the drive for the unionization of Japanese laborers.

Takano's *Shokkō Shokun ni Yokosu,* written in early 1897, is one of the most trenchant and moving appeals ever made in the history of the Japanese labor movement. Fresh in language and thought, devoid of the deadening jargon of labor polemics, and clear in its presentation of the fundamental issues, it embodied all Takano's hopes and fears for the future of his countrymen.

"You workers . . . ," he cried out, "are people without capital who provide a living for others than yourselves. One of your arms and one of your legs are, so to speak, devoted to the support of society. When you meet with some misfortune and are disabled or when you become infirm with age and can no longer work, you are immediately deprived of the means of earning a living and are turned out into the street. Should death overtake you, your wives and your children are hard put to stay alive. In this state of affairs you are really as helpless as a candle in the wind."[5] He then explained the procedure for organizing trade-unions, drawing largely upon the example of the American Federation of Labor, and the mutual benefit system practiced by work-

[4] Tekano Fusataro [sic], "Labor Movement in Japan," *American Federationist,* I, no. 8 (October 1894), p. 164. For the text of this article see also Kublin, *Meiji Rōdō Undō-shi no Hito-koma,* pp. 3-11.

[5] For the Japanese text of *Shokkō Shokun ni Yokosu* see Katayama and Nishikawa, *op.cit.,* pp. 18-27. The English quotation is taken from my partial translation of the pamphlet published in Theodore W. De Bary, ed., *Sources of the Japanese Tradition,* New York, 1958, pp. 807-811.

ers in the United States. Takano's effort was worthy of a veteran agitator.

In their quest to prod the workers of Japan into action and to focus the attention of the public upon the social dangers raised by the process of industrialization, the Friends of Labor did not limit themselves to the publication of a mere pamphlet. An open meeting, sponsored by the group, was held in the quarters of the *Kinki-kan* in Tokyo on April 6.[6] On this occasion Takano, as the main speaker, reiterated the message of *Shokkō Shokun ni Yokosu.* This gathering, which was attended by "several hundred workers," has unfortunately been overlooked by almost all Japanese labor historians, yet the event marked the real opening of the labor movement in Japan.

Despite its historical importance, Takano was not greatly impressed by the results of the gathering. "It cannot be said that the meeting has done much toward the labor movement in this country," he observed, "but it serves as a foundation for future work."[7] When, however, he considered the prospects for "future work," Takano was deeply unhappy. Of immediate concern was the difficulty of securing funds, without which the program of public assemblies sponsored by the Friends of Labor would have to be abandoned. To obtain contributions from wage-starved workers was nearly impossible. And in a letter to his friend Samuel Gompers, Takano grieved over his inability to find a "financial angel." "I hope," he wrote in concluding his lament, "we will not be forced to abandon the idea of holding meetings."[8]

Adding to the problems of the Friends of Labor was the onset of a business recession in 1897. In all industrial societies efforts to promote trade-unionism during times of depression

[6] Takano Fusataro, "Our Organizer in Japan," *American Federationist*, IV, no. 4 (June 1897), p. 77. For the text of this article see also Kublin, *Meiji Rōdō Undō-shi no Hito-koma*, pp. 47-49.

[7] Takano, "Our Organizer in Japan," p. 77.

[8] *ibid.*, p. 78.

have usually been unavailing. Nevertheless, as strikes continued to flare up, Takano and his friends pressed on with their campaign to organize the workers. This was a fateful decision, one which in the long run was to have unfortunate results. It was Japan's tragedy that the first significant attempt to organize trade-unions occurred in a period when economic conditions were inopportune.

The adverse conditions notwithstanding, Takano and his comrades pressed ahead with their project. Takano himself was persuaded to move from Yokohama to Tokyo and to direct the activities of the Friends of Labor. For the next few months he scurried about the city, attempting to enlist the cooperation of intellectual and civic leaders who might be of assistance in "educating" the workers. Shimada Saburō, a liberal journalist and politician, and Suzuki Junichirō, a professor of economics at Tokyo Imperial University, were thus induced to join the Friends of Labor. An unusually valuable ally was found in Sakuma Teiichi, the wealthy and progressive owner of one of Tokyo's largest printing houses. It was under these circumstances also that Katayama was sought out by Takano and persuaded to throw in his lot with the burgeoning labor group.

In the spring of 1897 Katayama was not, it should be recognized, very well informed about labor unions. He had never revealed any special interest in industrial-labor problems during his stay in the United States, though he had, to be sure, met the famous Tom Mann during his brief visit to England in the summer of 1894. Katayama's heart still lay in social and settlement-house work, in kindergarten education, and in municipal reform. Despite the hopes placed in him by the Friends of Labor, he himself disclaimed any competency in the labor field, insisting that his talent and skills were vested rather in "social problems."[9] But being well on the road to the life of a "do-gooder," he

[9] Katayama Sen, *Jiden*, Tokyo, 1954, p. 217.

could not resist the invitation to participate actively and prominently in a worthy social enterprise. In this frame of mind Katayama with his typical zeal began the career of a trade-union organizer that was to win him lasting fame in his country.

Japan's first trade-union organizers, including Katayama, were, though radicals within the context of Japanese conditions, essentially moderate in their beliefs. Being basically social reformers, they did not consider the capitalist system to be inherently evil. Not of "proletarian" background or status themselves, they believed nevertheless that laborers had a right to a decent living and to hope in life. When they undertook to promote a trade-union movement, they had no intention of stirring up social discord but rather sought to work for the elimination of the abuses in working conditions which were fomenting strife in the industrial world. It is not surprising that for a brief period businessmen and government officials in general viewed their activities tolerantly, if not with complete indifference.

By the summer of 1897 it had become possible for the group to take positive action in the labor field. On June 25 a public meeting, attended by some twelve hundred workers, was held in Kanda, Tokyo. Addresses were presented by Jō Tsunetarō, Sakuma Teiichi, and Matsumura Kaisuke. It was at this time that Katayama delivered his maiden speech on labor affairs, his talk being appropriately entitled "The Necessity for Labor Solidarity."[10] At the conclusion of the proceedings Takano, as spokesman for the Friends of Labor, then called upon members of the audience to join in the establishment of an association to promote the formation of trade-unions. Only forty-seven of the laborers present, a rather discouraging number, responded to the appeal.[11]

With a small group of intellectuals as leaders and with less

[10] Katayama and Nishikawa, *op.cit.*, p. 27.
[11] Watanabe Kango, *Meiji Shakai Undō-shi*, Tokyo, 1955, p. 34.

than a hundred workers as members the *Rōdō Kumiai Kisei-kai* (Society for the Promotion of Trade-Unions) was organized on July 7. Though the new association revealed in its outlook the strong influence of the American Federation of Labor, it was nevertheless designed to cope with the specific realities of the Japanese industrial-labor world. The purpose and function of this organization have commonly been misunderstood; it was not a trade-union *per se* but, as its name clearly denotes, a society for the encouragement of trade-union organization. The leaders of the Society thought of it as a "trades union school."[12] As such, it undertook to provide education in labor problems for workers, who were then expected to agitate among their fellows to the end that a trade-union be organized in their craft. The Society also strove to coordinate the activities of trade-unions and devoted itself to the advancement of the common interests of labor.

At its first meeting on July 7 the *Rōdō Kumiai Kisei-kai* prepared a tentative constitution and elected its officers and functionaries. As the prime movers in the creation of the labor association, Takano Fusatarō, Jō Tsunetarō, Sawada Hannosuke, and several others were honored with the posts of secretaries. It was also decided to continue with the program of public forums to educate the public and the workers. For this purpose contributions were to be solicited. By the end of July it was possible to sponsor a second meeting of workers, which was convened in the YMCA hall in Kanda. As a result of addresses and appeals delivered by Takano, Jō, Katayama, Shimada, and others, the *Rōdō Kumiai Kisei-kai* gained a small number of new recruits.[13]

[12] Takano Fusataro, "Prospects of the Japanese Labor Movement," *American Federationist*, IV, no. 9 (November 1897), p. 210. See also Kublin, *Meiji Rōdō Undō-shi no Hito-koma*, p. 56. Among Japanese labor historians Professor Ōkōchi Kazuo has been almost alone in noting this essential point. See his *Reimei-ki no Nihon Rōdō Undō*, Tokyo, 1955, pp. 148-149.

[13] By early September 1897, Takano estimated the number of mem-

Inspired by evidences of their headway, inconsequential as they may have appeared to the public at large, the Society held its first regular monthly meeting on August 1. The constitution of the organization was now formally adopted and Takano was elected Secretary-General. In recognition of his efforts to further the aims of the new labor movement Katayama was appointed to the Board of Directors and made a member of all education committees.[14] And since it seemed that the *Rōdō Kumiai Kisei-kai* showed promise of becoming more than a mere gathering of intellectuals, a continuing program of agitation was planned. In the fall of 1897 public meetings were, accordingly, sponsored two and three times monthly and the area of activity was soon extended to nearby Yokohama.

It would be an exaggeration to maintain that with the birth of the Japanese labor movement Katayama had at long last discovered his place and purpose in life. For some time to come labor agitation was but one of a multitude of his activities aimed at the advancement of the social welfare. He continued to carry on his work at Kingsley Hall, to engage in the educational programs of the *Kumiai* Church, and to lend his time and energy to various progressive study groups which continued to mushroom in Tokyo's fertile intellectual world. But it was characteristic of the conscientious Katayama that, when he associated himself with a social project, he spared no effort in his participation. Having been coopted into the *Rōdō Kumiai Kisei-kai* in the summer of 1897, he immediately immersed himself in intensive study of Western trade-union movements in general and of Japanese industrial-labor conditions specifically.

During this earliest phase of his life as a trade-union organizer Katayama's views on labor matters did not differ

---

bers of the Society to be 450. See Takano, "Prospects of the Japanese Labor Movement," p. 210.

[14] Katayama and Nishikawa, *op.cit.*, pp. 29-30.

significantly from those upheld by the younger Takano. Like the Secretary-General of the *Rōdō Kumiai Kisei-kai,* whose labor creed was "trade-unionism, pure and simple," he yearned for a peaceful and orderly growth of industrial capitalism in his native land. And like many of the leaders of the labor movement Katayama fervently hoped that Japanese businessmen and workers would profit from the "errors" of Western capitalism by anticipating the social evils that accompanied the rapid extension of industrialism. "The old barrier of seclusion and narrowness, [sic] will soon pass away before the new and broad system of industry," warned Katayama. "But how it will come to pass, [sic] is the gravest problem that weighs upon the intelligent thinker. Will the change come in the form of evolution or revolution? Or will the difficulties and struggles that may fall upon the head of labourers be left to natural and economic forces? Can they be averted by careful prevention and comprehensive reform?"[15]

Katayama's queries about the course and consequences of industrialization in Japan were really rhetorical. As a confirmed optimist, he could only believe that the rule of reason would prevail. "Let us," he suggested, "crush the *ill tempered* [italics mine] capitalist at the outset, and try for a healthy and harmonious growth of capitalism and labour."[16] The advantages of an intelligent industrial-labor policy were too obvious, he argued, to admit dispute. If the "capitalist class know that their ultimate interest is the same with that of labor," mutual understanding and cooperation would assure both employer and worker a fair stake in the economic growth of the nation and also hasten the development of Japan into the greatest industrial power in Asia. Much like Takano, Katayama did not, when he joined the labor movement, consider himself a champion of a socially partisan

[15] Sen Katayama, "Labour Problem Old and New," *Far East,* II, no. 10 (October 1897), p. 488.

[16] *ibid.,* p. 490.

cause but rather a forward-looking citizen striving for the broad welfare of his country and his countrymen.

If at the beginning of the Japanese labor movement Katayama and Takano saw eye to eye on the need for the organization of trade-unions, they were poles apart in temperament, personality, and intellectual conviction. Takano was a hard-headed realist free from illusions about the tremendous obstacles that had to be surmounted in the construction of a trade-union movement. Understanding that the government and most businessmen would tolerate the organization of workers only as long as their interests were not immediately and directly endangered, he knew only too well, on the basis of his observations in the United States, that a gigantic struggle loomed ahead. He preferred thus to steer a moderate and cautious course, to win concessions and reforms gradually, and, above all, to avoid political entanglements and unnecessary provocation of the workers' political and industrial foes.

Katayama was, however, of a cut completely different from Takano. Possessing a magnanimous opinion of human beings, he was unable, despite his own harsh experiences in industrial America, to think the worst of capitalism and its foremost beneficiaries. Not having as yet been buffeted about by state and business power, he tended to minimize the strength of the opposition. To him it seemed necessary merely to place before the public the "facts" of the existing industrial-labor situation to foster a positive change in attitudes on the part of employer and worker. Where Takano was wary and carefully scouted the enemy camp before acting, Katayama was impatient. With his attention centered upon the urgent need for reform in working conditions rather than upon the ranks of the opposition, he plunged ahead bravely, if at times almost recklessly. Throwing himself into the program of labor agitation, he spent every spare moment in studying, lecturing, and writing upon the paramount issues.

During the fall of 1897 the *Rōdō Kumiai Kisei-kai* intensified its sorties into the labor arena. The enlistment of new members as well as the founding of trade-unions proceeded slowly, for the very idea of challenging employers on the terms of work was still too daring for the overwhelming number of laborers. By the late fall, however, a major breakthrough was achieved when hundreds of ironworkers employed in public and private foundries in Tokyo agreed to establish a union. December 1 was a memorable day for Japan's trade-union pathfinders. At a grand inauguration ceremony staged in the YMCA quarters in Kanda, the *Tekkō Kumiai* (Iron Workers' Union) was formally established, congratulatory messages being presented by leaders in public, business, and professional life. The new union, with almost twelve hundred members, soon became the largest and probably the strongest trade-union formed in Japan before the outbreak of World War I.[17]

On the very day the Iron Workers' Union was founded the first issue of its newspaper, the *Rōdō Sekai* (Labor World) was published. This first labor newspaper in Japan, edited by Katayama, was bilingual, containing both Japanese and English sections. Appearing bimonthly for the next four years, it was, like similar journals in Europe and America, oriented toward the needs and interests of workers. In the opening number Katayama proclaimed feelingly, if somewhat magniloquently, the purpose of the paper:

"The people are silent. I will be the advocate of this silence. I will speak for the dumb; I will speak for the silent ones; I will interpret their stammerings; I will interpret the grumblings, the tumults of the crowd, the complaints, the cries of men who have been so degraded by suffering and ignorance

[17] See Katayama and Nishikawa, *op.cit.*, pp. 74ff. and Takano Fusataro, "A New Trade Union in Japan," *American Federationist*, IV, no. 12 (February 1898), p. 272. The complete text of the above article will also be found in Kublin, *Meiji Rōdō Undō-shi no Hito-koma*, pp. 70-72.

that they have no strength to voice their wrongs. I will be the word of the people. I will be the bleeding mouth from which the gag has been snatched. I will say everything."[18] With his ensconcement as editor of the *Rōdō Sekai,* an office which provided him with unprecedented opportunities to speak in the name of labor, Katayama was vaulted into a position of leadership in the trade-union movement rivaling that of Takano alone.

The *Rōdō Kumiai Kisei-kai* was greatly heartened by its coup in sponsoring the Iron Workers' Union, and attempts were shortly made to encourage the formation of branches in other cities and towns. During the early months of 1898 action was taken to stir up the workers in other crafts and trades. As might have been predicted, no progress was made in the organization of operatives in the relatively well-advanced textile industries, whose women and child laborers comprised at least half of the industrial labor force of the country. The mobilization of highly skilled artisans was, however, more successfully carried out. In March a brilliant victory was scored when the engineers of the Japan Railway Company were able to combine after waging a hard-fought and bitter strike. Their union was named the *Kyōsei-kai* (Treatment Improvement Association). Other unions were formed by the invasion of such traditional guilds as the ship-carpenters, plasterers, furniture-makers, and doll-makers.[19] By the time of the first anniversary of the writing of *Shokkō Shokun ni Yokosu* it appeared that the foundations of a trade-union movement had been laid down in Japan.

In the spring of 1898 the *Rōdō Kumiai Kisei-kai* decided to sponsor an "athletic meet" in beautiful Ueno Park. Though the avowed purpose of the affair was to stimulate the morale of union members and to strengthen their feelings of solidar-

[18] As quoted in Sen Katayama, *The Labor Movement in Japan,* Chicago, 1918, p. 39. A Japanese translation of this work will be found in Katayama and Nishikawa, *op.cit.,* pp. 303-382.

[19] *ibid.,* pp. 51-55.

ity, it may be suspected that the trade-union leaders hoped to present a public show of the expanding labor movement. To forestall adverse criticism and to preclude possible police intervention, however, rules of behavior, covering the time from the assembly of the workers for a parade through the city streets until the conclusion of the events in Ueno Park, were drawn up in detail. April 3 was the date originally set for the gala event but it was later changed to April 10, the thirtieth anniversary of the transfer of the imperial capital from Kyoto to Tokyo.[20]

Regrettably for the carefully devised plans of the *Rōdō Kumiai Kisei-kai* the suspicion and hostility of the metropolitan police were soon revealed. Several weeks before the scheduled celebration Takano was summoned by the police authorities and informed that the labor demonstration would not be permitted. In the next few weeks further conferences were held but, despite the assurances and remonstrations of Takano and the intercession of the highly influential Shimada, the police officials refused to extend their authorization. In the face of this firm opposition the directors of the *Rōdō Kumiai Kisei-kai,* unwilling to provoke a clash that might cast the labor movement into disfavor with the public, reluctantly canceled the parade and athletic meet. It was a disheartening setback for the fledgling organizers.

Though the officers of the *Rōdō Kumiai Kisei-kai* were unwilling to antagonize the Tokyo police, Katayama was aroused to indignation by the discriminatory action. Pointing out that other groups and associations were not forbidden to conduct parades and demonstrations, he quickly proceeded to arrange for a public display of organized labor. On the morning of April 10, taking his place at the head of about three hundred members of the Iron Workers' Union, he led

[20] Note the comments in Takano Fusataro, "Labor Notes from Japan," *American Federationist,* v, no. 6 (August 1898), p. 118. See also Kublin, *Meiji Rōdō Undō-shi no Hito-koma,* p. 86.

the column along the boulevard beside the Imperial Palace. After saluting the Emperor, who did not deign to present himself, with resounding cheers, the workers then continued on to Ueno Park to enjoy a picnic under the blooming cherry trees. The entire affair was conducted in orderly fashion and, if it was not, strictly speaking, an act of defiance of the Japanese state, the episode did represent a token challenge of its arbitrary officials.[21]

Until the Cherry Blossom Picnic Affair in April 1898, Katayama had been a peaceable and law-abiding citizen with a respectful attitude toward the imperial government. He had never been guilty of an irreverent thought or act toward the throne or its illustrious occupant nor, for that matter, was he to be contumelious toward the imperial personage or institutions for some years to come. In the years immediately after the Sino-Japanese War he was still a staunch imperialist and nationalist and would unquestionably have resented imputations against his patriotism and loyalty to the state. The jolt given the trade-union movement by the police in the spring of 1898, however, affected him deeply. Thereafter his passive annoyance with officious and highhanded policemen and bureaucrats gradually gave way to resentment and antagonism, and in the next few years his writings were increasingly colored by scornful and derisive comments upon the thought and behavior of imperial officials.

Men without Katayama's deep wellsprings of compassion and lacking his stern sense of social justice would surely have been easily dismayed by the obstructions and exasperations experienced by Japan's pioneer trade-union organizers. He, however, responded magnificently to both triumph and defeat. Every advance in the line of labor's ranks, no matter how halting or trivial, worked upon him like a powerful

[21] For an account of this episode in Japanese labor history see Katayama, *The Labor Movement in Japan,* p. 45.

stimulant and impelled him forward. If sophisticated social and intellectual leaders were sometimes slightly amused by his ecstatic predictions about labor's future, his exuberance was nevertheless occasionally contagious. He did not, on the other hand, consider reverses to be irremediable and as signifying the arrival of doomsday. Though he was disappointed, he was rarely discouraged or infuriated by checks to his plans, which he stubbornly construed as challenges to the mettle of his faith.

Given his sanguine disposition, Katayama was not hard-put to see progress in the organization of trade-unions, particularly after the successful founding of the Iron Workers' Union. Other labor leaders were more reserved in their judgments. By the dawn of the twentieth century about twenty thousand of Japan's workers had been brought into the union fold.[22] Most of the new trade-unions were small, having fewer than five hundred members. Of the larger unions the iron workers, ship-carpenters, wood-sawyers, longshoremen, printers, plasterers, and railway engineers and firemen were noteworthy. Yet it must be recognized that almost all the trade-unions were founded in either Tokyo or Yokohama and that the number of organized laborers totaled less than five per cent of those who could even by the loosest criteria be deemed industrial workers. But perhaps the major setback to labor during this period was the failure of organizers to make the slightest penetration into the relatively large textile mills, where alone workers existed in sufficient strength to swell the trade-union movement into a tide.

If Katayama was able to derive satisfaction from the slow growth of trade-unions, it was because he was not, like most other labor leaders, exclusively concerned with the labor movement. He did not, accordingly, evaluate progress in the organization of workers merely by counting heads. When

[22] This is Katayama's estimate. *ibid.*, p. 44.

he traveled about the country, visiting the cities and towns in the vicinity of Tokyo, in the northern prefectures and Hokkaido, and in the Kansai and the far southwest, he soon discovered that the impact of industrialism extended far beyond the great urban industrial centers. Factory production and modern technology were, he noted, destroying the traditional way of life in all parts of the land. And what Katayama learned in his discussions with Japanese workers everywhere, what he observed in the old and new manufacturing establishments, and what he took away from his studies of Western social movements heightened his sense of urgency.

It was not necessary to be a social crusader to be shocked by the conditions of labor common in the factories of Japan in the late nineteenth century. Nor does it matter that these working conditions were probably more a carryover from the norms which had prevailed for centuries in cottage industries and urban workshops than a concomitant of the new industrialism. More perturbing was the growing impersonality of industrial-labor relations and the simultaneous erosion of time-honored customs and practices which had in previous years ensured workers a modicum of security and decent treatment. Katayama's anxiety over the spread of physically harmful and spiritually degrading conditions of work, his concern with the sprouting of social evils directly attributable to industrialism, and his alarm at the immediate and long-range effects of factory life upon society as a whole pervade the columns of the *Rōdō Sekai* and his many other periodical pieces of the time. At the same time his maturing comprehension of the complexities of social reform soon led him to extend the direction and scope of his agitational activities.

Katayama and other leaders of the *Rōdō Kumiai Kisei-kai* hoped that a factory act, protecting the basic interests of workers, would be passed by the Imperial Diet. Such a law had from time to time been considered by the state oligarchs before the Sino-Japanese War but because of a lack of immediate need and enthusiasm, the proposals had never been enacted into legislation. The only factory acts in effect before the formation of the *Rōdō Kumiai Kisei-kai* were municipal ordinances intended to protect the interests of employers against "trouble-makers." For all practical purposes these statutes were addenda to the standing police ordinances. But with the growth of industrialization during the war with China and particularly with the outbreak of industrial-labor friction after the conflict the imperial government again considered the feasibility of factory legislation. Its efforts were unfortunately fruitless.[23]

The first national factory law ever to get beyond the mere talking stage in Japan was drawn up in the Ministry of Industry and Agriculture of the government of Count Okuma in the fall of 1897. Designed for submission to the Imperial Diet in November of the following year, ample time was allowed for review of its provisions by interested businessmen and bureaucrats. Arrangements were, in fact, made to place the recommended legislation for appraisal by chambers of commerce throughout the country as well as by the Higher Agricultural, Commercial, and Industrial Board. Slim as were the prospects of securing Diet approval of the bill under the most favorable circumstances, it was patent that the wily Count Okuma did not wish to risk antagonizing unnecessarily the propertied groups directly concerned.

The proposed factory law was divided into five sections, each containing specific provisions to protect basic interests of employers or employees. The first part, defining the scope of the act, restricted its applicability to factories engaging over fifty workers and, if deemed necessary, to other plants

[23] For a review of the Japanese government's concern with factory legislation before 1897 see Ishii Ryosuke, *Japanese Legislation in the Meiji Era,* trans. and adapted by William J. Chambliss, Tokyo, 1958, p. 559.

where dangerous or other peculiar conditions of labor were common. Since most Japanese workers toiled in "factories" with fewer employees than the stipulated number, they were in effect excluded from the coverage of the bill and it is understandable, accordingly, that the leaders of the *Rōdō Kumiai Kisei-kai* demanded that its scope be extended to include all factories. That many employers and their government supporters considered the recommended legislation too broad in its covereage is, on the other hand, not surprising. The problem of determining where to draw the dividing line, if any, in the coverage provided by factory acts vexed government, business, and labor for many years.

The second section of the factory act under consideration required employers to adopt safety measures for the prevention of accidents from dangerous machinery. Provision was also made for a system of inspection by government officials. In the third portion of the bill the employment of children under the age of ten was subjected to restrictions, while the number of daily working hours for youngsters under the age of fourteen was, except in "special circumstances," to be limited to ten. Employers were also to be required to furnish at their own expense educational facilities for their employees below the age of fourteen. This section also defined the area of liability of the employer for accidents suffered by his workers and called for the issuance of workmen's certificates to prevent the piracy of labor by unscrupulous mill-owners. The fourth section set forth regulations for the maintenance of apprentice systems, and the final part of the act spelled out the functions of factory inspectors. It was proposed that, once the legislation was passed by the National Diet, it go into effect on July 1, 1899.[24]

[24] For the text and commentaries upon the proposed factory act the following should be consulted: Katayama and Nishikawa, *op.cit.*, pp. 39ff.; Takano Fusataro, "Proposed Factory Act in Japan," *American Federationist*, IV, no. 11 (January 1898), pp. 250-252; by the same author, "Factory Legislation in Japan," *American Federationist*, V, no. 10 (De-

Close examination of the proposed factory act by Katayama, Takano, and their confreres in the *Rōdō Kumiai Kisei-kai* soon convinced them that, though it singled out for corrective action several of the most glaring and objectionable abuses in working conditions and industrial-labor relations, the bill was not only inadequate but, in some instances, inimical to the best interests of the workers. Being half-hearted in its approach to the problems of child labor, leaving the employee unprotected in his relations with his employer, and ignoring various outstanding evils in the factory system, it was difficult for most trade-union leaders to argue that half a bill was better than none. A campaign of protest, extending through the spring and summer of 1898, was, accordingly, launched. Katayama and his staff on the *Rōdō Sekai* carried on a running attack upon the proposed act, advocating liberalization of many of its measures. Conferences were held with government officials, petitions were presented to appropriate government agencies, and in public lectures and forums a concerted effort was made to inform the public of the nature and implications of the impending legislation. Though it may not be stated with certainty that the *Rōdō Kumiai Kisei-kai* was solely responsible, it is nevertheless clear that the original proposals were finally amended to the benefit of factory workers.

It may, in retrospect, be surmised that the agitation for the modification of the government's factory bill was too successful. Upon submission of the legislation for the approval of the Imperial Diet, the fears and opposition of its overwhelmingly conservative members were immediately aroused. It was rejected with dispatch. This decision not only crushed the immediate hopes of the *Rōdō Kumiai Kisei-*

---

cember 1898), pp. 200-201 (these two articles are reprinted in Kublin, *Meiji Rōdō Undō-shi no Hito-koma*, pp. 105-108, 109-111); and Tetsuya Hayakawa, "The Necessity of Enacting a Law for Labourers," *Far East*, II, no. 12 (December 1897), pp. 657-662.

kai but it underscored the widespread lack of sympathy for regulatory factory legislation by a regime favorable to business and industrial interests. No change in the temper of the Imperial Diets of Japan was manifested until 1911, when a lukewarm and equivocating Factory Law, to become operative only after the passage of a five-year period, was approved.

If the defeat of the factory act of 1898 was distressing to the *Rōdō Kumiai Kisei-kai,* it was fatal to the future of the struggling Japanese trade-union movement. Katayama, Takano, and other friends of labor, having aroused a small segment of the workers and excited their hopes for improved and more secure conditions of employment, were now to pay the price for their agitation. Convinced that the Meiji government was not interested in ameliorating their lot, disappointed workers started in 1899 to abandon the *Rōdō Kumiai Kisei-kai,* while the organization of new and the expansion of old trade-unions slowed down perceptibly. Simultaneously, civic-minded leaders who had invested their time and effort for a year and more on behalf of the helpless workers began to drift away and to turn their attention to other affairs. In the late fall of 1898 Takano, who had moved to Yokohama to organize a cooperative store for workers, remained in the seaport city to direct the new enterprise. It was left to Katayama, accordingly, to rally the shattered ranks and to inspirit the flagging hopes of labor.

CHAPTER IX

SOCIALIST AGITATOR

In November 1898, a new organization, the *Shakai Shugi Kenkyū-kai* (Society for the Study of Socialism), was quietly founded in Tokyo. Katayama was one of the original members. Lest its purposes be misunderstood, the association in its charter proclaimed its aims to be "the study of the principles of socialism and whether or not they may be applied to Japan." Membership in the club was declared to be open to those who were "in accord with the objectives of the Society, whether or not they agree with the teachings of socialism."[1] It was thus made unmistakably clear that the *Shakai Shugi Kenkyū-kai* was devoted to the study and not to the propagation of socialism.

Though socialism and its ideological variations were not completely unknown in Japan during the earlier years of the Meiji period, interest in Western radical thought was extremely sporadic before the end of the Sino-Japanese War. The reasons for the general indifference to the reformist and revolutionary ideas, which were then coming into vogue in Europe and America, are not too hard to find. Socialist theories were ignored because they dealt with problems which were not held to be of immediate or critical importance by national spokesmen. Political and intellectual leaders were not oblivious to the growing social distress in the rapidly expanding cities and especially in the overcrowded countryside but the paramount issue, dwarfing all others in the discussion and debate of the seventies and eighties, was

[1] The founding of the *Shakai Shugi Kenkyū-kai* is discussed in Hyman Kublin, "The Origins of Japanese Socialist Tradition," *Journal of Politics*, XIV, no. 2 (May 1952), pp. 261-262 and in Hayashi Shigeru, "Nihon ni okeru Shakai Shugi Kenkyū Sōshiki no Shotai," *Shakai Kagaku Kenkyū*, [I], no. 1 (1948), pp. 58-100. See also Kishimoto Eitarō, ed. *Meiji Shakai Shugi Shiron*, Tokyo, 1955, pp. 69ff.

the definition of the nature of the national polity. This task overwhelmingly dominated the thought and energies of dispassionate statesmen and ambitious politicians alike.

The Meiji oligarchs, groping their way toward the construction of a modern nation-state, did not always see eye to eye on matters of methods and tactics. Ideologically, however, they were essentially conservative and, after restlessly but patiently probing about for a durable rationale for state and monarchy, they embodied their philosophical synthesis in the Constitution of 1889. Their foes outside the government, opportunistic and self-seeking as they doubtless were, still did not enjoy a completely free choice of campaign weapons. Though they were ready to play the self-assumed role of a loyal opposition and to serve, if summoned, as His Imperial Majesty's first ministers, they had no intention of sharing power with politically activated but uncontrollable masses. Clamoring for popular rights for all but seeking in a parliamentary system of government a means of facilitating control of the state by a new minority, they propounded the liberal philosophies of the English or French schools.

Disdained by the titans of Meiji statecraft and politics, the study of socialism became the province of a miscellany of scholars, journalists, and churchmen. When prominent religious and lay writers like Katō Hiroyuki, Kozaki Hiromichi, Sakai Yusaburō, and Tokutomi Sohō lingered over the radical social theories evolved in nineteenth-century Germany, France, and England, it was not necessarily because they were moved by a sense of philosophical rapport. These first Japanese students of Western socialism were rarely converted ideologically; even less frequently did they advance to the point of advocacy. They were rather inspired by the discovery of new sources of scholarly exercise, by the challenges posed by theoretical problems ignored or obscured in the more familiar systems of thought, and by the opportunity to acquire deeper understanding of major nuances of the history and civilization of the West. Needless to say, neither their writings nor those of several other academicians and clergymen exerted any appreciable influence upon the social and economic thinking of the period.[2]

A lively interest in socialism became evident in Japan only after the end of the conflict with China in 1895. The closer attention now paid to Western radical ideas and movements was, it must be stressed, but a single aspect of a much more pervading concern with social policy and social problems. The "impact" of industrial capitalism and the consequent stresses created in Japanese society were to a large extent responsible for the upsurge of interest in these matters; it is easy, however, to exaggerate the influences of the Sino-Japanese War. What should not be overlooked is the cumulative effect of some thirty years of intellectual growth and change. Since the days of the Meiji Restoration a full generation had run its course. The foundations, if not the superstructure, of a modern nation-state had been firmly laid down, new vistas of national achievement had been gradually opened, and intellectual horizons had been steadily extended. The entire era had been marked by creative vigor and, given the directions of the drive toward modernization, a flowering of thought was perhaps inevitable.

The intellectual, scholarly, and artistic activities of the

[2] The growth of interest in socialism and social problems before the Sino-Japanese War is reflected in a vast amount of Japanese literature. The following studies will be found particularly useful: Kyōchō-kai, *Saikin no Shakai Undō*, Tokyo, 1929, pp. 1-19; Kimura Tsuyoshi, "Nihon Shakai Shugi-shi," *Shakai Mondai Kōza*, VIII (1926), pp. 27-50; Kada Tetsuji, *Nihon Shoki Shakai Shisō no Kenkyū*, Tokyo, 1933, pp. 153-159; Asō Hisashi, "Meiji Taishō Shakai Undō Shōshi," in Shibusawa, Eiichi *et al.*, *Meiji Taishō-shi*, 15 vols., Tokyo, 1929-1930, III, pp. 330ff; Akamatsu Katsumaro, *Nihon Shakai Undō-shi*, Tokyo, 1955, pp. 5-29; and Kaji Ryūichi, *Meiji no Shakai Mondai*, Tokyo, 1955, *passim.* For an interesting study of the Rev. Dwight W. Learned, a Western pioneer in the introduction of radical social thought into Meiji Japan, see Sumiya Etsuji, *Nihon Keizai-gaku Shi no Hito-koma: Shakai Seisaku Gakkai wo Chūshin to Shite*, Tokyo, 1948, pp. 95-115.

nineties in Japan underscore the arrival at maturity of the creative endeavors of an older generation. At the same time the appearance on the public stage of an impressive number of younger men, restless and dissatisfied with the existing state of affairs, suggests that the burning political and philosophical issues of the first half of the Meiji period had begun to cool. A Constitution had been promulgated, parliamentary government had been introduced, the "unequal treaties" with the Western powers had been renegotiated, and the national interest had, temporarily at least, been successfully upheld in Korea. Many young adults, finding abundant opportunities for the realization of their ambitions in government, business, the professions, and the armed services, were content to drift with the tide of the times. Still, a small minority found the age wanting in individual challenge and desperately craved a sense of purpose and mission. Wandering about in search of a faith and a cause, some of them found their *raison d'être* in socialism.

The pioneers of the socialist movement of the late Meiji period were not simply rebels and nonconformists. Intellectually restless and emotionally sensitive, their adolescent years had been spent in unbroken quests for philosophical systems which would satisfactorily explain both ontological problems and social phenomena. All of them had to a greater or lesser extent been grounded in Confucian humanism, had explored the gospel of Christianity, and had initially responded to the promise of liberalism with enthusiasm. Insofar as their desire for spiritual and psychological fulfillment is concerned, Christianity was in most instances found to be sufficient but it was personal needs as well as the humanitarian imperatives of their religious faiths which turned their minds to social reform and socialism.

The founders of the *Shakai Shugi Kenkyū-kai* were all Christians.[3] Though a few members were ardent believers

[3] This point was made explicitly clear by Abe Isoo, one of the

in the social gospel, not one had either a deep knowledge of the character of social problems or more than a vague familiarity with the principal socialist theories of Europe and America. Katayama and Abe Isoo were doubtless the best informed members of the club.[4] Yet even they could not but be aware how aptly they personified the wisdom of the old Japanese adage that in the land of the blind the one-eyed is king. Accordingly, from the very beginning the Society placed exclusive emphasis upon study and education. Taking their cue from the English Fabian Society, the members met monthly in the library of the Unitarian Church in Tokyo to engage in discussion and to listen to lectures on the lives and teachings of Western socialists.[5] The addresses, presented by religious and lay leaders, were occasionally published in church and secular journals, thereby familiarizing a growing number of intellectuals and students with the principles and purposes of socialism.

Katayama was strongly influenced in his social activities and thinking by his participation in the *Shakai Shugi Ken-*

---

founders of the socialist study group. Note his retort to Kōtoku Shūsui, as quoted in Kosaka Masaaki, ed., *Japanese Thought in the Meiji Era,* trans. and adapted by David Abosch, Tokyo, 1958, p. 324.

[4] Abe Isoo, one of the outstanding socialists of modern Japan, was born in 1865. After graduating from Doshisha University in Kyoto, he studied at the Hartford Theological Seminary in the United States as well as in Europe. Returning to Japan, he served as a Christian minister in Okayama for several years. Then from the late nineteenth century until his death in 1949 he was a professor on the staff of Waseda University, acquiring great fame as a scholar of social problems, as a prolific writer on socialism, and as an organizer and leader of sundry left-wing movements and parties. Though no definitive biography of Abe has yet been written, the autobiography of his early years, *Shakai Shugi-sha to Naru made,* Tokyo, 1932, is well worth reading.

[5] Karl Kiyoshi Kawakami, *The Political Ideas of Modern Japan,* Iowa City, 1903, pp. 184-185. Kawakami's discussion of the socialist movement in the aftermath of the Sino-Japanese War, appearing in this work, is a condensation of his piece, "Socialism in Japan," *International Socialist Review,* II, no. 8 (February 1902), pp. 561-569. Since his treatment of the subject is replete with factual errors and dubious interpretations, it should be read with extreme care.

kyū-kai but not in the manner that has commonly been alleged or assumed. Neither his new relationships nor his broadened studies resulted in his conversion to socialism; he was already a socialist, albeit of the Christian variety. He was, moreover, no philosophical gadfly flitting after the intellectual fads of the moment. The principal result of his involvement in the study group was a sharpened perception of social problems and a strengthened belief in the corrective possibilities of Christian socialism. He now not only began to note more feelingly social abuses and inequities of the type which had aroused the indignation of churchmen in America and Europe but also to spy out injustices and evils which were embedded in Japanese ways and customs.

Being above all a man of compassion, Katayama responded more quickly to the promptings of his heart than to the dictates of his mind. Given to omnivorous reading, he was not scornful of bookish learning nor was he averse to engaging in intellectual give-and-take in public debates and private seminars. But, unlike many of the academics, clergymen, and educated laymen with whom he was to become involved in running exchanges, he was temperamentally unable to draw a neat, dividing line between faith and action. For him to believe was to do. And believing wholeheartedly in the Utopian destiny of mankind, in the inevitable advent of a Kingdom of God on earth, he not only looked forward patiently to the regeneration of man through the gospel of Christianity but also insisted simultaneously upon the purification of society through reform. Translation of his faith into action had already drawn him into settlement-house work, primary and adult education, and trade-union organization. He now advanced along the much wider front of general social reform.

When Katayama began to promote the welfare of the "masses" at about the turn of the twentieth century, there was no lack of noble causes to attract his support. As manager of Kingsley Hall he continued to provide programs of religious instruction for the young and old and particularly to provide opportunities for workers in the slums of Kanda to advance themselves educationally.[6] When outraged citizens raised a cry against the opening of brothels in the workers' district at Omiya, a suburb of Tokyo, he threw his weight behind a general antiprostitution campaign. But his most important work was in the labor field where he soon overshadowed all other organizers and agitators. As secretary-general of the Iron Workers' Union and as editor of its organ, the *Rōdō Sekai,* he did not cease to clamor for legislation to outlaw objectionable working conditions and to protect the helpless worker. At workers' rallies, in public demonstrations, and in journals of opinion he intensified his pleas for public recognition of the "rights" and interests of labor. Mindful too of the worker's needs and interests outside the factory and mill, he lent words of encouragement to the incipient cooperative-store movement and urged upon all who would listen the necessity for instituting municipal ownership of public utilities. Japanese workers had never known so fervent and fearless a friend.

Katayama's opinions on social problems and particularly his activities in support of them were not endorsed by the entire membership of the *Shakai Shugi Kenkyū-kai.* The most unwavering cooperation was forthcoming from Abe, Kinoshita Naoe, and Kawakami Kiyoshi. Most members were opposed to any action other than scholarly discussion, while many Christian clerics and laymen stubbornly refused to

[6] For reasons which are worthy of speculation Japanese scholars have neglected to pursue Katayama's career as manager of Kingsley Hall after his founding of the settlement house. Since social work was for some years after 1897 to be an important part of his life, this oversight is inexcusable. Not even the recent lengthy biography of Katayama, which entirely omits consideration of the first thirty-five years of his life, touches upon his continuing association with Kingsley Hall. See Kishimoto Eitarō *et al., Katayama Sen,* 2 vols., Tokyo, 1959-1960.

stray from the straight and narrow path of theological and spiritual affairs. In their eyes the social ideas and crusades of Christianity's "left wing" in Japan entailed not only a dilution but a perversion of the aims and teachings of their faith. The criticism of Christian socialism voiced by Uchimura Kanzō, founder of the increasingly influential *Mukyōkai* ("Churchless" Church), was indicative, if not wholly representative, of the misgivings over the outlook of Katayama and Abe. "Christianity deals with heaven," he argued, "while socialism tries to reform this world." The first duty of man is "to reform himself" through faith "and then to reform society."[7]

The inability of Katayama to secure major support for social reform from prominent Christian leaders was in many ways a blessing in disguise. Though many Christian pastors and laymen were as individuals held in high esteem by the Japanese community, Christianity itself was not so well regarded. Antagonism toward and suspicion of the alien religion were not uncommonly transferred to the various Christian social and educational enterprises. But, irrespective of the indifference and opposition raised by salvation-oriented spiritual leaders to his work and ideas, Katayama had to contend with more formidable foes. Preeminent among the enemies of socialism, apart from the state itself, was the *Shakai Seisaku Gakkai* (Association for the Study of Social Policy), which was headed by the redoubtable academicians, Kanai En and Kuwata Kumazō.

The *Shakai Seisaku Gakkai* had been organized in 1896 by a group of Tokyo Imperial University professors and government bureaucrats whose social and economic thinking had been molded by the German theories of *sozial-politik.* Accepting the capitalist system as just and efficient but urging the necessity of reform so as to head off industrial strife and radical movements, they took a stand midway between

[7] Kosaka, *op.cit.*, p. 339.

the extremes of economic liberalism and socialism. The position of the association was set forth in its prospectus as follows:

"Since the spirit of extreme self-interest and of free and unrestricted competition gives rise to widening gulfs between rich and poor, we reject the principles of *laisser faire*. We are also opposed to socialism because its plans for the destruction of capitalists and for the overthrow of the existing economic system would be detrimental to the fortunes of the nation. We believe that, if the present system of private property is maintained and if, within its limits, class friction is prevented by the exercise of state power and by the exertions of individual citizens, we may look forward to the continuation of social harmony."[8]

Kanai and his followers in academic circles and in the imperial government, having no intention of stirring up widespread controversy, made no concerted attempt to carry the fight for their social policy into the public arena. Devoting themselves to the study of the "scientific principles" of *sozial-politik* and of their applications in the nations of the West, they confined themselves to seminar discussions and to the writing of learned treatises. Narrowly focused as their efforts were, they nevertheless exerted a broad influence upon the social and economic thought of scholars and state officials, to whom the ideal of the "harmony of capital and labor" seemed, from the point of view of the national interest, to be practical and wise. The concern of the social policy school was, like that of the Meiji state, primarily the advancement of the "fortunes of the nation" and only secondarily the promotion of the general welfare of the people.

[8] The complete name of the organization was *Nihon Shakai Seisaku Gakkai*. The circumstances of its founding are well presented in Sumiya, *op.cit.*, pp. 262-263. The text of the objectives of the association, from which my translation has been made, will be found on pp. 263-264 of the same work.

Equally important as the unsympathetic view of the needs and interests of the infant industrial class and as the fundamentally authoritarian approach to the problem of insuring social peace held by Kanai and Kuwata were their strictures against Katayama and his program of socialism and social reform. It may well be appreciated that, to scholastics surveying the industrial-labor scene from the Olympian heights of Tokyo Imperial University, the energetic Christian socialist was a dangerous rabble-rouser and potential troublemaker. That they held no respect for Katayama's intellect was made clear by the well-known pundit, Yamaji Aizan. Katayama has the patient, plodding "mind of a cart-horse," he sneered. And despite the fact that Katayama had taken at best but a half step beyond a stand of "trades-unionism, pure and simple," he was sharply attacked by the proponents of social policy and branded as a peddler of pernicious "socialism."[9] The accusation was in many respects unfounded but, what was even more unfortunate, it was leveled by scholars whose opinions carried considerable weight. The leaders of the *Shakai Seisaku Gakkai* were, to be sure, not exclusively responsible but there can be no doubt that from this time on Katayama and his social reform projects were smeared with the taint of radicalism, while the charge of "socialism" was for years thereafter sufficiently damaging to retard the most innocuous movements for social improvement.

If the advocates of *sozial-politik* looked upon Katayama's social ideas disapprovingly, his efforts on behalf of trade-union organization did not escape the attention of the Meiji government. In February 1900, for reasons that are not completely clear, the state acted suddenly and swiftly to choke off the infant labor movement by introducing a new and revised Public Peace Preservation Law. Although the

[9] See especially Kawai Eijirō, *Meiji Shisō-shi no Ichi-Dammen*, vol. IX in *Kawai Eijirō Senshu*, Tokyo, 1949, pp. 307-311 for a clear-cut exposition of Kanai's opposition to Katayama's socialist position.

legislation actually liberalized police regulations for the arrangement and conduct of public meetings and demonstrations, it struck a death blow at the trade-unions. In effect, the law, which remained in force for more than two decades, did not prohibit the organization of labor combinations; it rather rendered them completely impotent by forbidding workers and their leaders to engage in the primary activities of trade-unions. Until after World War I labor groups in Japan could, as a result, function only as fraternal or mutual-benefit associations.

The anger and indignation of organized laborers and of the scattering of socialists over the Public Peace Preservation Law was well expressed by Katayama in the columns of the *Rōdō Sekai.* "The law provides carefully clauses," he protested, "that will enable police authorities to stop, to punish and to fine working men who speak or agitate for wages, and hours of labour. Working men, hereafter, will be completely under mercy of employers, they can not ask for higher wages or shorter hours without violating the law in question. There will be no room left to working men to organize themselves into a Union, because the law forbids, with a threat of sever [sic] punishment of fine and hard labor the labor agitation of any form whatever."[10] It is understandable that the long period during which these police ordinances remained in effect is known in Japanese labor history as "Ankoku Jidai," or the "Dark Ages."

The passage of the Public Peace Preservation Law has been subject to various constructions. The most common explanation, advanced not only by Marxist but also by other historians, has it that the act was a naked demonstration of the burgeoning power of industrial capitalism. Although it would be foolish to reject this interpretation categorically,

[10] *Rōdō Sekai,* III, no. 5 (March 1900). See also Alfred Stead, *Great Japan,* New York, 1906, p. 230, which does not accurately reproduce the wording of the original text.

it may be argued that it raises more questions than it answers. At the dawn of the twentieth century, with industrialization more a goal than an actuality in Japan, it is improbable that the Meiji government was frightened by the "power" of a working class which constituted not more than one per cent of the total population.[11] By the most generous estimate, too, it is doubtful that the aggregate of trade-union members exceeded twenty thousand in the thirty-third year of Meiji. And for all the images commonly conjured up of a labor force seething with unrest the basic fact remains that during the entire calendar year preceding the passage of the Public Peace Preservation Law only fifteen strikes, involving about 4,300 workers, occurred.[12] When the Meiji state established tight controls over trade-union operations, it may well have responded to the pressures of alarmed businessmen but whether the basic purpose was to protect the interests of industrialists is, in the light of the prevailing circumstances, open to question.

The intent of the new police regulations of 1900 may be determined by examining the legislation as a whole.[13] With this perspective it becomes quite clear that the act was not designed, as is so often implied, basically for the suppression of trade-unions. Not merely labor organizations but, more important, political associations came under its purview. From the moment parliamentary government had been inaugurated in 1890, political parties, locked in a struggle for power with the authoritarian state, had sought greater freedom for their activities by campaigning for the modification of the Public Peace Preservation Law of 1887, described by a commentator as "one of the most arbitrary and

[11] See ch. VIII, n. 2.

[12] The pertinent statistics are presented in Murayama Shigetada, *Nihon Rōdō Sōgi-shi*, Tokyo, 1947, p. 224.

[13] The complete text of the Public Peace Preservation Law, known in Japanese as *Chian Keisatsu-hō*, will be found in Hioki Norio, *et al.*, *Nihon Hanrei Taisei*, 24 vols., Tokyo, 1935-1937, XXII, pp. 37-52.

repressive laws ever enacted by the government since the Restoration."[14] After a decade of effort they finally succeeded in forcing through the National Diet the passage of new and revised legislation, abridging the stringent controls over political parties and their activities. Since trade-unions had come into being only after the introduction of the older law and no comprehensive regulations for their restraint were in effect, advantage was doubtless taken of the opportunity to provide the necessary police authority in the act of 1900. If the restrictions imposed upon labor organizations were inordinately severe, it was obviously because neither the oligarchs nor the political parties had any interest in serving as champions of the working class, which was still sufficiently weak to be ignored.

With the labor movement stifled so soon after its formation, trade-unionists and socialists were compelled to review their situation. For Takano, to whom the trade-union was the *sine qua non* for the emancipation and uplift of the industrial proletariat, the setback seemed to be irretrievable. Acknowledging the futility of further struggle and having no illusions as to what lay in store for the hapless Japanese worker, he withdrew completely from the labor field and spent the few remaining years of his life in China as a foreign correspondent for the Yokohama *Advertiser*. For Katayama and other socialists, whose dedication to reform transcended their commitments to organized labor, a decision such as Takano's was impossible. Their alternatives could not be measured by the yardstick of practicality but only by the criteria of their Utopian beliefs. What was at stake was not their political sagacity, intellectual acumen, or common sense but the worth and integrity of their convictions.

Whatever the other indictments lodged against Katayama

[14] George E. Uyehara, *The Political Development of Japan, 1867-1909*, New York, 1910, p. 182.

as a thinker and theoretician, he was never accused of betraying his principles. It could thus have been predicted that, when the legal door for trade-union activities was closed to him, he would not retreat to Kingsley Hall and its politically unobjectionable program of religious, social, and educational work. And since he wholeheartedly believed in combining knowledge and faith with action, it was to be expected that he would not resign himself to the role of pundit on socialist and labor affairs for readers of the *Rōdō Sekai* and other progressive journals. If he had for a short while uncertainties about a new course of action, they were resolved by the particulars of the Public Peace Preservation Law. Though agitation for the improvement of wages and working conditions was strictly forbidden with the threat of stern penalties, public meetings, mass demonstrations, and propagandistic discussion were permissible "within the limits of the law." Like labor leaders in Western nations whose attempts to advance the interests of workers had been blocked by state legislation, Katayama soon decided to transfer the fight to the political arena.[15]

Katayama's decision to engage in a competition for parliamentary power was shared by other trade-unionists and socialists. "The very oppressive features of the Police Law against the working classes," he recalled many years later, "caused these classes and their friends to feel an urgent need of obtaining universal suffrage in Japan. With this

[15] The new tactics forced upon Japanese labor leaders were explained in the *Rōdō Sekai* as follows: "There is, however, one thing left to the working man to do with a [sic] some hope that is to work for the immediate repeal of the law in the next session of the Diet. To do this effectively is to carry the battle into the enemy's camp by changing the labor agitation to the political agitation. The law gives people a greater freedom in political activity in holding political meetings and forming political associations. Thus we can not fight against oppression and tyranny of employers in the economic field . . . but we can and must secure our inborn rights and heritage under the red flag of labor politics that is Socialism." *Rōdō Sekai*, III, no. 5 (March 1, 1900). See also Stead, *op.cit.*, p. 231, whose quotation varies in minor respects from the original.

purpose we organized an Association for Universal Suffrage. Many prominent men came into the Association. The Tokyo Barbers' Union and the Nippon R. R. Workers' Union joined. . . . . At the same time, we preached Socialism at the workingmen's meetings, perhaps with more zeal and enthusiasm than we showed for trade unionism. . . . There was then more freedom of speech for labor and Socialist politics at public meetings than there was freedom on the subject of trade unions, strikes and the boycott, since the latter were directly concerned with the existing industries of the country."[16] As a result of this concerted campaign the Nippon Railroad Workers' Union in March 1901, formally proclaimed its belief that "Socialism is the only ultimate solution of the labor problems" and indicated its willingness to support a movement for universal suffrage.[17]

The irrepressible Katayama was joined in the new political campaign by several Christian socialists as well as by Kōtoku Shūsui and Sakai Toshihiko.[18] This small band of social reformers was unhappily aware of the limitations of the *Shakai Shugi Kenkyū-kai* and its sedate program of study; there was, it was recognized, no possibility of converting the group to a course of political action. These socialists realized, moreover, that, though they themselves were engaged in literary and journalistic occupations and were able

[16] Sen Katayama, *The Labor Movement in Japan,* Chicago, 1918, pp. 59-60.

[17] *ibid.,* pp. 60-61.

[18] Kōtoku Shūsui, also known as Kōtoku Denjirō, was born in Kōchi on the island of Shikoku in 1871. Strongly influenced in his youth by the radical popular rights theories then in vogue and especially by the teachings of the liberal thinker, Nakae Chōmin, he had by the close of the nineteenth century shown evidence of a brilliant, if erratic, intellect. With the passage of the years he drifted continuously to the left, ultimately becoming the leader of the anarchist movement in Japan.

Sakai Toshihiko, born in 1870, was a school teacher turned journalist. Strongly affected by the radical philosophical currents of the late nineteenth century, he became a well-known social critic and one of the first systematic students of Western socialism.

to articulate their dissatisfaction with prevailing social and political conditions, their protests would remain unheeded unless they were pressed in more positive and systematic fashion. Consequently, during the months following the institution of the new police laws a small group, composed of Katayama, Abe Isoo, Kinoshita Naoe, Kawakami Kiyoshi, Kōtoku Shūsui, and Sakai Toshihiko, began to meet in the offices of the Iron Workers' Union to plan the organization of a new political party.

Despite the outward appearance of camaraderie, the "socialist coalition" formed in the spring of 1901 rested upon precarious ideological foundations. Four of the members, including Katayama, were devout Christians holding socialist convictions that were fundamentally humanistic and humanitarian. The social thought of Kōtoku and Sakai, inchoate as it was at the time, was, on the other hand, largely a derivative of radical French liberalism and materialistic French and German socialism. If the "majority" could not accept many of the underlying philosophical premises of the "minority" without doing violence to the axioms of their faith, their own spiritual idealism was the constant butt of Kōtoku's derision. Even at this early stage in his tempestuous career the young social critic was well along the way toward the almost morbid hatred of Christianity he was to nourish to the very day of his tragic death. It is apparent that only an immediate and common end held the strange socialistic group together.

By the spring of 1901 a platform for the forthcoming *Shakai Minshu-tō* (Social Democratic Party), setting down immediate and long-range objectives, had been hammered out. Seasoned reformers and revolutionaries in Europe and America would have found much to gladden their hearts in the statement of aims, for it embodied many of the goals they themselves had striven to achieve over the span of a half century and more. Though it is difficult to pinpoint the specific influence of Western socialists and Communists, "Utopian and scientific," it is evident that Katayama and his associates were strongly indebted to Lassalle, Marx, Engels, Proudhon, Ely, George, American Christian socialists, and English Fabians. The knowledge of the Japanese socialist pioneers was not entirely first-hand, being partly derived from summaries and commentaries.

The final text of the declaration of purpose of the *Shakai Minshu-tō* was written by Abe, who used as a model the Communist Manifesto of Marx and Engels.[19] In the opening paragraphs, which singled out for stinging criticism many chronic abuses in the Japanese social and economic system, the tone of the entire pronunciamento was set. After the preliminary remarks the eight ultimate aims of the new political party were tersely listed: universal brotherhood; disarmament and international peace; abolition of political and economic distinctions; public ownership of land and capital; public ownership of communication and transportation facilities; equitable distribution of wealth; equality of political rights; and free state-supported education for the people. Since it was understood that these goals could not be quickly attained, the organizers of the *Shakai Minshu-tō* concluded their manifesto by presenting twenty-eight demands for social and political reform. It was intended that these demands provide the ammunition for day-to-day political battle.

Viewed in retrospect, the immediate targets of Japan's first Social Democrats seem more a well-founded indictment of

[19] "It [the platform] contains a long preliminary discussion on the defects of the present social regime . . . modelled on the manifesto of the Communist Party as formulated by Karl Marx and Frederick Engels in 1848." Kawakami, *op.cit.*, p. 187. See also Kawakami, p. 563. The Japanese text of the program appears in Asahi Shimbun-sha, *Meiji Taishō-shi*, 6 vols., Tokyo, 1930, I, pp. 211-213, and in Kishimoto Eitarō, ed., *Meiji Shakai Undō Shisō*, 2 vols., Tokyo, 1955, I, pp. 155-159. An English translation will be found in Kawakami, *op.cit.*, pp. 564-565. See also Chitoshi Yanaga, *Japan since Perry*, New York, 1949, p. 235, for a summary.

the failures and betrayals of the liberals and an unflattering commentary upon the Meiji state's callous disregard for the plight of workers than a program of political action of misguided and visionary radicals. Nine of their specific demands called for the enactment of legislation to protect the basic interests of workers, particularly of women and children, and to outlaw subhuman conditions of labor. An additional six insisted upon political reforms such as universal suffrage, secret ballot, proportional representation, and introduction of the referendum. Most of the remaining items in the Party's platform were socialistic but of varying degree of extremism. The proposals for the abolition of the House of Peers, the upper house in the National Diet, and for reduction of the size of the armed forces were certain to raise considerable controversy.

Counting upon the support of trade-union members, other unorganized workers, and progressive citizens in general, Katayama and his five allies announced the launching of the *Shakai Minshu-tō* on May 21, 1901. The declaration of aims was published in the *Rōdō Sekai* and in four other metropolitan Tokyo newspapers. But scarcely had these papers appeared on the newsstands than the organizers of the Party learned that their efforts had been for naught. By the order of Baron Suematsu, Minister for Home Affairs, the *Shakai Minshu-tō* was suppressed, circulation of the newspaper editions carrying the offensive manifesto was prohibited, and charges of violation of the national press laws were lodged against the responsible editors.[20] The life of Japan's first Social Democratic Party may thus be measured in mere hours.

It is easy, perhaps too easy, to construe the extinction of the *Shakai Minshu-tō* as but another of the numerous

[20] Since most of the newspapers had their editions on the streets before the police order was handed down, many of the offensive issues escaped confiscation. Asō, *op.cit.*, p. 337.

demonstrations of the arbitrariness of the Meiji state. To do so, however, makes it impossible to understand the government's tolerance of many other expressions of social and political dissent during the decade and a half after the Sino-Japanese War. For all the posthumous exaltation of Katayama, Kōtoku, Sakai, and other reformers and rebels of the Meiji period as valiant fighters for the cause of social democracy, it is most likely they were viewed as nuisances and cranks and not as reckless revolutionaries by Japanese officialdom. The later Meiji oligarchs and political party chieftains may well have had shortcomings of intellect and character but they cannot seriously be accused of lack of political sophistication. The socialistic demands of the Social Democrats can only have struck them as the mouthings of eccentrics. There was no need, moreover, for them to consider seriously the call for improvement of working conditions. When the government of Premier General Katsura quashed the new political party, it was because Katayama and his fellow socialists touched upon several issues of critical political sensitivity.

The *Shakai Minshu-tō*, with its sights directed toward the establishment of a socialist society, could never, in view of the existing conditions in Japan, have acquired more than the proportions of a splinter political party. Practically ignoring the peasantry, who constituted about seventy-five per cent of the population, too advanced in its ideas for the urban workers, and having no appeal for most businessmen, professionals, and intellectuals, the socialist "vanguard" had no real prospect of making an appreciable impact upon Japanese political life. But when it raised demands for political reform, which were more or less in consonance with the aims of the stronger and politically dangerous liberal and democratic forces, the fate of the *Shakai Minshu-tō* was sealed. Most of its program could be shrugged off without a second thought; its appeal for change in the existing political system and, particularly, for universal suffrage could not. And at the very moment the government was desperately attempting to check the expansion of tsarist Russia in nearby Korea and Manchuria, the insistence of the socialists upon the reduction of the armed services could appear to be little less than seditious. Its democratic and antimilitarist and not its socialist posture doomed the *Shakai Minshu-tō.*

Though Katayama was not unable to read the political handwriting on the wall, he did not always succeed in interpreting it correctly. At times of crisis and actual disaster in his career, instead of examining the facts and drawing sober and hard-headed conclusions, he could as often as not be expected to be forthcoming with a confession of faith. This virtue of detecting a ray of hope, when others saw only gloom, spared him innumerable heartbreaks. Thus, though the dissolution of the Social Democratic Party was difficult to assess otherwise, he ingenuously evaluated the blow as the "best means of waking up the people."[21] It was, on the contrary, indisputable that the repressive act of the state closed the last effective method for Katayama and his allies to rally mass support for their movement. As in other countries, so too in Japan; the socialists could aspire to gain popular backing only by winning immediate and substantial benefits for the workers through trade-union agitation or political action. Now rebuffed in their attempt to transform the economic into a political struggle and refusing even to contemplate a resort to revolutionary tactics, they had no legal alternative but to fall back upon "education."

To implement their plans of inculcating in the people a basic knowledge of socialism, Katayama and his friends decided to work through the *Shakai Shugi Kyōkai* (Socialist Association). This organization had been founded in the

[21] Sen Joseph Katayama, "The Labor Movement and Socialism in Japan," *International Socialist Review,* II, no. 3 (September 1901), p. 189.

closing months of 1900 by a small group of socialists dissatisfied with the limited program and objectives of the *Shakai Shugi Kenkyū-kai.* Emphasizing the study of socialism but also determined to carry on an active program for its dissemination, the group now vigorously undertook to hold regular meetings, to sponsor public lectures in Tokyo and other cities throughout the country, to encourage the writing of tracts as well as of scholarly treatises, and to facilitate the translation and publication of the basic writings of Western social theorists. Though the members of the *Shakai Shugi Kyōkai,* the first organization in Japan devoted solely to the spread of socialism, never exceeded one hundred in number, they succeeded during the almost three years of their dedicated activity in arousing an interest in socialism in many parts of the land.[22]

Katayama played a notable role in the drive to whip up understanding of socialism and its purposes. It would perhaps not be too much to say that the months from the summer of 1901 to the fall of 1903 were one of the happiest and most self-satisfying periods in his entire political career. Though there was much to be done, there were still countless evidences of progress and achievement. While he continued to keep many irons in the fire and could never say no to an invitation to support a new and worthwhile cause, his major enterprise during the year or so after the death of the *Shakai Minshu-tō* was the creation of a socialist publication of regular and frequent issue. There were, as his own writings as well as those of various other socialists attest, no serious obstacles in the way of publication outlets, for many of the larger newspapers and journals of opinion were not reluctant to tack with the tides of public interest. But what

[22] The organization and program of activities of the *Shakai Shugi Kyōkai* are discussed in Kyōchō-kai, *op.cit.*, p. 22. See also Watanabe Kango, *Nihon Shakai Undō-shi*, Tokyo, 1955, pp. 44-46 and Kimura Tsuyoshi, *op.cit.*, IX (1926), pp. 61-62.

Katayama wanted above all was an organ which the socialists could call their own.

In setting up the first socialist daily in Japan it was necessary for Katayama to assume personally not only the major responsibility for arrangements but also the heavy financial obligations. The Iron Workers' Union was fortunately most cooperative. In the summer of 1901 it was announced that its paper, the *Rōdō Sekai,* which had appeared bimonthly for more than three years, would be discontinued with the publication of its one-hundredth number and replaced, with the December issue, by a new socialist daily. "The free use of the Iron Workers' Headquarters was given us," Katayama recalled, "the second floor being given over to editorial and composing rooms. Our office occupied the first floor front and in the back rooms the paper was printed. . . . It cost just one thousand dollars to get types, machines and other necessary equipment."[23] Original plans changed, however, and the first number of the *Naigai Shimpō* was not issued until January 1, 1902.

It cannot be said that Japan's first daily socialist newspaper was a success. Though it received modest support from workers, university students, and a scattering of curious intellectuals as well as first-rate articles contributed by the founders of the defunct Social Democratic Party, the journalistic venture had to be terminated after only two months. Katayama attributed the failure of the *Naigai Shimpō* to a number of unforeseen difficulties, the most important being the general lack of business experience of the staff and his own flagging health, which did not permit him to give the paper the attention required. On April 3, 1902, publication of the old *Rōdō Sekai* was resumed on a bimonthly basis. Lasting less than a year, the paper in its final issues introduced Japanese readers to the writings of such eminent European authors and critics as Zola, Millerand, and Vander-

[23] Sen Katayama, *The Labor Movement in Japan,* p. 67.

velde. In the following year it was replaced by a new journal, *Shakai Shugi* (Socialism).[24]

Most exciting to Katayama was the growing number of opportunities to address gatherings of workingmen in different areas of the country. Unlike many of the other socialist leaders, he believed that socialism was essentially a workers' movement and that there were dangers in directing it along a path of pure intellectualism. He did not hesitate to applaud the appearance of many new books and studies on socialist topics but he sensed that their philosophical orientation and their elegant and technical language, edifying to the highly educated, were meaningless to semiliterate laborers. Katayama himself did not neglect his pen; he was one of the most productive writers of his day. But he was never so contented as when he was able to confront an assembly of interested workers to speak about their problems in simple and sympathetic terms.

Katayama's "proletarian" approach to the propagation of socialism led before long, if not to a rift, to an estrangement from many of the socialist intelligentsia. As he shuttled back and forth between Tokyo and its satellite cities and towns and as he undertook tours to the north and west to lecture before trade-unions and at public meetings, he acquired a practical knowledge of social and labor conditions and an intimate familiarity with the concerns of the worker which were probably unrivaled at the time. He was doubtless overshadowed among intellectuals and university students by other more brilliant, even more penetrating, radical writers but few, if any, socialists commanded his popularity among the "masses." But if he enjoyed a modest success in popularizing socialism and in transmitting its spirit to the working class, it was at the cost of a growing distrust

[24] For the history and vicissitudes of the radical press, particularly of the *Rōdō Sekai*, *Naigai Shimpō*, and *Shakai Shugi*, during the Meiji period see Watanabe Yoshimichi and Shioda Shōbei, *Nihon Shakai Shugi Bunken Kaisetsu*, Tokyo, 1958, pp. 38, 48.

on the part of armchair theoreticians, who were quick to dismiss him as a lowbrow.

By the beginning of 1903 points of tensions, more critical than the friction between the intellectuals and the popularists, began to emerge within the socialist movement. If Katayama's outlook, not to speak of his position as Secretary-General of the Iron Workers' Union, demanded a conception of socialism scorned by the academicians, his staunch Christian faith, which colored his ideology, engendered irreconcilable differences with Kōtoku and his followers. After several years of intensive study, during which his socialist views took on sharper focus, the young journalist on the *Yorozu Chōhō* had finally become a convinced Marxist. Kōtoku's shift in thought may be measured by reference to his *Teikoku Shugi* (Imperialism), a fundamentally humanistic critique published in 1901, and his *Shakai Shugi Shinzui* (The Essence of Socialism), a lucid review of historically materialistic socialism which appeared in 1903.[25] From the point of view of this pioneer Japanese Marxist, the Christian basis of the socialism upheld by Katayama, Abe, Kinoshita, and Kawakami marked them as Utopian idealists.

Kōtoku, who lacked the mellow sensitivity of Sakai Toshihiko, then also turning toward Marxism, was particularly given to mordant jests at the religious faith of the Christian socialists. In one of his later works Kinoshita Naoe, one of the most gifted socialist writers and orators of the Meiji period, related an unusually sharp exchange with Kōtoku on the subject of Christianity. These two young men, together with Katayama, were traveling by train to Yokosuka to ad-

[25] These two works have fortunately been reprinted in recent years. *Teikoku Shugi* is most commonly available in the Iwanami Bunko edition (Haku 112), Tokyo, 1959. *Shakai Shugi Shinzui* is available in the following editions: Iwanami Bunko (Haku 114), Tokyo, 1959; Kōbun-dō (Atene Bunko 11), Tokyo, 1949; and in Kōtoku Shūsui, *Shūsui San Meicho*, Tokyo, 1947, pp. 69-130. This last edition has been used in this study.

dress a meeting. Kōtoku, according to Kinoshita, turned to him and remarked,

"'Kinoshita, why don't you give up God! If you'd only do this, I'd gladly untie your shoelaces for you!' Kotoku's voice was thin, but as sharp and penetrating as an owl's. I hesitated to answer. Katayama came to my assistance. 'Kotoku, be careful that you yourself are not vanquished by God!' There was a half smile playing about Katayama's lips as he made this somewhat scornful rejoinder. Without even listening to Katayama's words, Kotoku continued, 'I'll make you give up God yet! I really will!' Speaking thus, Kotoku narrowed his almond-shaped heavy-lidded eyes and sat staring determinedly. Katayama and myself, though we were both Christians, were separated in that I was unaffiliated, a sort of tramp, while Katayama was an upstanding church member."[26] Their philosophical differences apart, a breach between the gentle but strong-minded Katayama and the doctrinaire and probably neurotic Kōtoku was sooner or later bound to occur.

Having been continuously engaged in the study of socialist theories since the days of the *Shakai Shugi Kenkyū-kai,* Katayama himself had, like Kōtoku, Sakai, and also Abe, made tremendous strides toward the mastery of Western socialist theories. That he had left behind him the "water and gas socialism" he had advocated while under the spell of his collegiate enthusiasms was made abundantly clear by the summer of 1903. In July one of his most important works, *Waga Shakai Shugi* (Socialism to Me), was published at about the very time Kōtoku's *The Essence of Socialism* was rolling off the press.[27] The two books are of unsurpassed

[26] The anecdote was originally set forth in Kinoshita Naoe, "Katayama Sen Kun to Boku," *Chūō Kōron,* XLVIII, no. 12 (December 1933), pp. 302-303. The quotation cited is from the translation appearing in Kosaka, *op.cit.,* pp. 326-327. See also Morito Tatsuo, *Nihon ni okeru Kirisuto-kyō to Shakai Shugi Undō,* Tokyo, 1950, p. 111.

[27] This work is available in various editions. The most handy are

value not only for the light thrown upon the thought of the two not overly friendly socialist rivals but also because they foreshadowed a rupture of major dimensions in the later history of the socialist movement.

From the standpoint of theoretical clarity Kōtoku's *Shakai Shugi Shinzui* must be rated the finest exposition of Marxist historical materialism written in Japan before the Russo-Japanese War. Revealing a consummate grasp of Marx's teachings about the causes and nature of revolutionary social change, his study neglected, nevertheless, to take into account several of the cardinal theses of "scientific socialism." Curiously enough, though he understood the importance of means and modes of production in determining social organization, the phenomena of "contradictions" in class-based societies, and the historical unfolding of class struggles, he minimized the revolutionary role of the industrial proletariat and its "historical mission" to overthrow the capitalist system. European socialists would surely have been stunned by his appeal to patriots, men of good will, and revolutionary intelligentsia to work for the acquisition of parliamentary power by means of universal suffrage.[28]

Katayama's *Waga Shakai Shugi* is much longer than Kōtoku's study, dealing more extensively not only with the evolution of industrial capitalism but also with its ramifications in the principal institutions of society. It is apparent that Katayama had come under the heavy influence of Marxist theory, though, it should be pointed out, the precision of his understanding has been questioned by scholars.[29] If he accepted Marx's finding that the degradation of the industrial proletariat was an inevitable product of the capi-

Katayama Sen, *Toshi Shakai Shugi—Waga Shakai Shugi,* ed. Kishimoto Eitarō, Tokyo, 1949; and *Katayama Sen Tazoe Tetsuji Ni-Shu,* ed. Kishimoto Eitarō, Aoki Bunko 259, Tokyo, 1955, pp. 19-126.

[28] See the critique by Watanabe and Shioda, *op.cit.,* pp. 45-46.

[29] The commentary by Kishimoto, ed., *Katayama Sen Tazoe Tetsuji Ni-Shu,* pp. 264ff., is well worth study.

talist system and that the emancipation of the working class was contingent upon the destruction of industrial capitalism, some of his conclusions indicated a stubborn resistance to the implications of historical materialism. Thus, he sought to reconcile his Christian faith with "scientific socialism" by insisting that "true religion and morality could not be enjoyed to the full until socialism had been brought into the world."[30] As long as man remained a pawn of capitalism, he maintained, these humane pleasures were only to be half tasted.

What particularly distinguished Katayama from Kōtoku and, indeed, from all other Japanese socialists of the times was his ready perception of the key role of the proletariat in bringing about the socialist millennium. Only through the power of the working class, properly organized, directed, and instilled with a sense of its "historical mission," he argued, was it possible to expedite the overthrow of capitalism and the advent of the socialist revolution. This does not mean that Katayama was a proponent of forceful and violent methods; on the contrary, he utterly refused to consider their use. To attain the great goal of socialism he preferred to rely upon parliamentarism and particularly upon the general strike, that great mythical political tactic which then and for many years to come captivated the imagination of innumerable Western revolutionaries. Long after he had abandoned some of his most firmly held beliefs his faith in the wisdom and necessity of these political weapons remained unshakable.[31]

Had he written no other work, *Waga Shakai Shugi* would have merited Katayama a place as one of the most advanced socialist thinkers of Meiji Japan. There were still critical problems with which he had to wrestle. Such issues as the Emperor system, imperialism, nationalism and internationalism, and war and peace could not be glossed over, particularly in the light of the political trends within his own country. As

[30] *ibid.*, p. 113.
[31] Katayama, *The Labor Movement in Japan*, pp. 119-120.

a Japanese, Christian, and socialist he had probably reached as advanced a position on these vital questions as conflicting loyalties to nation, creed, and ideology would permit. Neither rational analysis nor tortured soul-searching could, however, provide the solutions to his dilemmas. If there were to be any answers, they were to be forthcoming primarily from the events of life.

CHAPTER X

PACIFISM AND WAR

Upon his return to Japan from the United States in 1896, Katayama had lost little time in joining the small band of good Samaritans intent upon uplifting the wretched masses. As a devout Christian socialist, he had accepted as an article of faith the lofty ideal of the common brotherhood of man and in his many projects on behalf of church and society had striven to further the social welfare of his fellow Japanese. If his resolution had not been weakened by continual setbacks, the times had nevertheless been severely trying, so much so that his thought on basic social problems had undergone gradual modification. Nothing better epitomized his continuing ideological readjustment than his shifting position on the issue of war.

During the final phase of Katayama's sojourn in the United States and Europe, Japan had become embroiled in war with imperial China. As opposed to the Manchu regime, where apathy toward the conflict was widespread, in Japan the nation rallied to lend united support to the government and remained steadfast in its determination to see the hostilities through to a successful conclusion. By tacit consent political disputes were put off for the duration of the hostilities and even inveterate malcontents declined to embarrass the state by provoking public debate on the problems raised by the war. How Katayama viewed the struggle with China at the time battle actually raged on the Asian continent is not known but he personally had no reason to question the righteousness of his country's cause. From statements made at the termination of the struggle, however, there is no doubt that he rejoiced in the triumph of Japan and was pleased by its effects upon the international position of his motherland.[1]

[1] Katayama was greatly pleased by the outcome of the war with

Like many of his fellow citizens, Katayama soon learned that the Sino-Japanese War had not only left unresolved the dilemma which Korea posed for Japanese foreign policy but also that military victory had raised many new issues vital for the future of his country. Before long it became apparent that the Meiji state, buoyed up by the successful prosecution of its first major war in modern times and by new and broader vistas of international power and prestige, was determined as never before to foster the growth of its political, military, and economic might. And the Japanese army and navy, increasingly confident with each defeat inflicted upon China, no longer hesitated to demand larger allocations for the expansion of the armed forces. In this drive for power and strength the government repeatedly made it clear that popular opposition to its policies would in no circumstances be permitted to get out of hand.

Shortly after the passage of the Public Peace Preservation Law, which severely circumscribed opportunities for social protest and agitation, events on the adjoining continent dramatically demonstrated that the war with China had provided no durable solution to the *Chōsen Mondai.*[2] With the elimination of China as one of several alien manipulators of the government of the "Hermit Kingdom" a sharp struggle for political ascendancy over the peninsula country set in between Japan and Russia. Distasteful as Chinese control had previously been to the Japanese government, the prospect of Russian hegemony over Korea was frightening. In 1900 the occupation of Manchuria by tsarist troops gave sub-

---

China, believing that Japan's victory would hasten the elevation of Japan to the position of "Great Britain of the East." Sen Katayama, "Labour Problem Old and New," *Far East*, II, no. 10 (October 1897), p. 477.

[2] During the Meiji period the challenge to Japanese foreign policy posed by Korea was commonly designated the *Chōsen Mondai* or "Korea Problem." For an incisive analysis see Hilary Conroy, "*Chōsen Mondai:* the Korean Problem in Meiji Japan," *American Philosophical Society, Proceedings,* C (October 1956), pp. 443-454.

stance to Japanese alarm over Russian ambitions on the nearby continent. Never since the middle of the nineteenth century, when the warships of Western powers had sailed defiantly into Tokyo Bay, had the national security of Japan seemed to be more gravely threatened. When repeated urgings and protests failed to bring about Russian evacuation of China's northeastern provinces, Japanese political and military leaders resigned themselves to the inevitability of an armed clash.

By the fall of 1903 fears of Russian imperialistic intentions were loudly voiced, and outspoken nationalists, fired by a sense of mission, undertook to excite passions for war among the people. In the face of the apparently irresistible force of government and public opinion many perennial critics of state policy wavered, while newspapers, which had hitherto specialized in vilification and dissent, now thought it expedient to jettison the cause of peace. Most fateful for the subsequent development of the socialist movement was the breach on the issue of war which occurred on the staff of the *Yorozu Chōhō,*[3] one of the most widely read of the Tokyo dailies.

Kuroiwa Ruikō, owner of the *Yorozu Chōhō,* was one of the most resourceful and, in some ways, opportunistic newspaper publishers of the Meiji period. Having a sense for news and a flair for ferreting out topics of public interest, he had little trouble in attracting some of the most promising and exciting writers of the day to his staff. Combining an appeal to the avante-garde with sensationalism and thriving on controversy and dissent, the *Yorozu Chōhō* not only built up a circulation which was the envy of the entire Japanese newspaper world but was influential in setting the tone and pace of high-level popular discussion. As long as the matter of war or peace hung precariously in the balance, Kuroiwa

[3] The name of this newspaper is commonly misread by modern scholars as *Man Chōhō*. The correct pronunciation is *Yorozu Chōhō*.

was not averse to lending the columns of his paper to the interests of pacifism. But when conflict with tsarist Russia seemed to be unavoidable and, moreover, imminent, the *Yorozu Chōhō* abruptly switched its policy on October 8, 1903.[4] With this unexpected turnabout the small but vociferous antiwar groups in Japan were compelled hurriedly to establish new programs and methods of opposition.

The rejection of militarism and war may not be rated highly among the social values of Meiji Japan. Condemnation of human strife had not for centuries been enunciated militantly by the many Buddhist sects and by the last half of the nineteenth century Buddhist exhortations had only the faintest influence in conditioning the attitudes of the Japanese people toward war. If the post-Restoration creed of Neo-Shinto nationalism did not, on the contrary, explicitly extol war, it did exalt military spirit and ideals as the noblest embodiment of patriotism and loyalty to the Emperor. The Meiji oligarchs also persistently summarized their policy in the shibboleth *Fukoku Kyōhei* (Rich Country, Strong Army) and, despite the state of the nation's finances, provided funds to strengthen the military and naval forces. When protests against policies of war were raised by political leaders, they were rarely couched in religious or moral categories but, as was evident in the maneuvers of the so-called peace party in the dispute over Korean policy in 1873-1874, in terms of the practicality of military involvement at the time.[5] Similar considerations underlay the scattered objections to the war which impended with China in 1894.

Religious, humanitarian, and ideological scruples over the use of military force for the settlement of international

[4] Kimura Tsuyoshi, "Nihon Shakai Shugi-shi," *Shakai Mondai Kōza*, IX (1926), p. 62; Matsushita Yoshio, *Hansen Undō-shi*, Tokyo, 1954, pp. 11-12; and Sen Katayama, *The Labor Movement in Japan*, Chicago, 1918, p. 82.

[5] This problem is excellently discussed in Nobutaka Ike, "Triumph of the Peace Party in Japan in 1873," *Far Eastern Quarterly*, II, no. 3 (May 1942), pp. 286-295.

disputes emanated in Meiji Japan from the teachings of foreign faiths and philosophies which only slowly acquired currency. The paramount influence was unquestionably Christianity. Japanese Catholics and Protestants were, however, no different from their fellows in faith in the United States and Europe in refusing to adopt an unequivocal stand against war, Katayama himself being a typical example for many years. The torment of the Japanese convert to Christianity in search of a position on the problem of war which would reconcile the demands of intellect, faith, and country is excellently seen in the career of Uchimura Kanzō, one of the outstanding Christian lay leaders of modern Japan.

As opposed to the religious pacifism which was derived from the dictate of moral duty, Japanese socialists of diverse ideological inspiration—Lassallian, Fabian, and Marxian—had by the opening of the twentieth century moved toward antiwar postures which rested upon theories of class struggle and materialistic interpretations of history. The most extreme and strident antiwar views were indisputably set forth in 1901 by Kōtoku Shūsui in his volume, *Imperialism.*[6] When war with Russia seemed increasingly probable in the closing months of 1903, Katayama's antiwar position straddled those of Uchimura and Kōtoku: his compassion for man as the perennially helpless victim of war, derived from teachings of his religious faith, was reinforced intellectually by a materialistic ideology whose ultimate conceptions of man and God he could not completely accept.

Until the reversal of its policy the *Yorozu Chōhō* had fulfilled journalistically the antiwar purposes of religious idealists, humanitarians, and variegated socialists. No sooner was the fateful decision made known, however, than the propon-

[6] It should be observed that Kōtoku's socialist beliefs were still inchoate, his attack on imperialism being essentially humanistic. By 1903, however, he had reached a Marxist position on imperialism and war.

ents of pacifism and the foes of war were compelled to find ways and means to serve the demands of conscience and intellect. Thus, after vowing never again to contribute to the columns of the *Yorozu Chōhō,* Uchimura demonstrated his rejection of state policy on war and militarism by a self-imposed silence which was as eloquent, if not so effective, as words.[7] For their part, Kōtoku and Sakai Toshihiko announced their intention, at a meeting of the *Shakai Shugi Kyōkai* held on the evening of October 8, of resigning their positions on Kuroiwa's newspaper. At the same meeting the society passed a resolution stating its opposition to a conflict with Russia.[8]

Within a few weeks it became clear that Japanese socialists had not spoken their last word on the subject of international conflict. As the socialists regrouped their meager and dwindling forces, it was apparent that the struggle against war would be continued on both the domestic and world fronts. Upon resigning from the *Yorozu Chōhō,* Kōtoku and Sakai immediately organized the *Heimin-sha* (Commoners' Society) for the express purpose of campaigning for socialism and peace. To publicize their opinions the *Heimin Shimbun* (Commoners' Newspaper) was founded, Sakai being editor and publisher. In the statement of policy, which appeared in the first issue on November 15, 1903, the paper proclaimed its intention of "arousing the sentiments of the masses, within the limits of the law." The *Heimin Shimbun* was by all odds the most forceful and exciting radical journal published in Japan before the post-World War I era.[9]

[7] Uchimura's pacifist views are lengthily analyzed in Kosaka Masaaki, ed. *Japanese Thought in the Meiji Era,* trans. and adapted by David Abosch, Tokyo, 1958, pp. 344ff.

[8] "Socialism Abroad: Japan," *International Socialist Review,* IV (1903-1904), p. 501.

[9] The *Heimin Shimbun* has fortunately been completely reprinted. See Hattori Shisō and Konishi Shiro, eds. *Heimin Shimbun,* 4 vols., Tokyo, 1953-1958. On the *Heimin-sha,* which issued the newspaper and carried on other serialistic activities, see Nakamura Katsunori,

For several months Sakai, Kōtoku, and other socialists waged a desperate up-hill struggle in the *Heimin Shimbun* to convince the Japanese people of the horrors and folly of war. In colorful and hard-hitting phrases they sought to depict the perfidy of capitalists, the avarice of war contractors, and the callousness and corruption of politicians. And in more direct efforts to whip up public indignation they repeatedly reminded the people of the staggering numbers of the innocent proletariat who would be sacrificed on the battlefields of the continent and expressed their sympathy for the many widows- and orphans-to-be. With its limited circulation and influence the *Heimin Shimbun* could, however, actually do nothing to halt the march of events and on February 9, 1904, Russia and Japan were at war.

As in 1894, when war had broken out between Japan and China, Katayama was thousands of miles from home when the Russo-Japanese War began. On December 29, 1903, after completing a tour of the mining communities in Hokkaido, he embarked upon his second journey to the United States and Europe.[10] On several occasions during the next few months he offered reasons for his decision to leave his homeland at so critical a moment in the history of Japanese socialism. Even he would probably have agreed that there was no pressing urgency to undertake, as he announced he would, organizational work among Japanese emigrants in the United States. But of far greater moment was his stated intention of attending the forthcoming national convention of the American Socialist Party, which was to be held in Chicago, and of participating in the proceedings of the Sixth Congress of the Second International, scheduled to convene

---

"Heimin-sha to Sono Zaisei Jijō," *Hōgaku Kenkyū*, XXXII (December 1958), pp. 20-56; and by the same author, "Heimin-sha no Kaisan to Danatsu," *Hōgaku Kenkyū*, XXXIII, no. 2 (February 1960), pp. 521-541.

[10] Yamagiwa Keiji; *Kinoshita Naoe; Ichi Senkaku-sha no Tatakai to Nayami*, Tokyo, 1955, p. 138.

in Amsterdam in August 1904. He was, it may be conjectured, hopeful of ensuring that the crucial problem of war or peace in the East would be accorded proper attention in the high councils of Western socialism.

There is no questioning the weightiness of the considerations underlying Katayama's decision to go abroad in 1903. Yet the suspicion remains that the journey was as much a flight as a mission. "I am worn out after an unceasing toil of seven years," he shortly thereafter confided to Kawakami Kiyoshi, "and I need a good rest." And besides, he continued, "what is the use of preaching socialism when the whole nation is intoxicated with . . . false glory . . . ?"[11] To say that he was stampeded by the ever louder drum-beats of war which were echoing throughout the length and breadth of Japan would be an exaggeration. It is plausible, however, that he was troubled, more than he cared openly to admit, by the prospective ordeal of attempting to work in close cooperation with Kōtoku and other antiwar zealots in the *Heimin-sha*. Though he had never concealed his admiration for the fearless and rebellious spirit of the young journalist, he was nevertheless irritated by Kōtoku's cynicism, his caustic speech, and his cold intellect. Purposeless as it was to quarrel with Kōtoku, it was as trying to engage in common action with him. Unfortunately, each was to go his own way during the epochal days of the Russo-Japanese War but Katayama may well have concluded that he had no alternative. Only in the United States and Europe, he probably believed, was it possible to find the aid and comfort in formulating a position on war which would satisfy the many doubts and torments generated by his religious faith, his political ideology, and his patriotic sentiments.

Upon arriving in San Francisco, which he had last seen more than eight years before, Katayama sought out several

[11] Karl Kiyoshi Kawakami, "Japanese on American Farms," *Independent*, LIX (October 26, 1905), p. 966.

of his old friends whom he tried to persuade to form a socialist cadre.[12] Then, after a very brief stay, he pushed on to Texas for the purpose of observing at first hand the agricultural enterprises which had but recently been started with great expectations by a vanguard of peasant emigrants from Japan. Here he tarried for several months, working as a waiter in a Japanese restaurant in order to earn money for his passage to Europe and striving as always to plant an interest in socialism among his countrymen.[13] With the coming of spring he left for Chicago, where the élite of American socialists were gathering for a national convention. Though he arrived without any fanfare and presumably without advance notice, his presence was noted on the second day of the meeting. By acclamation of the delegates he was invited to fill a seat of honor on the platform.[14] From all indications Katayama's role at the convention was purely symbolic and, when the proceedings were completed, he departed for the East Coast. Shortly thereafter he sailed for Europe.

A study of the statements and writings of Katayama during the first six months and more of 1904 reveals an unending search on his part for cause to justify his own unquenchable optimism. But, as diplomatic and military affairs unfolded in harsh reality, he refused to accept the dictum of events, resorting instead to wishful thinking and self-delusion. Thus, in one of his very first declarations on the prospects of war and peace, which was published at about the time of his arrival in California, he strove to reassure himself as well as his readers by scouting the prize of battle which was being greedily eyed by the governments of both Russia and Japan. "I do not personally believe," he wrote, "that the occupation

[12] Oka Shigeki, "Katayama Sen to Amerika," *Kaizō*, XXXII, no. 8 (July 1951), p. 77.

[13] *ibid.*, p. 77.

[14] National Committee of the Socialist Party, *Proceedings of the National Convention of the Socialist Party Held at Chicago, Illinois, May 1 to 6, 1904*, Chicago, 1904, p. 24.

of Manchuria by Russia is a question of life or death for Japan. Far from it: Japanese workers have no vital interest in the matter. They do not wish to engage in mutual slaughter with the Russian workers for the possession of Manchuria and even Korea. We are certain that the Russian workers think as we do on this question."[15] He then added a deceptively comforting observation:

"I cannot foresee with certainty what will come out of the present crisis, but it seems probable to me that there will be no war, for the moment at least, because the great majority of the Japanese people are opposed to it, especially the proletariat who are convinced that it would result in the immediate rise in the cost of the necessities of life. . . . The workers as well as the peasants in Japan are equally hostile and I believe that in the face of these sentiments on the part of the great mass of the population the government will not be able to undertake war despite the desire of certain capitalists."[16] Less than a month after this confident forecast appeared in the French press, Japanese naval forces carried out a surprise attack against the Russian fortress at Port Arthur.

Like most socialists of the day who were in principle opposed to international war, Katayama was a proponent of parliamentary obstruction and of the general strike to give weight and meaning to the grand ideal of socialism. But, as he himself knew, these otherwise powerful weapons of political coercion were denied to Japanese socialists and workers and the collision with Russia had not been averted. Realities could not, however, be completely avoided and Katayama sought consolation in predicting the positive advantages that would

[15] Sen Katayama in the symposium "La guerre russo-japonaise et le socialisme international," *Mouvement Socialiste*, XII, no. 134 (March 15, 1904), p. 340. Katayama's opinion, published in this journal, originally appeared in *Aurore* (January 11, 1904) before the outbreak of hostilities.

[16] *ibid.*, pp. 341-342.

accrue to the Japanese socialist movement as a consequence of the war then raging in southern Manchuria.

The struggle in the East, Katayama assured the socialists of America and Europe, would expedite the growth of the socialist movement in Japan. Once the people awakened, as they inevitably would, to the realization that it was they who paid the price in blood and taxes for victories on the battlefield which availed them nothing, they would learn an unforgettable lesson. Understanding the message which peaceable agitation had failed to inculcate, they would turn from the capitalists and politicians, who had deluded and betrayed them with promises of vain rewards, to their socialist friends. By prosecuting their selfish war, Katayama believed, the capitalists and their adherents were actually forging the engines of their own destruction.[17]

In a world dominated by capitalism, socialists believed, international war could only redound to the immediate profit of the financiers and industrialists. In keeping with this tenet Katayama was at first ready to aver, like many of his comrades in Japan, that the outcome of the war was of no particular concern to him. But, like numerous Western socialists of the times, he soon came to sense that in the issue of victory or defeat for Russia or Japan there were practical implications for the decline of capitalism and the ascendancy of socialism. Despite the fact that both Russia and Japan were denounced as capitalistic, warmongering states, it was thus necessary to make a choice between two evils. And so, following the lead of European socialists who saw defeat hastening the downfall of Russia, the most powerful despotism in Europe, if not in the world, Katayama began to look forward to a Japanese victory. "Now the war is going on in a brutal manner," he stated. "I am opposed to this war, but as a Japanese I do not

[17] Sen Katayama, "Le socialisme au Japon," in Secrétariat Socialiste International, *L'organisation socialiste et ouvrière en Europe, Amérique et Asie,* Brussels, 1904, p. 460.

wish Japan to be beaten by Russia who in the past treated the Jews as she has in Kishineff, and is still dealing with Fins [sic] in the most brutal fashion, and moreover she has shot down many laborers during strikes."[18]

If Katayama was after considerable groping to find the solution to his dilemma by condemning the Russo-Japanese War in principle but by supporting a Japanese victory as the lesser of two evils, Kōtoku and his socialist circle in Japan did not retreat from their uncompromising position. Even after war had been declared, the *Heimin Shimbun*, in a series of impassioned editorials and articles, continued week after week to attack the policy of the Japanese government. In their dogged fight Kōtoku and Sakai luckily secured the help of the brilliant young intellectual and writer, Nishikawa Kōjirō, and of Kinoshita Naoe, author of the widely read socialist novel, *Hi no Hashira* (Pillar of Fire). Their diatribes and "exposés," such as "The Results of War," "The Delusions of the Soldiers," and "The Heavy Burden of Patriotism," severely rankled the government but, as long as the *Heimin Shimbun* conducted its campaign "within the limits of the law," the authorities could do nothing to check the criticism and abuse.[19]

No unusual foresight was needed to predict that the Japanese state would not interminably tolerate the tirades of the staff and contributors of the socialist newspaper. In the twentieth issue of the *Heimin Shimbun* an editorial, "Ah, Woe! The Rising Taxes," was published, which at last provided the police with the legal opening they had been seeking.[20] The

[18] Sen Katayama, "Les socialistes japonais et la guerre," *Mouvement Socialist,* XII, no. 135 (April 15, 1904), p. 458; and Sen Katayama, "Attitude of Japanese Socialists toward Present War," *International Socialist Review,* IV, no. 9 (1903-1904), p. 514.

[19] These articles were published in the following issues of the *Heimin Shimbun*: "Sensō no Kekka" ("The Results of War"), no. 14 (February 14, 1904); "Heishi no Byūsō" ("The Delusions of Soldiers"), no. 15 (February 21, 1904); and "Aikoku no Omoni" ("The Heavy Burden of Patriotism"), no. 17 (March 7, 1904).

[20] "Aa Zōzei" ("Ah, Woe! The Rising Taxes"), *Heimin Shimbun,* no. 20 (March 28, 1904).

sale and circulation of the objectionable number were prohibited, charges were entered against Sakai, the publisher, and proceedings were initiated to close down the paper. In a decision handed down by the First Criminal Division, Tokyo District Court, on April 5, Sakai was adjudged guilty of violating the national press laws and sentenced to three months in jail.[21] The *Heimin Shimbun* was, moreover, ordered to discontinue its business.[22] When the decision was appealed, however, Sakai's sentence was reduced to two months and the ban on the paper was lifted.

Having failed in their efforts to stifle the *Heimin Shimbun*, the police now resorted to tactics of harassment. By March 1904, the newspaper, largely read by sympathetic intellectuals and students, had built up a steady circulation of about forty-five hundred, of which a little more than one thousand were spoken for by direct subscribers and the remainder accounted for by distributors and newsstands. Subscribers were now called upon by agents of the police and "advised" to patronize other newspapers, while dealers were intimidated and cautioned to desist from handling the pernicious journal. As a result of this pressure the circulation of the *Heimin Shimbun* dropped to about thirty-seven hundred by June, though, surprisingly enough, the number of direct subscribers actually rose by several hundred.[23]

The maneuvers to destroy the *Heimin Shimbun* elicited reproof and mockery from the socialists, who tirelessly insisted that Japanese officialdom was being ridiculously zealous in its efforts to end the antiwar crusade. On June 12, 1904, the

[21] Asahi Shimbun-sha, *Meiji Taishō-shi*, 6 vols., Tokyo, 1930, I, p. 220. For an interesting account of this episode see also the preface to Kinoshita Naoe, *Hi no Hashira*, in Yamamoto Mitsuo, ed. *Shakai Bungakushū*, vol. XXXIX of *Gendai Nihon Bungaku Zenshū*, Tokyo, 1930, p. 338. Kinoshita's novel has also been republished in the Iwanami Bunko series (Midori 264), Tokyo, 1959. In this edition see pp. 3-5.

[22] The newspaper was permitted to continue publication pending final disposition of the case by the courts.

[23] Shirayanagi Shūko, *Saionji Kimmochi Den*, Tokyo, 1929, p. 486.

attitude of the militant pacifists was summarized in a scolding editorial: "When one thinks that there are not more than two hundred professed Socialists in Japan, it seems strange that the Government is nervous over their propagandism. . . ." Moreover, the editors added, "If Socialists were reckless enough to resort to violent actions, it would be quite proper for the Government to use police force for the sake of social peace, but not one accusation of this kind can be brought against them. Are they not denouncing war all the time, because they believe that *no violent action is justifiable at any time*? We may say, without much exaggeration, that all Japanese socialists are peace-lovers in the extreme sense, and they are exactly the people for whom no police authority is required. Publicity is our motto, and nothing is kept secret among us. If the Government were to prosecute us by using proper methods we would not be severe in our criticism, but unjust and dishonourable means have been used to disgrace our name, and we cannot let it pass unnoticed."[24]

The battle against the war in Japan was by no means limited to journalistic castigation of the government of Premier General Katsura Tarō. In keeping with the tradition and expectancy of the followers of the Second International, Kōtoku and Sakai issued on March 13, 1904, a proclamation of sympathy with their oppressed Russian brethren, clearly indicating that they and their followers had adopted an unequivocating stand against the war. "Dear Comrades," their historic message began, "your government and ours have recently plunged into war to carry out their imperialistic tendencies, but for us Socialists there are no boundaries, race, country or nationality. We are comrades, brothers and sisters, and have no reason to fight. Your enemies are not the Japanese people, but our militarism and so-called patriotism. . . . We cannot foresee which of the two countries will win, but the result of the war will

[24] *Heimin Shimbun*, no. 31 (June 12, 1904). See also Alfred Stead, *Great Japan*, New York, 1906, p. 238. The italics in the quotation are mine.

be the same—general poverty, new and heavy taxes, the undermining of morality, and the extension of militarism. *Therefore, it is an unimportant question which government wins.*" [Italics mine.][25] For the small band of idealists grouped about the *Heimin Shimbun* the repudiation of war was an absolute principle. They saw no need to search for practical political advantages or to choose reluctantly between two manifest evils.

The straight-forward Japanese pronouncement, which was answered in a similar if not identical vein by Russian Social Democrats in their newspaper *Iskra,* won the acclaim of socialists throughout the world.[26] The *Volkszeitung*, a German-language socialist paper in New York City, in fact, reprinted the Japanese text for the admiration of its readers. Several months later the members of the *Heimin-sha* addressed an appeal to the various delegates who were then preparing, as was Katayama in the United States, to proceed to Amsterdam where the international congress of socialists was soon to get under way. Each of the participating representatives was enjoined "to urge the Government of his country to take steps to bring the war to an end speedily."[27] But being aware that socialists in other countries could under the circumstances actually do very little to bring pressure to bear against the

[25] The proclamation originally appeared in the *Heimin Shimbun,* no. 18 (March 14, 1904). The Japanese text of the quotation cited may also be found in Kimura, *op.cit.*, IX, 72, and in abbreviated form in Shirayanagi, *op.cit.*, p. 493. The version cited above is the translation appearing in "The Socialists of Japan to the Socialists of Russia," *Arena,* XXXII (1904), p. 322. See also Katayama, *The Labor Movement in Japan,* pp. 87-89.

[26] Kimura, *op.cit.*, IX, p. 73; and Shirayanagi, *op.cit.*, p. 494. For an English translation see Katayama, *The Labor Movement in Japan*, pp. 89-90. In the many effusions of good will the ideological implications of this exchange between the Japanese and Russian socialists have commonly been overlooked. For a discussion of this basic issue see below, Ch. XIII, n. 6.

[27] Isoh Abe [Abe Isoo], "Socialism in Japan," in Shigenobu Okuma, ed. *Fifty Years of New Japan,* 2 vols., London, 1909, II, p. 507.

Russian and Japanese states, they were counseled to use their "pens and tongues" as effectively as possible.

From the West came a message which tremendously heartened the pacifists in the East. On June 27, 1904, Count Tolstoi's stirring condemnation of the practice of war in general and of the Russo-Japanese War in particular was published in the London *Times.* The article of the world-famed Russian writer and philosopher, "Bethink Yourselves," created a sensation in the press of Europe and the United States, where it was extensively reprinted and commented upon. In Japan it was translated and published in the *Heimin Shimbun* in August.[28] Since Tolstoi enjoyed immense prestige in Japanese intellectual circles, "Bethink Yourselves" was excitedly received, so much so that the *Heimin Shimbun* found it necessary to run off reprints. Although Japanese socialists gratefully welcomed Tolstoi's support in the struggle to bring the war to an end, the fiery Kōtoku was reserved in his praise. The dogmatism, which was soon to lead to his isolation from the mainstream of the Japanese socialist movement, was already strongly foreshadowed.[29]

It seems clear in retrospect that by the summer of 1904 the exigencies of war had served to sharpen the ideological positions of Japanese socialists, especially of Katayama and Kōtoku. Fortunately, the distance which separated them and the impossibility of intimate communication prevented the occurrence of an open breach. But, however cognizant the rank and

[28] *Heimin Shimbun,* no. 39 (August 7, 1904). Katayama, *The Labor Movement in Japan,* p. 93, erroneously gives the date as August 27.

[29] Kōtoku's criticism of "Bethink Yourselves" was expressed in the next issue of the *Heimin Shimbun.* "Tolstoi," he wrote, "ascribes the cause of war to the debasement of man and, accordingly, desires to save him by teaching repentance. We socialists attribute the cause of war to economic competition and, thus, we seek to prevent war by abolishing economic competition. For this reason we are not completely in accord with Tolstoi." Kōtoku Denjirō [Shūsui], "Torusutoi-Ō no Hisen-ron wo Hyō-su," *Heimin Shimbun,* no. 40 (August 14, 1904). For a reprint of this piece see "Kōtoku Shūsui-hen," in Yamamoto, *op.cit.,* XXXIX, p. 205.

file of Japanese socialists may have been of the true situation, socialists in the United States and Europe, who were not familiar with the fine but vital details of Japanese affairs, were unable to detect the serious discordance. Insofar as the Second International interested itself in the issues raised by the Russo-Japanese War, it was commonly believed that an undivided front was being maintained under the most difficult conditions by their comrades in the East. When Katayama arrived in Amsterdam to attend the Sixth Congress, he was, accordingly, accepted without contradiction as the representative and spokesman of an ostensibly united Japanese movement.[30]

For Katayama personally the Sixth Congress at Amsterdam was one of the most gratifying and memorable events of his lifetime. As the only Asian in attendance at an international gathering made up exclusively of Europeans and Americans, to some of whom he was already known through his many articles in the socialist papers, he was a showpiece of inestimable worth. Showered with attention, sought out by the veteran leaders of the European socialist parties, feted and lionized, he was able to brush aside for a while the dispiriting memories of the petty bickerings and harassments which had been his lot as a socialist in his homeland. But the most flattering of all tributes was bestowed upon him at the very opening of the Congress proceedings. Inspired by his presence, the assembled delegates enthusiastically elected him first vice-president of the convocation, Henri Van Kol of Holland and Georgii Plekhanov of Russia being chosen president and second vice-president respectively. Katayama was probably the only Asian

[30] Katayama was not the first Japanese to attend a congress of the Second International but he was the first Japanese delegate of a recognized movement. The second assembly of the Second International, held at Brussels in 1891, had been attended by Sakai Yusaburō, a prominent liberal and pioneer in the social movement of Meiji Japan. See Junshiro Asari, "The Development of the Social Movement and Social Legislation in Japan," in Inazo Nitobe and others, *Western Influences in Modern Japan,* Chicago, 1931, p. 313.

ever accorded such high recognition in the entire history of the Second International.

The various gestures of recognition extended to Katayama at Amsterdam, gracious as they doubtless were, may perhaps have proved only that the hard-boiled leaders of Western socialism had not completely rejected bourgeois amenities. Had he carried out the duties of his honorary office in conventional manner, it is not unlikely that he would in later years have provided only the subject matter for an occasional and inconsequential recollection. But during the very first session of the Congress he became an actor in an historical drama which has ever since gladdened the hearts of socialists the world over. Van Kol, flanked on the speaker's platform by Katayama and Plekhanov, expressed his joy in his opening address that, at a time when the governments of Russia and Japan were waging war, Russian and Japanese socialists had declared themselves for peace. Suddenly the Russian delegate, in a move observable by the entire assembly, reached across the paunchy girth of the chairman and took Katayama by the hand. The electrified audience burst into thunderous applause.[31] "Symbolically, the Russian proletariat was shaking hands with their [sic] Japanese fellow wage slaves."[32]

When Van Kol concluded, he was followed to the rostrum by Katayama, who recounted the history and growth of the Japanese socialist movement. His sarcastic comment that there

[31] Secrétariat Socialiste International, *Sixième congrès socialiste international tenu à Amsterdam du 14 au 20 Août 1904; compte-rendu analytique,* Brussels, 1904, p. 18.

[32] Daniel De Leon, *Flashlights of the Amsterdam Congress,* New York, 1929, p. 43. De Leon, the veteran American socialist who was present at the assembly, has offered, perhaps maliciously, an explanation of Plekhanov's dramatic move. According to him, the audience was being lulled to sleep by Van Kol's address. In an inspired attempt to resurrect the situation the Russian delegate conceived this gesture of the international solidarity of workingmen. "It was a well thought demonstration, the work of a flash of genius," De Leon pronounced. "Apart from rousing the Congress from the languor it was drooping into, and driving it to frenzied applause, the handshake . . . was a pathetic rebuke to capitalism."

were three thousand socialists on the police registers in Japan evoked laughter from the delegates, who well knew that the figure was grossly exaggerated. And then sufficiently inspired by the previous proceedings and in a mood of brimming camaraderie the Congress, taking note of the appeal raised earlier by Japanese socialists, passed a resolution affirming its intention to "take measures to check the spread and progress of the war."[33] Actually, however, the Congress was in no position to implement the resolution. Furthermore, there was no enthusiasm for a full-scale debate, and the problem of international war was, for all practical purposes, tabled. It was not until the summer of 1914 when, brought into the open again by the outbreak of the European war, it disrupted the uneasy unity of the socialist world.

Amsterdam was the high point of Katayama's trip to the West during the Russo-Japanese War. Not only was the constant adulation a tonic for his sagging morale but his timely appearances in America and Europe had a profound influence upon his own subsequent career as well as upon the history of the Japanese socialist movement. In addition to crystallizing his hitherto inchoate ideas on the universal brotherhood of the proletariat and making him thereafter a confirmed internationalist in outlook, the trip won him the prestige in the circles of international socialism he was never to enjoy in the more restricted confines of his native movement. For some

[33] A positive step along these lines was taken several months later by the French socialist leader, Jean Jaurès, who, on the occasion of the sailing of the Russian Baltic fleet for the Far East, demanded in the Chamber of Deputies that France maintain a strict neutrality and render no assistance to the naval vessels of her ally. How instrumental Jaurès was in influencing French policy in the matter is a moot point but it is clear that Russia received far less aid than she had hoped for. The action by Jaurès may be construed as being in conformity with the resolution of the Sixth Congress but it should be observed at the same time that Jaurès, like other European socialists, favored victory for Japan. His move, which could only hinder the Russian war effort, was most welcome to the Japanese. It is ironic that the Katsura government, which was then persecuting its own radicals, should have been grateful to the French socialists.

years to come Western socialists, concerned with the revolutionary role of industrial proletariat and not with affairs in "backward" countries like Japan, were to reveal a personal interest in Katayama but rarely in the socialist movement it was believed he represented. Sen "Joe" Katayama was, in short, to be transfigured by the socialists of the Occident into a solitary symbol of proletarian struggle against tyranny and oppression in remote Asia.[34]

After his visit to the Low Countries, Katayama made his way back to the United States. It is indeed puzzling that few serious attempts have been made, particularly by his most devoted admirers, to explain his failure or unwillingness to return to Japan to join Kōtoku, Sakai, and Nishikawa in their frenzied fight to bring about a cessation of hostilities.[35] Whatever the reasons for this neglect may be, his innumerable biographers and eulogists have neither posed the problem nor, more importantly, the implications of the answer. When all is said and done, there is no doubt that after the Amsterdam Congress Katayama decided to sit out the war in the United States and to be a spectator to the desperate and futile struggles of his ideological comrades at home in Japan. Kawakami Kiyoshi surely put his finger on the matter when he noted that, while Katayama lags "behind no person in his devotion to socialism," he is, nevertheless, "exceedingly law-abiding, and shrinks from radicalism of a fire-and-blood nature."[36]

It is a striking and incontrovertible fact that Katayama, who has been extolled over the years as the embodiment of the antiwar movement in modern Japan, was never in his homeland for a single day during the course of any of the foreign conflicts in which his country was involved during his own

[34] Joseph was Katayama's baptismal name. He rarely used it, though some of his published articles are on occasion signed Sen Joseph Katayama.

[35] Though the Amsterdam Congress completed its proceedings in August 1904, the Treaty of Portsmouth, concluding the Russo-Japanese War, was not signed until September 1905.

[36] Kawakami, *op.cit.*, p. 966.

lifetime. During the Sino-Japanese War of 1894-1895, when he was in England and the United States, he had not, to be sure, been opposed to the policy of his government but at the time of the Russo-Japanese War he chose to be a voluntary exile in America. In World War I he was an expatriate in California and New York and, when late in his life the Japanese Kwantung Army recklessly embarked upon the conquest of Manchuria, Katayama was living as a refugee in Soviet Russia. Though his absences from his native land during some of its most momentous periods of history were partly fortuitous, personal and ideological considerations may not be completely ignored. What is necessary, above all, is a more precise understanding of his position on the issue of war which constantly shifted, subtly but significantly, through the span of many years.

By the late summer and early fall of 1904 Katayama had asked himself whether any worthwhile purpose was to be served by returning to Tokyo. Grieved by the very act of war, he had, nevertheless, come to the conclusion that, socialist opposition or not, the conflict with Russia would sooner or later run its course and that, from the long-range interests of both Japanese and international socialism, a Japanese victory over Russia was to be preferred. It was this type of temporizing with principle that had years before tripped Karl Marx himself and prepared the way for the unbroken record of controversy and equivocation of the First and Second Internationals on the issue of war. But however wise or dangerous his solution may have been, Katayama, having taken his stand, could see no reason to return to Japan. If he could not now bring himself to support wholeheartedly the position advocated by the hard core of the *Heimin-sha*, neither was he minded to split the precarious unity and pathetically weak ranks of Japanese socialism by pressing for the acceptance of his own views. Justifiable and unselfish his intentions may have been but his decision cost Katayama dearly in terms of prestige and influence in the Japanese socialist movement.

From the perspectives of Texas, where he lived during the remaining months of the Russo-Japanese War, Katayama followed the tortured course of the antiwar movement which the members of the *Heimin-sha* continued to prosecute daringly but futilely. To take their crusade more directly to the people than was possible with the insignificant circulation of the *Heimin Shimbun* Kōtoku and Sakai periodically staged public forums and protest meetings. Most of these gatherings were held in Tokyo, usually in the hall of the YMCA building. These assemblies, which were surprisingly well attended according to the socialist press, were closely watched by the suspicious police, who evidently believed that revolutionary conspiracies might be plotted. At times the speakers were peremptorily interrupted and on one occasion, at least, the police, attempting to drag Sakai from the platform, were, despite the pleas for restraint by the socialist leaders present, set upon by the furious audience.[37] In addition to this agitation, antiwar pamphlets were printed for mass distribution, students, it is said, taking advantage of their vacation periods to distribute them in the rural areas.[38]

The simmering exasperation of the government rose to a boiling point in November 1904. That the Japanese state was provoked by the criticism of the *Heimin Shimbun* there can be no doubt. But to understand the outburst of oppression at this time it is necessary to bear in mind that nerves were strained because of the bloody repulses of the Japanese army,

[37] "Socialism Abroad: Japan," *International Socialist Review,* v (1904-1905), p. 439.

[38] Abe, *op.cit.*, II, p. 509. The students distributing the radical literature were presumably not Abe's. During the Russo-Japanese War the Christian socialist leader created a nation-wide stir by leading the Waseda University baseball team on a sports tour of the United States. Kimura Ki, ed. *Japanese Literature; Manners and Customs in the Meiji-Taisho Era,* trans. and adapted by Philip Yampolsky, Tokyo, 1957, pp. 253-255.

which had stalled on the approaches to Port Arthur, and by the news that the Russian Baltic fleet had sailed for Far Eastern waters. Thus, when there appeared in the November 6 issue of the *Heimin Shimbun* such articles as "An Announcement to Primary School Teachers," "Confusion of the So-called Patriots," and "The Attitude of the Educator towards the War," the police responded by forbidding the sale and circulation of the offensive edition, by instituting legal charges against the responsible writers and editor, and by initiating action to shut the publication down completely.[39]

Not in the least daunted by these official actions, the staff of the *Heimin Shimbun* proceeded to lay plans for an unforgettable commemoration of the first anniversary of the paper. It was decided to publish a bound volume of the first fifty-two numbers of the *Heimin Shimbun*; to bring out in the anniversary edition of the paper on November 13 a complete translation of the Communist Manifesto, enriched with pictures of Marx, Engels, Lassalle, Bebel, Kropotkin, and Tolstoi; and to cap the occasion with a garden party. The police had no legal grounds to prohibit the sale of the bound volume or to prevent the publication and distribution of pictures of Europe's most famous revolutionaries but they acted promptly to forbid circulation of Marx and Engels' Manifesto.[40] Lodg-

[39] "Shōgaku Kyōshi ni Tsugu" ("An Announcement to Primary School Teachers"); "Iwayuru Aikoku-sha no Rōbai" ("Confusion of the So-called Patriots"); and "Sensō ni tai-suru Kyōiku-sha no Taidō" ("The Attitude of the Educator towards the War"), *Heimin Shimbun*, no. 52 (November 6, 1904). It was the first article in particular to which the police objected. Kimura, *op.cit.*, IX, p. 75; and Shirayanagi, *op.cit.*, p. 487.

[40] The word "communism" first appeared in a Japanese work in 1870 and the first Japanese biography of Karl Marx was probably written by Nishikawa Kōjirō in 1902. Although the Communist Manifesto was circulated in Japan in foreign-language editions, the translation published in the *Heimin Shimbun* was the first complete rendition into Japanese. Police authorities were generally indifferent to the availability of radical literature in western languages but translations into Japanese immediately captured their attention. See Gustave Eckstein, "Le premier congrès socialiste japonais," *Mouvement Socialiste*, no. 121 (June 1, 1903), p. 208. Until 1914 works of the following western writers were sup-

ing new charges of violation of the national press laws against the socialist paper, the police also forbade the holding of the garden party.

The antiwar movement in Japan reached its peak with the publication of the anniversary edition of the *Heimin Shimbun* and thereafter rapidly declined. Despite all their efforts, the socialists could not save their paper, much less Kōtoku and Nishikawa, from the wrath of the government. In December the two radicals, together with Sakai, were arraigned before the first Criminal Division, Tokyo District Court, and fined for publishing the Communist Manifesto.[41] In January 1905, the socialists, anticipating the suppression of their organ, sought unsuccessfully to secure a license for a new weekly. Then in the sixty-fourth issue of the *Heimin Shimbun* the publishers, "struggling to hold back their tears," sadly announced the voluntary discontinuance of the paper. As a parting gesture of defiance the socialists, borrowing a page from the life of Marx and his journal, the *Neue Rheinische Zeitung*, printed the final number of the paper in bold red type. The *Chokugen* (Plain Talk), a small socialist monthly, was designated the new official journal of Japanese socialism.

Kōtoku and Nishikawa fought a losing battle through the courts against the charges leveled against them on the preceding November 6. On March 28, 1905, they entered prison for five and seven months respectively. Though an outcry was raised by some of the great Tokyo dailies, which argued that the government was needlessly creating martyrs and by its oppression only inspiring those socialists who were still at liberty, the two unrepentant agitators were required to serve their full sentences in prison.

With the jailing of Kōtoku and Nishikawa the Japanese antiwar movement lost its spark and verve. The *Chokugen*

---

pressed when translated: Sombart, Zola, Blatchford, L. G. Deutsch, Marx, Engels, Tolstoi, and Kropotkin.

[41] The text of the judicial decision appears in Asahi Shimbun-sha, *op.cit.*, I, pp. 221-228.

continued to clamor for peace until the very end of hostilities but it never became an adequate replacement of its predecessor, the *Heimin Shimbun*.[42] A pathetic challenge was hurled at the government in May with the entrance of Kinoshita Naoe into the political lists as a socialist candidate in the general elections. That he received only thirty-two votes in the total of more than sixteen thousand cast was due, his comrades charged with much truth though with utter lack of realism, to police interference with his political campaign. Kinoshita's political effort really marked the demise of the Japanese socialist campaign for peace during the Russo-Japanese War.

Despite their valiant and, at times, fanatical efforts, the members of the *Heimin-sha* and their sympathizers were neither instrumental in preventing the outbreak of war with Russia nor in hastening the advent of peace. Their crusade waged over a period of almost two years nonetheless represents as fine an example of unselfish devotion to a noble cause as may be found in modern social history. If their results were meager, there is no cause for scorn. Coping with a people who did not question the practice of war or the government's alluring promises of great rewards in the event of victory, the task was too formidable for the small group. The net achievement of the die-hard pacifists was probably best summed up in the simple tribute—or epitaph—of Katayama in distant America. "It is perhaps the first time in the history of Japan," he said in humble pride, "that the cry, 'Down with war,' has been raised in the land of the samurai."[43]

[42] For an excellent, detailed discussion of *Chokugen* see Nakamura Katsunori, "Shukan Shimbun *Chokugen* Sō-mokuji to Kaisetsu," *Hōgaku Kenkyū*, XXXII, no. 8 (August 1959), especially pp. 46-53.

[43] Katayama, "Les socialistes japonais et la guerre," *op.cit.*, p. 456. He was not, however, completely unable to distinguish between the publication of socialist writings and their effect upon the people. Not many months before he had made this clear. "People," he wrote, "are crazy after the war news, they will not turn their ears to the voice of Socialists nor read much of their Socialist literature." Katayama, in the American *Social Democratic Herald*, as quoted in "The Socialists of Japan and the War," *Comrade*, III (August 1904), p. 239.

The Treaty of Portsmouth in September 1905, which ended the Russo-Japanese War, aroused in Katayama and the Japanese socialists the grim satisfaction of vindicated prophecy. When the terms of the peace agreement were made public, the Japanese people, who had little suspected how urgently their government leaders desired peace, were stunned for a moment by the absence of provisions for Russian indemnities. In Tokyo especially the more grievously disappointed citizens erupted in a riot of anger. Mass protest demonstrations, recalling those which had occurred in Petrograd but a few months before, soon led to clashes with the police, while infuriated groups roamed the streets attacking government offices, overturning police boxes, and setting fires. The Japanese state, frightened by the outbursts, was compelled to declare martial law and to bring in reinforcements to restore order. To Kōtoku, who had just been released from prison, the spectacle of a "sea of fire and blood" was a triumph.[44]

Peace meant, however, much more to the socialists than an occasion to congratulate themselves upon their political omniscience. Though he was appalled by the carnage that victory had entailed, Katayama was able to draw comfort from the heavy blow that had been struck at tsarist reaction and autocracy and from the prospect that a disillusioned Japanese people would henceforth be more receptive to the blandishments of socialism. Kōtoku, too, was even more strongly convinced that the masses could never win in war.

Yet, apart from the apparent validation of personal beliefs, war and peace in 1904-1905 impelled Japanese socialists to evaluate their thought and activity in the light of their expectations and with the wisdom of retrospection. Here especially was the most important consequence of the postures

[44] Kōtoku Denjirō [Shūsui] to Albert Johnson, September 8, 1905, in H. Havel, ed. "Kotoku's Correspondence with Albert Johnson," *Mother Earth*, VI, no. 6 (August, 1911), p. 184. See also Hyman Kublin, "Kōtoku Shūsui no Ichi Beijin Anakisuto e no Shokan-shū," *Shakai Kagaku Kenkyū*, IX, no. 1 (June 1957), p. 115.

on war taken during the conflict, for it seems clear that the war had a greater effect upon the socialists than the socialists upon the war. In great measure the individual experiences and reactions of Japanese socialists during the Russo-Japanese War hastened the rise of the sharply conflicting theoretical and tactical lines which were to emerge once the hated Katsura had given way to the more indulgent government of Prince Saionji in 1906. All the contradictions and antagonisms which had been submerged in the idealism of the earlier but shakily united movement now flared up in internecine controversy.

CHAPTER XI

THE LONELY YEARS

At the Amsterdam Congress of the Second International Katayama enjoyed the spotlight for an all too brief moment. But within a few days after the close of the socialist conclave he disappeared from public notice and remained in obscurity for the next year and a half. This sudden lapse into political oblivion has been passed over in almost complete silence by his biographers who for inexplicable reasons have shown only faint curiosity about his whereabouts during this time. Unfortunately Katayama, whose tracks in life after 1895 may generally be followed with no more than ordinary difficulty, has left only fragmentary evidence of his activities during this period. If the scanty information available does nothing to embellish the popular image of Katayama as a dedicated and irrepressible social revolutionary, it does provide invaluable glimpses of a pattern of behavior completely in keeping with his character.

With his business in Europe concluded and with the conflict in the East showing no signs of an early decision, Katayama was in no hurry to make his way back to his native land. His views on the Russo-Japanese War apart, it is possible that the untimely death of his wife Fude, not long before he had departed for America, removed whatever qualms he may have had about prolonging his stay abroad indefinitely. Be this as it may, when the proceedings at Amsterdam ended, he spent the next few weeks traveling about in Holland, Belgium, and France, presumably familiarizing himself with the state of affairs of the local socialist movements. By the early fall he returned to the United States, where the lackadaisical presidential campaign of 1904 between Theodore Roosevelt and Judge Alton B. Parker was running its dreary course.[1]

[1] The Chronology (*Nempu*) in Katayama Sen, *Jiden*, Tokyo, 1954, p. 347, notes for the year 1904 only that Katayama attended the

Shortly thereafter he went on to Texas where he remained for more than a year.

Katayama's life in Texas, spent intermittently from early 1904 until January 1907, can only be designated as bizarre. To fathom his purposes it must be pointed out that since his return to Tokyo in 1896 he had been intensely interested in encouraging emigration by his countrymen to the United States. Not only had he written and lectured widely toward this end but he had also established an orientation program at the Kingsley Hall settlement house. Not even his involvement in trade-union and socialist agitation had been able to divert him from the aim of helping his compatriots to find a better life overseas. After spending a few months in Texas in early 1904 his enthusiasm had been so fired by the agricultural settlements founded by some Japanese speculators and emigrants in 1903-1904 that he decided to return and remain awhile after he had attended the Amsterdam Congress.

At the time Katayama settled down for an indefinite stay in Texas, a small number of Japanese communities and farms were in existence at League City, Alden, and Webster to the south of Houston, at Palestine in the north, at Garwood in Colorado County, and at Del Rio on the Mexican frontier far to the west.[2] Almost all the holdings were worked by owner-operators. At Garwood, however, Hashimoto Junzō, the brother-in-law of the Consul-General of Japan in New York, used

---

Amsterdam Congress. His return to the United States is erroneously listed under the entry for 1905. That he was back in America by October 1904, having spent about two months in Europe after the close of the Congress, is made clear by one of his letters of the period. See his communication, "Beikoku Tayori," dated "Texas, November 1 [1904]," in the *Tobei Zasshi*, IX, no. 1 (January 3, 1905), p. 18.

The volume number of *Tobei Zasshi* is part of a consecutive series of periodicals including the earlier *Rōdō Sekai* and *Shakai Shugi* as well as the later *Amerika*.

[2] *ibid.*, pp. 18-19. See also Yoshimura Taishirō, "Tekisasu Nihon-jin," *Tobei Zasshi*, IX, no. 1 (January 3, 1905), pp. 8-10. Katayama himself bought a tract of land at Aldine. K. K. Kawakami, "Japanese on American Farms," *Independent*, LIX (October 26, 1905), p. 964.

locally hired hands, while at Del Rio the Japanese farmers leased their land. These ventures had aroused more than mere curiosity, for they were inspected from time to time by fairly well-known entrepreneurs and politicians from Japan.

The efforts of Japanese settlers to raise rice in Texas met with results ranging from extraordinary success to abysmal failure. On Hashimoto's farm, where the initial investment was heavy because of meticulous regard for methods of cultivation, the yields per acre were, at the outset at least, amazing. It has been claimed that he was able to raise almost forty bushels of rice per acre, a harvest which has rarely been exceeded even in Japan itself. Though few other farmers were able to derive such gratifying rewards, there were evidently sufficient instances of conspicuous success to encourage the settlers to continue their work. Japanese peasants and farm managers had persuasively demonstrated that, provided adequate amounts of water were available, there was no insuperable obstacle to the commercial cultivation of rice on the plain lands of Texas.

How Katayama passed his time during the fourteen months he lived in or near Houston is not completely known. It is clear, however, that he diligently sought out various Japanese farmers in the area and carefully studied the economics of their enterprises. This information, together with reports on the plans and problems of Japanese settlers in other parts of the state, provided the material for lengthy letters which he wrote for publication in the journal, *Tobei Zasshi* (Introducing America), a bimonthly issued in Tokyo.[3] This magazine, which he had launched in 1905, was designed to assist Japanese pre-

[3] The file of this rare periodical used by the author is in the Waseda University Library in Tokyo. References to it are fairly common in the literature on the Japanese social movement but there is little evidence that it has been consulted by Japanese scholars, who have generally relied upon the better known *Heimin Shimbun*. Equally neglected as a source of information on Katayama's life and thought is the less well known and almost never used successor of *Tobei Zasshi,* namely, *Amerika.* A file of this periodical will also be found in the Waseda University Library.

paring to go to the United States.[4] A good part of his remaining time was apparently spent in study and writing, his principal work of this period being his *Bankoku Shakai-tō* (The Socialist Parties of the World). This book was a product of his European tour. Needless to say, he could not refrain from discussing socialism with whoever would listen, be it one of his own countrymen or a local member of the American party. Letters from friends at home and newspapers and journals from Japan and Europe kept him abreast of socialist developments.

Firsthand investigation confirmed Katayama in his belief that Texas offered a bright future for Japanese settlers. Since Okazaki Tsuneyoshi, owner of a restaurant in Houston, professed to share his optimism, the two aspiring promoters decided to return to Japan to encourage their countrymen to migrate to America's largest state. The details of their plans are vague and it is not always clear how they themselves were to be recompensed for their time-consuming efforts.[5] In any event, Katayama and Okazaki left Houston, probably in December 1905, for San Francisco.[6] There at the home of Oka

[4] *Tobei Zasshi* is mentioned only discursively in the comprehensive study of source materials on the Japanese socialist movement made by Watanabe Yoshimichi and Shioda Shōbei, *Nihon Shakai Shugi Bunken Kaisetsu*, Tokyo, 1958, pp. 48-49. No mention is, moreover, made in this work of the journal, *Amerika*. On *Tobei Zasshi* see also the entry and annotation in Cecil H. Uyehara, *Leftwing Social Movements in Japan; an Annotated Bibliography*, Tokyo, 1959, p. 31; this work also neglects to mention *Amerika*.

For the objectives of *Tobei Zasshi* see Katayama's letter, "Beikoku Tayori," dated "Texas, December 23 [1904]," published in the journal, IX, no. 2 (February 3, 1905), pp. 15-17.

[5] Oka Shigeki, "Katayama Sen to Amerika," *Kaizō*, XXXII, no. 8 (July 1951), p. 77.

[6] Oka Shigeki, who met with Katayama at this time, does not explicitly cite the date of his arrival in San Francisco. He merely indicates that, when Kōtoku Shūsui arrived in the city in December 1905, he and Katayama got together for a chat. *ibid.*, p. 77. The Chronology in *Jiden*, p. 348, however, specifically states that Katayama was in the "Golden Gate" city in late November. Though it is possible the Chronology is correct, it is unlikely in view of Kōtoku's precise account of his meeting with Katayama, which he dates December 26, 1905. "I

Shigeki, the publisher of a local Japanese-language newspaper, Katayama, who was not overly pleased, met his old ideological antagonist, Kōtoku Shūsui.[7]

No extended exchange of political and philosophical views was necessary to convince Katayama that Kōtoku and he had come to a final parting of the ways. Not only was the radical journalist his old surly self but there was no mistaking that the two social revolutionaries had drifted even further apart since their last meetings in the fall of 1903. The more significant change was, however, evident in the outlook of the younger man. Kōtoku's futile antiwar struggle against the state and his confinement in prison during the final five months of the conflict had not chastened him at all but rather had hardened his spirit of defiance. Ideologically the most important consequence of his stay in jail had been a turn toward the theories of anarchism, which he had begun to study avidly, if erratically.[8] It was, as a matter of fact, his desire to enrich his knowledge of this extremely Utopian philosophy, which had been explored only superficially in Japan, that had prompted his trip to the United States.

The split between Katayama and Kōtoku was far more serious than a personal quarrel. More important, it symbolized the crystallization of ideological and tactical differences of conviction which had been latent since the inception of the socialist movement. Agreement on the need for social revolution in Japan and common but not united opposition to an authoritarian state had for a number of years prevented deep-

---

come to the United States," remarked Kōtoku, "and he returns to Japan." See Kōtoku's communication published in *Hikari* as quoted in Tanaka Sōgoro, *Kōtoku Shūsui; Ichi Kakumei-ka no Shisō to Shōgai*, Tokyo, 1955, p. 287.

[7] Oka, *op.cit.*, pp. 77-78. See also Tanaka, *op.cit.*, pp. 287-288.

[8] Contrary to a widespread belief, Kōtoku had shifted from Marxian socialism towards anarchism even before his visit to the United States. See his letter to Albert Johnson, dated August 10, 1905, in Hyman Kublin, "Kōtoku Shūsui no Ichi Beijin Anakisuto e no Shokan-shū," *Shakai Kagaku Kenkyū*, IX, no. 1 (June 1957), pp. 112-113.

rooted antagonisms from flaring into the open. Even the "united front," maintained under the exigencies of the Russo-Japanese War, had been more apparent than real and had endured as long as it did partly because of the self-imposed silence and restraint of several socialist leaders. But sooner or later, when the context of political conditions changed, these conflicts of a fundamental nature were bound to burst forth.

Unsatisfactory and, perhaps, even distasteful as his meeting with Kōtoku in San Francisco was, Katayama, accompanied by Okazaki, returned to Japan in January 1906, with much to look forward to.[9] He was eager to see again his motherless children who had for the preceding two years and more been under the care of his old friend Iwasaki. And having been absent from his country during a most momentous period in its history he was understandably impatient to observe for himself the far-reaching changes he knew had taken place in countless aspects of national life. In addition to these matters of direct personal interest, he was anxious to move ahead as rapidly as possible with his emigration project and to take stock, unquestionably with considerable uneasiness, of the socialist situation.

Had it not been for his own beliefs, Katayama might well have had substantial cause for encouragement when he studied the social and political scene in Japan upon his return home. The socialist movement had been almost hopelessly fragmented by the pressures of the Russo-Japanese War, but it was also noticeable that the Treaty of Portsmouth, which had almost traumatically disabused the Japanese people about the decisiveness of their victory, had awakened undisguised popular wrath. In coping with postwar mass demonstrations and daily journalistic denunciations of his handling of the peace negotiations, Premier Katsura had resorted to the same heavy-

[9] According to Kōtoku, Katayama sailed from San Francisco on December 30, 1905. Tanaka, *op.cit.*, p. 289.

handed, repressive measures used so successfully against the socialists during the hostilities. But what the emergency of war had previously sanctioned the embittered Japanese people would no longer condone, and the resulting wave of popular indignation and protest so severely shook his government that in January 1906, at about the time Katayama debarked at Yokohama, General Katsura was forced to resign as Premier. Perhaps only the socialists could fully appreciate the sardonic jest of history when Prince Saionji Kimmochi was designated to form a new cabinet. For just twenty-five years before he had, when buoyant with an enthusiasm for liberalism acquired after a decade's sojourn in Europe, been compelled to abandon publication of his "radical" newspaper at the suggestion of the Meiji Emperor himself.[10]

Prince Saionji, in addition to having a sound and sympathetic understanding of political liberalism, was at the same time far better apprised than most leading statesmen of the Meiji period of the nature of Western civilization. To him socialism was not merely the creature of demagogues and visionaries but rather the normal concomitant of social growth in industrial societies.[11] He realized, accordingly, that socialist doctrines could seize the imagination and kindle the dreams of people only when the conducive social conditions prevailed and that state repression could check but never extinguish a social movement engendered by the very processes of industrial evolution. It is likely, too, in view of his own political philosophy, that he believed the cause of retarded liberalism might be furthered with socialist support. Shortly after he organized a new government Saionji let it be known, consequently, that the state would not frown upon peaceful political activity by the socialists.

Saionji, being responsible for the destiny of Japan, had no intention of tolerating subversive activities within the state.

[10] Yosaburo Takekoshi, *Prince Saionji*, Kyoto, 1929, p. 56.
[11] Shirayanagi Shūko, *Saionji Kimmochi Den*, Tokyo, 1929, p. 99.

He obviously hoped that the socialists would limit their efforts to the conventional agitation of political parties. He was not unaware that his unprecedented policy of "coddling" radicals was considered even by his loyal following in the *Seiyū-kai* party as rash and dangerous, that it furnished the intransigent General Katsura and other staunch defenders of state interest with political ammunition, and that the outcome of the experiment was dependent not so much upon a tolerant state as upon the decidedly unpredictable behavior of crusading zealots.[12] Like many a policy born of idealism, Saionji's was far from ideal; on the other hand, given his purposes, the alternatives left him with little choice.

With the indulgent permission of the Saionji government, several socialist groups acted quickly to organize political parties. On January 14, 1906, Nishikawa Kōjirō and Higuchi Den successfully submitted an application for the establishment of the *Nihon Heimin-tō* (Japan Peoples' Party), their stated objective being the promotion of universal suffrage. This was shortly followed by the petition of Sakai Toshihiko and Fukao Shō, also approved, for the formation of the *Nihon Shakai-tō* (Japan's Socialist Party). In order to achieve unity of the socialist ranks thirty-five representatives convened in the office of Dr. Katō Tokijirō on February 24. From the discussions and compromises, in which Katayama participated, a relatively united party, the *Nihon Shakai-tō* emerged with the primary aim of "advocating socialism within the limits of the law."[13] The socialists were now able after almost five years of denial to resume the struggle for their goal through the medium of political action.

Katayama's long-held views on campaign tactics were given

[12] Note the conversation among the leaders of the *Seiyū-kai*, one of the principal political parties, in the fictive biography of Saionji: Bunji Omura, *The Last Genro; the Statesman Who Westernized Japan*, Philadelphia, 1938, pp. 276-278.

[13] Kishimoto Eitarō, *Nihon Rōdō Undō-shi*, Tokyo, 1953, p. 79. See also Sen Katayama, *The Labor Movement in Japan*, Chicago, 1918, p. 104.

the seal of vindication at the birth of the *Nihon Shakai-tō*. "As I foresaw that . . . misfortune might happen if we went too far in our tactics," he said, "I . . . persuaded my fellow comrades in drafting the constitution of the Socialist Party in February 1906, to insert a clause—'We advocate socialism within the limit of the Law.' My contention was that in Japan a law-abiding socialist could most forcibly and ably advocate socialism. Our workers were not educated in the tactics of the labor movement and therefore [we] should go slow in order to lead and educate them.[14] A majority of the socialist leaders present at the historic meeting, averse to jeopardizing their newborn political existence, accepted this practical counsel. For the while at least Katayama's stock among his fellow socialists was raised.

The *Nihon Shakai-tō,* whatever its prospects for gradual growth may have been, did not enjoy substantial popular support at the time of its organization. Too many of the members of the Executive Committee were intellectuals and journalists with incredibly naïve illusions about the nature and extent of their influence. Few of them, it is certain, understood the thinking and behavior of the workers as well as Katayama did. And if some of the founders of the new party were not unwilling to accept a police estimate of some twenty-five thousand socialists in Japan, he cynically observed that the "government might have reported more socialists in order to get an appropriation for suppressing them."[15] He was, moreover, not at all misled by the type of "intellectual" who was drawn to socialism, noting that "a large majority of comrades have been young men, especially students who would [because they were minors] be excluded from a formal political party."[16] For his part Katayama preferred to rely upon the workers.

It cannot be said that the *Nihon Shakai-tō* compiled an im-

[14] Katayama, *The Labor Movement in Japan,* pp. 115-116.
[15] *ibid.,* p. 104. [16] *ibid.,* p. 105.

pressive record of achievement during the first year of its existence, though for a brief moment after the launching of the party its name was made known throughout Japan. On March 15 the socialists sponsored a mass meeting in Tokyo's famous Hibiya Park to protest a proposed increase in carfare on the local trolley system. Katayama, who wrote a small pamphlet for the occasion, claimed an attendance of over ten thousand people, which is probably not unlikely. After several socialist speakers had excited the audience by their strong denunciations of the streetcar owners, the inflamed crowd went on a rampage, attacking and destroying the properties of the company. The government was sufficiently impressed by the mass outburst to deny the petition for a raise in fares. "It was," boasted Katayama, "the first victory for the red flag in Japan."[17]

Despite its signal triumph in protecting the interests of the public, Katayama was not overly excited by the prospects of the *Nihon Shakai-tō*, the socialist leaders still being too heavily committed to intellectualism to change their ways. Katayama thus decided to press ahead with his plans to promote emigration to the United States. Securing funds from the ever faithful Iwasaki to cover his own financial obligations, he then became deeply involved in a fraudulent scheme of the unconscionable Okazaki.

For reasons which before long were to become clear Okazaki assumed the burden of recruiting a group of emigrants who were to be settled in a community of their own making on the outskirts of Houston. For this purpose the enterprise was publicized in Okayama Prefecture, where both he and Katayama had lived during their younger days. Thirty peasant families were each induced to contribute one thousand yen, to be used on their behalf for the purchase of agricultural land in Texas. Accounts of the extremely rich rice yields ob-

[17] *ibid.*, p. 106. A very valuable account of this affair is Kimura Tsuyoshi, "Nihon Shakai Shugi-shi," *Shakai Mondai Kōza*, XI (1927), pp. 97-100.

tained by Japanese who had already settled down in various parts of the state were apparently most convincing. In July, after Okazaki finally managed to secure the necessary passports for the emigrants, Katayama was persuaded to go ahead to Houston and to make arrangements for their arrival. Waiting about in Texas for many months, it dawned on him at last that he had been duped by his partner. Only the shameless, allegedly somewhat richer, Okazaki but no peasants from Okayama ever appeared.[18] In February 1907, Katayama, mortified by the experience, hastened back to Japan. One may well understand why he never thereafter breathed a word of the affair.

Humbled and embarrassed by his own naïveté, Katayama had, nevertheless, other disturbing matters to consider when he returned to Tokyo. On February 17, just two days before he landed at Yokohama, the annual meeting of the *Nihon Shakai-tō* had been held on the occasion of the first anniversary of the party. Attended by practically all important socialist leaders of the late Meiji period, including Kōtoku, who had returned from America in the preceding June, it was the most fateful conclave of socialism in Japan before the end of World War I. Even before the beginning of the proceedings it was evident that many members were determined to fight for fundamental revisions in the statement of party aims, which had been adopted a year before. The future course and the very life of the party depended on the outcome of the debates.

The challenge to party policy and tactics was hurled by the inimitable Kōtoku. The Executive Committee, having been

[18] For a discussion of this entire episode see Oka, *op.cit.*, p. 78. In his very widely read book, *The Labor Movement in Japan*, p. 116, Katayama laconically skips over the months from the summer of 1906 to February 1907, during which period this affair unfolded, in a single sentence. "Unfortunately," he wrote, "I was absent after June of that year and arrived at Yokohama two days after the Socialist Party meeting [of February 17, 1907]. The Chronology in the *Jiden*, p. 348, incorrectly dates Katayama's return from America in March.

faced with the impossible task of reconciling conflicting demands, finally placed before the gathering its recommendation that the first article in the party's constitution be amended to read: "We advocate, first of all, the achievement of socialism." The phrase, "within the limits of the law," vital to the continuation of the legal existence of the party, was dropped. Specific objectives were basic change in the existing social system, modification of the Public Peace Preservation Law, universal suffrage, opposition to militarism, and opposition to religion. Kōtoku, who had been powerfully swayed by the anarcho-syndicalism of the IWW during his stay in the United States, immediately made clear his dissatisfaction with these proposals.[19]

Kōtoku's attack upon the standing declaration of aims of the *Nihon Shakai-tō* as well as his fight against acceptance of the amendments proposed by the Executive Committee have been vividly recounted by Sakai. "The argument against parliamentary tactics delivered by Kōtoku . . . ," he wrote, "was indeed one of the great orations of our times. Contending in ill health with the bitter cold, he fought for the adoption of his new position. Swept by waves of emotion, sparks flashing from his eyes and fire erupting from his mouth, ever stronger, ever swifter, he cast a spell over the entire audience for almost an hour."[20] His plea, which was based upon anarcho-syndicalist concepts, called for an explicit rejection of universal suffrage and parliamentarism in general. Insisting that these tactics were futile for the realization of social revolution, he urged instead upon the strongly moved assembly resort to "direct action" and the general strike. A third resolution, submitted by Tazoe Tetsuji, went to the opposite extreme, recommending recognition of the primacy of universal suffrage. In the

[19] For the text of the proposed new party platform see Kishimoto, *op.cit.*, p. 86, and Kimura, *op.cit.*, XI (1927), pp. 106-107.

[20] Sakai Toshihiko, "Shakai-tō Taikai no Ketsugi," *Shin Heimin Shimbun*, February 17, 1907, in Sakai Toshihiko, *Sakai Toshihiko Zenshū*, no. of volumes unknown, Tokyo, 1933, III, p. 274.

end the original proposal, brought in by Sakai, received twenty-eight votes, as opposed to twenty-two for Kōtoku's and only two for Tazoe's.[21] It had been demonstrated beyond doubt that moderate methods no longer carried weight with the socialist captains.

Katayama was grieved by the shift in tactics approved by the majority of the leaders of the *Nihon Shakai-tō.* Had he himself been present at the meeting, he would surely have sided with Tazoe. Though he well understood that frustration and desperation had helped evoke strong support for Kōtoku's anarcho-syndicalist views, he also knew that, being so extreme, these novel ideas could only increase the gulf between the radical intellectual leaders and the working class. After the Bolshevik Revolution, but not in 1907, Lenin would doubtless have castigated Kōtoku's approach to revolutionary struggle as "left-wing infantilism." On the other hand, Katayama also perceived that the stand taken by the majority, "a compromise between two extremes," was nonetheless an invitation to political suicide, for it precluded for all practical purposes any hope of implementing the remaining objectives of the party. It came as no great surprise to Katayama when the government, discovering the decision of the socialists to reject action "within the limits of the law," took immediate steps to suppress the *Nihon Shakai-tō.*

With the interdiction of the second socialist party in Japanese history the movement on which it was based was riven beyond any possibility of repair. For many years to come the state, incorrigibly suspicious of the intentions of the socialists, adamantly refused to authorize the establishment of a new political organization. But even had permission to found another party been requested and forthcoming, it is a moot point whether such approval would have been of any avail. The proceedings of February 1907 revealed that the ideological and tactical differences of the doctrinaire leaders had

[21] *ibid.*, III, p. 274, and Kimura, *op.cit.*, XI (1927), p. 108.

become so solidified that unity within a political party was improbable. The movement for social revolution had been subordinated to the "logic" of academic theories, and it is difficult to escape the conclusion that for the following decade and more reformers and revolutionaries in Japan were more interested in defeating one another in polemical arguments than in awakening and leading the proletarian masses.

Before plunging into the struggle for the emancipation of the workers of Japan, in which he had really played only a minor role since the end of 1903, Katayama decided to put his family affairs in order. With all his traveling and moving about he had not been able to pay attention to his children to whom he was not much more than a familiar name. On May 12, 1907, accordingly, he remarried, his second wife being a country woman, the thirty-one year old Hara Tama of Aomori, the northernmost province of Honshu.[22] She was not only the stepmother of the young Kan'ichi and Yasuko but also gave birth to Katayama's second daughter, named Chiyoko, in January 1908. It would be a strain on the truth to say that she enjoyed her home and family life with her middle-aged husband; during his fourth trip to the United States some years later she left him without regret.

A deep cause of sorrow to Katayama in the spring of 1907 was the suppression by the government of the newspaper *Nikkan Heimin* (Commoners' Daily). For the first time in more than five years the socialists in Japan found themselves without a journal. The *Nikkan Heimin* had more or less continued the practice, if not the policy, of an exclusively socialist publication which Katayama had fostered successively with the *Rōdō Sekai*, *Naigai Shimpō*, and *Shakai Shugi*. In October 1903, when the *Shakai Shugi Kyōkai* had been disbanded under the pressures of the war looming with Russia, its place had been taken by the *Heimin-sha* (Commoners' Association), founded by Kōtoku and Sakai. Their antiwar paper, the famous

[22] Katayama Sen, *Jiden*, Tokyo, 1954, p. 349.

Heimin Shimbun, had then become the mainstream of Japanese socialist expression until it was closed down by the police in January 1905 on charges of violation of the national press laws. Though Katayama was a member of the editorial board and an occasional contributor to the *Heimin Shimbun*, he had nevertheless sought to maintain an independent organ by founding the *Tobei Zasshi* in 1905, afterward renamed *Amerika*.

With the termination of the *Heimin Shimbun* and the jailing of Kōtoku and Nishikawa and, particularly, with the end of the Russo-Japanese War the emergence of ideological differences had been stimulated. During the final phase of the struggle with the tsarist empire socialists who had not been cowed continued their propaganda in the tiny paper, *Chokugen* (Plain Talk), which met its pathetic end during the disturbances in Tokyo in September 1905. In the next few months several new publications, representing distinct philosophical orientations but accepting contributions from socialists of varying shades, were started. The *Kaben* (Fire Whip), which lasted about eight months, had a pronounced bent toward literature and philosophy; the *Shin-Kigen* (New Era), edited by Abe Isoo and Ishikawa Sanshirō, was the organ of Christian socialism; and the *Hikari* (Light), headed by Nishikawa Kōjirō and Yamaguchi Yoshizō, continued to uphold the Marxist position laid down by the extinct *Heimin Shimbun*.[23]

When the political atmosphere became somewhat more favorable after the founding of the *Nihon Shakai-tō*, the socialists gradually slackened in their determination to promote their individual viewpoints in separate and relatively expensive journals. As a result, the *Nikkan Heimin*, with an editorial board representing disparate socialist viewpoints, was

[23] For notes on the socialist papers founded shortly after the Russo-Japanese War consult Watanabe and Shioda, *op.cit.*, pp. 57-60, and Uyehara, *op.cit.*, pp. 39-40. Nakamura Katsunori, "*Hikari* Sō-mokuji to Kaisetsu," *Hōgaku Kenkyū*, XXXIII, no. 6 (June 1960), especially pp. 39-42, is also useful.

launched in January 1907. Because of the sharp divisions in the socialist ranks, however, the paper aroused strong resentments. Katayama charged that the "editorials . . . were dominated by Comrade Kōtoku's influence but there were many comrades who advocated political action. . . ."[24] And during the following weeks, he wrote, "I watched the work of my comrades in the Daily Heimin, only contributing articles from time to time. I was sorry to see this movement become more and more radical and extreme."[25] Shortly after the paper published several of the addresses delivered at the February meeting of the *Nihon Shakai-tō,* it was ordered by the government to discontinue operations.

Max Nomad, the well-known scholar of socialist history, has commented, in reference to the large number of newspaper writers who have engaged in radical movements, that journalism has not been the maker of revolutionaries but that revolutionaries have often tended to become journalists. How well this observation is exemplified in the career of Katayama! Without a socialist journal assuring publication of his thoughts and observations of the moment he was a lost soul. To him it was absolutely necessary, if success were ever to be achieved, constantly to enlighten the worker about the coming social revolution. When the *Nikkan Heimin* was brought to its unhappy end in the spring of 1907, his own response was easily predictable. In June, together with Nishikawa, he founded the *Shakai Shimbun* (Social News), which continued to have a precarious existence for more than four years.[26]

[24] Katayama, *The Labor Movement in Japan,* p. 116.
[25] *ibid.,* pp. 116-117.
[26] In recounting (*ibid.,* p. 118) the founding of this new journal Katayama has not played fair with non-readers of Japanese. "After these difficulties," he wrote, "there appeared two socialist papers, one in Tokyo published by Comrade Nishikawa and myself with two other comrades, and another at Osaka by Comrade Morichika. The one was called Shaksi Shimbum [*sic: Shakai Shimbun*] (Socialist News) the other Osaka Heimin." It need not be argued that Katayama was perfectly well aware that *Shakai Shimbun* means Social News (Newspaper) and not Socialist News. What this suggests is that Katayama was

Insofar as philosophy and tactics are concerned, the ideas set forth by Katayama in the *Shakai Shimbun* from 1907 on reflect the peak of his development as a socialist before the Bolshevik Revolution of November 1917. Accepting Marxism as his guiding theory and believing wholeheartedly in the "historical mission" of the proletariat class to overthrow the capitalist system and to usher in the socialist era, he also supported the positions of the mainstream of the Second International. His socialist orthodoxy thus led him to reject the anarcho-syndicalism and "propaganda by deed" (upheld theoretically at least, by Kōtoku and his followers in the *Ōsaka Heimin*), which was launched by the extreme left wing at about the same time as the *Shakai Shimbun*. Insisting stubbornly that the working class in Japan was still politically too immature to play a militant revolutionary role, he inveighed against counsels of force, violence, and direct action and urged instead the pursuit of the aims of trade-union organization and of universal suffrage by legal means. Though he believed, as a matter of theory, in the use of the general strike, he did not consider Japanese workers ready to exploit effectively this method of revolutionary coercion.

The two wings of the socialist movement, each with its own publication, engaged in an intense but not necessarily acrimonious rivalry during the fall and winter of 1907-1908. In addition to conducting separate programs of lectures, which were never heavily attended, the contending factions also cooperated occasionally to sponsor debates in which the "experts" pitted their knowledge and oratorical skills against one another. Katayama, it must be admitted, was hard pressed to defend his position in these debates. He was, moreover, not only unsuccessful in winning over new supporters but he was also unable to replace the loss of several of his most valuable allies. One by one his political friends

from the outset of this publishing venture most anxious to avoid providing the police with the slightest excuse to close down his paper.

had died, drifted away, become estranged, or shifted to the camp of anarcho-syndicalism. Although it probably would have made no difference in the long run, in 1908, when the factional struggle within the radical ranks began to assume an unprecedented bitterness, he was deprived of the backing of two able fighters who had rendered yeoman's service in the socialist wars. For all practical purposes he was for some years isolated ideologically from the leaders of the social movement.

Katayama's break with Nishikawa, to whom the responsibility of editing the *Shakai Shimbun* was entrusted, was a major setback for parliamentarist socialism. The facts of the dispute are not easily ascertained.[27] It is a matter of record, however, that, while Nishikawa champed against the moderate policy of Katayama, the latter accused his old friend of harboring a secret "anarchist" in their group, known in the Japanese socialist world as the *Doshi-kai.* As a result of the quarrel Nishikawa and his clique broke away in February, set up another club with the same name, and also began to publish a rival paper, the *Tokyo Shakai Shimbun.* This tempest in the socialist teapot did not blow over quickly. The fury of the personal and polemical exchanges is well illustrated by an English-language news item appearing in the *Tokyo Shakai Shimbun* in March 1908.

"25 members of the Tokyo Socialist Doshi Kwai," the notice reads, "met at the house of Comrade Nishikawa and unanimously passed a resolution excluding Mr. Katayama from their party. . . . The above resolution is necessary because our foreign comrades might think Mr. Katayama representative of socialists of Japan, while, in fact, it is far from the case.

[27] Katayama's account of his break with Nishikawa is succinctly presented in *The Labor Movement in Japan,* pp. 125-126. For more detailed discussions of the issues involved note particularly the following: Ōkōchi Kazuo, *Reimei-ki no Nihon Rōdō Undō,* Tokyo, 1955, pp. 183ff.; Arahata Kanson, *Nihon Shakai Shugi Undō-shi,* Tokyo, 1948, pp. 221-224; and Kishimoto, *op.cit.,* pp. 108-110.

First, he is not socialist in the strict sense, but a lukewarm raformer, secoond, his character is so narrow, so niggard, so mean and lustful, and above all so cruel toward his friends, I mind you to his friends, that there are few who will side with him."[28] This assault upon his socialist beliefs and personal character, obviously intended to discredit Katayama among European and American comrades, had no prospect of achieving its purpose. When all is said and done, the fact remains that, as long as he continued to adhere to the Second International, no other Japanese Marxist could ever hope to challenge or undermine his standing among Western socialists.

An even more grievous loss to Katayama than the critically needed support of Nishikawa was the death of Tazoe Tetsuji on March 24, 1908, at the age of thirty-four. Born in Kumamoto and a graduate of the Nagasaki school system, he had studied in the United States from 1897 to 1900 at Baker University and at the University of Chicago. As a Christian socialist of unquestioned integrity and intellectual brilliance, he had from the moment he joined the socialist movement succeeded in winning the unstinting respect of all his fellow workers. At the historical meeting of the *Nihon Shakai-tō* in 1907 he had, in the absence of Katayama, waged a valiant but futile battle for parliamentarism. Despite the overwhelming defeat of his resolution, he continued to enjoy the esteem of all socialist factions, his skill as an economist and as a theoretician enabling him to meet his antagonists on equal terms. At the news of his death, friends and foes alike wept in common grief.[29]

[28] The denunciation appeared in the *Tokyo Socialist [Tokyo Shakai Shimbun]* on March 15, 1908. It is reprinted in Ōhara Shakai Mondai Kenkyū-jo, *Nihon Shakai Shugi Bunken*, Tokyo, 1929, pp. 230-231. The spelling is as in the original.

[29] For a brief sketch of the life and thought of Tazoe, who is unfortunately overlooked in many studies of the Japanese socialist movement, see Kishimoto Eitarō, ed. *Katayama Sen—Tazoe Tetsuji Ni-Shū*, Tokyo, 1955, pp. 289-290. For a touching memorial to Tazoe by his ideological foes, note *ibid.*, pp. 287-288. A brief but useful biographical

During 1908 the socialist movement experienced further misfortunes. On June 22 the contentious factions agreed to call a truce in order to celebrate the release from prison of Morichika Umpei, the editor of the *Ōsaka Heimin* who had fallen afoul of the national press laws. For a few hours rivalries were forgotten as the proponents of parliamentarism and of direct action convened for congratulatory speeches in the auditorium of the *Kinki-kan* in the Kanda district of Tokyo. But, when the audience was leaving the building at the conclusion of the program, several youthful adherents of Kōtoku's group, known as the *Kinyō-kai*, suddenly unfurled two huge red banners emblazoned with the slogans "Anarchism" and "Common Property under Anarchism." At the same time they launched into the revolutionary song "The Chain of Wealth." In a moment a contingent of policemen, posted nearby in anticipation of a demonstration, swooped down upon the gathering crowd and, after a brief tussle for control of the flags, arrested a considerable number of the socialists and anarchists. What had opened as a day of revolutionary camaraderie closed in a major disaster.[30]

The "Red Flag Affair" of June 22, 1908, is surely one of the most shameful and disgraceful episodes in the history of the Meiji period. Though it is undeniable that a few of Kōtoku's anarchist followers were recklessly provocative, it is also apparent that the police officials were ridiculously apprehensive. The unfounded anxieties of the law-enforcement agents were, moreover, outweighed by their consequent vindictiveness. Fourteen members of the direct action group were prosecuted by the state, found guilty, and subjected to

---

note appears in Sakisaka Itsurō, *Kindai Nihon no Shisō-ka*, Tokyo, 1954, p. 269.

[30] For the circumstances of the "Red Flag Affair" see, *inter alia*, Kyōchō-kai, *Saikin no Shakai Undō*, Tokyo, 1929, p. 33; Arahata, *op.cit.*, pp. 228-233; Watanabe Kango, *Nihon Shakai Undō-shi*, Tokyo, 1955, pp. 55-57; Sakai Toshihiko, *Nihon Shakai Shugi Undō-shi*, Tokyo, 1954, pp. 193-196; and Katayama, *The Labor Movement in Japan*, pp. 132-133.

prison sentences ranging from one to two years. The list of those convicted reads like a "Who's Who" in the history of the early Japanese revolutionary movement. Doubtless the grossest miscarriage of justice was the arrest and imprisonment for two years of Sakai Toshihiko and Yamakawa Hitoshi on the judicial presumption that "they must have been the leaders." Though Kōtoku had not been caught in the net of police vengeance, the "Red Flag Affair" left his direct action movement seriously paralyzed.

Three weeks after the clash between the anarchists and the police the government of Prince Saionji fell. On July 14 General Katsura, appointed premier for the second time, set up a government which remained in power for more than three years. No sooner had he assumed office than the soldier-politician, counting upon adverse public reaction to the imbroglio precipitated by the direct actionists, let it be known that his regime had no intention of permitting radicalism to flourish. Katsura had even stronger reason to believe his draconian policy toward socialism would meet with public approval. During the preceding year large-scale and violent strikes had broken out spontaneously in several of the largest copper mines in the country and had been suppressed by army troops only after tremendous destruction had been wrought. Though the socialists had had no hand in the outbursts of the cruelly exploited miners, it was widely insinuated that their agitation had been responsible. A harsh and systematic policy to extinguish socialist radicalism was thus introduced in July 1908.[31]

[31] The attitude and tone of policy of the Katsura regime toward socialism and radicalism in general have inimitably been depicted by Takekoshi, *op.cit.,* pp. 236-237. "Later, in the time of Katsura's second Ministry [1908-1911]," this close friend and confidante of Prince Saionji wrote, "an American book entitled 'Socialism' was translated at the Home Department. The translation was mimeographed to be distributed among the officials of the Home Department and the Governors of the Prefectures for their information in dealing with the socialists, though the original, which treated of socialism in a general

With the onset of closer controls and stern repression by the police under Premier Katsura the dispute between Katayama and Kōtoku, between parliamentarism and direct action, was reduced even more than before to purely academic proportions. At no previous time in the entire history of the Meiji period had it been so difficult for political nonconformists to carry on their work. The movements of radicals were now carefully watched. "Detectives and policemen," Katayama wrote, "hounded them day and night. Comrade Kotoku was weak in health, but his house was guarded by four policemen, two in front and two in the rear. . . . Everyone who visited him was forced to give his name, and then this person was also followed by a detective."[32] Katayama himself fared no better. "At one time," he recalled, "there were two policemen always after me; one at the back of my house and the other opposite . . . as a janitor in the school."[33] If a detailed record of his comings and goings during these years was ever kept, it was unquestionably prepared for his dossier at police headquarters.

When circumstances permitted, Katayama, always with the view of advancing political consciousness and understanding, lectured before workingmen's groups. Since there were usually police agents in the audience, who did not even bother to make themselves inconspicuous, it was necessary for him to be exceedingly discreet. At these meetings during 1908-1910 he later reminisced, "I spoke mostly on the material finance and on economic subjects, always interpreted

way, was an indifferent book sold openly in America, the mimeographed copies of the translation were all marked with red print 'Strictest Secrecy' and taken great care of. The official attitude which was like that of one who stops his ears while he steals a bell or of a cat that shuts her eyes while she steals cream, was laughable, but while the mentality which regarded even the word 'socialism' with horror was worse then [sic] ludicrous . . . it was lamentable." The language is as in the original.

[32] Katayama, *The Labor Movement in Japan*, pp. 133-134.

[33] *ibid.*, pp. 134-135.

in the light of Socialism. We could not mention words such as labor strikes, labor organizations, boycott and socialism or revolution. But we expressed revolutionary socialist thought in a round-about fashion. By such means as these we carried on our propaganda work. . . ."[34] But however favorable an interpretation he placed upon these talks, they had little effect.

Katayama was severely criticized for the views and tactics he advocated during these years of trial in the socialist movement. The charges lodged against him, usually by ultra-leftist Marxists, not to speak of anarchists and syndicalists, were really none other than those raised by extremist factions in opposition to the mainstream policies of the revolutionary movements in Europe. He was thus accused of upholding reformism, of supporting the "bourgeois" theory of *sozial-politik*—in short, of betraying the cause of proletarian revolution. Such censure was neither fair nor warranted, for it stemmed from a confusion of his objectives with his tactics. It may well be that his efforts could not but be vain as long as he persisted in staying within the limits of the law but this does not mean that other methods would have produced more satisfactory results. For all the pompous pronouncements of his antagonists, the entire history of Japan for the next decade and more reveals that, in view of the prevailing political and socio-economic conditions, no other road to social revolution led to even a modicum of success.

Until the "Red Flag Affair" socialists had rarely been prosecuted in the courts for offenses other than violation of the press laws and, when found guilty, had been subject to fines and relatively moderate prison terms. The excessive punishments meted out after June 1908, however, sharply underlined Premier Katsura's warning that a heavy brake would be placed on all radical activity. Socialists and

[34] *ibid.*, pp. 128-129.

anarchists were thus confronted with the unenviable choice of being completely above suspicion or of becoming political martyrs. And that the Japanese state was almost hysterically determined to stamp out all manifestations of what it considered to be leftist extremism became sensationally evident with the unfolding of the infamous "High Treason Case" in May 1910. No additional warning of what lay in store for subversive revolutionaries was thereafter necessary.

The *Taigyaku Jiken*, or "High Treason Case," as the incident is known in modern Japanese history, was not rivaled even by the later Sacco-Vanzetti Case in the United States as a travesty of justice. Though mountains of literature have been written about the episode, not all the basic facts have yet been established beyond a reasonable shadow of doubt.[35] It is nonetheless clear that four of Kōtoku's disciples, convinced by the teachings of Russian anarchists that the Emperor-myth had to be destroyed in order to hasten the great social revolution, began to plot the assassination of the Meiji Emperor. Unluckily for the conspirators their plans were discovered by the police who immediately began to round up more than a score of well-known anarchists. Among those placed under arrest and indicted for conspiracy to commit high treason was the ailing Kōtoku, held to be the leader of the plot.

When the *Taigyaku Jiken* is separated from the multitude of irrelevant issues that have been dragged into the case, it

[35] Since the end of World War II an extraordinary number of books and periodical studies concerning Kōtoku's life and thought has appeared in Japan. Many of his books and miscellaneous writings have also been reprinted. A substantial part of these recent studies is polemical in nature and Marxist or Communist in orientation, testifying probably to the intense desire of the left wing in Japan to discover symbols and traditions of revolution and "democracy" in modern Japanese history. Japanese radicals, in short, have tended to equate opposition to the old authoritarian state with social democracy. Perhaps the most useful among the new studies of Kōtoku are the following: Tanaka, cited above; and Shioda Shōbei, *Kōtoku Shūsui no Nikki to Shokan*, Tokyo, 1954.

seems incontrovertible that the Japanese state under Premier Katsura was determined to exploit its opportunity to end the anarchist movement. To achieve this purpose it was necessary to incriminate Kōtoku. There is absolutely no doubt that he was a thorough-going anarchist and a believer in "direct action" and "propaganda by deed" but few scholars have ever seriously entertained the thought that this ivory-tower revolutionary had ever gone beyond a theoretical justification of terror and violence.[36] But, whatever his philosophical doctrines may have been, the state was extremely hard put to prove its charges, so much so that it resorted to the most questionable judicial procedures, including the introduction of faked evidence. The trial, held in secret, finally concluded with a judgment holding Kōtoku and twenty-three of his comrades guilty. In January 1911, twelve of the convicted "conspirators" were sentenced to imprisonment for terms of long duration; Kōtoku and eleven other defendants were hanged three days after sentence had been passed with a haste that was decidedly irregular.

One may well understand Katayama's horror at the fate of Kōtoku and many of his principal followers. Though he had always looked with disapproval upon anarchist and anarcho-syndicalist ideas and had himself been attacked by their Japanese proponents, he was nevertheless shocked by their cruel political murder. In Japan only a few voices were raised in protest against the government's conduct of the trial. When socialists in Europe and America loudly expressed their indignation at the proceedings, the government, completely missing the point, sought to give assurances that its measures were directed only against anarchists. But no sooner had Kōtoku and his followers been executed than the police, hoping to blot out the last vestiges of radicalism, began to persecute the socialists with unconcealed fury. "All

[36] For a thoughtful appraisal of this problem see Nobutaka Ike, "Kōtoku: Advocate of Direct Action," *Far Eastern Quarterly*, III (May 1944), pp. 222-236.

books on socialism," Katayama stated, "were confiscated and all the public libraries were ordered to withdraw socialist books and papers. Even moderate papers like ours [the *Shakai Shimbun*] were severely censored and a few months after the said trial it was practically suppressed by the authorities."[37]

With the disposition of the "High Treason Case" the social movement in Japan came to an abrupt halt. Radical activities were so thoroughly circumscribed that the disputes over theory and particularly over the issue of tactics, which had agitated socialists and anarchists for the preceding four years, were reduced to a mere topic of dinner conversation. In the following months of 1911 Katayama, Sakai, Abe, and a few other socialists could do no more for the cause of social revolution than to behave circumspectly and meet occasionally for club discussions. Katayama, who had been employed for the previous year as a staff contributor to the *Tōyō Keizai Shimpō*, a well-established progressive and crusading newspaper, continued to write, though cautiously, about social and labor problems. At the same time he sought to find an outlet for the expression of ideas and observations, which could be published in Japan only at excessive risk, in several of the leading socialist journals of Europe and America. His many articles in the widely read *Die Neue Zeit* and in the *International Socialist Review*, mild in tone as they frequently were, testified that his socialist spirit had not been completely crushed.[38]

It was perhaps asking too much of Katayama to confine himself to the sedate routine of commentator on social affairs. He had never considered journalism as an end in itself but rather as a means to encourage social action. By the end of

[37] Katayama, *The Labor Movement in Japan*, p. 140.

[38] Katayama's writings published in foreign periodicals at this time will be found listed in Hyman Kublin, "A Bibliography of the Writings of Sen Katayama in Western Languages," *Far Eastern Quarterly*, XI (November 1951), pp. 72-73.

the year, consequently, he became deeply involved in a movement to secure an increase in wages for the employees of the streetcar companies in Tokyo, whose schedules of pay and working conditions were notoriously poor. On the day before the New Year the transit companies were suddenly confronted with a superbly organized strike which effectively curtailed public transportation in the city. At a loss to deal otherwise with the solid front presented by the strikers, the trolley owners capitulated on January 4, 1912, offering a satisfactory settlement. This was one of the outstanding victories of "organized" labor during the entire Meiji era.

Katayama was one of the first to learn—and one of the first to admit—the extremely heavy cost of victory in the Tokyo Streetcar Strike. On January 15, together with more than sixty others suspected of complicity, he was arrested by the infuriated police. Arraigned in court, where he was singled out as one of the ringleaders, he was charged with incitement to strike. The Public Peace Preservation Law, which had for years hung over his head like the sword of Damocles, had finally fallen. On April 30, after he had already been detained in jail for three and a half months, Katayama was condemned to five months' imprisonment, the punishment to begin from the day of sentence. It was the heaviest sentence meted out.[39]

There is much about Katayama's part in the great strike of 1912 that is puzzling. Since few other Japanese, including the police, were so familiar with the detailed provisions of the Public Peace Preservation Law, he must have realized beforehand that to become involved in agitation leading to strike action was to court government reprisal. And because he was

[39] For Katayama's version of the strike see *The Labor Movement in Japan,* pp. 143-144. More extensive discussions of the Streetcar Strike will be found in Kishimoto Eitarō *et al., Katayama Sen,* 2 vols., Tokyo, 1959-1960, I, pp. 303ff., and in Hattori Shisō, *Monogatari Nihon no Rōdō Undō,* Tokyo, 1953, pp. 56-62. Note also the entries in the diary of the sculptor, Tobari Kogan, quoted in Miyakawa Torao, "Katayama Sen to Tobari Kogan," *Rekishi Hyōron,* no. 102 (February 1959), pp. 66-69.

not unaware of the edgy temper of the police since the arrest and trial of the anarchists, it is impossible that he expected to be dealt with lightly. What may be suggested is that Katayama, stung by the ceaseless criticisms of the direct actionists, may have deliberately invited state persecution in order to prove in an unmistakable way that he too could be self-sacrificing. No demonstration of the power of workers, moreover, could have been better calculated to arouse the anger of the police than a transit strike conducted during the New Year holidays. "A better understanding," Katayama later commented, "was brought about by the streetcar strike in which *those comrades who were considered moderate and tame,* caused by their agitation a great strike that shocked bourgeois society."[40] If, as has been intimated, he wished to make a point, he was quite successful. Rarely thereafter was Japan's oldest socialist leader subjected to personal and polemical attack by his fellow revolutionaries.

Katayama's months of confinement in Chiba Prison were a severe ordeal. Having been accustomed to a busy daily routine he was now compelled to change entirely his pattern of life. The long hours were partly whiled away in reflection and reminiscence; it was at this time that he began to write his *Jiden* (Autobiography), setting for himself a pace of two pages per day. By the time of his release, however, he had managed to finish only forty pages and it was only after a long interruption that the book was finally completed. Luckily he was not required to serve out his term, for in early September, when a general amnesty for prisoners was proclaimed upon the death of the Meiji Emperor, he was set free.

Upon coming out of prison, Katayama was not long in concluding that all life had been snuffed out of the social movement. The public, which had been subjected to annoying inconvenience when the streetcar strike had been held during

[40] Katayama, *The Labor Movement in Japan,* pp. 144-145. Italics are mine.

the New Year season, was now prepared to believe the worst of socialism. Even though mass protests against government policies were conducted at the time, there were no citizens ready to speak out in defense of radicals. Workers, too, were more fearful than ever of raising their voices against profit-hungry employers. From an all-time high in 1907, when fifty-seven strikes involving 9,855 workers had occurred, industrial-labor clashes fell in number to twenty-two, with 2,100 participants, in 1913.[41] The "long cold winter" had set in for socialism.

For many months Katayama struggled to avoid acceptance of the obvious. He continued to write for the *Tōyō Keizai Shimpō* but a mere glance at his articles of this period makes it clear that he had no interest in his work. Journalism had become simply a means of earning a living. Only in his occasional pieces published in socialist journals abroad is it possible to catch glimpses of the unbroken rebel. And, as an added irritant, the police did not for a moment relax their vigilance. By the spring of 1914 Katayama finally made his fateful decision. Since life had literally become unendurable, there was no alternative but to leave Japan.

[41] Murayama Shigetada, *Nihon Rōdō Sōgi-shi*, Tokyo, 1947, pp. 224-225.

CHAPTER XII

ONCE MORE AMERICA

In July 1914 the war which Europe had for years anticipated with dread began and, with little suspicion of the long and protracted holocaust that lay ahead, the Great Powers proceeded to spar for the knockout blow that would have the "boys home for Christmas." Less than a month later the government of Japan, aware of the utter helplessness of the Kaiser's possessions in the Pacific and alert to the "golden opportunity" for imperial expansion, declared war upon Germany. At about the same time Sen Katayama sailed from Yokohama for the United States.[1]

This was Katayama's fourth and last journey to America but the outlook was changed from that of his previous visits. For perhaps the first time in his long and checkered socialist career his thoughts were not primarily concerned with the plight of the proletariat, then butchering one another on the bloody battlefields of distant Europe. Katayama, the selfless socialist, had customarily looked upon his personal problems with aristocratic disdain. A moment had at last arrived, however, when personal adversity could no longer be ignored.

Throughout his long life Katayama, determined not to entertain doubts, had refused to harbor regrets. Thus, when he had as a young man left Japan in 1884 to seek an education in the United States, he had been able to forget easily his many years of privation and to face the unknown with the

[1] Most literature about Katayama is vague concerning the date of his departure from Japan. According to the Chronology in Katayama Sen, *Jiden,* Tokyo, 1954, he sailed from Yokohama on September 9, 1914, and arrived in San Francisco on the 28th. These dates are confirmed in Watanabe Haruo, *Nihon Marukusu Shugi Undō no Reimei,* Tokyo, 1957, p. 224, which adds also the information that he traveled aboard the *Sado Maru.* In Kishimoto Eitarō *et al., Katayama Sen,* 2 vols., Tokyo, 1959-1960, II, pp. 19-21, 393, it is furthermore indicated that he landed at Seattle on the 25th and from there went on to San Francisco, arriving on the 28th.

naïve confidence that was ever to evoke both the admiration and despair of his friends. Again, on the occasion of his departure from his homeland on the eve of the Russo-Japanese War, he had looked forward to the future with an ingenuous optimism that belied his advancing years. And during his third trip to America, following the conflict with tsarist Russia, it had not occurred to him that his fanciful hopes had no prospect of justification. But, in the summer of 1914 when he sailed for the United States, Katayama's spirits were depressed. He was approaching his fifty-fifth birthday with no trade or profession other than socialism, with no resources other than his political faith and his dubious reputation.

Friends of Katayama in the United States were informed in the press that he planned to attend the International Socialist Congress scheduled to be held in Vienna in the fall. It is not unlikely that he nursed the dream that, with a new imperialist war at hand, he might be able to reenact the sensational role which had won him international fame at Amsterdam in 1904. It soon became clear, however, that the outbreak of the great European war had shattered whatever solidarity there might have been in the ranks of the Second International. During the Russo-Japanese War socialists everywhere had been quick to express their condemnation of what was, after all, a local conflict waged in a remote corner of the world. But with the preservation of their own motherlands at stake in 1914 socialist parties in all the belligerent states self-righteously rallied to the support of their governments, splinter groups alone doggedly upholding a stand against the war. In the United States, which was not as yet involved, the seeds of crisis had also been sown but, for the moment, though a few socialists bolted from the radical camp, the American party remained loyal to its antiwar position.

Katayama's decision to leave his homeland was prompted by his fervent wish to aid the international socialist movement in preventing the spread of the conflict in Europe. The early frustration of his hopes, however, induced him to remain in the United States where political conditions still permitted the public conduct of antiwar agitation. Nevertheless, Katayama had other pressing reasons for quitting Japan; it was these less publicized considerations as well as his ideological convictions which led him to assume the role of a lonely expatriate. What the veteran Japanese socialist sought in the United States and Europe was not primarily further renown but rather desperately needed refuge.

Stubborn and dauntless a fighter as he was, Katayama had by the summer of 1914 been driven to the verge of despair. He was not completely discouraged by the course of affairs in Japan, yet he could not foresee an immediate improvement in his personal and political prospects. Distressed by the chauvinism that was sweeping his country, by the pitiless persecution of the Japanese police, and by his inability to support himself and his family, Katayama had at last been compelled to admit that for a socialist in Japan life had become "almost unbearable." Vindictive police in his homeland, he bitterly complained, did not hesitate to "poison the mind" and to threaten reprisals for the employer rash enough to hire known socialists. "No institution," Katayama wryly commented, "wishes to have the footprints of the police department about its doorsteps."[2]

Katayama's plight was poignantly expressed in a letter written from San Francisco to the famous English socialist leader, H. M. Hyndman, whom he had first met at the Amsterdam Congress.[3] "I am really driven out of my country because of socialism," he lamented. "Financially it was impossible for me to get a living in Japan." But, he added in that spirit of self-sacrifice that the wealthy English radical sought so futilely to awaken among the downtrodden of England, "If

[2] Sen Katayama, "What It Means To Be a Socialist in Japan," *International Socialist Review*, XIV (February 1914), pp. 467-468.

[3] The complete text of this letter will be found in H. H. Hyndman, *The Awakening of Asia*, London, 1919, pp. 190-192.

I could devote my life for . . . the working classes I would [have] suffered every privation and poverty, but . . . I was too well known to the authorities. . . . I was utterly helpless for the rest of my life in Japan." Hyndman could only think it ironic that the same Japanese government that granted asylum and assistance to the harried revolutionary leaders of China hounded its own political dissidents into exile. It did not occur to him to speculate why, among the several radical political leaders in Japan, Katayama alone thought it necessary to seek sanctuary abroad.

On arriving in the United States Katayama discovered that to be a Japanese in California was in many ways no different from being a socialist in Japan. For almost twenty years ignorant and calculating nativists in the "Golden State" had insisted upon calling the Japanese immigrant to account for the reproductive "sins" of his progenitors. Proud and sensitive Japanese, hoping only for opportunities to earn an honest living, had continued to suffer indignity and abuse without redress and many a delicate memory had been lastingly scarred by wanton acts of bigotry.

The discrimination of Californians against Japanese settlers had caused serious tension between the United States and Japan. Partially smoothed over by the "Gentlemen's Agreement" of 1907, which placed upon the Japanese government the responsibility of controlling the emigration of its subjects to the United States, the dispute was rekindled in 1913, about a year before Katayama's arrival in San Francisco. To the great embarrassment of the federal government the state legislature passed the discriminatory Alien Land Laws, which specifically restricted the rights of Japanese citizens to purchase and own land. In Washington the blatantly unfair legislation, striking directly at industrious and efficient Japanese farmers, aroused sharp protests from the Japanese Ambassador, while in Japan itself bellicose nationalists undertook to whip up demonstrations against the United

States. Not since the years immediately after the Russo-Japanese War had relations between the United States and Japan been so severely strained.

As a Japanese in California Katayama could expect to receive only the treatment of a second-class resident. Despite this, he refused to share in the resentment of his countrymen, both in Japan and in the United States, over the Alien Land Laws. Throughout the furore he held fast to the cynical and disinterested view of the confirmed international socialist. Mindful of Marx's warnings about the cunning exploitation of nationalistic sentiments by the "ruling classes" and cognizant of his own government's expert manipulation of the political and racial emotions of the people in the past, Katayama declined to be taken in by what he termed "patent trickery." To him the controversy, fraught with jingoism and "entirely bourgeois in nature," was a mask for deeper and more sordid motives.[4]

Katayama had long since passed the stage when he could view the policies and statements of the Japanese government with other than suspicious eyes. He found it impossible to believe that it would, even at the strong urging of influential persons "entertained by the rich Japanese on the Pacific Coast," concern itself with so picayune a problem as anti-Japanese discrimination in California, unless it had a hidden and sinister purpose. It was clear, to Katayama at least, that the Japanese authorities were deliberately magnifying the issue so as to raise a scare of war between the United States and Japan. Had not the government, he questioned rhetorically, played upon the fears of the masses on many occasions to secure ever larger appropriations for the military and naval forces? The entire episode, he was quick to charge, was an obvious hoax.

Assuming, but not with complete validity, that American

[4] Sen Katayama, "California and the Japanese," *International Socialist Review,* XIV (July 1913), p. 31.

socialists were sympathetic toward the workers of Japan, Katayama tried to reassure them. Japanese laborers were, he proclaimed, not easily deceived. Engaged in a continuing struggle to exact their daily pittances from the "greedy capitalists," they cared not a whit "whether a few hundred Japanese in California may or may not own the land." The anti-American demonstrations encouraged by the Japanese government to protest the treatment of Japanese emigrants on the Pacific Coast were, according to Katayama, ignored by Japanese workers, being attended mainly by "students or loafers."[5] Though in Japan, where memories of the scandalous misuse of the naval appropriations in 1912 were still fresh, this explanation might perhaps have had a convincing ring, it can scarcely have endeared Katayama to California Japanese experiencing the direct effects of the detested Alien Land Laws.

Keeping himself aloof from the struggle to secure fair economic opportunity for Japanese emigrants, Katayama's most pressing problem upon his arrival in California was, ironically, "to get a living." Since frugality had always been for him a virtue born of necessity, he had no problem in satisfying his own minimal needs. But the thought of his wife and children in Japan, branded by the possession of his name and subject to the constant vigilance of the police authorities, was an unfailing source of worry. It was not that he was a particularly devoted husband and parent. He was not. For years socialism had been his first and only love and oppressed mankind his true and only heir. He had both shirked and shifted his familial responsibilities. But, now that he was in the United States, thousands of miles from home, his eyes were sharply opened to a neglect that had for years been painfully evident to many of his friends.[6]

No sooner was he settled in San Francisco than Katayama

[5] *ibid.*, p. 32.

[6] See particularly the comments by H. Vere Redman, "Sen Katayama," *Contemporary Japan,* II (March 1934), pp. 668-680.

set about earning sufficient money to bring his older daughter, Yasuko, to the United States. Though she was not yet fifteen years old, she aspired to become a professional dancer. Her ambition was probably stirred by the example of her half-cousin, Hara Nobuko, who had already taken the first successful steps to become an opera singer. Realizing that opportunities for a favorable marriage for his daughter would be limited in Japan as long as he continued to engage in radical agitation, Katayama hoped that Yasuko would be able to embark upon a career in the United States which would in time make her financially independent. With this lofty aim in mind he brought Yasuko and Nobuko to San Francisco in the spring of 1915 and then attempted to make arrangements for their performance at the World's Fair which was scheduled to open shortly in the city.

Katayama's grandiose hopes for his daughter were never realized. Though Yasuko and Nobuko, belles in a preponderantly masculine community, were warmly greeted by the Japanese in California and an initial concert was successfully presented, they never succeeded in rousing the enthusiasm of the American entertainment and cultural world. Nobuko, moreover, found herself unable to look approvingly upon her uncle's political activities. Cool in her relations with him, she made no attempt to conceal her antagonism from Yasuko, who was strongly under her influence. A family rift resulted several years later.[7]

In California Katayama engaged in a continuing struggle to support himself and his family. His employment opportunities were restricted not only by his age but also by the fact that he was a marked man in the United States. For a brief while after his arrival he bent his efforts and exploited his friendships to secure the position of secretary of a projected confederation of Japanese organizations in the West Coast

[7] Oka Shigeki, "Katayama Sen to Amerika," *Kaizō*, XXXII (July 1951), p. 79.

area. The consular officials of the Japanese government, however, apprised of his political record, blocked the appointment. That he was, because of his notoriety as an agitator, *persona non grata* to many Japanese residents in California and adjoining states did not facilitate his chances. He had consequently to resign himself to irregular and usually menial work.

It is difficult to determine the many types of employment Katayama undertook during the more than two years he lived in California. If he was not, strictly speaking, a migrant laborer, it is clear that he did not hold any job very long. At times he worked as a cook and as a street-cleaner. For a while, too, he ran a day-store in Oakland, taking on daily piecework and doing odd chores in the neighborhood. In a frantic attempt to earn more than his customary trivial wages he once decided to try farming, stirred probably by the prosperous example of many of the Japanese settlers in California. This venture, however, was never carried through.[8]

Partisans of Katayama charged that the local Japanese vice-consul blocked his plans to earn a living by farming and his efforts to organize a union of Japanese laborers in the San Francisco area. Katayama was consequently not only denied employment by wary Japanese businessmen but also ostracized by Japanese workers who had no wish to become involved in political controversies. Similar accusations of harassment of Japanese "radicals" on the Pacific Coast were to be made during the next few years. Japanese officials, it has been asserted, were bold enough in one case to kidnap an especially defiant emigrant and to ship him home to Japan.[9]

[8] On the various types of jobs held by Katayama in California see *inter alia,* Watanabe Haruo, *Katayama Sen to Tomo ni,* Tokyo, 1955, p. 29; Kishimoto *et al., op.cit.,* II, pp. 25-26; and Ishigaki Eitarō, "Katayama Sen to Sono Doshi-tachi," *Chūō Kōron,* LXVII, no. 14 (December 1952), p. 232. These memoirs of Ishigaki are part of a series of six articles appearing in the *Chūō Kōron* between June and December 1952.

[9] The so-called "Ota Incident" is discussed in Oka, *op.cit.,* pp. 80-81. The version by Katayama, "Japanese Socialists in America," *American*

How much credence should be given to these extraordinary charges? It may well be assumed that the Japanese government was irritated by the activities of known and potential "trouble-makers" in the Japanese communities in the United States, especially at a time when it was trying to secure the abolition of the legislation discriminating against its citizens. But, be this as it may, it must not be forgotten that authoritarian governments have always been vindictive toward their political refugees and hypersensitive to their criticisms, innocuous though they frequently are. Japanese officialdom had, to be sure, nothing to fear from the behavior of its emigrants on the Pacific Coast, or anywhere in the United States, for Japanese settlers in America have been outstandingly law-abiding. Nevertheless, the interference of the Japanese state in the lives of its citizens in the United States aroused the very adverse publicity the government in Tokyo was anxious to avoid.

His political aims apart, Katayama had more personal reasons to resent the unwelcome attention lavished upon him by Japanese consular agents. Successful in finding only intermittent and poorly paying jobs, he could not rise above a hand-to-mouth existence. The result was a tragic reenactment of the type of family rift which had brought so much unhappiness to Katayama's own childhood years. His wife in Japan, struggling to provide for herself, Kan'ichi, and Chiyo and annoyed incessantly by the police, finally decided to forsake him. Divesting herself of his notorious name, she drifted back to her native village. Katayama never saw her again. Kan'ichi, his son and heir, was not, however, completely neglected, for, when he came of age a few years later, he entered Keio University. He died in 1921, with only a dim memory of his absent father.

Labor Year Book, New York, 1916, pp. 137-138, is also useful. There are slight variations in his account in the same work for 1917-1918, pp. 290-291.

The problems of a livelihood did not for long prevent Katayama from pursuing the activities which were as inseparable a part of his socialist life as his political faith. Outwardly there seemed to exist boundless opportunities for agitational work in the United States. The American Socialist Party had grown tremendously since its organization in 1900 and branches were to be found in every state of the Union. Though the Party generally accepted the leadership of the inimitable Eugene V. Debs, it resembled, with its myriad factions and variegated followers, its many European counterparts, being possessed of an infinite capacity to accommodate almost anyone who dubbed himself a "socialist."[10] In view of his interests as well as his past associations Katayama soon identified himself with the left-wing internationalists represented by the *International Socialist Review.* Its publisher, Charles H. Kerr of Chicago, was one of Katayama's oldest friends in the United States.

Like many a foreign-born socialist dwelling permanently or living in exile in the United States Katayama was neither deeply interested in nor did he really understand American culture and life. For all the years that he had and was to live in the United States, there is little evidence that he ever acquired a sound grasp of the dynamics of American history and society. Though he earned his board and room in the country which had given him an education and a sanctuary, his heart and mind always remained in distant Japan and, insofar as his political activities were concerned, the United States represented at best a haven from which he could work for the cause of Japanese socialism. Narrowly equating social progress in America with the advance of its socialist movement but having only a distorted view of American life, he

[10] For rich and colorful sketches of the American Socialists of this period Joseph Freeman, *An American Testament; a Narrative of Rebels and Romantics,* New York, 1936, should be consulted. Theodore Draper, *The Roots of American Communism,* New York, 1957, chs. II-III, is also invaluable.

was unable to detect the mainsprings of American socialism itself. Only a thorough-going internationalist like Katayama could assume, and quite erroneously, that socialists in the United States were deeply concerned with the trials of their ideological brethren in Japan.

With this fundamental illusion Katayama, as one of the few Japanese socialists whose faith had not been shattered, sought to keep the flickering light of Japanese socialism burning and to give assurance to comrades in the United States and throughout the world that the struggle against the capitalist system in his homeland had not been abandoned. Before many months had passed, he resumed the role he had so often played before and which he could continue to perform without great fear of contradiction, namely, that of "expert" and interpreter of Japanese developments to politely curious but lamentably ill-informed American socialists.

Katayama's first opportunity to play his part on the American socialist stage came in the summer of 1915, when Suzuki Bunji visited the United States. Suzuki was an anomaly in Japan: a trade-union leader in a country that permitted trade-unions to exist as long as they did not engage in the primary activities of trade-unions. In 1912 he had, with the assistance and advice of an American Unitarian missionary, Clay Macaulay, organized the *Yuai-kai* (Friendly Society) in Tokyo. The *Yuai-kai* was not really a trade-union but rather, as its name indicated, a benevolent association of workers functioning more or less in the manner of the English mutual-aid societies. Its stated objectives were the improvement of the general welfare of workers and the encouragement of more harmonious relations between employer and employee. At the time of Suzuki's visit to the United States membership in the *Yuai-kai*, which now had branches throughout Japan, had risen to about 6,500 men and women. By early 1916 membership passed the 10,000 mark.

To its many critics in Japan the *Yuai-kai* was a clumsily

disguised "company-union." The accusation was, however, rather unfair. When it is considered that trade-unions were for all practical purposes forbidden by the Public Peace Preservation Law of 1900 and that the hostility of the government and police toward radical organizations had not waned since the "Anarchist Conspiracy" of 1910-1911, the futility of attempting to establish a conventional trade-union should seem evident. Suzuki and his followers believed, accordingly, that the *Yuai-kai,* with all its obvious shortcomings, could perform a socially useful purpose and that, when the political and legal atmosphere had changed for the better, the organization could be transformed into a *bona fide* trade-union. Until this step could be taken, however, they maintained that the *Yuai-kai* could not only help the worker in a practical way but also familiarize him with many of the problems of trade-union organization and activity he would some day have to face. In these circumstances it was deemed necessary to avoid arousing the animosity of both businessmen and police.[11]

In the United States Suzuki was widely greeted as a trade-union leader, though he was scarcely more a representative or spokesman for the workers of Japan than was Katayama. On August 27, 1915, he addressed the San Francisco Labor Council, one of the most powerful labor groups on the Pacific Coast. There is little doubt that Suzuki presented at this time, as in other speeches delivered during his tour of the United States, a much too roseate picture of the labor situation in Japan. Two days later the indignant Katayama rose to "expose" this "tool of the capitalists." Speaking before a

[11] Suzuki Bunji and the *Yuai-kai* are excellently and objectively studied by Nakamura Katsunori, "Suzuki Bunji to Taishō Rōdō Undō," *Hōgaku Kenkyū,* XXXII, no. 1 (January 1959), especially pp. 50ff. This study is continued in *Hōgaku Kenkyū,* XXXII, nos. 2-3 (March 1959), pp. 21-45, and XXXII, no. 6 (June 1959), pp. 35-64. For Suzuki's account of the founding and purpose of the *Yuai-kai,* see Suzuki Bunji, *Nihon Rōdō Undō Hattatsu-shi,* pp. 15-16. This lengthy pamphlet in the possession of the author gives no place or date of publication and is apparently an offprint from a journal of the very late Taishō period (*ca.* 1925) or of early Showa (*ca.* 1926-1927).

gathering of local socialists he denounced the *Yuai-kai* as a "paper-union" and a "mere aggregation of names."[12] Further diatribes against Suzuki and the *Yuai-kai* by Katayama were in the following weeks published in the American socialist press. Labor journals were, however, far more sympathetic and Suzuki was cordially received by trade-union leaders throughout the United States.

Katayama was not consciously a dishonest person. But like many a social revolutionary beset by constant discouragement he engaged in a continuing game of self-deception. With a philosopher's stone of his own devising he was able, as the occasion demanded, to transmute his fondest wishes into self-evident realities. Never was this characteristic of Katayama more evident, or more needed, than in the course of his denunciation of Suzuki, when he attempted to contrast the feebleness of the *Yuai-kai* with a picture of a swelling socialist movement in Japan. The truth of the matter was that in 1914-1915 the Japanese government, which could never be charged with a lack of vigilance in radical affairs, was as little perturbed by activities of socialists as Japanese businessmen were by those of the *Yuai-kai.*

When Katayama had left Japan for the United States in 1914, not much more of the socialist movement existed in Japan than forlorn hopes and fading memories. So reduced were the socialists in numbers and spirit, so thoroughly were they cowed by the wartime government of Japan, that they were capable of bestirring neither themselves nor the masses. The occasional voice of defiance was promptly silenced, the passing act of bravado immediately punished. The faint-hearted had melted away and the die-hards had turned to the comforts of philosophy. Katayama's hopes and pronouncements to the contrary, the socialist movement in Japan was in a state of suspended animation.[13]

[12] Katayama as quoted by Austin Lewis, "The 'Japanese Problem,'" *New Review,* III (November 1, 1915), p. 274.

[13] Japanese socialists themselves commonly designate the period from

While Katayama surveyed the socialist situation in Japan for signs of encouragement, he watched the national economy for evidence of impending capitalist disaster. Only the economic distress which was the concomitant of war, he felt, would induce the oppressed masses to see through the vanity of nationalism and to perceive, once and for all, the tawdriness of military victories. Every symptom of economic unrest and dislocation in Japan was thus eagerly seized upon as an incontrovertible substantiation of his hopes. That Japan was "suffering in many ways" because of the outbreak of the world conflagration, that "industries shut down because of a lack of European supplies while others closed up because of lack of business," and that "thousands of people were out of work" evoked grim satisfaction in the elderly socialist.[14] To hope for the best it was now necessary for Katayama to pray for the worst.

As opposed to his sanguine depiction of the socialist movement, Katayama's description of economic conditions in Japan during the early months of World War I was not entirely a figment of his wishful thinking. With Japan's entrance into the epochal conflict, her already unbalanced economic system was thrown further askew. The all-important rice market sagged, vital silk production fell off sharply, and export industries crumbled as Japan's foreign trade received the initial heavy impact of the world-wide war.

The economic dislocation was, however, of short dura-

---

the "High Treason Case" of 1910-1911 to the end of World War I as "the long cold winter" (*Fuyu no Jidai*). During the war years about a half dozen socialist papers and journals were published for varying lengths of time, the most important being the monthly *Hechima no Hana* (January 1914—August 1915) and especially the monthly *Shin Shakai* (September 1915—January 1920). For a retrospect of this period by Sakai Toshihiko, editor of the *Shin Shakai,* see his communication in the *Kommunistische Internationale,* II (1921), p. 152.

[14] Sen Katayama, "The War and the Japanese," *International Socialist Review,* XV, no. 5 (November 1914), p. 287.

tion. Energetic action by the Japanese government had by the spring of 1915 helped pave the way for an industrial and commercial boom, though an agricultural recovery was not fully brought about until the following year. War contracts, placed by both the Japanese and Allied governments, the opening of many new markets in Asia, Africa, and Latin America, and the establishment of new heavy industries inaugurated an era of unprecedented economic expansion and business prosperity. By the time World War I was ended, Japan had established her position as not only one of the foremost political and military powers but also as one of the great nations of the world.

Japan's tremendous industrial and commercial expansion during World War I was understandably not a completely smooth process. The immediate shock of the hostilities as well as the subsequent adjustments created severe stresses which were felt by the entire nation. Shortages of consumer goods, soaring prices, inflation, wage scales lagging behind a constantly rising cost of living, and a host of other problems helped to awaken a vast social unrest and to underscore the heavy cost of economic growth. Particularly hard hit were industrial workers and salaried employees in the cities, for whom the war actually entailed a gradual reduction in their standard of living. Nothing more succinctly illustrated their dissatisfaction with living conditions than the unbroken rise in the number and intensity of industrial strikes. In each of the years 1917 and 1918 respectively more strikes, involving a greater number of participants than during the entire period from 1897 to the beginning of World War I, broke out.[15] Such developments sustained Katayama's faith and reinforced his belief that the final victory would be his.

For Katayama to hope was to act. It was not enough to attack and rebut an infrequent antagonist from the homeland,

[15] Murayama Shigetada, *Nihon Rōdō Sōgi-shi,* Tokyo, 1947, pp. 224-226.

or to be occasional consultant on things Japanese for American comrades. Socialism and its propagation were the very *raison d'être* of his life and to deny him opportunity to give overt expression of his convictions was tantamount to a condemnation to spiritual and emotional starvation. Like his ideological confreres in Europe and America, he was never happier than when he was able to plunge into and lose himself in an endless frenzy of everyday socialist work, never more self-satisfied than when he could steal another moment from his daily routine which could be devoted unstintingly to the furtherance of the great cause. But never, save during his months in prison in Japan, had it ever been so difficult for Katayama to devote himself to socialism than during his San Francisco days.

When Katayama came to the United States, he had cherished plans of organizing Japanese workers and of recruiting them into the camp of socialism. One cannot help but be reminded of the Chinese revolutionary, Dr. Sun Yat-sen, whose plots to overthrow the Manchu rulers of his homeland had been supported for years by his countrymen overseas, especially in America. But Katayama's prospects of enrolling new socialist followers on the West Coast and elsewhere in the United States were not so promising. The alertness of Japanese consular officials was, though important, not decisive in thwarting his efforts.[16] The small number of

[16] Japanese socialists have charged that Katayama's activities with the Day Laborers' Union, an organization of Japanese workers, were not long in bringing him to the attention of the Japanese Consul in San Francisco who "made his life not only unpleasant, but his work for organization impossible." Japanese, it is alleged, "who came in touch with Katayama were classed as suspects and those who lived in the same house were told to leave. . . . The Day Laborers' Union . . . was forced to denounce him." S. J. Rutgers, "An Introduction to the History of the Labor Movement in Japan," *International Socialist Review*, XVIII (July 1917), pp. 37-38. Similar words are used by Louis Fraina in his Introduction to Katayama's *The Labor Movement in Japan*, Chicago, 1918, p. 25. See also the rather fanciful interpretation of Arakawa Jitsuzō, *Katayama Sen; Sekai ni okeru Kare ga Chii to Taiken*, Tokyo,

Japanese immigrants was clearly a major obstacle; the nature of the occupations they pursued was equally pertinent. Being largely farmers and small businessmen who had found a measure of prosperity, if not necessarily security, Japanese residents in the United States were understandably reluctant to jeopardize their good fortune by engaging in activities apt to antagonize further their nativist critics. There was, it may thus be suggested, no compelling reason for the Japanese government to be apprehensive about Katayama's radical influence in America.

The lack of a warm response of the Japanese in California to his political activities unquestionably spurred Katayama to continue his propagandistic agitation. During 1914 he had written a number of articles, dealing with the common themes of Japanese society and culture, for the *International Socialist Review*. These "human interest" sketches were, on the whole, politically innocuous. If the American reader were not apprised of Katayama's stormy background, he might easily have concluded that the author was an itinerant free-lance writer catering to American curiosity about Japan. Save for an occasional comment with ideological nuances, these articles might have been published with no embarrassment by such reputable and widely read journals as *Harper's* and the *Atlantic Monthly*. It is consequently not beyond belief that the publisher of the socialist magazine, Charles Kerr, who would ordinarily have scorned such material, commissioned Katayama to write the series, thereby permitting him to earn some desperately needed money in a dignified manner.[17]

1930, p. 199. A more dispassionate view is presented by Oka, *op.cit.*, p. 80. The Day Laborers' Union was really little more than a club with a numerically insignificant membership.

[17] Katayama's articles in the *International Socialist Review* and in other American journals during these years are listed in Hyman Kublin, "A Bibliography of the Writings of Sen Katayama in Western Languages," *Far Eastern Quarterly*, XI, no. 1 (November 1951), p. 73.

At the beginning of 1915 Katayama's writings resumed their blatantly polemical character, being especially prepared for publication in *Shin Shakai* (The New Society), a small paper of limited circulation launched by Sakai Toshihiko and other socialists in Japan in January 1915. Until early 1918 Katayama despatched a steady flow of communications and letters to the journal, commenting upon Japanese and socialist developments in the United States, interpreting trends in the European war from a socialist point of view, and recounting his personal experiences in America for the information of his circle of friends in Japan. In turn, he received papers, magazines, and letters which posted him on Japanese affairs in general and upon the vicissitudes of the enfeebled socialist movement in particular. This information from his homeland, though far from encouraging, soon led Katayama to consider the publication of a paper of his own but, because of his financial condition, it was not until the middle of 1916 that he was able to bring out the first issue of the *Heimin* (Commoner).[18]

Projected as a monthly journal, the *Heimin* actually appeared irregularly until its discontinuance in early 1918. To broaden its appeal its features were prepared bilingually. Though Katayama was assisted at the outset by Nonaka Masayuki, an immigrant residing in Los Angeles, and by Oka Shigeki, an old-time friend who published the Japanese-language newspaper, *Hokubei Shimbun,* in San Francisco, Katayama himself was, for all practical purposes, responsible for setting up and issuing the entire paper. "With almost no help from any source," the *International Socialist Review* announced, [he] . . . writes copy . . . prints it with his own hands, and circulates it as best he can. . . ."[19] Carrying

[18] "Socialist Work Among American Japanese," *International Socialist Review,* XVII (October 1916), p. 250.

[19] "Help Needed for Work in Japan," *International Socialist Review,* XVIII (March 1917), p. 569. See also Oka, *op.cit,* p. 82, and Watanabe, *Nihon Marukusu Shugi Undō no Reimei,* pp. 27-28.

news of political developments in Japan, calling for the unionization of Japanese workers, and advocating the cause of socialism, the *Heimin* was oriented toward what Katayama assumed were the true interests of Japanese residents in the United States. Save for a few scattered issues, the newspaper does not seem to have been preserved.

From the beginning of his publication venture Katayama had tremendous difficulty in securing a reading audience for the *Heimin*. Most Japanese in the United States preferred to read the *Hokubei Shimbun*, which for more than a quarter of a century from the time of its first appearance in 1908 was the most popular Japanese-language newspaper in America. Apart from a small number of Katayama's Japanese acquaintances, subscribers to the *Heimin* were mainly sympathetic American socialists whose interest was not unmixed with amusement over his increasingly quaint use of the English language.[20] Ignored by most Japanese in the American Far West, the *Heimin* also failed to attract supporters after its transfer to New York City in early 1917. Nevertheless, for whatever the designation was worth, Katayama's newspaper was considered the organ of Japanese socialists in America and added to the lengthy roster of foreign-language publications devoted to the spread of socialism in the United States.

For all Katayama's strenuous efforts, few Japanese in the United States ever heeded his call to socialism. After more than two full years of diverse agitation and propagandistic endeavor, it is problematical that he succeeded in winning more than a handful of recruits for his political movement. An appraisal of these new followers indicates, moreover, that, with at best a few exceptions, Japanese converts to socialism rarely acquired deep and lasting convictions. Quixotic romantics, incorrigible opportunists, and helpless neurotics, Katayama's newly found comrades on the Pacific Coast

[20] See A. H. Howland, "A Japanese Socialist Paper," New York *Call* (December 10, 1916), p. 8.

sooner or later became disenchanted, while those who returned to Japan were not long in vanishing into obscurity. Among those who remained steadfast in their loyalty were Nonaka Masayuki and Nikaidō Umekichi, later known in the history of Japanese socialism as disciples in the direct line of Katayama.[21]

Generally fruitless as were Katayama's many projects to create a socialist movement among the Japanese, they did have one immeasurably important consequence. Katayama became a name increasingly familiar to socialists in the United States. Woefully ill-informed and really disinterested in developments in Japan, they tended nevertheless to identify Japanese socialism with his personal activities and to place implicit faith in his interpretations of significant events. What is astonishing is that, apart from his clear-cut position on the war then raging in Europe, these socialists, whether they were native Americans, foreign-born immigrants, or exiles enjoying a refuge of indefinite duration, were wholly ignorant of the specific nature of his political thought. But the fact that he was militantly opposed to war was enough to win him recognition in the centers of radical socialism as one of the "grand old men" of the international socialist movement.

His enhanced reputation as a fighter for the proletariat cause as well as his distinct value as a symbol of unsullied international socialism probably saved Katayama from an ultimate pauper's grave in California. In the late fall of 1916 he received a telegram from S. J. Rutgers, a leader of the left-wing faction of the Dutch Socialist Party, urging him to come to New York City. Although the two men had known each other since the days of the Amsterdam Congress, friendship alone cannot explain Rutgers' renewed interest in Katayama or his willingness to provide him with the funds

[21] For notes on both Nonaka and Nikaidō see Watanabe, *Nihon Marukusu Shugi Undō no Reimei, passim.*

for the long trip across the American continent. The Japanese veteran most likely suspected that he had been chosen to play a part in a political maneuver planned by the Dutch revolutionary but whether he was informed or not is not important. There was assuredly no vital reason for Katayama to remain on the West Coast. In November 1916, accompanied by his daughter, he left San Francisco.[22]

In retrospect, it is clear that Rutgers understood Katayama as no Western socialist ever did. Since he himself was primarily a theoretician, he had no strong regard for the intellect of the Japanese socialist, recognizing his inability to cope with the hair-splitting problems of revolutionary theory. But Rutgers respected Katayama's indomitable spirit and his long and almost unrivaled experience as an agitator.[23] Because of these latter qualities the Dutch revolutionary shrewdly saw in Katayama an invaluable ally, or to put it less generously, a tool, for an enterprise he then had in mind. It is doubtless a measure of Rutgers' own desperation that he was willing to turn to the aging Japanese whose best revolutionary years were already behind him.

Rutgers, clever as he was, could not have known that because of Katayama's long absence from his homeland his ties with the social movement had become fragile. He surely did not appreciate that Katayama was rootless as a revolutionary in Japan and that he did not enjoy in his home country the reputation accorded him in the West. With Rutgers' invitation to Katayama, it may be concluded, the fading

[22] Oka, *op.cit.*, p. 82. This writer is, however, in error when he dates Katayama's departure from San Francisco "at the end of January, 1917." Watanabe, *Katayama Sen to Tomo Ni*, pp. 226-227, is doubtless correct when he fixes Katayama's departure in November, adding that he went via Los Angeles, where he visited Nonaka, and Arizona, where he called on his half-brother, Mizuno Yoshio. It is also known that he stopped off in Chicago to see his friend Charles Kerr. Katayama probably reached New York in mid-December 1916.

[23] This assessment is frankly stated by Rutgers in his "Introduction to the History of the Labor Movement in Japan," *op.cit.*, p. 37.

political warrior was given a new span of revolutionary life which necessitated lending his name and fame to cynical exploitation during his remaining years. But, given the circumstances in which he found himself, Katayama, being human, could not refuse; the alternative was oblivion.

CHAPTER XIII

THE END OF SOCIALISM

During the long and agonizing years of World War I New York City was the common meeting ground for radicals of many political shades and hues. For the rebel, the crusader, and the nonconformist in general, opportunities for the expression of pet social schemes and political platforms were, as nowhere else in the United States, available at every hand and turn. In the city's numerous auditoriums, where overflowing audiences regularly gathered to listen to earnest lectures and heated debates, native-born reformers, restive over the many failures of the American dream, rubbed shoulders with immigrants whose political faiths summarized the hopes and disappointments of a century of Old World millenarianism. Union Square in Manhattan had long since become world famous as an arena for nightly political jousts alfresco and in hundreds of kiosks scattered about town newspapers and journals collectively presented the rich spectrum of unorthodox social theory. Offered a chance for political resurrection, Katayama did not need a second invitation to quit the relatively provincial San Francisco.

Overjoyed with his new lease on political life, Katayama set out for New York. The long trip across the American continent was broken by a brief stop in Chicago, where he called upon his old friend, Charles Kerr, at the offices of the *International Socialist Review*. And, once he had arrived at his destination, he was, Rutgers has recently recalled, installed in "a quiet room in our home near the Ocean" in the Manhattan Beach section of Brooklyn.[1] He was not, however, a simple house guest of his political patron, for when he was not engaged in writing, conferences,

[1] S. J. Rutgers as quoted in Oakley C. Johnson, "In Memoriam: Sen Katayama," *Political Affairs*, XXXVIII, no. 12 (December 1959), p. 47.

and agitation, Katayama, whose more prosaic skills could not be ignored, served as cook in the Rutgers' household. It was as odd a relationship as may be found in modern revolutionary history but the arrangement, which permitted Katayama to support himself and his daughter, apparently worked with considerable success.

S. J. Rutgers, whose life became intimately involved with Katayama's, was much younger than his Japanese comrade. At an early age he had committed himself to revolutionary politics and, after joining the Dutch Social Democratic Party, had thrown his support behind its radical faction, commonly known as the "Tribunists." Since 1909, when this group of extremists had broken away from its more moderate parent body, its members had been strongly sympathetic toward Lenin and his Bolshevik followers in the Russian Social Democratic Party. With the outbreak of World War I the "Tribunists," though they were not in agreement with him on all basic issues of revolutionary socialism, were nevertheless some of his staunchest allies in the struggles within the Second International. Clear-cut evidence of their position and views was presented at the Zimmerwald Conference of September 15, 1915, when the Dutch minority faction backed Lenin's unsuccessful drive to organize a Third International and "to transform the imperialistic war into a civil war." Several years later, in 1918, the "Tribunists" founded the Dutch Communist Party and, in 1919, became charter members in the newly launched Third, or Communist, International.[2]

In 1915 Rutgers settled down in New York City. Well supplied with funds, he carried on an active propaganda

[2] For the background of the "Tribunists" Olga Gankin and H. H. Fisher, *The Bolsheviks and the World War; the Origins of the Third International,* Stanford, 1940, *passim,* is most helpful. See also Martin Ebon, *World Communism Today,* New York, 1948, p. 200, and Franz Borkenau, *European Communism,* New York, 1953, pp. 32-33.

campaign.[3] From the moment of his arrival in the United States he strove constantly to awaken American socialists to the prospects for the future of socialism that had been raised by the war and to convert them to a revolutionary position. As early as 1915 he had, with this aim in mind, published in the *International Socialist Review* and in the *New Review* a number of articles dealing with the issues posed by the Zimmerwald Conference. In 1916 he helped to found the extremely radical Socialist Propaganda League in Boston, using the militant Lettish immigrants as a cadre, and was also instrumental in the establishment of the *Internationalist* as its political organ.[4] By such means Rutgers sought to exploit the fissures within the sprawling and decentralized American Socialist Party and to construct bases of strength for the Zimmerwald Left within the Second International.

Considerations of this type unquestionably induced Rutgers to seek out his old acquaintance, Katayama. On the surface, at least, there seemed to be hope that the aid of the Japanese socialist might be enlisted in the project to rally a revolutionary left wing within the American Socialist Party. Katayama's dramatic act at Amsterdam during the Russo-Japanese War had become an epic in the history of the Second International. Since 1914 he had, moreover, revealed sympathy for the more radical elements in American socialism, which clustered about Kerr's publication in Chicago. But what was of immediate importance was the possibility that the Japanese

[3] According to Watanabe Haruo, *Katayama Sen to Tomo ni*, Tokyo, 1955, p. 30, Rutgers was engaged in foreign trade in New York City. Though this may be true, the Dutch revolutionary was actually a civil engineer who later put his training to practical use in the cause of Bolshevism. "My work in Soviet Russia," he wrote at a later time, "brought me into frequent contact with engineers in the employ of the Soviet organization for Public Works." S. J. Rutgers, "The Intellectuals and the Russian Revolution," in Lenin, Bukharin, Rutgers, *The New Policies of Soviet Russia*, Chicago, [1921], p. 84.

[4] S. J. Rutgers, "Vstrechi s Leninym," *Istorik Marksist*, nos. 2-3 (42-43), (1935), pp. 85ff. A translation of this important article, prepared by Hyman Joseph of New York City, is in the possession of the author. See also Gankin and Fisher, *op.cit.*, pp. 565-567.

veteran, who was really the only Japanese, or Asian, socialist relatively well known to the rank and file of the Second International, might be converted to the revolutionary program of the "Tribunists" and the Bolsheviks. In the deadly maneuvers being waged within the councils of international socialism the extremist minorities could not afford to ignore the potential endorsement of anyone who could be dubbed the representative of a national socialist party, even if for all practical purposes it did not exist.[5]

Rutgers' scheme of winning the allegiance of Katayama cannot but have been tinged with deep uncertainties. It was not enough to know that the Japanese rebel was opposed to war; a similar position might have been ascribed to many socialists in Europe and America. Vital to the Dutch radical's aims was whether Katayama's rejection of international strife was based on conventional antiwar convictions or upon a thoroughly revolutionary outlook. Fastidious a theoretician as he was, the Dutch left-wing leader could not have had any illusions about Katayama's antiwar record and views, for, from the viewpoint of a "Tribunist" or of a Bolshevik, Katayama's stand on the issue of war since 1904 could easily have been dismissed as a species of "bourgeois pacifism."[6] Rutgers'

[5] It should of course be borne in mind that the extreme revolutionary wing of the Second International was far from being an organized party in the sense conceived by Lenin. In 1916 this fanatical group was little more than a splinter organization.

[6] Lenin's position on World War I, as stated at both the Zimmerwald and Kienthal Conferences, was fundamentally and diametrically opposed to Katayama's. The vital difference in the views of the Bolshevik leader and the Japanese socialist lies not in their theoretical opposition to "imperialistic war" but in their antagonistic "programs" toward the conflict then raging in many parts of the world. Katayama desired peace and a cessation of the slaughter of fellow proletarians; Lenin's program called for the transformation of a bloody "imperialist war" into an even bloodier "class war." Few socialists in the Second International could see any sanity in a course of action that could only mean the exchange of a holocaust for a hecatomb.

The conflicting views of Lenin and Katayama had been foreshadowed as early as the Russo-Japanese War, at which time the Japanese socialists had carried out an exchange of letters with the Russian Social Demo-

basic task was to discover whether his Japanese friend was a genuine revolutionary and, if he were not, to make him one.

In view of his purposes, it is easy to understand why Rutgers went to such great pains to reshape Katayama's political life. Within a very brief time after he had come to New York the Japanese socialist was introduced to the élite of Russian and American revolutionary radicalism by his Dutch mentor. Possibly as early as December 1916, he met Alexandra Kollontai, Lenin's "agent" in the United States, who attempted to convert him to the Bolshevik position on war and revolution.[7] That Katayama did not quickly succumb to her persuasion is clear. On January 11, 1917, Madame Kollontai reported in a letter to the Bolshevik leader, then surveying the

---

cratic Party. In the Japanese letter it is stated: "We object absolutely to using military force in our fighting. We have to fight by peaceful means, by reason and speech." With these sentiments Katayama generally concurred but, since the Russo-Japanese War had broken out, he had thought it best to look forward to a Japanese victory as the lesser of two evils. Lenin, however, had been unequivocating. "Force against force," he had thundered, "violence against violence. And in saying this we speak neither as nihilists nor terrorists. But in the present instance this question is of secondary importance." Though it has not been definitely proved, it is commonly believed that this statement, published in *Iskra,* came from the pen of Lenin. For the complete texts of the Russian and Japanese letters see Sen Katayama, *The Labor Movement in Japan,* Chicago, 1918, pp. 88-90.

[7] Watanabe, *op.cit.,* pp. 30-31. Watanabe is, however, incorrect in stating that Trotsky came to New York "in the fall of 1916" and that Katayama met him as soon as he himself arrived in the city. Theodore Draper, *The Roots of American Communism,* New York, 1957, pp. 80-81, satisfactorily fixes Trotsky's arrival in New York from Barcelona on January 13, 1917, about four weeks after Katayama's arrival from the West Coast. Moreover, Katayama's first meeting with Trotsky did not, as Watanabe states, take place on the second floor of a synagogue on Manhattan's East Side but in Brooklyn, at the home of Ludwig Lore, on the evening of January 14, 1917, little more than twenty-four hours after the Russian revolutionary's arrival in the United States. The meeting to which Watanabe refers must have taken place at a slightly later time. Watanabe is also incorrect in indicating that Katayama met Trotsky before he had established relationships with Madame Kollontai, Bukharin, and other Russian revolutionaries in New York. Watanabe has, however, slightly corrected his chronology of these events in his later *Nihon Marukusu Shugi Undō no Reimei,* Tokyo, 1957, pp. 227-228.

course of the world-wide war from a vantage point in neutral Switzerland, only that the Japanese was shifting "in the direction of the Zimmerwald Left."[8] Although this information is admittedly vague, what is implied is that Katayama, directly confronted for the first time by the doctrines and program of Bolshevism, was not ready to make the full and daring leap to the position of organizational separatism and mass violence advocated by Lenin. Katayama had good cause to be wary: though his experience in the applied tactics of revolutionary struggle was far broader, he was no match for the Bolshevik captain in matters of abstract revolutionary theory.[9]

A few days after Madame Kollontai's report Katayama was invited to attend a meeting of ultra-leftist socialist leaders. On the evening of January 14, 1917, he accompanied Rutgers to a gathering at the home of Ludwig Lore in Brooklyn. Among the approximately twenty radical chieftains present, of whom eleven have been identified, were the Americans, Louis Fraina and Louis Boudin, and the Russians, Nikolai Bukharin and Leon Trotsky. The inimitable Trotsky, who had been expelled from Spain a few weeks earlier, had debarked in New York only on the day before the meeting. The objective of the conference was to explore the possibilities of consolidating the badly fragmented left-wing groups in the United States and to devise a mutually agreeable program of action.[10] In the extended debate to determine the future direction of American radical socialism it was, strangely enough, the Russians, Bukharin and Trotsky, who set the alternatives and wrangled over them. Katayama was a close and deeply interested ob-

[8] Gankin and Fisher, *op.cit.*, p. 576.

[9] Equally responsible for his hesitancy was the fact, as Katayama himself admitted, that he was unable for some time to grasp the theoretical subtleties of the various positions adopted by the contending factions at Zimmerwald and Kienthal. See Watanabe, *Katayama Sen to Tomo ni*, p. 31.

[10] Katayama's account of this historical gathering is presented in his article, "Morris Hillquit and the Left Wing," *Revolutionary Age*, II, no. 4 (July 26, 1919), p. 6. See also Draper, *op.cit.*, pp. 80-82.

server. At issue was the question whether a separate left-wing organization was to be established, as urged by Bukharin, or whether the radical socialists in the United States were to be integrated as a bloc within the American party. How Katayama voted on the latter proposal, successfully pressed by Trotsky, is not specifically known but his activities during the immediately following months strongly suggest that he sided with the majority.

The glosses latterly furnished by his eulogists to the contrary, there is no reason to believe that Katayama was overly influenced by his new Russian acquaintances. Nor does it seem that he was stampeded into accepting the extreme ideological views of either Bukharin or Trotsky, by whose theoretical subtleties he was bewildered and dazzled rather than convinced. Needing time to appraise the fare of new revolutionary ideas, he was, however, quick to approve the plan of action proposed for the invigoration of the left wing. If, as seems most likely, he opposed Bukharin's demand for an independent group, it was doubtless because he had no wish to precipitate an irreparable split in the American Socialist Party which, despite its many inner conflicts, remained united in its opposition to war. Furthermore, having been a journalistic agitator for two decades, he could have raised no objection to Trotsky's recommendation to launch a new publication of the radical left.[11] But what probably elicited his greatest enthusiasm were the moves made to forge a link, through Madame Kollontai, between the left wing of American socialism and Lenin's minority faction in Europe. At this juncture in his career he at last conceded that the Second International, whose ideals he had upheld for so many years, was beyond revival.

The associations which Katayama formed with American

[11] The problem of determining specifically Katayama's position at the meeting of January 14, 1917, is complicated by Trotsky's omission in his autobiography of any reference whatsoever to Katayama. Consult Leon Trotsky, *My Life*, New York, 1929.

and European revolutionaries in New York during the winter of 1916-1917 had a vital effect both upon his own political future and upon the later history of the Japanese socialist movement. He was, in the first place, to establish relationships which became personally invaluable once the Bolsheviks had seized power in Russia and set about organizing the Third International with its program of world revolution. Secondly, Katayama was accorded a position of leadership in the regrouped left wing in the United States and was, accordingly, strategically situated when the group undertook to found the American Communist Party. Last but not least, he was presented with a powerful challenge to his basic socialist convictions, one which demanded that he burn his ideological bridges behind him.

As in the case of Lenin and other revolutionary leaders, events rather than preconceived theory shaped Katayama's decisions. The unexpected outbreak of revolution in Petrograd in March and America's entry into the war in the following month fomented crisis in the rank of the American Socialist Party. Though, to be sure, an uncompromising antiwar resolution was passed with an overwhelming majority vote at the Party's national convention in St. Louis in April, the issue of war or peace, as in the case of the European socialist parties in 1914, split American socialism beyond repair. American socialists quickly divided into proponents of militant antiwar action, advocates of moderate and temperate opposition to the hostilities, and "apostates transferring their ideological baggage to the camp of chauvinism." Here was written the last sorry chapter in the history of the Second International and its forty-year quest for an impregnable position on international war.

The ruptures in the American Socialist Party were of immense benefit to Katayama. The steady flight of the leaders and the wholesale desertions from the rank and file soon changed the nature and makeup of American socialism as a political organization. The vacuum created on the higher levels of the Party not only facilitated the incredibly rapid rise of young, ambitious, and inexperienced men but also hastened the emergence of a new majority faction in the Party in the form of the autonomous foreign-language federations. A large part of the membership, as a consequence, broke definitively with whatever roots the American Socialist Party may have had in American life and traditions and embarked upon programs of action which were either distasteful or incomprehensible to the overwhelming mass of the American people. Thus, although the moderate wing of the American Socialist Party was for a few years more able to enlist the support of diverse sympathizers, the left wing, to which Katayama aligned himself, could not succeed in "capturing" more than its own original following.

By the spring of 1917 Katayama was wholeheartedly committed to the program of propaganda and agitation of the left wing of the American Socialist Party. It is doubtful, however, that he had completely come to terms with Bolshevism as an ideology. For the moment, at least, the opportunity for action and struggle, which was presented by the solidification of the left wing, was of almost greater importance than meticulous analysis of theoretical revolutionary problems. Not to be overlooked was the consideration, always uppermost in his mind, that involvement with the radical left in America and, through it, with the Bolshevik faction in Europe held out the inviting prospect of a springboard for future work in Japan. During his years of exile in the United States he had not for a moment forgotten the cause of socialism in his native land.

With his shift to the left-wing camp Katayama was rejuvenated as a revolutionary. In the spring of 1917, when Madame Kollontai, Bukharin, and Trotsky left the United States to participate in the struggle for power in Russia, he began to work closely with the young and as yet unknown new leaders of American radicalism. His reputation as a "proletarian fighter," as a "true internationalist," and as a dauntless and uncompromising foe of "imperialist war" was now exploited to the utmost. When in May the *Class Struggle*, a monthly revolutionary journal, was launched with the financial assistance of Rutgers, he was appointed a contributing editor.[12] When the Socialist Propaganda League of Boston transferred its headquarters to Brooklyn, where it was more easily able to carry on its agitation, Katayama was recruited as a charter member of the reorganized group. When the *New International*, edited by the precocious and ambitious Louis Fraina, was barred from the United States mail as "seditious," Katayama readily came forward to lend his support to the *Revolutionary Age*, which was hurriedly established in its place. And when the *Radical Review* made its appearance in August, he was called upon to express his support for its policies in the opening issue. Though his many polemical pieces during these months were uncommonly jejune and scarcely clarified the primary issues which were wracking the American Socialist Party, they were nevertheless gratefully received by the left wing as opportune expressions of revolutionary solidarity.

Wrapped up in many enterprises to hasten the consolidation of the American left wing, Katayama was constantly busy during the spring and summer of 1917. Yet, with the encouragement of Rutgers, he undertook to write his most influential and widely read book. In July, after an absence of several years, he returned to the columns of the *International Socialist Review* with the first installment of a series, *The Labor Movement in Japan*. Two more parts of the longer study were printed before the magazine had to suspend publication when its distribution in the mail was

[12] During the following two years Katayama wrote four articles for *Class Struggle*. For precise data on these and other pieces written by Katayama in the United States during these years see Hyman Kublin, "A Bibliography of the Writings of Sen Katayama in Western Languages," *Far Eastern Quarterly*, XI, no. 1 (November 1951), pp. 73-74.

prohibited by the federal government. Despite the interruption, however, the entire series was issued as a small book in the following year by the firm of Charles Kerr in Chicago.[13]

If Katayama is well known to Western socialists and to students of Japanese trade-union history in the United States and Europe, it is largely because of his book *The Labor Movement in Japan.* A "necessarily brief and incomplete" review, as he himself called it, of the socialist and labor movement in Japan from 1897 to 1912, the volume is both partisan and self-serving. Katayama may perhaps be excused for exaggerating his own contributions and his influence upon the social movement in his native land but it is regrettable that he saw fit to minimize, even to ignore, the roles and achievements of other equally outstanding labor and radical leaders such as Takano, Kōtoku, Sakai, Abe, Nishikawa, and others.[14] The true value of the book, it must be stressed, rests less upon its sketchily recounted events and its extremely debatable historical interpretations and more upon the light thrown on Katayama himself. The tendentious character of the book notwithstanding, it has been cited more uncritically as a primary source in studies of the Japanese labor movement of the period than probably any other document.[15]

[13] The periodical series, never completed, appeared in the *International Socialist Review* in the issues for July, August, and September 1917. The Introduction was written by Rutgers. When the entire series was published as a book, Louis Fraina wrote a new Introduction. For an intimate note on Katayama's writing of the volume see Watanabe, *Katayama Sen to Tomo ni,* pp. 49-52.

[14] Only the inimitable Kōtoku is not passed over lightly.

[15] *The Labor Movement in Japan* has been translated into Japanese on several different occasions. The handiest edition is in the Iwanami Bunko series (*Haku* 87). Translated by Yamanabe Kentarō under the title *Nihon ni okeru Rōdō Undō*, Tokyo, 1955, this edition also contains an earlier collaborative work of Katayama and Nishikawa Kōjirō, *Nihon no Rōdō Undō,* which was first published in 1901. A less well-known translation is by Kishimoto Eitarō, "Katayama Sen to Meiji Rōdō Undōshi," *Keizai Ronsō*, LXI, no. 3 (September 1947), pp. 35-60, LXII, no. 3

The Labor Movement in Japan was written for the edification of American readers, who, being utterly unfamiliar with Japanese affairs, cannot have been expected to be sober in their judgments. Though the book was not widely reviewed or commented upon in the United States, probably because the attention of American radicals was focused upon the dramatic events then unfolding in Russia, Katayama still was praised. The most generous accolade was bestowed by the celebrated writer John Reed, who unabashedly proclaimed the book "one of those invaluable historical works which for the first time set forth the real history of the real people of a country."[16] His implication to the contrary, the young Reed, who had not yet reached the point of disenchantment with Bolshevism, has never enjoyed in the United States, or anywhere for that matter, a reputation as an authority on the "real" history of the Japanese people. It may be suspected, moreover, that Katayama's was the first book about Japan he had ever read. But neither Reed nor his coterie of admirers, then racing along on the tide of revolution, was especially embarrassed by such considerations.

For all his efforts on behalf of the left wing in the United States during the greater part of 1917 it is difficult to determine precisely what Katayama considered the immediate objectives of his agitation. Thrilled by each success scored by his fellow fighters in the vanguard of socialism, he had not resigned himself to an indefinite and aimless struggle in the American revolutionary movement. But whatever uncertainties he may have had about the prospects of Bolshevism and about the purposes of his own work were resolved, as in the case of numerous other radical activists, by the

(September 1948), pp. 24-70. Still a third edition will be found in Katayama Sen Seitan Hyakunen Kinen-kai, *Katayama Sen Chosaku-Shu*, 3 vols., Tokyo, 1959-1960. Unfortunately, none of these various translations is critically edited and many of Katayama's errors of fact are passed over in silence.

[16] See Reed's review in the *Liberator* (March 1919), p. 44.

epochal events in Russia in November 1917. The news of the Bolsheviks' seizure of power and their proclamation of the establishment of a workers' state turned what had been a flickering ray of hope for Katayama into the firm and guiding light of his life.

In the winter of 1917-1918 Katayama was probably one of the very few socialists in Europe and America to grasp the world-wide implications of the Bolshevik Revolution. More so than Lenin and his followers, old and new, who were almost exclusively concerned with the revolutionary promise of the industrial proletariat of Europe and who dabbled in American and Asian affairs largely for purposes of organizational politics, Katayama, having been involved in the socialist struggles of three continents, could view the Bolshevik coup with a universal perspective. If he could rejoice in the prospect that the red banner would before long wave throughout the dominions of the deposed tsar, he also sensed that the gigantic wave of revolution would sooner or later roll far beyond the borders of dying imperial Russia. For Katayama the November Revolution augured not only the "liberation of the oppressed" of Russia and of Europe but also of America, Asia, and Japan.

Heartened immeasurably by the incredibly favorable turn in the fortunes of the Bolsheviks and more confident than ever before that his campaigns in the social movement of his native land had not been entirely in vain, Katayama's activities now began to assume specific political focus. What had to be done seemed clear. Revolution in Japan, he now believed, was not merely possible; it was inevitable. He continued, thus, to cooperate closely with leaders of the American left wing, who were moving gradually toward the organization of a Communist Party, and to maintain with great difficulty liaison with the Bolshevik captains in Europe, then making plans for the inauguration of a Third International. But, above all, he kept a close watch upon affairs in Japan. If revolution were destined to erupt in his homeland, he was determined not to be caught unprepared to exploit the historical opportunity.

Had it not been for the magnificent prize which lay in the political offing, Katayama would have had little cause to be sanguine during the final months of World War I. His personal circumstances must surely have mocked his grandiose dreams. In the spring of 1918, when the ever faithful Rutgers left for Russia to jockey for position in the high revolutionary councils, Katayama and his daughter moved to a small and barely furnished apartment in Manhattan. No longer able to fall back upon the financial aid of his Dutch friend, he now had to support himself with irregular jobs as cook in private homes and local restaurants. On one occasion he opened a popcorn stand in Coney Island, a venture which was unsuccessful. For a brief while too he earned a pittance by hawking the *New International* on the streets of New York and at public forums sponsored by various left-wing groups.[17] Despite his unprepossessing life, however, he found numerous encouraging opportunities in his Manhattan locale to carry on revolutionary activities which deluded him into believing that his sufferings were worth while.

In Manhattan, Katayama was, for the first time since his arrival from California, effectively situated to form close relationships with some of the local Japanese immigrants. It was no new experience to be shunned by the businessmen among his countrymen, who, being informed about his "traitorous" background, refused to offer him either employment or backing for his political enterprises. His presence, however, quickly became known to a few Japanese workers who lived in the neighborhood. Lonely, homesick, and not at all resigned to living out their years in the United States, they clung together clannishly, seeking their recreation and diversions within their own community. Residing in the same

[17] Gankin and Fisher, *op.cit.*, p. 567.

rooming houses, maintaining cooperative dining halls, and organizing innumerable clubs to foster their common interests, their habits of living were somewhat typical of the first-generation of European immigrants who had settled in the great cities of America. From the ranks of these socially uprooted and intellectually restive Japanese, Katayama slowly constructed a small but hard core of personally devoted followers, more or less committed to the advancement of socialism and revolution.[18]

To the ideologically unanchored young Japanese in New York City Katayama was a political luminary who had already left his imprint upon the history of their country. Though some of them would not for fear of police retaliations have sought out his company in Japan, they did not suffer from these inhibitions in the United States. Before long, accordingly, Katayama was drawn into the social and intellectual routines of the Japanese community, while his own apartment became the frequent meeting place for small political discussion groups. World politics, Japanese affairs, and socialism were common topics of debate; in view of his wide-ranging knowledge and unique experience, his opinions were understandably accorded a special deference. That he was in communication with well-known socialist leaders in Japan, whose letters he permitted his disciples to read, and that he was known to have a speaking acquaintance with chieftains in the American and Bolshevik

[18] Since the end of World War II several of Katayama's old cronies have published their reminiscences of their former years in the United States. The following books and articles will be found particularly valuable: Watanabe Haruo, *Katayama Sen to Tomo ni,* Tokyo, 1955; Kondō Eizō, *Komuminterun no Misshi,* Tokyo, 1949, pp. 3-69; Suzuki Mosaburō, *Aru Shakai Shugi-sha no Hansei,* Tokyo, 1958, especially pp. 114-122; and Ishigaki Eitarō, "Amerika Hōryō Yonjū Nen," *Chūō Kōron,* XLVII, no. 7 (June 1952), pp. 198-212; no. 8 (July 1952), pp. 218-225; no. 9 (August 1952), pp. 224-232; no. 10 (September 1952, pp. 209-217; no. 11 (November 1952), pp. 246-254; and no. 14 (December 1952), pp. 232-241. Subtitles of the above articles are omitted for the sake of brevity.

revolutionary movements also strengthened the esteem in which he was held by his radically inclined compatriots.

Among the members of the study group which gradually gravitated around Katayama were several Japanese who in later years became prominent in the socialist and revolutionary movements in Japan. For a short while Kondō Eizō was especially close to the "Rojin" (Old Man), as Katayama was affectionately called. Kondō was born near Tokyo in 1883. Roaming about the United States, studying and working, for more than fifteen years, he had finally drifted into socialism. Settling down in New York in 1917, he soon became a central figure in the local Japanese club. Taguchi Unzō had, like Kondō, led a vagabond's life. After knocking about Asia and Europe, he had come to New York where he joined Katayama's socialist group. Inomata Tsunao was a graduate of Waseda University. After serving in the Japanese army, he studied economics at the University of Wisconsin where he became a socialist. While he was a graduate student at Columbia University, he joined forces with Katayama.

Odd and varied as were the antecedents of Katayama's intimates in New York, none had perhaps so odd a background as Mamiya Sueyoshi. Constantly in search of the novel and romantic, he had, after working as a merchant seaman, sought adventure as a cowboy in the American West. Disillusioned by the hard and lonely life, he had then migrated to New York City where he became one of Katayama's most devoted disciples. Nonaka Masayuki, who had assisted Katayama in the publication of the *Heimin* in California, also came East to continue his socialist activities. Last but not least, Watanabe Haruo and Ishigaki Eitarō were associates of Katayama at this time and in their later years became some of the principal biographers of the Japanese socialist leader.[19]

[19] Biographical sketches of several of these Japanese intimates of Katayama appear in Noguchi Yoshiaki, *Musan Undō So-tōshi Den,* Tokyo, 1931, *passim.*

Not all the Japanese immigrants and travelers who played a part in Katayama's study group accepted socialism as a political faith. Some steadfastly refused to change whatever political or economic convictions they already had, while others drew the line at accepting the ultra-leftist doctrines advocated by Katayama and his few unwavering comrades. Perhaps the outstanding example of ideological resistance was encountered in Takahashi Kamekichi, a brilliant young graduate of Waseda University, who was employed by the famous *Tōyō Keizai Shimbun* as its American correspondent. Though he personally liked the old Japanese socialist leader and constantly visited him in his home, he refused to espouse the Bolshevism which was steadily taking a grip on Katayama.[20] In the socialist club too the doctrines of Lenin soon divided the members into contentious factions, the minority, known as the "Bolsheviks," being led by Katayama.[21]

It seems clear in retrospect that Katayama, who was not in this respect different from almost all left-wing leaders in the United States, moved very slowly toward Bolshevism. Though it is difficult to be positive, there are grounds for the belief that he committed himself to Lenin's movement before he had a thorough understanding of the ideology entailed. The fact remains that, despite the Bolshevik revolutionary's resounding victories in Russia since November 1917, his peculiar theories were but imperfectly known in the United States, considerable time being required before his basic writings became commonly available in the United States. During the interim months and even years many radicals and would-be revolutionaries in America deemed themselves Bolshevik adherents, notwithstanding their holding beliefs which had been categorically rejected by Lenin in his polemical jousts in Europe. What unquestionably appealed most strongly to Katayama was that Lenin's formula for

[20] Watanabe, *Katayama Sen to Tomo ni,* pp. 26-28.
[21] *ibid.,* p. 27.

proletarian revolution had been justified by events in Russia and that the Third International he was determined to establish held out promise for a similar triumph in Japan.

Events in their homeland in the summer of 1918 convinced Katayama and the members of the "Bolshevik" faction in New York that they had been pursuing a correct ideological course. In early August a group of housewives in Japan, incensed by the continuously rising price of rice, set off a series of nation-wide demonstrations which increased in violence and fury during the following six weeks. In more than a hundred cities and towns throughout the country angry workers and their families joined in the "August Rice Riots" in protest against the widespread war-profiteering and inflation. Defying the government which had served them so poorly, mobs of outraged citizens attacked rice shops, warehouses, government offices, and newspaper plants. In the face of this massive wave of sacking, destruction, and incendiarism national and municipal authorities were stunned, for a brief while actually cowed, but by mid-September martialed troops and police succeeded in reestablishing law and order. Never before in the history of modern Japan had state authority been treated to such mass impudence and scorn.[22]

It mattered little to Katayama that the "Rice Riots" brought about the downfall of the Terauchi government in Japan. Nor was he impressed by the emergency measures taken by the Japanese state to reduce the price of rice and to check the inflationary spiral. These were, in his opinion, merely the conventional steps of an authoritarian state to soften the indignation of its aroused subjects. But the unmistakable evidence that the masses in Japan had at long last awakened

[22] For a detailed study of the "August Rice Riots," see Kyōchō-kai, *Saikin no Shakai Undō*, Tokyo, 1929, pp. 686ff. Katayama's own reaction and interpretation of the disorders may be studied in his article, "A Japanese Interpretation of the Recent Food Riots," *Class Struggle*, II, no. 5 (December 1918), pp. 600-606.

to the realization that they had been victimized by the war policy of their government was cause for elation. State and business leaders might well have been jubilant over the tremendous expansion in industry and foreign trade since 1914 and the army and navy surely had reason to be satisfied by the extension of Japanese power on the Asian continent and in the central Pacific but the "Rice Riots" and the rising incidence of industrial strikes attested, according to Katayama, to deep-rooted dissatisfaction among the workers. Their unprecedented demonstrations of protest, following so soon after the proletariat revolution in Russia, suggested to him that the day of reckoning for Japanese capitalism and imperialism was at hand.

The happenings in Japan understandably raised the spirits of Katayama and his Bolshevik band in New York. With the end of World War I in November 1918, political and social strife, engendered by both hope and despair, also became widespread in many countries throughout the world. In defeated Germany fanatical Communists, led by Karl Liebknecht and Rosa Luxemburg, engineered the abortive Sparticist revolt and shortly thereafter Bela Kun sought to found a Soviet regime in the dismembered Hungarian Empire. In distant China, restive under war-lord rule, nationalistic intellectuals and students were infusing new life and courage into a prostrate land, their nation-wide demonstrations against the Paris Peace Treaty in May heralding the regeneration of their country. And in Japan and the United States popular discontent was revealed in a rash of industrial strikes, political clashes, and general social restiveness. The prayers of countless people to the contrary, there was to be no return to normalcy.

With World War I at an end, the statesmen of the victorious allied powers gathered in Paris and sought there to reconstruct the shattered world system. At the same time Katayama and his friends came to the conclusion that the moment had arrived for decisive action on their part. A division of responsibility was, accordingly, worked out. Kondō, who was thought, because of his age, to be somewhat wiser and more experienced in political affairs than the other young and recent converts to socialist revolution, agreed to return to Japan and to establish contact with the old-time veterans of socialism. With their assistance he was to attempt to organize a Communist Party in Japan. In May 1919, he left San Francisco for Tokyo.[23]

Katayama decided, on the other hand, to remain in the United States. Once again, as at the close of the Russo-Japanese War, he hesitated to return home at a crucial juncture in the history of the Japanese social movement. Whether it would be fair to charge him with political cowardice is a moot point. Considering his critical views on the nature of the Japanese social order and his often reiterated insistence upon the need for fundamental changes, he could not convincingly have argued that conditions in his native land were premature or inopportune. At no time since the Meiji Restoration some fifty years before was Japan so widely swept by mass dissent and social protest as at the close of World War I. Since the beginning of 1917 the number of industrial strikes had risen uninterruptedly, attaining an all-time high in 1919 when almost five hundred work stoppages took place. In the daily newspapers the government was attacked for its oppressive and inept policies and for its alleged condoning of corrupt and racketeering practices. Students on college campuses and intellectuals in the nation at large led the protest against the authoritarianism of the state, and organized clubs to agitate for political and social reform. And with Germany and its allies decisively defeated the government could no longer muster even lukewarm popu-

[23] Kondō, *op.cit.*, pp. 54-55, 69. The account presented by Rodger Swearingen and Paul Langer, *Red Flag in Japan, International Communism in Action,* 1919-1951, Cambridge, 1952, p. 10, is also useful.

lar support for the blatantly opportunistic adventures of the Japanese army in eastern Siberia. Rarely, it may be held, had the prospects for mass revolution in Japan seemed more inviting.

In view of the unprecedentedly favorable conditions for social upheaval in Japan Katayama must certainly have had strong reasons for not hastening home immediately after the close of World War I. But, though he sought to justify his decision by pointing to the urgent tasks which remained to be done in the United States, there was also perhaps an explanation which he could share only with himself. No one realized better than he that, when he had fled in despair from his homeland more than four years before, his popularity and influence had sunk to their nadir. And he must have known in his heart that, unlike his die-hard comrades in Japan, who had courted the oppression of the state in order to keep alive the socialist cause, he himself had elected to battle against Japanese militarism and imperialism from the safe and secure sidelines of the United States. Was there any wisdom, he may well have asked himself, in returning to Japan where there was every likelihood he would be subject to nasty accusations and innuendoes?

For all his modesty and humility, which his acquaintances never failed to extol, Katayama cherished the good opinion and esteem of his fellows. Though he had always been disinterested in the trappings and perquisites of status and power and had succeeded in transforming the humble circumstances of his life into a value system, there was nothing he feared so much as scorn and disparagement, particularly from those whom he himself held in open or secret regard. Uncertain about his home-coming reception in Japan, he may well have persuaded himself to postpone his return to a time when he would be invulnerable to invidious criticism from new and old-time political antagonists. It was far more sensible, he must have concluded, to assure the place of leadership in the coming and decisive struggle for a Communist Japan, which he can only have believed was rightly his, by cementing his relationships with the general staff of the crystallizing international movement. When the historical bid for power was made in Japan, might he not, like the former expatriate Lenin, triumphantly return home to the frenzied cheers of his revolutionary countrymen?

In 1919 there existed ample outlets for Katayama's energy, zeal, and ambition in the ruthless forays and scrambles within the left wing in the United States. Too much, however, has probably been made of his purely minor and really peripheral activities during this period by his Japanese biographers, no doubt because he did not confide completely in his Japanese associates. That he had been marked for a key role in an imminent revolutionary thrust of history-making proportions was becoming more evident but, until the decisive moment for action arrived, patience was necessary. After so many years of disappointment, he was willing, to be sure, to bide his time but he could scarcely afford to wait too long. With the close of the year his sixtieth birthday would be at hand and revolutions, he knew, were commonly made by and for youth.

While he looked forward to coming events with great expectancy, Katayama turned nostalgically to a review of his past. Since his prison days in Tokyo he had been engaged in the writing of his autobiography but because of the countless vicissitudes in his life and the heavy demands upon his time the project was periodically interrupted. At the urging of his close friends he now resumed work on his reminiscences. Writing without full benefit of his personal papers and records and not having access to the intimates of his earlier years who could refresh his memory of the bygone days, his autobiography was as difficult a literary undertaking as he had ever attempted. Even Katayama would probably have agreed that the book he had in mind, one of the most important he had ever sought to produce, was never completed in wholly satisfactory form.[24]

Anyone familiar, if only in passing, with Katayama's life can only conclude that his *Jiden* (Autobiography), is one of the strangest works ever written by a prominent revolutionary. Reminiscences in its tenor have from time to time been written by Bolshevik small fry, who have been granted their meed of commendation from both revolutionary power politicians and the ideologically devout. It would be difficult, however, to point to an autobiography in a similar vein produced by any other Marxist-Leninist worthy. In different political circumstances Katayama's story of his early life would prob-

[24] Katayama's autobiography, or *Jiden,* has been published in various editions and translations. Originally edited by Ishigaki Eitarō, one of his New York intimates who was deemed to be literarily gifted, the account of Katayama's life, covering the period from his birth through 1899, was first published in the well-known journal *Kaizō* in 1922. It was next issued in book-form in the *Kaizō Bunko* series (Series II, no. 103) in December, 1931. A third edition was published on February 20, 1949, in *Katayama Sen Senshu,* vol. I (no subsequent volumes seem to have been issued). This edition, appearing under the sponsorship of the *Nihon Kyōsan-tō Tōshi Shiryō Iin-kai* (Committee on Source Materials Relating to the History of the Japan Communist Party), also contains several commendatory statements and news items from the Communist newspaper *Akahata.* A fourth edition, with apparently no changes from the second edition, was brought out on October 31, 1949; it had the same sponsor as the third edition. A fifth edition, to which has been added some of Katayama's important published articles, several letters, a Chronology, and brief explanatory essays by Yamanabe Kentarō and Hirano Yoshitarō, was published by the *Iwanami Shoten* in Tokyo on February 10, 1954, and reprinted on August 5, 1954. This edition has been followed in this study.

It should be noted that in the *Iwanami Shoten* edition the frontispiece is identified as a photograph of Katayama at the age of twenty-five; it is clearly the picture of him appearing in the classbook of 1892 at Grinnell College. It is possible that Katayama, in order to save money, used an older picture for his class album.

A sixth edition of the *Jiden* was published in the three-volume set of his collected works issued in Tokyo in 1960 on the occasion of the centennial of his birth. For the particulars see the Bibliography.

What seems to have been a Russian translation of the *Jiden* was published in Moscow in 1926. Under the title *Moya Zhisn* (My Life) it is described as being eighty pages long, appearing in or under the auspices of the *Moskovskii Rabochii* (The Moscow Worker).

ably have been dismissed as "bourgeois," a play for the applause of the masses. If the book has continued to be read by innumerable non-Communists and Communists alike, it is unquestionably because it possesses the dual virtue of stirring the sympathies of the former without being damaging to the political needs of the latter. It should not be inferred that this was Katayama's deliberate intent.

A reading of Katayama's Autobiography quickly reveals, much to one's amazement, its essentially nonpolitical character. It is, accordingly, of limited value for the study of his revolutionary career and the growth of his social thought. Lest his readers open his book with false expectations, his purpose in writing is set forth at the very outset, namely, to explain himself as a father and as a human being to his children whom, he guiltily realized, he had heartlessly neglected because of his long and undivided absorption in the affairs of the world. "I propose to recount, frankly and without embellishment," he begins the Autobiography, "the story of my life, ordinary, of no particular interest, and commonplace as it has been."

"My purpose is quite simple, really nothing unusual. Let me say at this point that I am looking for neither the approbation nor the criticism of others. My sole aim is to tell my beloved children in detail something about the place where their father was raised and about his own parents, some of the facts about the days of his youth, about the places where he lived during his adult years, and about the things he has done."[25] It must be admitted that, having initially made his objective clear, Katayama adhered faithfully to his course.

The *Jiden* is, despite its many shortcomings, the most enduring of Katayama's works. True, it is discursive and sententious, and not free from exasperating gaps and digressions. But its saving grace is its disarming candor, its lack of pretentiousness, and its power to evoke genuine sympathy.

[25] Katayama, *Jiden,* p. 3.

Katayama understood himself as well as any man may and, though he did not always like what he knew, he did not seek to conceal his many personal faults. He readily discloses his resentment of his father, while he speaks tenderly and, at times, with stricken conscience about his mother. He confesses to his envy of his older brother, recalling after so many years his terror and pleasure at the sight of Mokutarō receiving a severe spanking from their furious father. Wistfully and with proper shyness he reminisces about his first "love," a teen-age girl near Hadeki whom time could never make him forget. But he tells us, above all, without suggestion of self-pity, about his struggle for an education and his quest for a place of worth in the world. Perhaps it was fortunate that he never completed his Autobiography, which breaks off at the beginning of his controversial socialist career, for the story of his life during his first forty years may still be read as the tale of an indomitable individual born into an indifferent world.

Katayama's work on his Autobiography was interrupted by fast-moving events in the United States and Russia. During the final months of 1919 the lines of battle within the American left wing had been sharply pitched and the vicious and gruelling struggle for control of the revolutionary movement in the United States was well under way. At the same time Bolshevik leaders in Russia, having consolidated the earlier victories in their drive for final power, had had opportunity to assess the conditions and prospects for the expansion of revolution into Europe and beyond. It is apparent that Lenin and his lieutenants, beguiled by the relative ease of their successes in Russia, were unjustifiably sanguine in their hopes for revolutionary gains in the United States. Be this as it may, the Bolsheviks pressed ahead with plots for the conquest of the citadel of capitalism and Katayama found himself drawn ever more deeply into a web of international intrigue and conspiracy.

It may well be the advantage of hindsight that warrants the conclusion. Still, it is amazing to note how grossly the emerging Communist groups in the United States underestimated the forces of resistance to revolution in the aftermath of World War I. It is, on the other hand, equally astonishing that governmental authorities, exaggerating the peril to the democratic and capitalist system, permitted themselves to be stampeded into as rash and unnecessary repressive action as has ever been taken in American history. On New Year's Day, 1920, agents of the federal government unleashed a multi-state assault upon the headquarters of leftist political groups, arresting a bewildering variety of Communists, Socialists, Anarchists, Syndicalists, and sundry other suspected agitators and trouble-makers. Katayama, who had been passed over in the initial raids, dared not press his luck too far. Alerted to the impending danger, he fled from New York City and went into hiding.

CHAPTER XIV

TOWARD BOLSHEVISM

Until the Palmer Raids of early January 1920, Sen Katayama had enjoyed a respite from police surveillance and harassment for more than five years. Whether the Japanese revolutionary had been marked for apprehension by the agents of the Attorney-General of the United States is not known but the news of mass arrests of political radicals throughout the country, conveyed to him by alarmed friends, was sufficiently foreboding to convince Katayama that escape from New York City was his sole course of safety. Hurriedly packing a few belongings and taking on a disguise, he boarded a train for Atlantic City on January 3 and there found refuge in the home of his countryman, Naitō Kansaburō. Katayama remained in hiding in the resort city for the next four months.[1]

What were the activities during the year or two preceding the Palmer Raids that led Katayama as well as his closest intimates in New York to conclude that he could not, save through flight, avoid being taken into custody by agents of the federal government? This question, of paramount importance for an understanding of his revolutionary career, has never been entirely answered by either Japanese or Western historians. Japanese biographers have persisted in relying upon the self-centered reports of Katayama's fellow revolutionaries in the United States who themselves reveal not only the grossest misunderstanding of the nature of the social unrest in the post-World War I United States but also a lack of knowledge of his relationships with American and European revolutionary leaders of the times. Western

[1] Watanabe Haruo, *Nihon Marukusu Shugi Undō no Reimei*, Tokyo, 1957, pp. 107-108. The hiding place in Atlantic City was suggested by Taguchi Unzō, who had worked there during the summer vacation season.

scholars have, on the other hand, been uninformed about the widely ramified scope of his revolutionary undertakings, particularly as they were related to developments in distant Russia and Japan. Katayama's role as a leader in the international Communist movement from 1919 to 1922 has, as a result, been either ridiculously exaggerated or unjustifiably minimized. What part then did he play in the momentous revolutionary events of these years?

It is clear that the most fateful decision Katayama ever made was to accept the invitation of S. J. Rutgers to move to New York City in the late fall of 1916. Had the Japanese socialist decided to remain in California, the most earth-shaking political upheaval of modern history—the Bolshevik Revolution—would have passed him by unnoticed. Once he was in New York, however, he not only came into contact with many of the principal leaders of America's socialist left wing but he was also brought to the direct attention of conspirators who were to be the master minds of the Bolshevik seizure of power and the organization of the international Communist movement. While Katayama's doings with the members of the Russian left wing as well as with Rutgers were brought to a temporary halt when one by one they left the United States for Petrograd and Moscow, he continued to work closely with the prime movers of the solidifying left wing in the United States.

It is perhaps a fair estimate of the situation that, with the exception of Rutgers, Katayama's future revolutionary lot was affected most lastingly by the almost incomparable Louis Fraina. Born in 1894 in a small village in southern Italy, Fraina came to the United States when he was only three years old. Raised in a poverty-stricken home in the lower East Side of New York City, his formal education did not extend beyond elementary school. Thereafter he educated himself, showing a marked preference for the literature of social protest and revolt. By the age of fifteen the precocious but intellectually erratic youngster had advanced into and beyond the frontiers of conventional socialism and then for some years was a confidante and fellow worker of the ideologically volatile Daniel De Leon, chieftain of the ultra-radical Socialist Labor Party. During the earlier years of World War I Fraina, an outspoken critic of the Second International, continued to shift further to the left, reaching by the time of America's entrance into the conflict as extreme a revolutionary position as perhaps any other American of the day.[2]

Whether or not Katayama was well acquainted with the writings of Louis Fraina before his arrival in New York is difficult to establish. It is interesting to note, however, that the political views of the young intellectual and agitator were in many respects not substantially different from those of Katayama's old competitor, the anarcho-syndicalist, Kōtoku Shūsui. This would seem to suggest that during the winter of 1916-1917, when the old Japanese socialist first met Fraina, he was far better prepared to grasp and comprehend the revolutionary theories of the young Italian-American than those of Trotsky or Bukharin. It must also be borne in mind that, despite his occasional meetings with the future leaders of the Bolshevik Revolution, Katayama was never strongly swayed by them during the brief time that he associated with them. All evidence, direct and implicit, tends, on the contrary, to support the thesis that the ideological impulses which moved him toward a revolutionary socialist position emanated first from Rutgers and, after the Dutchman's departure from the United States in the spring of 1918, from Fraina.

[2] For Fraina's youthful years see especially Theodore Draper, *The Roots of American Communism*, New York, 1957, pp. 61-62. David A. Apter, "Lewis Corey: a Portrait of an American Radical," *Columbia Library Columns*, VIII, no. 2 (February 1959), pp. 4-5, is also useful. When Fraina abandoned Communism and left the Party, he changed his name to Lewis Corey.

In the months following the meeting of left-wing leaders at the home of Ludwig Lore in early 1917 such strong-minded men as Rutgers, Fraina, and Katayama did not see eye to eye on all ideological matters of fundamental importance. Perhaps Rutgers alone had an understanding of the theories of Bolshevism which were still generally unknown in Russia, Europe, and the United States. Fraina was doubtless equally extreme in his doctrines but, since his thought had evolved along an anarcho-syndicalist course and his knowledge of Leninist teachings was still imperfect, his main ideas converged with Rutgers' primarily on opposition to imperialism and war.[3] Katayama was clearly the most moderate of the trio, for though he was willing to concede the ineffectiveness of the Second International and to acknowledge its failure to cope with the vital issue of war and peace, he was unable for some time to reach an alternative position.

If Katayama required more time and especially the persuasion of historical events to advance to a truly revolutionary posture, his own belief in the need to consolidate the diverse left-wing groups in the United States facilitated cooperation with the theoretically more radical Rutgers and Fraina. His sense of urgency was quickened, too, by America's entry into the war and by the resulting confusion in the American Socialist Party. Thus, by the late spring and summer of 1917 Katayama, as has been seen, joined with Rutgers and Fraina, striving to rally the extreme left and to publicize its program. Shortly thereafter Rutgers, provided with letters of introduction to Katayama's old socialist comrades in Japan, left for Russia. While Rutgers had generally preferred to remain in the background, the energetic Fraina, strongly supported by the Japanese veteran, soon became one of the mainstays of American revolutionary socialism.

[3] Note the remarks of Apter, *op.cit.*, pp. 7-9.

Like many socialists in the United States Katayama and Fraina moved more positively toward the camp of Bolshevism with the news of Lenin's successful coup in November 1917. Although Katayama had only the most general knowledge of the nature of Bolshevism, he still did not hesitate to hail the Leninist seizure of power as a glorious victory of the Russian proletariat and as the advent of a socialist millennium for oppressed mankind.[4] Presumably he did not acquire a more precise understanding of the essence of Leninism until somewhat later in 1918, when Fraina published the first collection of the Bolshevik leader's latest writings in English.[5] It was not, accordingly, until the end of the year at the earliest that Katayama could have acquired any real insight into the thinking of Lenin. What he learned he apparently approved, for his exposition of Communist doctrines during the following months resulted in his being designated as the leader of the "Bolshevik wing" among the Japanese socialists who gathered in his rooms in Manhattan for discussion and debate.[6] Apart from evidences of his new thought in various periodical pieces of 1919-1920, moreover, Katayama's growing enthusiasm for Bolshevism may be noted in his Japanese version of Lenin's *State and Revolution,*

[4] "Russia is our great hope for the moment," he said. "The revolution must be maintained, not only for Russia's sake but for the sake of the proletariat of all lands. It seems dark now, but we will triumph yet. The idea is taking root, the workers can never be the same as they were before the revolution. There are many disappointments ahead for us, but we are used to them and we will not give up hope." Katayama, as quoted in: E. W. McAlpine, "Russian and Japanese Socialists Join Hands despite Looming Clash," The *World,* [Oakland, Calif.] (March 22, 1918), pp. 1, 5.

[5] Draper, *op.cit.,* p. 107. See also Leo Gruliow, "Lenin and Lewis Corey (Louis Fraina)," *Columbia Library Columns,* VIII, no. 2 (February 1959), p. 15. Katayama's small band of Japanese in New York apparently did not undertake a serious study of Lenin's writings until 1919.

[6] Watanabe Haruo, *Katayama Sen to Tomo ni,* Tokyo, 1955, p. 27; and Ishigaki Eitarō, "Katayama Sen to Sono Doshitachi," *Chūō Kōron,* LXVII, no. 14 (December 1952), p. 236.

designed for the edification of his compatriots in the United States as well as in his homeland.

These activities of Katayama, carried on during the period of about two years after his transfer from San Francisco to New York City, were not productive of any far-reaching effects upon left-wing socialism in the United States nor upon the political behavior of Japanese socialists and other immigrants scattered about Brooklyn and Manhattan. They are, on the contrary, of greater import in underlining his gradual shift from the more moderate and, perhaps, ideologically restrained position of left-wing socialism, which could still be accommodated within the spectrum of the Second International, to the more militant and revolutionary outlook of the proponents of a Third International. Yet the acquisition of a new social and political point of view could not furnish Katayama with any lasting intellectual or emotional comfort, for he was above all a man of action rather than of ideas. It was inevitable, given his character, that he would work zealously for the establishment of political groups to implement his beliefs.

The problem confronted by left-wing socialists like Katayama had first been posed unequivocally by Lenin at the Zimmerwald Conference of 1915, namely, to abandon the Second and to create a Third International devoted to the furtherance of revolution as defined by the Bolshevik faction. Though Katayama himself may well have reflected about the imperatives of the challenge from time to time, they surely could not have failed to cross his mind at the historic gathering of left-wing leaders in Brooklyn. But, implicitly or explicitly, Lenin's proposal had been rejected as the commanders of the extreme left decided to work for the consolidation of the left-wing groups within the American Socialist Party which still adhered to the Second International. During the next two years, when the American party was split by the involvement of the United States in the war, when Bolshevik victories augured the successful founding of a "workers' state," and when opportunities for the extension of "proletarian revolution" became unprecedentedly promising, many left-wing champions in the United States were tantalized by second thoughts. By the winter of 1918-1919 movements were afoot everywhere to bury the Second International.

Of left-wing leaders in the United States few became more deeply involved than Katayama in the widely spread plans and plots to shatter the Second International and to replace it with an organizational apparatus inspired, if perhaps not dominated, by the Bolsheviks in Soviet Russia. Because many of Katayama's movements and activities were cloaked in secrecy and his plans had to be altered occasionally in the light of unanticipated turns in events, it is possible to determine the interrelationship, if not necessarily the exact sequence, of his many ambitious schemes on behalf of his newly adopted Communist cause. These undertakings of Katayama, which were the capstones of the more than three decades of his life invested in social reform and revolution, were threefold: to assist in the construction of an American Communist Party; to work for the creation of a Communist Party of Japan; and to support the world-wide objectives of the Communist, or Third International.

In the desperate maneuvers and political in-fighting engaged in by the founding fathers of the American Communist parties Katayama, as a general without an army, did not for some time play a major role. Whatever modest influence he was able to exert was probably felt more by leaders of the various left-wing factions and claques, especially by the rapidly rising Louis Fraina, than by rank and file followers, with whom he was not on intimate terms. Given the state of affairs within the American Socialist Party, no other line of action was open to Katayama. And once the leaders of the left wing insisted that self-proclaimed revolutionaries stand up and be counted on the fundamental issue of control and policy of the American Socialist Party, there was little need for him to hesitate.

In the winter of 1918-1919 such left-wing leaders as Louis Fraina, John Reed, and Charles E. Ruthenberg began to deploy their forces in the open struggle to direct the course of the American socialist movement. But if the left-wing captains enjoyed widespread grass-roots support within the party, largely because of the backing of the Slavic-language federations whose prestige and presumption had soared with the Bolshevik Revolution, it was soon made clear that the right wing and "centrist" leaders were not to be easily stampeded and crushed. In May a thorough-going "purge" of the Party was initiated by the opposition camp led by the New York lawyer, Morris Hillquit, shattering once and for all whatever unity the Party still retained and leaving the organizational machinery in the hands of the right wing. Henceforth there was to be no turning back; socialism and Bolshevism had come to a final parting in the United States.

Having been effectively outflanked by Hillquit and his allies, left-wing chieftains gathered together in New York City in June to review the crisis and to devise a new strategy. The net result of the meeting, however, was neither greater unity within the left wing nor a common policy which could rally the "purged" Communists but rather the hardening of a new split destined to plague both the incipient American movement and the Communist International for the next four years. On the one side, representatives of the English-speaking groups, assuming rather ingenuously that Hillquit and his lieutenants could still be overturned and the American Socialist Party "captured" by the left wing, were reluctant to press for the immediate formation of a Communist Party, preferring to resume battle at the national socialist convention scheduled for September 1. On the other side, the minority, composed of delegates from the foreign-language (Slavic) federations, clamored for the immediate launching of an American Communist Party. Voted down, the minority faction stalked out of the meeting and shortly announced its plans to sponsor a convention on August 30 for the purpose of launching a new party. The socialist movement had now been divided into three contentious groups.[7]

Since the initial thrusts Katayama had followed the offensives and counteroffensives on the battlefield of American socialism with rapt attention. To him there was no confusing friend and foe. Having committed himself to the furtherance of the purposes of the Third International, there was no mistaking the "villainy" of Hillquit and socialists of his ilk who blindly and stubbornly insisted upon resisting the "tide of history." In July Katayama made known his disagreement with the right wing in a scathing attack upon its leader and his policies.[8] In scoring Hillquit for flaunting the wishes of perhaps a majority of socialists the Japanese radical, who had obviously not as yet fully grasped the deeper meaning of the Bolshevik concept of "democratic centralism," doubtless evoked a responsive chord among thousands of infuriated Party members. But in assailing Hillquit and his followers for interpreting erroneously the mood of the American people and the prospects for a workers' revolution in the United States Katayama was guilty of a doctrinaire position, of succumbing to what Lenin himself was slightly later to castigate as "infantile leftism." In those days when social radicalism approached the historical cross-

[7] The struggles and wrangles of the left-wing leaders are skilfully traced in Draper, *op.cit.*, chs. 8-9. For another workmanlike account see Daniel Bell, "The Background and Development of Marxian Socialism in the United States," in D. D. Egbert and S. Persons, eds. *Socialism and American Life*, 2 vols., Princeton, 1952, I, 318ff.

[8] Sen Katayama, "Morris Hillquit and the Left Wing," *Revolutionary Age*, II, no. 4 (July 26, 1919), p. 6. This is one of the most important writings of Katayama during the period of his transition to Bolshevism.

roads in the United States Katayama, by now an incorrigible wishful-thinker, pointed out the wrong direction.

In misconstruing widespread dissatisfaction with the high cost of living which followed the end of World War I for seething fervor for a revolutionary change in American life, Katayama was no different from the small number of native-born and immigrant radicals who vainly confused their hopes with social realities. The key error committed by the left wing, dazzled by the initial triumphs of Bolshevism, was to assume that the United States could be equated, insofar as the likelihood of proletarian revolution is concerned, with Russia or Germany or Hungary, or even as Katayama drew the conclusion, with Japan.[9] The United States was no decadent autocracy crumbling under the heavy impact of war. Its cities had not been ravaged and destroyed in the frenzy of battle. Its land had not been pitted and gutted by bomb and shell. There were no hordes of demoralized and defeated soldiers, no desperate and rebellious armies of peasants, no riotous and revolutionary masses of workers. Such well-established facts suggest that it was not really repression or even the divisions in the ranks of the ultra-radical left but rather their total lack of understanding of the depths of faith of the American people in their democratic, capitalist system, all its defects notwithstanding, that predestined the abysmal failure of the embryonic Communist parties. Rarely in the history of the international Communist movement, it may be maintained, has a group of Communist leaders more fallaciously misinterpreted the "objective conditions" than the would-be revolutionaries in

[9] Katayama's shift from Marxism to Leninism is succinctly revealed in his following observation. "From Russian experiences," he declared, "it is fully proved that the Bolshevist ideas are much more easily applied in a country where capitalism is not so fully developed as in England and America." And, so, he continued, "we have a better prospect of having Bolshevism in Japan and in Mexico." Sen Katayama, "Radicalism in Japan," *Gale's Magazine,* III, no. 3 (October 1919), p. 4.

the United States in the aftermath of World War I. And Katayama may be counted among the politically errant.

Considering the character of the social and economic unrest in the summer and fall of 1919, it probably made little difference in the long run whether the majority or minority policy of the left wing prevailed. Both factions suffered from the delusion that American capitalism could be laid to rest simply by reading its obituary. By the turn of September the break of the extreme left from the American Socialist Party was formally confirmed and the once promising political movement of the socialist giant, Eugene V. Debs, was mortally wounded. When the Slavic-language federations, led by Fraina, proclaimed the establishment of the Communist Party of America, the English-speaking groups countered with the formation of the Communist Labor Party. At a moment when the Communist movement in the United States could least afford disunity, its forces were rent by conflicting organizations, programs, and ambitions.

America's first Communist parties enjoyed only four months of relative freedom of action before the Palmer Raids. Despite the many warning signs, particularly in the form of arrests of radicals by federal and state authorities during the fall of 1919, the scope and fury of the nation-wide blow struck by the Attorney-General on the night of January 2, 1920, caught its many victims by surprise. Within a matter of hours more than 4,000 alleged radicals and revolutionaries in thirty-three cities had been arrested. In New York City alone about four hundred men and women were apprehended.[10] The "Red Scare" had seemingly given way to officially spurred hysteria.

Katayama was lucky enough to escape detention. Why? No attempt was apparently made by federal agents to secure his arrest and he was able to remain in the city without embar-

[10] The "Palmer Raids" are ably discussed in Robert K. Murray, *Red Scare; a Study in National Hysteria, 1919-1920,* Minneapolis, 1955, pp. 210-222. For the raids and arrests in New York City see especially p. 214.

rassment until his departure on the afternoon of January 3. It is unlikely that he was completely unknown to the officers of the General Intelligence Division of the Department of Justice who were in all probability responsible for determining who among the some 60,000 radicals listed in their files were to be taken into custody. Failing definite evidence to the contrary, it may well be that Katayama was not considered sufficiently important to warrant the attention of the Attorney-General's office. But whatever place the agents of the young J. Edgar Hoover may have accorded the Japanese revolutionary in their list of "dangerous radicals," it is fairly certain they were not completely apprised of the full extent of his activities to promote the interests of international Communism.

Deeply absorbed as Katayama was in schemes to solidify the left wing in the United States and to bring into being a Communist movement and party, he never failed to keep an eye upon developments in his homeland. There too, he had continued to hope, a revolutionary movement might some day be launched. It is thus not hard to appreciate his excitement when he learned of the "August Rice Riots" and of the outbreak of industrial-labor disputes which swept Japan once the European War had been brought to a close. If he did not hasten home immediately, it was surely because unprecedented opportunities for the promotion of revolution, in Japan and elsewhere, and for the advancement of his role of leadership very shortly became available. In January 1919, after long years of planning, Lenin formally acted to bring into existence the Third International, or Comintern. Now as never before, it seemed to Katayama, the workers of Japan would not have to struggle alone to overthrow the old oppressive order.

Partly because of his hope to participate in programs to extend the Bolshevik Revolution beyond its Russian locale and to integrate a revolutionary struggle in Japan with the broader international movement Katayama arranged, as has been seen, for a division of effort.[11] While he remained in the United States, where there were fewer physical obstructions than in Japan to the maintenance of liaison with the Bolshevik leaders in Europe, his young associate, Kondō Eizō, returned to Tokyo in May 1919. Though he was easily able to establish contact with several of Katayama's long-time comrades, Kondō immediately encountered almost unsurmountable obstacles in his efforts to form a Communist organization. Not only was social radicalism still, as in the prewar years, the domain of professional intellectuals tirelessly engaged in ideological sniping at one another but a strong current of anarcho-syndicalism threatened to wash away the wobbly pillars of Marxism. Furthermore, the new philosophy of revolution, Leninism, was not as yet known to even the avante-garde among Japanese leftists.[12]

After more than a year, marked by bitter contention and recrimination, the principal leaders of left-wing groups agreed to call a truce and to concentrate their puny strength in a drive to secure "democratic freedom" for the people of Japan. In the Socialist League, founded in the summer of 1920, there were to be found such uneasy allies as the ill-fated anarcho-syndicalist, Ōsugi Sakae; the irrepressible radical socialist, Sakai Toshihiko; Yamakawa Hitoshi, perhaps Japan's foremost Marxist theoretician of the day; and the staunchly individualistic former disciple of Kōtoku Shūsui, Arahata Kanson. Even if it had not been suppressed by the state less than a year after its formation it could have been anticipated that this united front of the political left would not endure.[13]

[11] See above, p. 254, for his understanding with Kondō Eizō.

[12] Because of the breakdown of communications between Japan and Soviet Russia it was not until some five years after Lenin's seizure of power that left-wing intellectuals in Japan began to acquire some familiarity with his basic writings. This paucity of Leninist materials will partly help account for the relatively great strength of anarcho-syndicalism in Japan in the immediate postwar years.

[13] On the founding and vicissitudes of the Socialist League note:

But Kondō's efforts had not been completely fruitless. As left-wing socialists acquired greater opportunities to delve into Leninist literature and as their antagonisms with the more moderate socialists on the right and with the anarcho-syndicalists on the left were sharpened, the blandishments of the "secret emissary of the Comintern," an appellation later assumed by Kondō, met with some success. When he demonstrated through his affiliations with agents of the Communist International and by his participation in international congresses sponsored by the Soviet government the likelihood of political and financial support from Russia, radical socialists quickly edged toward acceptance of Bolshevik doctrines. After Kondō and several other delegates from Japan attended the First Congress of the Toilers of the Far East, convened in Moscow in January 1922, the groundwork was laid for the construction of a Communist Party of Japan.[14] Six months later, on July 15, Katayama's dream of a revolutionary party in his homeland was fulfilled.

The role which Katayama played in the foundation of the Communist Party of Japan is difficult to fix precisely. There is no doubt that he was not always a direct participant in the many maneuvers which preceded its birth, for during long periods of time between Kondō's arrival in Japan and the actual achievement of success he cannot have maintained close liaison with the various leaders of the left wing in Tokyo. Nevertheless, his very activities in the United States and elsewhere, uncoordinated as they may have been with the struggles of his comrades in Japan, point to a persistent effort to assist in the creation of a Japanese party intimately tied to the

---

Kondō Kenji, "Chinsen-ki Igo; Shakai Shugi Domei no Kaisan made," in *Nihon Shakai Shugi Undō-shi, Shakai Kagaku* (Special Issue), IV, no. 1 (February 1928), pp. 170-172; Akamatsu Katsumaro, *Nihon Shakai Undō-shi*, Tokyo, 1955, pp. 177-180; and Arahata Kanson, *Nihon Shakai Shugi Undō-shi*, Tokyo, 1948, pp. 284-287.

[14] The First Congress of the Toilers of the Far East is discussed more fully on pp. 290ff.

network of international Communism. To this end Katayama not only strove to form a Communist group among Japanese immigrants and visitors in New York, some of whom later became key leaders in the Japanese movement, but he himself also began to assume positions of responsibility within an expanding Comintern apparatus.

In the history of modern Japan Katayama obviously has many claims to fame. But whatever figure he may cut in the popular imagination and in the political mythology of his country, he will always be known as an apostle of the Communist International during the critical years when it labored to fashion a web of organizations and representatives in the five continents of the globe. He was, moreover, no mere transitory conspirator in the international revolutionary movement, but a member of the tried and tested group of Comintern trouble-makers and "trouble-shooters" on call for assignment wherever Communist political capital was to be made. Among the various other Asian operatives of the Comintern during the decade of the twenties he was perhaps rivaled for a brief while by M. N. Roy, the Indian nationalistic firebrand. Katayama alone, however, was called the "father of Asian Communism."[15]

To determine when Katayama was first drawn into the embryonic network of the Communist International is like attempting to pinpoint the starting place of a waterfall. Still, there is a strong presumption that his growing involvement in the international intrigues of Bolshevism stemmed from his close relationship with S. J. Rutgers. The Dutch revolutionary had quit the United States in the spring of 1918, going on to

[15] Katayama has also been dubbed the "father of the workers of Japan" and a "father of the Revolution." Nozaka Sanzō, "Katayama Sen," in Yasuda Tokutarō *et al.*, *Hikari wo Ageta Hito-bito; Minshu Shugi-sha no Shisō to Shōgai*, Tokyo, 1956, p. 51. Oka Shigeki, "Katayama Sen to Amerika," *Kaizō*, XXXII, no. 8 (July 1951), p. 82, notes too that he has been referred to as the "father of the workers of the world."

Tokyo.[16] After calling upon Katayama's old friend, Sakai Toshihiko, and other Japanese socialists, he made his way to Russia, arriving many months after the Bolshevik Revolution. During the following year Rutgers busied himself in plans for the promotion of international Communism. In November 1918, when the Bolsheviks took their first positive step to establish systematic relationships with revolutionaries in Asia by holding the First Congress of Communist Organizations of the East, Rutgers delivered a message from the Japanese socialists who were unable to despatch their own delegates.[17] Perhaps more importantly, the Congress passed a resolution calling for the creation of a Department of International Propaganda, one section of which was to be concerned with Japanese affairs.[18] It requires no great strain upon the imagination to conclude that Rutgers, with Katayama in mind, had a hand in the shaping of this proposal.

That Lenin, Trotsky, and other Bolshevik leaders were, like Rutgers, becoming more attentive to the need for exploiting revolutionary possibilities in the international arena was made evident about a month after the First Congress of Communist Organizations of the East. In December a formal decision was made to launch the Third International and in January 1919, an invitation was extended to thirty-nine Communist and other left-wing political parties and organizations throughout the world to attend the First Congress in Moscow in the following month of March. What is remarkable, yet not surprising, since he was more or less known to the Bolshevik leaders, is that Katayama, though not the head of any established party or flourishing organization, was called upon by name in the

[16] Kishimoto Eitarō *et al.*, *Katayama Sen*, 2 vols., Tokyo, 1959-1960, II, p. 397. This source also indicates that Rutgers left Yokohama on July 19 and that he arrived in Moscow at the end of September.

[17] Rodger Swearingen and Paul Langer, *Red Flag in Japan*, Cambridge, Mass., 1952, p. 7.

[18] Xenia J. Eudin and Robert C. North, *Soviet Russia and the East, 1920-1927*, Stanford, 1957, p. 78.

Bolshevik invitation to represent the "Socialist groups of Tokio and Yokohama."[19] While he was unable to attend the epochal conclave, Katayama could not but realize that he had been tapped for a role of leadership in the burgeoning world-wide network of Communist revolution. He decided, accordingly, to postpone his return to Japan indefinitely.

There was much to occupy Katayama's attention in the United States after the First Congress of the Third International had concluded its proceedings. In addition to engaging in the battle over policy within the left wing and lending his support to the drive for an American Communist Party, he worked ceaselessly to convert his countrymen in New York City to Bolshevism. Not only did he provide authoritative interpretations of developments in Russia for newly arrived Japanese travelers, who were referred to him by Ludwig Martens, the Soviet "Consul-General" in New York City, but he also sought to convince his Japanese acquaintances of the soundness of Leninist teachings.[20] And though he himself had believed for many years, like a faithful Marxist, that proletarian revolution could occur only within a mature capitalist system, he now insisted that the experience of Soviet Russia provided an historical example for the guidance of such underdeveloped societies as Japan and Mexico. Hope had become the wellspring of conviction.

By the end of 1919 Katayama had, for all his effort, succeeded in leading little more than a half dozen Japanese in New York City into the Bolshevik fold. But few in number as these recruits to Communism may have been, they rendered yeomen's service to their adopted ideal during the next few years. The young Taguchi Unzō, Watanabe Haruo, Ishigaki Eitarō, Inomata Tsunao, Mamiya Sueyoshi, and Nonaka Ma-

[19] A translation of the text of the invitation will be found in New York State Legislative Joint Committee Investigating Seditious Activities, *Revolutionary Radicalism,* 4 vols., Albany, 1920, I, pp. 418-419. These volumes are commonly known as the Lusk Report.

[20] K. Ishimoto, "Order Reigns in Soviet Russia," *Gale's Magazine,* II, no. 12 (July 1919), p. 5.

sayuki stood by Katayama in every trouble and trial, serving as his loyal lieutenants in the struggle to link Japan to the chain of Bolshevism. Long before the leaders of the left wing at home in Japan had made their fateful ideological shifts to the battle lines of Communism, these comrades of Katayama had taken their places in the vanguard of Bolshevik-style revolution.

Katayama's sundry activities to advance the Communist movement in the United States and abroad were abruptly interrupted by the Palmer Raids. Fearing arrest, he discreetly stayed in hiding in Atlantic City and, though he secretly returned to New York from time to time, he dared not show himself in public. Whether Katayama's anxieties were well founded is a moot point, for the hysteria suddenly raised by the Attorney-General's assault on political radicalism waned with even greater abruptness. Nevertheless, Katayama did not deem it prudent to return to his familiar political haunts in New York City until the end of April.

At the very time that he was in hiding, a Bolshevik project of deepest interest to Katayama was in process of unfolding in western Europe. Hoping to expedite the international dissemination of Bolshevism, to facilitate communication among Communist Party agents throughout the world, and to carry on preparations for the Second Congress of the Third International, planned for the summer of 1920, a propaganda bureau was contemplated for establishment in Amsterdam in January. The veteran revolutionary, Rutgers, had great hopes for this new center of Bolshevism designed to establish closer links with revolutionary headquarters and personnel in Europe, North and South America, and Asia. Here in early February a meeting of representatives of many Communist and left-wing Socialist parties as well as of the Comintern was held to consider plans for the Second Congress.[21] Though no Japa-

[21] Perhaps the most accurate account of the Amsterdam meeting will be found in Draper, *op.cit.*, pp. 233-235. The recollections of one

nese delegate was present, Rutgers was not oblivious to the hopes of his Japanese comrade in revolutionary arms.

Soon after he returned to New York Katayama and his small Communist group became part of a belt of transmission of revolutionary materials despatched by Rutgers' agency in Amsterdam. These Bolshevik publications were not only used for the further indoctrination of his own scanty following, but also forwarded to left-wing Socialists and Communist sympathizers in Japan where there continued to be a dearth of knowledge on Leninism. Though the pioneers of the Japanese Communist movement were ultimately able to obtain Bolshevik literature directly from Soviet Russia, in the beginning the cadre in the United States and, slightly later, various American Communists were instrumental in overcoming the initial difficulties.[22] In this indirect but vital way Katayama contributed to the advancement of Leninism in his native land.

During the remaining months of 1920 Katayama was not forgotten in the plans of the Communist International. Though he himself had not attended the Second Congress, he was nevertheless the subject of discussions among the Bolshevik chiefs who were strongly dissatisfied with the progress of the revolutionary movements in the Americas. In the first place, at the very moment when the Comintern was determined to strengthen its international apparatus and to tighten its control over constituent parties, the Second Congress was being treated to a dismaying spectacle. The cleavages within the American Communist groups continued to wrack the movement in the United States and to take on new forms with the passage of each season, and the quarrels were even carried

---

of the participants, the English Communist, John T. Murphy, *New Horizons*, London, 1941, pp. 84-92, are rather garbled and should be used carefully.

[22] Watanabe, *Nihon Marukusu Shugi Undō no Reimei*, p. 115. For the United States as a link in the transmission belt by which Communist materials were passed on to Japan see Swearingen and Langer, *op.cit.*, pp. 60-62.

into the conclave in Moscow. There the Bolshevik leaders looked on in consternation as delegates from three different factions heatedly disputed for recognition as representatives of the American party. Realizing that the internecine strife could not be permitted to continue, a mandate was issued to the American organizations, ordering them to negotiate a unity by the following October 10.[23] This injunction was more easily handed down than executed.

A second important decision taken at the Second Congress was to initiate a program for revolutionary organization and agitation in Central and South America where Bolshevik influence had not as yet made any significant penetration. This new direction of activity was most likely recommended by Michael Borodin and M. N. Roy who had fished in the troubled revolutionary waters of Mexico for many months before their participation in the Amsterdam and Moscow meetings.[24] To direct this new campaign the Comintern, distrusting the existence of a revolutionary headquarters in Amsterdam or, for the matter, anywhere outside Soviet Russia, proceeded to ensure its own control by appointing a special task force. Designated as the American Bureau and composed of Louis Fraina, Katayama, and the Lettish-American, Carl Johnson, the group was assigned responsibility for advancing the revolutionary movement in Central and South America as well as in Canada.[25]

Communications between Soviet Russia and the United States were almost as slow as those between Moscow and

[23] Draper, *op.cit.*, pp. 267-268.

[24] Borodin, who was to become Sun Yat-sen's principal revolutionary consultant in 1923, was at this time well along the road on his ill-fated career as a Comintern agent. His activities in Mexico and the Caribbean are recounted by Carlton Beals, *Glass Houses: Ten Years of Free-Lancing*, New York, 1938, pp. 45-51. Roy, who was to serve as a Comintern representative in China in 1927, reminisces about his Mexican days in a series of autobiographical articles in the *Radical Humanist*. See particularly the successive issues from February 15, 1953, through August 23, 1953.

[25] Draper, *op.cit.*, p. 269.

Tokyo. Not until the end of October, about two weeks after the deadline set by the Comintern for the achievement of unity, did the American parties first learn of the stern directive. And it was not until the end of December that Fraina, after the absence of an entire year in Europe, returned to New York City. Katayama probably learned of his new assignments at this time. In addition to being alerted to the possibility of representing the Comintern in mediating the dispute among the American Communist parties and being informed of his mission in Central America, he was also instructed to make arrangements for a delegate of the Japanese-American Communist cadre to attend the Third Congress of the Third International which was to convene during the coming summer.[26] It was now clear that Soviet Russia, after its many probing actions of the previous two or three years, had now resolved to step up the pace of its revolutionary efforts in the Far East.

The early months of 1921 were busy ones for Katayama. Pending the arrival of new directives from the Comintern, he made no serious efforts to induce the contending leaders of the American Communist groups to heal the breaches in their ranks. The problem of deciding upon representation of a Japanese delegate at the Third Congress was, however, taken under immediate consideration by Katayama and his comrades. Taguchi was finally designated, leaving for Europe in the spring.[27] Katayama himself also hurried to bring his life of six and a half years in the United States to a close. His daughter, Yasuko, then about twenty-two years old, was sent back to Japan in the care of her companion, Hara Nobuko.[28] And at the end of March the aged revolutionary himself set out for Mexico City with Louis Fraina. Save for a brief while

[26] Watanabe, *Nihon Marukusu Shugi Undō no Reimei*, pp. 114-115.
[27] *ibid.*, pp. 122, 242.
[28] Katayama's family problems and relations are discussed at length in Arakawa Jitsuzō, *Katayama Sen; Sekai ni okeru Kare ga Chii to Taiken*, Tokyo, 1930, pp. 217-221.

a few months later he never again set foot in the United States.

Katayama lived in Mexico City for almost eight months. No other period of his life is so obscure. During the remaining years of his life he rarely spoke about his experiences in Central America and in his voluminous writings there are only fleeting and parenthetical references to his Mexican days. Not even the members of his Communist circle in New York have cast any real light upon his movements and activities for, apart from oblique hints, which are probably based upon sheer speculation, they generally allude to little more than the importance of his appointment as Chief of the American Bureau of the Comintern. Furthermore in the literature on the post-World War I Communist and revolutionary movements in Latin America in general and in Mexico specifically the name of Katayama is mentioned only rarely and then vaguely. But fortunately Fraina, who kept his silence for about thirty years, has written at length about his escapades with Katayama south of the American border.

Fraina's tale of his final mission in the Communist cause is as strange as it is pathetic. Devoid of self-pity, it is the swan song of a revolutionary destroyed by the very forces of history he had confidently assumed he understood. His Achilles heel, like Trotsky's, was his theoretical brilliance which evoked the unstinting admiration of Lenin himself.[29] It would be too much to conclude that the American Communist movement would have fared more happily had he been its undisputed field marshal during its formative years, since not even his acknowledged intellectual power could have compelled the facts of American life to conform to his conceptual categories. If he committed a fatal error, it was in believing that in so opportunistic a movement as Bolshevism the strength of ideas would prevail over the weaknesses of men. Only when it was too late did he realize, as Katayama never did, that he had been

[29] Note Lenin's remarks in Gruliow, *op.cit.*, p. 15

made a sacrificial victim of the revolutionary politics he had espoused.

That Katayama was assigned by the Comintern to carry on revolutionary agitation in Mexico requires no particular comment. With his loyalty to the international Communist movement established beyond reproach, it could have been assumed that he would undertake his mission dutifully and with as good prospects for success as any agent of the Communist International. But if there were no pressing reasons to keep the Japanese veteran in the United States, it may not be convincingly argued that the young Fraina had no major role to play in the American movement. Though he was not yet twenty-eight years old, he had already left a permanent mark upon the course of Bolshevik revolution in the United States. It may well be, as Theodore Draper, one of the foremost historians of American Communism, has suggested, that Fraina's assignment to Mexico was engineered by his foes in order to isolate him from Communist affairs in the United States.[30] It was beyond doubt a sentence to political death.

In Mexico Katayama and Fraina were eyewitnesses to one of the great social upheavals of the twentieth century. Their task was to determine the direction of the heavy revolutionary tide, with its many crosscurrents and undercurrents, that was sweeping over the immense area south of the Rio Grande and to divert it into the channels of Bolshevism. It was a grand challenge, posing complex problems of social and political analysis comparable perhaps only to those which were simultaneously confronting Comintern agents in the war-lord ridden Chinese Republic. But while in China revolution in 1921 was still a floundering and inchoate force, the struggle in Mexico for a just way of life rested upon a strong, popular base and possessed a purpose, momentum, and inner dynamism which did not lend themselves to either subversion or diversion. Since 1911, when the despotic regime of Porfirio Diaz was

[30] Draper, *op.cit.*, p. 294.

overthrown, the power of popular revolution had gradually been strengthened until, during the years of the Carranza government, aim and focus were provided in the Constitution of May 1, 1917. It matters little whether Carranza's successors, Obregon, Calles, and Vasconcelos, were at heart opportunists or genuine champions of the people. Unable to resist the tremendous pressures for sweeping social change, they could advance only with the surge of the awakened Indians and mestizos of their country.

Though their superiors in the Comintern were manifestly oblivious to the fact, Katayama and Fraina arrived in Mexico at a most unpropitious time for the fulfillment of their orders. The political conditions and social climate had drastically changed since the visits of Roy and Borodin several years before. Katayama and Fraina came to Mexico too late to take advantage of the mass upsurge for a new deal in life and too soon to make Communist capital of the frustrations and setbacks which inevitably occur in popular revolutions. But to devoted apostles of Bolshevism such facts were neither obvious nor admissible and the elderly Japanese and the young Italian-American resolutely buckled down to the task at hand.

No sooner had Katayama and Fraina entered the arena of revolutionary politics in Mexico City than they had to return secretly to the United States on urgent business. As the time for the opening of the Third Congress of the Communist International neared and the divided American Communist movement showed no signs of progress or even effort toward unity, the Comintern refused to postpone action any longer. It had no intention of being politically embarrassed or harassed by wrangling American Communists either at the impending Congress or in the newly launched Red International of Trade-Unions. The team of trouble-shooters, Katayama, Fraina, and Carl Johnson, was thus instructed to bring the bickering factions together and to construct a united party without further delay.[31] As a result, the trio of Comintern agents attended a convention of delegates from the American parties at Woodstock, New York, at the end of May where, after a heated and protracted fight, an uneasy truce and coalition were brought about. Katayama and Fraina then returned to their post in Mexico City.

It was probably about this time that Fraina's ardor for the international Communist movement began to cool. Bitterly accepting the fact that he had been outmaneuvered in the struggle for leadership in the American movement, disenchanted by the changing character of the "proletarian revolution," and dismayed by the cynicism of its Russian masters, he was beset by doubts about the cause he had so faithfully served.[32] By the fall of 1921 his disillusionment was, for all practical purposes, complete and within the next six months he not only parted company with Bolshevism forever but quickly vanished into the anonymity of American life.[33]

However Fraina may have looked upon his Mexican assignment by the Comintern, Katayama had no need either to fret or regret. For while he continued to flirt with obscure revolutionary politicos of socialist and syndicalist persuasion, purchasing from them reports on the local revolutionary situation, he had many more important matters on his mind. During the summer he was in constant communication with his Japanese comrades in New York, discussing with them plans for the liquidation of their activities in the United States. Under the aegis of the Comintern, various congresses, calling for the more direct participation of the peoples of Asia, were being scheduled. There was now no longer any purpose in using Katayama as a handy man of the Communist International or to disregard the potential value of his loyal band.

In September 1921, Katayama's comrades in the United

[31] *ibid.*, p. 270. [32] *ibid.*, pp. 294-295.

[33] Fraina's subsequent career as scholar and writer is covered in his obituary in the New York *Times* (September 17, 1953), p. 29.

States began to wind up their affairs, soon after embarking individually or in small groups for Soviet Russia. Katayama himself left Mexico on November 12, overjoyed at the prospect of being immersed again in the revolutionary affairs of his native land.[34] That the ends of Bolshevism in Mexico had been furthered as a result of his stay is highly problematical, the principal memento of his visit being perhaps his writing of the introduction to a Spanish-language edition of Lenin's *State and Revolution*.[35] If Katayama did not choose to speak or write thereafter about his experiences in Mexico, the reason is perhaps self-evident. What was there for him to say?[36]

Katayama traveled directly to Soviet Russia, going via Paris and Berlin. When his train finally pulled into the railroad station in Moscow on December 14, the old Japanese revolutionary was treated to a heart-warming sight which compensated for the disappointments and rebuffs of more than two decades. On the platform a vast throng milled about an honor guard of the Red Army, waiting impatiently for the train to come to a halt. Amidst the many well-wishers on hand to greet the "grand old man" Katayama detected the faces of his Japanese comrades from America and of others from the homeland. But the official words of welcome were presented by a passing acquaintance of his New York days, Leon Trotsky, commander-in-chief of the world-famous Red Army. To lend even further importance to the occasion such Bolshevik dignitaries as Kalinin, Zinoviev, Radek, and Lunacharski were also present. Literally and figuratively, it was an impressive demonstration of the "red-carpet treatment" accorded by the

[34] Eudin and North, *op.cit.*, p. 145, are in error when they indicate that Katayama was in Moscow in November 1921. Leaving Mexico on November 12, he arrived in Moscow on December 14.

[35] Kishimoto *et al.*, *op.cit.*, II, p. 182.

[36] Katayama's letters to his friends in New York City were quite perfunctory; they present almost no real information about his activities in Mexico City. See his note to Bertha Inomata in *ibid.*, II, p. 181. See also Ishigaki Eitarō, *op.cit.*, p. 238.

Bolsheviks to visitors from abroad deemed useful in promoting Communist interests.

With his triumphal entry into Moscow Katayama's many flights and wanderings at last came to an end. The Soviet Union may well have provided him with a home and a haven for the remaining years of his life. But in a larger sense his eleven years in Russia were the end of the revolutionary trail for Katayama. For almost a quarter of a century he had enjoyed a free political hand and had acknowledged neither man nor movement as his master. Bolshevism, however, permitted no such latitude of choice. It was either serve or be destroyed.

CHAPTER XV

WITH THE COMMUNIST INTERNATIONAL

When Sen Katayama arrived in Moscow in December 1921, his sixty-second birthday was only a few weeks off. Almost a quarter of a century had passed since he had launched a career dedicated to the service of his fellow men. But if he cut a prestigious figure among the celebrities of the Bolshevik world, many of whom were young enough to be his children, it was not because they were well apprised about the particulars of his past life. It was enough that he had been one of the "grand old men" of the Second International, that he had thrown his weight behind the expanding Communist movement, and that he was, above all, Japanese, hence, Asian.

Katayama was highly valued by the high command in Moscow because of his potential usefulness to advance the Communist front in the Far East. This is quite clear from an appraisal of Bolshevik maneuvers in late 1921, at the very time that Katayama transferred his base of revolutionary operations from Mexico to Soviet Russia. Four fateful years had elapsed since the Leninist seizure of power in the tsarist citadel of Petrograd. Though the Red legions, headed by the amazing Trotsky, had succeeded in extending the Bolshevik hold over the far-flung Russian dominions, the campaign for world revolution had run into unexpectedly fierce opposition from capitalist regimes which refused to collapse in keeping with the confident forecasts of Communist theoreticians. The Bolshevik juggernaut had been brought to an abrupt halt.

Being preeminently a hard-headed realist, Lenin soon determined upon a shift in revolutionary tactics. At the Second Congress of the Communist International in 1920 the doctrine of simultaneous world revolution, upon which ardent Bolsheviks had for some years pinned their hopes, was replaced by a policy of attack upon the Achilles heel of capitalism, the colonial empires maintained by the great powers in Asia and Africa. Europe and the United States, as the fortresses of capitalism, were for the time being to be weakened by conventional political harassment. And within Soviet Russia itself the inauguration of the New Economic Program (NEP) in 1921 now signaled the beginning of a strategic retreat from the ultra-radical policy of "war communism."

Though the leaders of Bolshevism had been mindful of Asian affairs since the early days of the November Revolution, largely because of the Allied military expedition to Siberia and the subsequent Japanese grab for the Russian East, economically underdeveloped Asia had not loomed high in the revolutionary priorities of Communist ideologists oriented toward the industrial West. Despite the pronunciamentos of Bolshevik spokesmen, the fishing of Soviet Russia in ruffled political waters from Japan to Turkey, and the intrigues of agents of the Communist International, Lenin could really boast of no concrete successes in all of non-Russian Asia by the closing months of 1921. The few Communist parties that had been established after tremendous effort enjoyed no more than nominal existence. In addition to being ridden by ideological forces inimical to Marxist-Leninism, these infant political groups exercised no perceptible influence in their respective societies. Soviet Russia and the Communist International were thus in dire need of organizers to construct the vanguards of revolutionary movements and parties among the peoples of the East. It is no wonder that, when the Bolsheviks began to direct their attention to Asia, their thoughts soon turned to Katayama. If they were ready to use him for whatever purposes their plans demanded, he in turn was not unwilling to be used.

The official ceremony and fanfare marking Katayama's advent in the capital of Communism was an augury of the role which had been marked out for him. Quickly installed in the famous Hotel Luxe, the home and headquarters of many a foreign Communist dignitary during the twenties and thirties, he was in short order posed before the eyes of the Communist world as a revolutionary hero of the foremost standing. Paraded before the public, popularized in the press, he was also ushered into the highest political councils of Soviet Russia and the Communist International where he was repeatedly called upon to address the top-ranking leaders of the revolutionary movement. And when he was received in private audience by the foremost Bolshevik chieftains, including Lenin himself, it was made plain for all to see that the veteran revolutionary had been accorded the status of a luminary in the Communist galaxy.[1]

While Katayama was making the rounds of officialdom in Moscow, the Comintern was engaged in projects to strengthen the machinery of revolution in the East. Just a few weeks earlier, in November, a preliminary meeting of the First Congress of the Toilers of the East had been held in Irkutsk in eastern Siberia. Taguchi Unzō, a member of Katayama's New York group, was one of the eleven Japanese who took part in the brief proceedings.[2] The formal work of the Congress, however, did not get under way until January 21, 1922, when the Irkutsk group joined with other delegates from Asian lands and peoples for a full-scale conclave in Moscow and later in Petrograd. On this occasion Katayama was thrust to the forefront of Asian revolutionary affairs and brought to the notice of revolutionaries from other Asian lands.

The First Congress of the Toilers of the Far East was attended by more than one hundred and fifty delegates. The very name of the conference as well as the number and type

[1] Katayama has recounted the circumstances of his first meeting with the Bolshevik leader in "With Comrade Lenin," Clara Zetkin *et al.*, *We Have Met Lenin* (Moscow, 1939), pp. 11-15.

[2] Rodger Swearingen and Paul Langer, *Red Flag in Japan, International Communism in Action, 1919-1951,* Cambridge, Mass., p. 12; and Xenia J. Eudin and Robert C. North, *Soviet Russia and the East, 1920-1927,* Stanford, 1957, p. 145. The number of Japanese participants varies according to the source.

of the various delegations revealed succinctly the immense difficulties of the Comintern in promoting its international objectives. In addition to a motley collection of would-be revolutionaries acting in the name of such peoples as the Buryats, Yakuts, Kalmuks, and Mongols of Siberia and the China border areas, more than a hundred Koreans, Chinese, and Japanese were present. The sixteen-man group from Japan was headed by Katayama and, were it not for the participation of five of his friends from New York, the Japanese delegation would have been strongly overshadowed by the numerically strong Koreans and Chinese. Interestingly enough, the Japanese contingent was itemized in the official roster of the Congress as nine Communists, four anarchists, and three members without specific party affiliation.[3]

The opening addresses, delivered by such well-known Bolsheviks as Zinoviev and Kalinin, set the tone of the entire Congress. Katayama, acting in the capacity of a representative of the Comintern, also presented a message of greeting. All introductory speakers emphasized the historical responsibility of Asian peoples to carry on ceaseless struggles for national liberation from the yoke of both Western and Japanese imperialism. By this policy the Bolsheviks hoped not only to inflict heavy blows upon their capitalist enemies and to soften them for the ultimate *coup de grâce* by revolutionary Communism but also to cater to the aspirations for national independence of revolutionaries throughout Asia. These tactics of Communist support of nationalist movements, whether bourgeois or proletarian, to the end that they be "captured" and diverted at the propitious moment along a Communist line, were pursued in Asia and elsewhere for many years thereafter.

[3] *Der Erste Kongress der kommunistischen und revolutionären Organisationen des Fernen Ostens, Moskau, Januar 1922,* Hamburg, 1922, pp. 12-13, gives a detailed breakdown of the various delegations and participants. See also Eudin and North, *op.cit.,* p. 145.

Once the ceremonial requirements had been disposed of, the members of the Congress buckled down to the serious analysis of the tasks of revolution in Asia. In the Japan section Katayama himself presented one of the major reports on political, economic, and labor conditions in his home land.[4] In his typically dull and dry style he recapitulated the history of the growth of capitalism and authoritarianism in modern Japan, laying the groundwork for a program of revolutionary action. His concluding note was in complete accord with the primary aim of the Comintern. "The task of the Japanese proletariat is for the present," he trumpeted, "to construct, together with the toiling masses of other lands in the Far East, a plan for a common struggle against the imperialists. . . ."[5]

For Katayama and his Japanese comrades the First Congress of the Toilers of the Far East was an exhilarating event. Especially pleasing to them was the firm acknowledgment of the Comintern, set forth in the final resolution of the proceedings, of the indispensable role of the Japanese proletariat in leading the epochal struggle against the forces of imperialism in the East. "There is no issue without Japan," Zinoviev bluntly declared. "The Japanese proletariat holds in its hands the key to the solution of the Far Eastern question."[6] This was not mere flattery by the Bolsheviks. Uninformed as they may have been about details of political and economic conditions in Katayama's native land, they knew that Japan was the most highly industrialized nation in Asia. The support of her working class was held essential to the victory of the socialist revolution.

Recognition by the Comintern of Japan's role in forwarding the cause of revolution in Asia also underscored the urgent need to bring a Communist Party into being in Japan itself. The continued failures of Japanese revolutionary leaders was

[4] *Der Erste Kongress*, pp. 71ff. [5] *ibid.*, p. 77.

[6] Swearingen and Langer, *op.cit.*, p. 13. See also Eudin and North, *op.cit.*, p. 224, for a slightly different wording.

in this respect somewhat awkward. While Katayama and his comrades had made little or no progress toward the realization of this basic objective, both the Chinese and Koreans had already founded working party organizations. During and after the Congress the formation of a Japan Communist Party was given the most serious attention.

Shortly after the Congress came to an end, about half the members of the Japanese delegation left for home.[7] Great hope was placed in two newcomers, Takase Kiyoshi and Tokuda Kyūichi, whose promise as revolutionary leaders had made a strong impression upon Katayama and the Comintern chiefs. But when the Japanese group finally reached Tokyo after an arduous and nerve-wracking journey, they discovered to their dismay that the political situation had drastically changed since their departure in the fall of the previous year. The police authorities, infuriated by the open agitation for the withdrawal of Japanese troops from Siberia, had at last taken stern measures to break up the Communistic band believed responsible. Kondō Eizō himself had been arrested and sentenced to jail. To launch a Japan Communist Party it was now necessary to start afresh.

Takase and Tokuda were no disappointment to their comrades in far-away Moscow. In response to their assignment they scurried about, seeking to rally diverse left-wing elements by giving assurance of Comintern support for a revolutionary movement. An organizational break-through was finally achieved when such eminent veterans as Sakai Toshihiko, Arahata Kanson, and Yamakawa Hitoshi were induced to take the lead. On July 5, 1922, the decisive step was taken when

[7] When the Congress ended, Katayama published his impressions of the gathering. See Sen Katayama, "The First Congress of Communist and Revolutionary Organizations of the Far East," *International Press Correspondence,* II, no. 15 (February 24, 1922), pp. 105-106. For the recollections of Watanabe Haruo, see his *Katayama Sen to Tomo ni,* Tokyo, 1955, pp. 110ff., and also his *Nihon Marukusu Shugi Undō no Reimei,* Tokyo, 1957, pp. 160ff. Note too the remarks of Suzuki Mosaburō, *Aru Shakai Shugi-sha no Hansei,* Tokyo, 1958, pp. 121-129.

the Japan Communist Party was established at a secret meeting in Tokyo.[8]

While his friends pushed ahead with the revolutionary movement at home, Katayama had a full stint of political work blocked out for him by the Comintern.[9] During the remaining months of 1922 he was frequently on the move. At the beginning of April he traveled to Berlin as a member of a Comintern delegation to an international congress. There an attempt was made to promote unity within the splintered ranks of revolutionary socialism.[10] Shortly thereafter he undertook the long trek to Chita in the Soviet East in order to revivify the propaganda campaign against Japanese interventionist troops. To the Soviet regime this was a critical assignment, for as long as Japanese military forces continued to remain in eastern Siberia and north Manchuria, it was impossible for the Bolsheviks to consolidate their hold upon Asiatic Russia.[11] Though there is no indication that Katayama's efforts were even moderately successful, the Japanese government began the evacuation of its expedition in the winter of 1922-1923. But not until two years later were Soviet Russia and Japan to conclude a treaty settling their outstanding differences.

These political sorties of Katayama, which were coupled

[8] Ichinose Masayuki, *Nihon Kyōsan-tō*, Tokyo, 1955, pp. 46-47; and Ichikawa Masaichi, *Nihon Kyōsan-tō Tōsō Shōshi*, Tokyo, 1955, pp. 69-71.

[9] For all the kudos that came his way and for all his busy assignments, Katayama was pathetically lonely in Moscow. He continued to long after "faces" from home and for the intimacies of family life. Note the remarks of John Murphy, *New Horizons* (London, 1941), p. 239.

[10] This was the abortive Berlin Conference of the International Union of Socialist Parties designed to unite the Second, Two-and-a-Half, and Third Internationals. See Jane Degras, ed. *The Communist International, 1919-1943: Documents*, 2 vols., London, 1956-1960, I, pp. 209, 337; and Kishimoto Eitarō *et al.*, *Katayama Sen*, 2 vols., Tokyo, 1959-1960, II, pp. 244-245.

[11] For his propaganda approach note Sen Katayama, "To the Soldiers of the Japanese Army in Siberia," *International Press Conference*, II, no. 45 (June 7, 1922), p. 338.

with the preparation of numerous articles and reports for the publications of the Comintern, were in a way preliminary to a much larger undertaking. Since progress was being made in the founding of new parties in Asian countries, the Comintern looked forward with eager expectation to its Fourth Congress, which was to open in Moscow in November. It was planned to use the occasion not only for a review of the political situations in the colonial countries of Asia and Africa but, more specifically, for the development of concrete programs of revolutionary action.

The Fourth Congress of the Communist International was a great moment in Katayama's life. At this time the delegation from Japan, led by Takase, formally applied for and received recognition of the recently founded Japan Communist Party.[12] It now became an integral member of the Communist International in good standing. After discussions with Katayama and other Comintern leaders the Takase group was instructed to draw up a detailed program of Party objectives upon its return to Tokyo. The Japan Communist Party was well on the way to becoming a functioning rather than a mere "paper" organization.

The Comintern cannot but have been deeply pleased by the speed with which the newborn Japan Communist Party acted to execute its orders. During the winter of 1922-1923 the directors of the still minuscule group, meeting in frequent sessions, quickly formulated regulations for the governance of the Party as well as a program of basic political aims. The statement, which was finally adopted at a meeting of the Party in March and subsequently approved by the Comintern, was sweeping in its demands. The Communists called, first of all, for the abolition of the Japanese monarchy and the imperial army as well as for the disbandment of the hated secret police systems. They demanded the confiscation of large landed estates and their redistribution to the poverty-stricken peasants.

[12] Ichinose, *op.cit.*, p. 48.

Finally, the Japanese Communists cried out for diplomatic recognition of the Soviet regime and for the withdrawal of all Japanese military forces from the Asian continent, Formosa, and Sakhalin.[13]

In their initial statement of objectives the founding fathers of the Japan Communist Party revealed themselves as consummate theoreticians but inept revolutionaries. If they hoped that their sweeping demands would give their movement a distinctive character and set it apart from other radical political groups, they surely did not fail. But there is little doubt that in their ultra-radicalism the pioneer Japanese Communists grossly misjudged the temper of the times and committed themselves to a political position which left them little free play to exploit such revolutionary opportunities as existed in Japan. This fatal weakness of subordinating political reality to the imperatives of theory was on many occasions in the future to cause serious dissension and defections from the Party.

In the spring of 1923 it was perhaps not unreasonable to assume that the Japanese people were ready to support drastic changes in the way of life that had been evolving at a rapid pace since the momentous days of the Meiji Restoration. At every hand there were unmistakable signs of social and intellectual grievance. In such great urban centers as Tokyo, Yokohama, Nagoya, Kyoto, Osaka, and Kobe clashes between industry and labor had become chronic. Industrial workers, plagued by the persistently high cost of living, needed no strong urging to defy the state by precipitating strikes. Though the number of work stoppages had declined from the record peak attained in 1919, in each of the following years of the Taishō era (1912-1925) almost as many strikes occurred annually as during the entire final two decades of the Meiji

[13] Nihon Kyōsan-tō Shi Shiryō Iin-kai, *Kominterun Nihon Mondai ni Kan-suru Hōshin-sho Ketsugi-shū*, Tokyo, 1955, pp. 9-10. See also Swearingen and Langer, *op.cit.*, pp. 16-17.

period. There were, moreover, no grounds for belief that the incidence of labor protest would soon abate.

In addition to being disturbed by the continued militancy of industrial workers, the Japanese government had good cause to be annoyed by the strident clamor for reform raised by social critics in academic life. On the campuses of the imperial and leading private universities resolute professors and students daily flaunted the state authorities by organizing clubs and launching journals to attack the policies of their unenlightened government. Many of these associations made no attempt to conceal their democratic, Marxist, or anarchist leanings. Denunciation of political and societal conditions filled the columns of the nation's press, while the younger generation in the larger cities and towns uninhibitedly demonstrated its rejection of outmoded traditions and customs. The Japanese state, it seemed, was at last being called upon to pay for its feverish drive toward modernization and world power.[14]

Katayama and many of the functionaries of the Comintern were not alone in being deceived by the shape of affairs in Japan. Many Japanese themselves, not to speak of experienced foreign commentators, were quick to conclude that the sharpening political consciousness of the intellectual élite and the working classes heralded happier conditions. Still others detected in the unprecedented outburst of radicalism the impending destruction of what was for them a satisfactory social order. But their ill-founded fears were perhaps as unjustified as the glowing hopes of the irreconcilable foes of the prevailing system.

The tasks faced by the Communist Party in Japan were fundamentally different from those confronting revolutionaries in almost all other countries in Asia. Though the fact of Japan's "special characteristics" was recognized by the Communists,

[14] For an excellent portrayal of this period Chitoshi Yanaga, *Japan since Perry*, New York, 1949, ch. 31, is excellent. Note also A. Morgan Young, *Japan under Taisho Tenno, 1912-1926*, London, 1928, pp. 279-286.

they did not know how to adjust to its implications. Of pivotal importance was Japan's unique history and ideological heritage. Just about every other people in the East was more or less subject to the influences or control of imperialist power. In these lands efforts for political and social change were preponderantly nationalistic and such radical movements as existed were strongly inspired by moderate Western thought and example. Both reformers and revolutionaries were engaged primarily in campaigns for self-government or independence and were on the whole content to settle for the political and social rights conventional in advanced Western societies. Whether they cooperated or competed with these nationalistic groups, Communists could always hope to make political capital by joining in the fight for emancipation from imperial hegemony.

The problem of Communists in Japan was radically different. Japan was not only an independent state, in full control of her sovereign powers, but also possessed an overseas domain of impressive proportions. The nationalistic sentiments of the people were, consequently, as susceptible to exploitation by the state and established political parties as by their implacable enemies on the left. In the late Taishō as well as during the following Showa era nationalism was, as a matter of fact, a more powerful weapon for conservatism than for radicalism. Furthermore, though the "logic" of Communist theory may have necessitated a pledge to abolish the Emperor-system, it was, from the point of view of practical politics, completely rash. The Japanese masses had no quarrel with their sovereign nor with the monarchical system of government. To call for their destruction was as politically indiscreet as to agitate for the elimination of marriage and the family. But, more important, no political proposal could have been better calculated to inflame the state authorities against the Communists than their treasonous proposition that the institution of the Emperor be jettisoned.[15] It was an open summons to repression. Finally, the Communist insistence upon the liquidation of the Japanese Empire was doubtless premature. There was at the time no popular distaste for the maintenance of the overseas colonial domains and little willingness to discard them. The Empire, on the contrary, was a source of deep national pride.

Furthermore, as opposed to the situation in almost all countries in Asia, Katayama's comrades in Japan found themselves arrayed against unusually powerful forces of opposition. The conservative political factions, strongly entrenched in the state and confident of massive backing from businessmen, bureaucrats, landholders, and peasants, could not easily be routed from their positions of dominance. Though they may have been willing to make minor concessions to the advocates of reform, they showed no intention of slackening their grasp upon the reins of power. As for the liberal and democratic leaders, their call for moderate reform was sufficiently attractive to numerous intellectuals and workers to reduce the political inroads the Communists might otherwise have made into these classes. And further to complicate the Communist task was the existence of a broad variety of proletarian organizations of socialistic persuasion. Holding down the political left and led by men of firm convictions they were to refuse, then and later, to accept a role subordinate to that of Communist interlopers supported by an alien power. Whether united or fragmented, these socialist groups were always too strong to be captured or crushed by the Comintern wing in Japan.

Whatever the prospects of the Japan Communist Party may have been, it was soon demonstrated that their very existence would not be tolerated by the state. As trade-union organizers, socialists, Communists, and anarchists stepped up the pace of

[15] The political delicacy of this issue was recognized by the founding fathers of the Party; it gave rise to endless debate. See especially the remarks of Ichinose, *op.cit.*, p. 51.

their activities in the spring of 1923, they were kept under the watchful eye of the police. In June the first of several crushing blows was struck at the radical movement. In a lightning raid, carried out with thoroughness, more than a hundred political, labor, and student leaders were arrested. Particularly hard hit by the coup was the Japan Communist Party, many of whose leaders continued to languish in prison months after the other seditious suspects had been released.[16]

Katayama's cohorts in Japan had no opportunity to recover from the shock of the police raids. The crisis in the Communist Party was, in fact, greatly intensified at the end of the summer. In September the huge metropolitan area of Tokyo was hit by a catastrophic earthquake. Amidst the widespread confusion and horror a disgraceful outrage, utterly senseless in its purposes, was perpetrated. Seeking a scapegoat for their passions and despair, roving mobs proceeded to attack and massacre the equally dazed Korean immigrants in the city, accusing them of looting, arson, and other heinous crimes. Perhaps the only Japanese in Tokyo not entirely befuddled by the turmoil were the police, who seized the chance to strike at the radical leaders again.

The police assaults of September 1923 literally crippled the fledgling Communist Party. With the exception of those leaders who were out of the country, barely a Communist of note escaped the political dragnet. "By this time," as has been aptly remarked, "a Party convention might well have been held at Ichigaya prison in Tokyo where . . . most of the important Communists had taken up forced residence. What was left could scarcely be called a Party."[17]

Not only were the Communists paralyzed by the new attacks, but, in the uproar of the disaster, ten trade-union organizers were seized by the swift-moving police and executed.

[16] Watanabe Kango, *Nihon Shakai Undō-shi*, Tokyo, 1955, p. 122; Sekine Etsurō, *Rōdō Undō Musan Seitō-shi*, Tokyo, 1954, pp. 95-96; Ichikawa, *op.cit.*, pp. 81-82.

[17] Swearingen and Langer, *op.cit.*, pp. 19-20.

No act of police sadism, however, exceeded in its brutality the slaying of Ōsugi Sakae, the renowned disciple of Kōtoku Shūsui. Arrested but a few months after his return from a European journey, the anarchist leader was cold-bloodedly strangled to death in his prison cell by a military police officer.[18] Radicals in Japan, chilled with horror by these events, were completely stripped of their remaining illusions about the nature of their "class enemies."

News of the debacle in Japan was slow in reaching the Communist high command in Moscow. Communications between Tokyo and the Russian capital were rather circuitous and couriers usually required a month and more to make the long trip in either direction. Not until late in 1923 did information about the repression and arrests of the Japanese Communists begin to reach Katayama and the Comintern. And still several more months elapsed before a complete report of the defeat and its even more alarming aftermath became available.

As a result of the arrests in the previous summer and early fall the ardor of many of the Japanese Communist leaders for Bolshevik-style revolution had quickly cooled. Overwhelmed by fear and discouragement, they had also begun to question the very need for the existence of a Communist Party in Japan. During the winter of 1923-1924 heated arguments were waged over the issue; Arahata Kanson, who had but recently returned from a tour of Soviet Russia, found himself almost alone in opposition to the main trend.[19] Finally in March the "dissolutionists," led by Sakai and Yamakawa, had their way, voting to liquidate the Party.[20] This was an extraordinary

[18] The brutal crime was compounded by the murder of Ōsugi's wife and nephew a few minutes later. Uemura Tai, "Ōsugi Sakae no Shisō to Shōgai," in Yasuda Tokutarō *et al.*, *Hikari wo Ageta Hito-bito*, Tokyo, 1956, p. 48; the details are given in A. Morgan Young, *op.cit.*, pp. 300-301.

[19] Arahata Kanson, *Kyōsan-tō wo Meguru Hito-bito*, Tokyo, 1950, pp. 42-46, presents a detailed account of the controversy.

[20] Ichikawa, *op.cit.*, pp. 84-85; and Ichinose, *op.cit.*, p. 55.

action, perhaps the only one of its type in the history of the Third International.

The disbandment of the Japan Communist Party took place at a most awkward moment for the Comintern. After having publicized the founding of the Party at the Fourth Congress, it may be easily understood that a report of its demise at the Fifth Congress, which was to be held in June, would have placed the Comintern in a foolish light. It is also possible that Bolshevik leaders, anxious to stress the line of a mounting wave of revolution in the East, were reluctant to acknowledge a contradictory development of major importance. To cope with the crisis in Japan a grim game of political make-believe was thus played. No announcement of the failure in Japan nor of the dissolution of the Japan Communist Party was made to the delegates at the Congress.[21] But realizing that some statement had to be made, since silence might well have aroused uneasiness, Katayama reported that the revolutionary movement in his home land was progressing satisfactorily.[22] His pretense was surely not the wishful thinking of a perennial optimist or of an aging revolutionary living in a world of dreams; it was conscious and premeditated deception.

At the very time that a cheerful front was being presented before the Congress, a special committee of the Comintern was meeting in private session to deal with the emergency in Japan. The report of the Japan Communist Party was not only rejected by the group but was strongly rebutted by the Japanese delegates to the Congress, Sano Manabu, Kondō Eizō, and Katayama. Refusing to accept as an accomplished fact the suspension of the Party agreed upon by a majority of its members, the committee decided instead to press for its rejuvenation. Finally, in November, Sano was instructed to return to Shanghai with Voitinski, Chief of the Comintern's

[21] Degras, *op.cit.*, II, p. 92.

[22] Swearingen and Langer, *op.cit.*, p. 20. Note also the statements of Katayama and Comintern leaders as quoted in Eudin and North, *op.cit.*, p. 275.

Far Eastern Bureau.[23] There, safe from the intrusions of the police, a concerted effort was made to revitalize the defunct branch of the Party in Japan.

In January 1925 a secret meeting of Japanese Communist leaders was held in Shanghai. In addition to Voitinski, Sano, and Heller, Chief of the Far Eastern Bureau of the Profintern, Arahata, Tokuda, Sano Fumio, and Aono Suekichi were present. Since none of these leaders had been in favor of the dissolution of the Party in the preceding year, an admission that the action had been an error was easily extracted by the Comintern representative.[24] In the next few days a new strategy for the Communist movement in Japan, the so-called Shanghai Thesis, was drawn up.[25] Its most significant feature was the recognition of the vital need to recruit workers into the Communist ranks and to involve them in posts of leadership. It is most likely that Katayama and the Comintern were responsible for this remedy for the ailing revolutionary movement which had not only been dominated but had mainly been composed of intelligentsia since its birth.

For all its urging and prodding the Comintern was unable to reactivate the Party in Japan. The crises, reverses, and defections that had wracked Katayama's comrades in Tokyo since the unforgettable summer of 1923 continued to recur for months after the Shanghai meeting. When Sakai Toshihiko had abandoned the Party after the disaster and returned to the socialist camp and Yamakawa had at the same time become a "right-wing deviationist" by shifting his activities to trade-union organization and parliamentarism, it had been a bitter pill for Communists to swallow. And now, after the Shanghai meeting came to a close, the "Group" was stunned by the desertion of Sano Fumio and Aono who balked at the

[23] Ichinose, *op.cit.,* p. 56.

[24] Eudin and North, *op.cit.,* p. 276; Arahata, *op.cit.,* pp. 47-48; and Ichinose, *op.cit.,* p. 56.

[25] For text see Eudin and North, *op.cit.,* p. 334.

ultra-radicalism of their fellow revolutionaries.[26] In the following months and years the defections from Communism in Japan were perhaps exceeded only in the equally unstable movement in the United States.

Arahata, Tokuda, and the other delegates had no sooner returned from the meeting in China when a new problem for the Communists arose in Japan. Alarmed by the growing strength of organized labor and by the spread of "dangerous thoughts," the government acted to toughen its police powers. In April a new Public Peace Preservation Law, passed by the National Diet, made it very clear by its warning of stern penalties for violators that the state would not stand by idly and permit radicals of any hue to agitate for the alteration or subversion of the public order and the national polity. Apart from causing the Communist Group to watch its very step and to move about in utmost secrecy, with consequent reduction in its political effectiveness, the legislation also forced the non-Communist left to adopt more moderate tactics in the political and labor fields. To defy the state, radicals soberly realized, was to court personal and organizational disaster.

The ominous Public Peace Preservation Law did not cause dismay among all Japanese Communists. On the contrary, some of them were further confirmed in their conviction that in a nation like Japan it was necessary for revolutionaries to work along secret and conspiratorial lines. But a dilemma was created when, on May 5, 1925, equally momentous legislation of the Diet came into effect. The introduction of universal suffrage was, with all its limitations notwithstanding, a political milestone in modern Japanese history. The number of qualified male voters was quadrupled, more than 10,000,000 subjects of the Emperor now receiving the franchise.[27] Whether the

[26] It is not always possible to determine precisely when Japanese revolutionaries decided to leave the Party and when, on the other hand, they were formally expelled.

[27] For discussion of the Universal Suffrage Law see Yanaga, *op.cit.*, pp. 405-406, and Hugh Borton, *Japan's Modern Century*, New York,

liberal, democratic, and socialist forces in Japan were strengthened by the suffrage bill is arguable, for it cannot be denied that the measure, a species of "Tory democracy," immeasurably reinforced the conservative political parties whose governments thereafter enjoyed a semblance of popular approval. Still, faith in parliamentarism and in open and legal competition for political power was, for a while at least, reaffirmed among the moderate democratic and socialistic groups. Communists, however, whose extremist program was anathema to the police, could not easily campaign for political support among the masses without exposing themselves to instant retaliation by the state. Theirs was an impossible position, and almost two years passed after the conclusion of the Shanghai conclave before the Japan Communist Party was at last reorganized.

To Katayama, who was far removed from the actual scene, the flounderings of the Communist leaders in Tokyo were as incomprehensible as the collapse of the Party was intolerable. Shortly after the Fifth Congress was terminated, he decided to take a close look at the entire revolutionary situation in the Far East. Accordingly, in the late fall, after a long vacation in the Caucasus Mountains in the company of Kondō, he set out for Vladivostok where he boarded a Russian ship for Shanghai. Though Katayama had a major hand in shaping the Shanghai Thesis, it does not seem that he personally participated in the deliberations. From Shanghai Kondō slipped into Japan to carry out a secret survey of the political and labor situation. Katayama went on to Nanking, which about three years later became the capital of the national revolutionary government of Chiang Kai-shek.[28]

Though he was primarily interested in the course of affairs

1955, p. 309. Yanaga indicates that the number of voters was increased from 3,300,000 to 14,000,000, while Borton states that the increase was from 3,000,000 to 13,000,000.

[28] Kishimoto *et al.*, *op.cit.*, II, pp. 285, 405.

in Japan, Katayama, as a high-ranking member of the Comintern, was also deeply concerned with developments in China and Korea. In the chaotic Republic of China the national revolutionary movement of Sun Yat-sen, in which the Comintern had a direct and heavy stake, was rapidly gathering momentum. Since the beginning of 1923, when the historical Sun-Joffe Agreement had been concluded, Soviet Russia had not only thrown the support of the Chinese Communist Party behind the "bourgeois" Kuomintang but had also provided the national revolutionaries with vitally needed technical and financial assistance. On the occasion of Katayama's arrival in China Michael Borodin, the Bolshevik agitator who had preceded him in revolutionary Mexico several years before, had been installed as one of the principal advisers to Sun. Members of the Chinese Communist Party, such as Mao Tse-tung and Chou En-lai, had also succeeded in securing key positions in the Kuomintang organization.

While Katayama did not make the trip to the headquarters of the Kuomintang at Canton in the far south, by traveling through many of the large cities in the Yangtze River area and in north China he was able to observe at firsthand the intensity of revolutionary fervor. There was no need for him to search for the social phenomena he wanted to see. On every side there was visible evidence of bitter hostility toward foreign capitalism and imperialism. That the defiant mood of workers was not a passing one was dramatically revealed in January by the stormy strike of textile workers in Shanghai against their foreign employers. During the following weeks and months industrial-labor disputes, political demonstrations, and clashes with police and troops continued uninterruptedly. Before Katayama left for Soviet Russia in March, traveling via Pukow, Tientsin, Peking, and then westward across Outer Mongolia, he had seen enough to convince him that the swelling revolution in China could not be checked.

The journey through China and Mongolia was a memorable adventure for Katayama and he took an almost boyish delight in recounting his experiences to his friends. But his mission had had a much more serious purpose which he had not for a moment failed to remember. Appraising revolutionary conditions in the Far East, he could not help but draw a comparison between the situations in China and his homeland. "The Communists in China today," he wrote, "present an appearance quite different from the so-called leaders of Communism in Japan. The former have the solid backing of the workers and peasants (of Kwangtung). . . . The labor movement in China is more steadfast than the Japanese and the Chinese workers are more strongly united. There are fewer instances among them of betrayal and scabbing."[29] Whether this comparison was either fair or correct is beside the point. But what may be surmised is that Katayama's disappointment in the proletarian revolutionary movement in Japan was much deeper than he cared to admit publicly.

For all his mixed feelings in the spring of 1925 Katayama was not completely discouraged. Following his return from China he resumed his efforts to regenerate the Communist movement in his homeland. For a brief while it seemed that the tactics set forth in the Shanghai Thesis, emphasizing the need for closer Communist liaison with the working class, were being proved correct. Communist agitators were making satisfactory headway in the labor movement and their influence was growing daily. But if they had reason to be enthusiastic about their repeated successes, their maneuvers had not gone unnoticed.

The new obstacles raised in the path of the Japanese Communists were created not simply by a hostile state armed with wider repressive powers than ever before but, more significantly, by antagonistic political and labor groups

[29] Quoted in *ibid.*, p. 286.

on the left. Sobered by the police attacks before and during the Great Earthquake, trade-unions and other proletarian organizations had acted quickly to curb the extreme radicals in their midst. Perhaps the most important shift to a policy of restraint was initiated by the *Dai Nihon Rōdō Sōdōmei* (General Federation of Labor) the nation's largest and most influential trade-union. Founded by Suzuki Bunji shortly after the end of World War I as a successor to the fraternal *Yūai-kai*, it had for several years upheld a radical and militant line. When the police authorities bore down upon leftist political and labor leaders in 1923, Suzuki and his supporters shortly thereafter recaptured control of the *Sōdōmei*. By early 1925, at the very time the Shanghai Thesis was being drawn up, the Suzuki faction was again firmly in power.[30]

At the Shanghai meeting of the revolutionary leaders it had not been considered too late to strive for the diversion of the *Sōdōmei* to an extreme leftist position. But by the time the Communists were ready to implement their plans they received a jolting blow. In May Suzuki and his moderate backers, determined to rid their federation of Communists and fellow travelers, took steps to expel the constituent trade-unions which were opposed to the policies of the majority.[31] The purged minority responded by establishing a competitive organization, the *Nihon Rōdō Kumiai Hyōgi-kai* (Japan Labor Union Council).[32] In the following October a small number of trade-unions, which had resisted the expulsion of the leftist elements but refused to join the new *Hyōgi-kai*, withdrew from the *Sōdōmei* and set up a third federation. The ranks of organized labor had been sharply and irretrievably divided.

[30] On the struggle within *Sōdōmei* see Kishimoto Eitarō, *Nihon Rōdō Undō-shi*, Tokyo, 1953, pp. 166-167; and Watanabe Kango, *Nihon Shakai Undō-shi*, pp. 79-80.

[31] Kishimoto, *op.cit.*, p. 180.

[32] Taniguchi Zentarō, *Nihon Rōdō Kumiai Hyōgi-kai Shi*, 2 vols., Tokyo, 1953-1954, I, p. 90; Hosotani Matsuta, *Nihon Rōdō Undō-shi*, 2 vols., Tokyo, 1948-1949, I, pp. 174-175; and Kishimoto, *op.cit.*, p. 180.

It is problematical whether the *Hyōgi-kai* was ever completely under the domination of the Communists. Yet because of its radical platforms, slogans, and behavior this trade-union federation with more than ten thousand members was frequently indistinguishable from a Communist organization. Its very existence as a separate entity in the world of leftist politics and labor was, nevertheless, a continuing source of worry to Katayama and the Comintern. However pleased they might otherwise have been to secure the sympathy and support of so many industrial workers, the cleavage in the forces of labor along distinctive ideological lines seemed to augur serious trouble for Communists determined to dominate and lead the labor movement. As long as other poles of attraction existed for the worker, it was realized that the Communist deployment on the political front would be severely impeded.

The implications of the split in the camp of organized labor became disturbingly apparent during the remaining months of 1925. With the introduction of universal manhood suffrage in the spring all opponents of the prevailing social order and political system had to review their methods. For the first time since the establishment of parliamentary government in 1890 the competition for political power had ostensibly been thrown wide open and critics of the state were given an opportunity, within the restrictions of the Public Peace Preservation Law, to make a bid for popular favor. With the unprecedented chance to present alternative choices to government policy, the leaders of intellectual, proletarian, and peasant groups now had to prepare to enter the arena of everyday politics.

The birth of Japan's proletarian parties had been foreshadowed as early as 1924. In anticipation of the passage of a universal suffrage bill the *Seiji Kenkyū-kai* (Association for the Study of Politics) had been organized in June. Headed by prominent socialists of different shades, the society prepared to lend its services to the formation of new political parties when the proper moment arrived.[33] More directly involved than the *Seiji Kenkyū-kai* in the swelling movement for mass political action was the *Nihon Nōmin Kumiai* (Japan Farmers' Union) which committed itself in July to the foundation of a political party to challenge the uncontested hold of conservatives upon local offices. By the time the suffrage bill had been passed the Farmers' Union, broadening its objectives, began to urge the formation of a united front with urban labor. The result of its efforts was the abortive Farmer-Labor Party. Organized on December 1, it was suppressed by the state on the very same day.[34] With this blunt warning the government of Katō Takaaki announced that it would not tolerate the existence of a political party with Communist leanings.

The non-Communist left struggled grimly for the next several years to create a viable proletarian party to represent the interests of workers and peasants. Its lack of success really mirrors the tragedy of the fight for responsible government in Japan during the so-called liberal twenties. With the omnipresent threat of repression constantly hanging over their heads, with the danger of Communist infiltration into their ranks constantly to be guarded against, and with their unfortunate propensity for ideological wrangling, the proletarian leaders were doomed to failure in their attempts to promote urgently needed reform. Unable to compose their differences and to combine at a time when only unity would have sufficed, they lost whatever slim chance they may have had to alter the balance of political forces within Japan.

The stirrings of the "masses" in Japan were followed with avid interest by the Comintern. Despite the disappointments in the trade-union field, Katayama and other Comintern

[33] Susuki Shigeto, "Seiji Kenkyū-kai no Rekishi-teki Nimmu," in *Nihon Shakai Shugi Undō-shi, Shakai Kagaku* (Special Issue), IV, no. 1 (February 1928), pp. 316-317.

[34] Yanaga, *op.cit.*, pp. 476-477.

strategists were convinced that opportunities for the extension of Communist influence were more promising than in many years. There were, however, a few outstanding issues that had to be resolved before the political situation could be fruitfully exploited. Not only were the Communist leaders still unable to reconstruct the Party but they had to contend with both left and right deviationist trends. The influence of Yamakawa, whose activity was concentrated upon the trade-unions, had to be countered and the ultra-radicalism of the rising theoretician, Fukumoto Kazuo, had to be curbed. Few as the Communists and their sympathizers were, they were in danger of being split into quarrelsome factions.

Fukumoto Kazuo was an archetype of the political theorists who have from time to time stormed into and bemused the world of Japanese radical intelligentsia. Having graduated from Tokyo Imperial University, where he had specialized in political science and economics, he was well versed in the writings of Marx and Lenin. In 1925, after he returned from a study tour abroad, during which he had joined the Communist Party in Germany, he launched his meteoric, if tragic, career as a theoretician.[35] Even if his principal conclusions were occasionally silly, he was a refreshing change from the generality of Communists who parroted Comintern phraseology. A prolific writer, he was immensely popular among academics and university students, by whom he was hailed as the new messiah of Bolshevism.

Had there existed a well-disciplined Party in Japan in 1925 and 1926, the young Fukumoto would have been quickly whipped into line. But Japanese Communists had been invariably frustrated in their attempts to resurrect their Party since the days of the Shanghai meeting. And at the time that Fukumoto was dazzling the extreme left with his

[35] Brief biographical sketches of Fukumoto will be found in Evelyn S. Colbert, *The Left Wing in Japanese Politics*, New York, 1952, p. 306; Swearingen and Langer, *op.cit.*, p. 25; and Eudin and North, *op.cit.*, p. 459.

polemical treatises, Arahata, Tokuda, Nozaka Sanzō, and several other die-hard leaders were cooling their heels in prison. His unorthodox ideas notwithstanding, the young professor succeeded, almost single-handedly, in revivifying the dormant Communist movement. By the summer of 1926 he had emerged as one of its acknowledged spokesmen.[36]

The Comintern, dejected as it was by the lamentable state of Communist affairs in Japan, could not even view Fukumoto as a mixed blessing. When everything possible had been said in his favor, the inescapable fact remained that his theories were contrary to the official thesis on Japan. According to the Comintern, Katayama's native land, ruled by a combination of "feudalistic landlords and monopoly capitalists" operating through the reactionary Emperor-system, had not as yet entered into an advanced stage of capitalist development. Since the necessary conditions for a socialist revolution were not extant, it was stipulated that a bourgeois-democratic revolution had first to be achieved. The task of the Communist Party was to aid in the attainment of this goal. Fukumoto, however, sought to "prove" that a mature capitalistic system existed in Japan and that Communists could aim immediately for a socialist revolution. From the point of view of the Comintern, this was ultra-leftism which could only lead to rash action setting back the entire Communist movement.

The heavy influence of "Fukumotoism" was brought home to the Comintern at the end of 1926. After very careful preparations a small number of Communists gathered together on December 4-5 at the remote hot-springs resort of Goshiki in Yamagata Prefecture in northern Honshu.[37] This secret conclave was actually the Third Congress of the Japanese Communists. In their hideout the assembled Communist

[36] See Koyama Hirotake, *Nihon Marukusu Shugi-shi,* Tokyo, 1956, pp. 28-29.
[37] Swearingen and Langer, *op.cit.,* pp. 25-26.

leaders formally reconstituted the Party and drew up a platform of thirteen planks. After more than two and a half years of fumbling and drifting the Communist movement had at last been given new body and direction.[38]

The elation of the Comintern over the decisive action in Japan may easily be understood. But its alarm at the ramifications of "Fukumotoism" upon Party tactics was shared by several older members who feared that the Party would soon be isolated from the proletarian and peasant masses. The anti-Fukumoto group stubbornly protested against an outlook which might have meant abandoning the potentially strong support of workers, peasants, and intellectuals to the non-Communist trade-unions, farmer-unions, study associations, and proletarian parties. Since so critical a dispute could obviously not be settled locally, Fukumoto and six other Communist leaders were called to Moscow in early 1927.[39] There the ideological deviationism within the Japanese movement was taken under study by a special committee of the Comintern. The result was foregone. After Fukumoto was subjected to relentless pressure and forced to confess the error of his thinking, a detailed report on the situation in Japan was prepared.[40] Later ratified by the Praesidium of the Comintern on July 15, this report, known as the "1927 Thesis," remained the official line until its modification in 1931.

In the thesis on Japan, set down by the Comintern in 1927, attention was first focused upon Japanese imperialism which, together with British and American imperialism, was deemed to be an immediate threat to both the Chinese Revolution and the Soviet Union. In Japan itself it was held there existed "the objective prerequisites both for a bour-

[38] Ichinose, *op.cit.*, p. 60.

[39] *ibid.*, p. 60: Kishimoto *et al.*, II, p. 302.

[40] For the 1927 Thesis, see Nihon Kyōsan-tō Shi Shiryō Iin-kai, *op.cit.*, pp. 12ff. See also Eudin and North, *op.cit.*, pp. 338-339, for pertinent extracts.

geois-democratic revolution . . . and for its transformation into a socialist revolution. . . ."[41] It was recognized, however, that "a tremendous obstacle and barrier is provided by [Japan's] ideological backwardness. . . . Neither the Japanese proletariat nor the peasantry have revolutionary traditions or experience of struggle. . . ."[42] The responsibility of the Japan Communist Party was therefore to harness the revolutionary power of the proletariat, peasantry, and urban petty bourgeoisie and to make this coalition "organizationally operative." Rejecting the deviationist and opportunistic tactics of both Yamakawa and Fukumoto, the Comintern stressed that "without an independent, ideologically tested, disciplined, and centralized mass communist party there cannot be a victorious revolutionary movement."[43] And apart from singling out the feudalistic landlords and monopoly capitalists as the principal class opponents of a bourgeois-democratic revolution, it was stoutly affirmed that the "communist party can develop only by fighting social-democracy," meaning the non-cooperative, non-Communist left.

In carrying on its drive for a bourgeois-democratic revolution the Japan Communist Party was instructed to apply "united front tactics." In essence, this entailed the mounting of a broad offensive against the ruling classes but with the express understanding that the Communist Party was to make use of the various mass organizations to fulfill its own objectives. In the struggle, the Comintern warned, the Party "must on no account efface its own features, and in no case yield to the influence of those it is fighting; it must preserve complete independence, ideological and organizational."[44] Having analyzed the situation in Japan and laid down a strategy for the coming contest for power, the Comintern finally set its stamp of approval upon the thirteen-plank pro-

[41] Degras, *op.cit.*, II, p. 397.
[42] *ibid.*, II, p. 397.
[43] *ibid.*, II, p. 399.
[44] *ibid.*, II, p. 400.

gram which had been devised at the Goshiki meeting in the preceding December.

With the Party reestablished and purged of deviationist influences and with its revolutionary strategy and tactics in order the Comintern now looked forward impatiently to the opening of political battle in Japan. For Katayama the campaign could not begin too soon. Aging rapidly and ill with heart disease, he knew that his time was running out.

CHAPTER XVI

NO FURTHER ROADS

During the many years that he lived in Soviet Russia Katayama met many of the leaders of the Japanese Communist movement. Journeying to Moscow as delegates to the periodic congresses of the Communist International or as couriers on special missions, such ranking Communists as Arahata, Sano, Tokuda, Takase, and Kondō spent long hours in discussion with the old campaigner. Being considerably younger than Katayama, these chieftains of Japanese Communism were the *nisei* and, in some cases, the *sansei* of the social revolutionary movement. Though they treated the veteran with deference, they at times found it hard to understand why he was accorded such high status in the brutally competitive world of Communism.

Occasionally silently nursed resentments against Katayama came out into the open. He had had his day and chance, it was bitterly charged. As an expatriate for years on end, it was claimed, he had lost intimate touch with the actual tide of affairs in the land of his birth. Some critics sarcastically asserted that he had never enjoyed a wide repute even during the peak of his prewar career and that he commanded no appreciable following in the Japan of the postwar era. Perhaps the most ungenerous of his Japanese denigrators might have been willing to overlook these shortcomings, had Katayama held a reputation as a social theoretician, probably the only superman recognized by Communist egalitarians. But not even his most devoted admirers, then and since, has ever attributed to him an extraordinary talent for juggling social abstractions.

Katayama's detractors were not completely unjustified in their allegations. Japanese Communists who performed the hard spadework of Party business and ran the perennial risks of arrest and imprisonment frequently found it difficult to appreciate the rationale for the role of leadership assigned to him by the Comintern. They may be excused for not taking very seriously the straight-faced explanation of Comintern officials that he was being rewarded for his many unselfish services to the cause of international socialism prior to and after the Bolshevik Revolution. Never known to be swayed by sentimentality, Lenin and his circle of cynical revolutionaries were more apt to settle political scores than to pay off political debts. If Katayama continued to retain the confidence of the Bolshevik general staff, it was because of eminently practical reasons.

First and foremost, the Comintern esteemed Katayama's loyalty to the international revolutionary movement. Unlike political adventurers who skipped in and out of the revolutionary team he represented neither a calculated risk nor a dangerous gamble. Once he had attached himself to the Communist cause, he had never deviated from the ordained course, shirked an assignment, however hazardous or perfunctory, nor wavered in the execution of his orders. It was accepted that he, too, had personal ambitions but he was never suspected of placing them above the broader aims of the revolution.

Katayama was also respected by the Bolsheviks as an unyielding internationalist. In practical revolutionary terms this meant that he could be counted upon to subordinate the struggle in Japan to the greater goal of bringing about a Communist world. By his labors in the United States, Mexico, China, and in the Comintern at large he had time and again shown his readiness to work for the ends of the international revolution anywhere and everywhere. No other Japanese in the service of the Communist movement was deemed so completely resistant to petty nationalism. Considering the high incidence of "right-wing deviationism" in Japan since the spring of 1923, Katayama's record was unassailable.

With all his evident failings Katayama was more useful to the Comintern than the common run of Communist leaders in Tokyo. Too many of his fellow workers in Japan, intrigued by the problems of revolutionary theory, were indifferent to the day-to-day tasks of revolutionary struggle. Katayama, however, had a rounded background almost unrivaled among the officials as well as the rank and file of the Communist International. As a labor organizer and agitator, propagandist and pamphleteer, courier and "trouble-shooter," he was a splendid example of the professional revolutionary whose classic profile had been sketched by Lenin almost a quarter of a century earlier. Having no other consuming interests or occupation, he had worked under the red flag in study groups, political parties, trade-unions, international congresses, and in the very streets of four continents. In the final analysis he may have been expendable, as the needs of Bolshevism demanded, but he was surely not easily replaceable.

Katayama's reliability was recognized by the Comintern in a somewhat unusual way. Despite the failure of his countrymen to maintain an approved Party during the first five years of his sojourn in Moscow, he was, in effect, granted a permanent position in the Comintern apparatus. After the Third Congress he served as a representative of the Japan Communist Party and at the Fourth Congress, when the Party received official status, he was elected to the Executive Committee of the Comintern (ECCI).[1] At the same time he was also appointed to a seat on the Praesidium; he was the only Asian and the only non-European assigned to this powerful twelve-man standing committee of the Comintern. At the Fifth Congress in 1924 and again at the Sixth Congress

[1] Jane Degras, ed. *The Communist International, 1919-1943: Documents,* 2 vols., London, 1956-1960, I, pp. 454-455. The only other Asian elected to membership in the ECCI but not to the Praesidium at the Fourth Congress was M. N. Roy of India. He was designated a representative of the "eastern countries."

in 1928 he was reelected to both of these high positions.[2] Few, if any, Communists from parties outside the Soviet Union ever served as long as Katayama on the Executive Committee of the Communist International during the first decade and a half of its existence.

As a ranking functionary of the Comintern Katayama was obviously more than a mere spokesman for the weak and discordant Japan Communist Party. Though he participated in the continuing deliberations of the Executive Committee and particularly of the Praesidium on all matters relating to the international revolutionary situation, his activities and writings denote that he was one of the Comintern's foremost experts and consultants on Asian and colonial affairs. Representing the Comintern at international congresses concerned with the problems of the East, serving as chairman and member of various committees to study Asian and colonial questions, and acting as a watchdog over the positions on colonialism adopted by the various national Communist parties, he had constant opportunity to underscore his worth to the Comintern hierarchs.[3] Specializing in international affairs and avoiding entanglement in the internal politics of the Russian Communist Party, he never failed to survive the

[2] *ibid.*, II, pp. 572-573. At the Fifth Congress Roy was elected a "candidate member" of the Praesidium of the ECCI. After the Sixth Congress Katayama was replaced by Katō (pseudonym for Sano Manabu) and Asano (pseudonym for Watanabe Masanosuke), the new representatives of the Japan Communist Party. But together with the prestigious Ottomar Kuusinen, Clara Zetkin, and Jules Humbert-Droz, he was accorded a "personal" place on the Executive Committee in tribute to his illustrious standing in the Communist International.

[3] See, *inter alia*, Sen Katayama, "Report and Resolution on the Egyptian S.P.," *International Press Correspondence*, III, no. 2 (January 5, 1923), p. 21; "Der Kampf des koreanischen Volkes gegen Japan," *Das Flammenzeichen vom Palais Egmont* (Berlin, 1927), pp. 146-148; and "Der antiimperialistische Kongress in Brüssel," *Rote Gewerkschafts-Internationale*, VII, no. 3 (March 1927), pp. 142-145. And for his role in the development of policy toward the negroes in the United States see especially Theodore Draper, *American Communism and Soviet Russia*, New York, 1960, pp. 348-350.

regular shakeups in the membership of the Executive Committee and its Praesidium.

Katayama's feat in ensconcing himself as a permanent fixture in the Comintern system is doubly impressive in view of the delicate political situation within the Soviet Union during the stormy years from 1924 through 1927. After the death of Lenin, who had dominated the Bolshevik movement since its inception, a vicious battle for his mantle developed in the Russian Communist Party. Partially masking the personal ambitions of such Bolshevik titans as Trotsky, Kamenev, Bukharin, Zinoviev, and Stalin the deadly fight was openly waged over policy on new as well as unresolved problems. Such issues as agrarian policy within the Soviet Union, the possibility of socialism within one country, the permanent revolution, and basic strategy in the Chinese Revolution could not be decisively settled, save after furious exchanges among the contenders for ultimate power. The personal political fortunes of all ranking Communists were drastically affected by the victories and defeats of the giants at the peak of the Party.

Katayama himself was perhaps no slower in reaching a position on the post-Lenin struggle for power than most other Communist dignitaries in the Soviet Union. It was not simply that he was as always cautious in matters relating to theory but that the many complex issues were not easily comprehended. He himself has, in addition, testified that, because of his limited facility with the Russian language, he could not always follow the lines of debate of the ideological contestants.[4] When, however, he finally came to his decision, he moved rapidly toward the Stalinist camp.

When the mighty Lenin passed away in January 1924 Katayama did not quickly transfer his allegiance to another chief in the Communist hierarchy. Though he was an official

[4] Kishimoto Eitarō *et al.*, *Katayama Sen*, 2 vols., Tokyo, 1959-1960, II, p. 290.

of the Comintern, he actually had limited associations with the top-ranking commanders of the Russian Communist Party. From the time of his arrival in the Soviet Union until the death of Lenin he personally met the Bolshevik leader on only a few brief occasions. His own work, centered in the Comintern, gave him few opportunities to establish close relationships with such Party men as Stalin, Trotsky, and Kamenev. He was, most likely, on the closest terms with Zinoviev and Bukharin who participated actively in the operations of the world-wide Comintern system. In short, Katayama was not deeply involved, personally or politically, with any of the would-be successors to the departed Lenin.

It has been intimated that the Japanese revolutionary was initially sympathetic toward Trotsky and his ambitions. While this may well be correct, it is possible to make too much of the presumed friendship between Katayama and the Russian. The two men were at best only casually acquainted with one another, Katayama being simply one of a multitude of revolutionaries Trotsky had met at one time or another during his long political career. The elderly Japanese had a high regard for the "bearded prophet" and valued his outstanding contributions to the success of the Bolshevik Revolution. Yet, it may be surmised, he was wary of the very qualities that had been responsible for Trotsky's commanding place in the revolutionary movement. Though he was not given to overt disparagement of intellectual radicals, believing that they had a necessary social role to play, he had a deeply ingrained distrust of their practical judgment. If he had displayed implicit faith in the leadership of Lenin, it was because the philosophical penchant of the first Bolshevik had been neatly balanced by his tough, down-to-earth realism. But Trotsky, a daring, scintillating, clever but none too shrewd revolutionary, could never have hoped to win, much more retain, his confidence and backing.

The Stalin of the mid-twenties was, on the other hand, a

power politician whom Katayama could follow without great qualms. The Georgian, it may be noted, had many of the characteristics, in greater richness, to be sure, of the Japanese himself. Patient and stubborn, methodical and single-minded, unpretentious and not without an earthy sense of humor, Trotsky's rival was a craftsman rather than an artist in the business of revolution. If he did not have the charisma of Lenin nor the personal magnetism of Trotsky, his iron will, organizing ability, and efficiency elicited wide respect from the workaday members and guardians of the Communist Party. Though it was his practice to take final counsel with himself, Stalin, unlike the egotistical Trotsky, had the indispensable talent of the successful politician, namely, a willingness to listen as well as to talk. As a result, he may occasionally have misjudged but he rarely underestimated his rivals, and his errors and failures, though numerous, were never politically fatal.

On the level of grand strategy for the extension of the Communist Revolution Katayama could test the feasibility of the conflicting opinions of Stalin and Trotsky primarily by reference to China and Japan. These were the societies which he professed to know best. From all indications Katayama seems to have been as enthusiastic over the progress of the revolution in China in the summer of 1925 as he was upset by the paralysis of the Communist group in Japan. He was, of course, aware that conditions in the two countries were fundamentally different.

In China the basic strategy for the furtherance of the Communist revolution had been devised even before the death of Lenin. Facing realistically the fact that the Chinese Communist Party was much too weak to bring about the completion of the bourgeois-democratic stage in the revolution by itself, Soviet Russia decided to support the Kuomintang in its drive to unify the country and to destroy the "baneful influence" of the imperialist powers. To help in the fulfillment of this primary task the Chinese Communists were ordered to desist from pursuing a completely independent course of action and to collaborate with the "bourgeois-nationalist" forces of Sun Yat-sen. At the decisive moment, when the "feudalistic war-lords" and their imperialistic backers were routed, the Communists were then to strike from within for control of the Kuomintang and divert the revolution along a socialist path. This plan of operations, favored by Stalin, remained in effect during and after Katayama's visit to China and, if he had any misgivings about its practicality, he did not voice them.

While the Comintern strategy was reluctantly applied by the Chinese Communists, it was vehemently assailed by the uneasy Trotsky. Arguing that a policy of collaboration with the "class enemy" would lead to disaster, that it was folly to trust the bourgeois leaders of the Kuomintang, he urged that the Chinese Communist Party keep its identity pure and pursue an independent revolutionary course. But though his own reservations about the reliability—or gullibility—of the Chinese Nationalist leaders were, as events later demonstrated, extremely well founded, his own policy of basing the revolution in China essentially upon the workers and peasants was hardly realistic. The Stalinist policy of a temporary united front between nationalists and social revolutionaries seemed at the time to be most promising of success.

However facilely Stalin and Trotsky may have attempted to settle the fate of the Chinese Nationalist Revolution, events in the spring of 1927 soberly demonstrated that Chiang Kai-shek and his followers in the Kuomintang were to have a word in the matter. At the very time that Katayama and the Comintern were engaged in weeding out the "errors" of "Fukumotoism" in the Japanese movement a catastrophe befell the Communist Party in China. In April Chiang, refusing to play the passive role cynically assigned to him by Stalin, proceeded to exert a gigantic squeeze upon the double-dealing Communists within the Kuomintang. As a result of massive arrests carried out by troops and police the ranks of the Nationalists were purged. Even though this forceful move caused a temporary split among the leaders of the Kuomintang, it was effectively healed before the end of the summer. The Party's left wing, discovering at last that it was being duped, parted company with its Communist allies and its Comintern advisers.

The Himalayan disaster in China which, to be sure, was not candidly acknowledged by Stalin and Bukharin for fear of strengthening Trotsky's hand, lent an extra note of urgency for positive action in Japan. With unity reestablished in their ranks and a strategy for a political offensive carefully blocked out in the "1927 Thesis," the Japanese Communist leaders returned from Moscow prepared to launch a major political offensive. Katayama hung with rapt attention upon every subsequent report from the Party in his homeland; he probably knew that this newest campaign was the "now or never" of his own long revolutionary career.

The formulation of a new Communist strategy for Japan in 1927 occurred at the very time that unprecedented opportunities for mass political action were opening up. Since the passage of the Universal Suffrage Law a few years earlier a number of proletarian parties had been founded by trade and peasant-union leaders, frequently in cooperation with leftist intellectuals. Though they issued their initial challenge against the old-line political parties in the local and prefectural contests of 1927, they looked forward with especial eagerness to the national general elections, scheduled for February of the following year. Here was a chance for the moderate and left-wing parties to publicize their platforms and to strike at the monopoly upon the National Diet held by the established conservative factions and claques. Thus, despite the omnipresent threat of the Public Peace Preservation Law the "proletarian" captains threw themselves into the contest with doubled vigor and determination. The resulting election campaign was without question the liveliest, most bewildering, and certainly most interesting Japan had known since the introduction of parliamentary government almost forty years before.

The Japanese Communists, no longer torn by dissension, responded to the unparalleled political situation with unusual confidence and boldness. By persistent effort Party men penetrated deeply into the ranks of organized labor, peasant-unions, campus and intellectual organizations, and even into governmental agencies. Special programs were devised to secure the backing of women and youth. As politicos, who really had had no prior practical experience, the Communists revealed remarkable skill in the techniques of popular electioneering and mass persuasion. Newspapers, campaign leaflets, wall posters, rigged public meetings—all revealed the presence of a hard-working Communist apparatus.[5] If the election campaign served no other purpose for the revolutionary movement, it widely advertised the existence of the Japan Communist Party.

Since its status was illegal, the Japan Communist Party could not engage in the heated campaign under its own colors. Its full support was thrown behind the Labor-Farmer Party, which was headed by the intellectual, Ōyama Ikuo, known to be extremely sympathetic to the Communist movement. Behind this leftist proletarian party the strength of Communist-dominated labor and peasant-unions, youth organizations, and cultural groups was marshalled. The success of the Communist campaign became evident when the election results were announced. Of the total of about one-half million votes cast for the half-dozen proletarian parties the

[5] Yokomizo Mitsuteru, *Nihon Shakai Shugi Undō-shi Kōwa*, rev. ed., Tokyo, 1932, pp. 206ff., presents a detailed account of the revived Japan Communist Party. Note also Watanabe Kango, *Nihon Shakai Undō-shi*, Tokyo, 1955, pp. 130-131, and Akamatsu Katsumaro, *Nihon Shakai Undō-shi*, Tokyo, 1955, pp. 226-230.

Labor-Farmer coalition obtained almost two hundred thousand. And of the eight candidates elected to office from the eighty-five nominated by the proletarian parties two were the nominees of Ōyama's party. None of the ten Communists running under its banner was, however, successful in his bid for political office.[6]

The 4.7 percentage of the total popular vote garnered by candidates of the proletarian parties did not make any significant dent in the power of the well-entrenched *Seiyūkai* and *Minseitō* parties which had for some years controlled the National Diet. But the extraordinarily impressive showing of the parties of the "masses" in their first plunge into open and active national politics could not but frighten the government. There was always the future to worry about. Thus, no sooner had the excitement of the elections started to wane than the state began to take hurried stock of the situation. On March 15, 1928, a day which has ever since been memorable in the history of the Japan Communist Party, the police initiated a sweeping drive to root out the leftist political menace.

The offensive launched by the government of Premier Tanaka Giichi, General of the Imperial Japanese Army, was far more pervading in nature and scope than the attacks against Communists and other radicals carried out almost five years before. Whereas the arrests of 1923 had involved only a handful of Communist, labor, and student leaders, the new campaign of repression and terror was gradually directed against literally thousands of Japanese citizens classified under the general rubric of "dangerous elements."[7] Before

[6] Evelyn S. Colbert, *The Left Wing in Japanese Politics*, New York, 1952, pp. 22-23. See too Chitoshi Yanaga, *Japan since Perry*, New York, 1949, p. 480.

[7] Nihon Kōgyō Kurabu, Chōsa-ka, *Nihon Kyōsan-tō Jiken Temmatsu*, pp. 41-42, indicates in its detailed listing that sixty-four individuals were ultimately arraigned on charges after the 1923 raids against the Communists. This pamphlet, marked "Secret," gives no place or date of publication but internal evidence suggests it was prepared in 1930.

the first wave of arrests were completed six weeks later not only had many hundreds of suspects been imprisoned but the Labor-Farmer Party, the Japan Labor Union Council, and other leftist organizations and publications had been compelled to suspend their activities.[8] The public did not have to be told that all-out war against "sedition" and "revolution" had been declared.

The Japan Communist Party, whose energetic role in the preceding elections had not passed unobserved, was singled out for special treatment by the alarmed and angered police. In the initial raids, carried out at all hours of the day and night, numerous Party members and sympathizers were rounded up. Though Tokuda Kyūichi, Nozaka Sanzō, and Shiga Yoshio were quickly apprehended, most Communist leaders succeeded, for a while at least, in escaping detention, either by going into hiding or by stealing out of the country to Soviet Russia.[9] Then, after having delivered these jolting blows, Tanaka's government took additional measures in June to strengthen the repressive powers of the Public Peace Preservation Law. By imperial decree more severe punishments, including the death penalty, were proclaimed against revolutionaries seeking to alter the national polity.

News of the political terror in Japan was conveyed to Moscow by Sano Manabu, who was later joined by Ichikawa Shōichi and Yamamoto Kenzō.[10] Their report on the Party crisis was even more upsetting since the Comintern itself

[8] In the wave of arrests, launched on March 15, five hundred thirty suspects were prosecuted. *ibid.*, pp. 41-42. According to Tokuda Kyūichi, however, about six thousand arrests were made, about twenty-five hundred of these people were jailed, and about seven or eight hundred were given sentences. See Tokuda Kyūichi and Shiga Yoshio, *Gokuchū Jūhachi-nen*, Tokyo, 1947, p. 53.

[9] For personal accounts of their arrests see Tokuda Kyūichi and Shiga Yoshio, *op.cit.*, pp. 53-54, 115-116. Tokuda's account is reprinted in Rironsha Henshu-bu, ed. *Tokuda Kyūichi Den*, Tokyo, 1955, pp. 103-104. Nozaka's report of his arrest will be found in his *Bōmei Jūroku-nen*, Tokyo, 1946, pp. 10-11.

[10] Ichinose Masayuki, *Nihon Kyōsan-tō*, Tokyo, 1955, p. 62.

was already agitated by an ominous shift in the foreign policy of Japan. Alarmed by the dramatic victories of Chiang's Nationalist forces, which in their bid for political unification had resumed their triumphant march northward toward Peking, the government of Premier Tanaka decided to intervene militarily in China. In May Japanese troops took up positions athwart the advancing Kuomintang armies in Shantung province, raising the possibility of a serious international incident. To the Comintern this display of Japanese imperialist power was perhaps far more disturbing than the Kuomintang's new policy of outright enmity for the shattered Chinese Communist Party.

In May the Political Secretariat of the Comintern's Executive Committee, completing its assessment of the situation, presented its recommendations for the struggle tactics to be pursued by the Japan Communist Party. There was no possibility of misunderstanding its view that, despite the tightened police controls of the Tanaka regime, no retreat would be tolerated. After meting out praise to the Japanese wing of the Communist movement for its success in resurrecting the Party as well as scolding it for its tactical "errors" vis-à-vis the various proletarian groups, the line of future political battle was delineated. "In order to be able to accomplish its new, great, and responsible tasks," it was announced, "the young communist party must strain every nerve to strengthen itself numerically and ideologically. Particular efforts must be made to strengthen and improve the illegal apparatus, in order to counter government action through the police and the judiciary to annihilate the communist party and all other revolutionary organizations. The party must take steps to improve its machinery, and at the same time let no legal opportunity slip for establishing contact with the masses as a means of extending and utilizing its ideological and organizational influence among the workers and poor peasants."[11] This was, in effect, a declaration of immediate and unconditional warfare against the Japanese government, to be waged by any and all means, "legal" and "illegal."

Furthermore, after calling upon the Japan Communist Party to strive for the reestablishment of the "revolutionary mass organizations" dissolved by state decree and for the defense of the Japan Labor Union Council and its leftist program, the method of attack upon Tanaka's foreign policy was laid down. "The communist party must make it clear to the workers," the resolution of the Political Secretariat stated, that "the Rodonominto group [Labor-Farmer Party] in parliament, because of their extreme numerical weakness, will be able to play an independent part only if they conduct an energetic struggle (supported by the communist party and the masses) against imperialism . . . Regardless of the difficulties they will encounter, the Rodonominto deputies must speak out against the robber war being waged by Japanese imperialism in China. . . ."[12] The concern of the Comintern was quite clear. Japanese military blandishments in China were considered not only a threat to the Chinese Revolution but a menace to Soviet Russia itself.

The direction of Comintern policy and the role assigned to the Japan Communist Party were spelled out repeatedly during the Sixth Congress of the Communist International, which opened on July 17, 1928. In his own address, delivered on the first day of the proceedings, Katayama asserted unequivocally that "the time has come to prepare ourselves for the fight against world imperialism which threatens our fatherland, the Soviet Union."[13] Still another Japanese comrade proclaimed that the "most important tasks the Communist Party of Japan faces on the international level are to make sure that not a single [Japanese] soldier remains in China. We must . . . counter all attempts on the part of the

[11] Degras, *op.cit.*, II, 444-445. [12] *ibid.*, II, 445.

[13] Rodger Swearingen and Paul Langer, *Red Flag in Japan*, Cambridge, Mass., 1952, p. 34.

Japanese bourgeoisie to interfere in the affairs of the Soviet Union . . . and transform the imperialist war into a civil war against the Japanese bourgeoisie."[14] And in the final resolutions of the Congress it was reiterated that the "Japan Communist Party . . . must make every effort to defend the Chinese Revolution and to combat the predatory policy of Japanese imperialism."[15]

The line which came out of Moscow in the summer of 1928 may only be deemed a summons to suicide on the part of the Japanese element in the revolutionary movement. It is difficult to escape the conclusion that the Comintern was ready to jeopardize and even to sacrifice the Japanese Party in order to fulfill the national interests of Soviet Russia. The Comintern officials were well informed about the stern penalties for revolutionary activity which had been introduced by the Tanaka government in June. That the Japanese state was not content merely to strengthen the Public Peace Preservation Law was indicated by the rapid and systematic organization of a nation-wide police apparatus to ferret out "dangerous elements and thought." In July the creation of the Special Higher Police agency in the Ministry of Internal Affairs signified that no stone would be left unturned to destroy individuals and groups suspected of "gnawing away at the vitals" of the established social order.

The subsequent history of the Japan Communist Party reads like the saga of a *banzai* charge against the impregnable ramparts of the Japanese state. Regrouping after the shattering spring arrests, the Party succeeded, despite unbroken harassment which picked off leaders as well as rank and file, in reconstructing its battered organization and carrying on frantic political battle.[16] But the proponents of

[14] *ibid.*, p. 34. [15] Degras, *op.cit.*, II, 463.

[16] According to Nabeyama Sadachika, *Watakushi wa Kyōsan-tō wo Suteta*, Tokyo, 1950, p. 127, the Communist Party succeeded in rebuilding its strength to the level held at the time of the raids in March of the preceding year. Nabeyama, a top-ranking leader of the Party was ar-

revolution could make no headway against the overpowering resources and grim resolution of the government. As a result of a second wave of mass arrests launched on April 16, 1929, and pressed for many weeks thereafter, the Japan Communist Party was for all practical purposes obliterated. "By the summer . . . ," it has been well observed, "nothing remained of the Party but a small group of desperadoes, advocates of total violence, determined to resist arrest at all costs."[17]

Not long after the Sixth Congress Katayama, after years of hope and effort, seems to have reconciled himself to the likelihood that the great revolution in his home country would not occur in his day. The attrition of the revolutionary movement in his native land, the threatening maneuvers of the Japanese army, and the reversal in the fortunes of the Chinese Communist Party were enough to convince him that a new struggle of immeasurable proportions with the capitalist-imperialist world lay ahead. Thus, he concurred in the desperate policy, laid down at the Sixth Congress, which required the feeding of countless victims into the maw of the Japanese police, believing that the greater aims of the Comintern would thereby best be served. For the foreseeable future the overriding duty of Communists everywhere was, as he himself had put it, to bend every effort for the defense of "*our* fatherland, the Soviet Union."

The shift in Katayama's revolutionary outlook was closely related to the change in his position within the Executive Committee of the Comintern which was arranged at the Sixth Congress. Instead of being appointed to his post as a

---

rested and sentenced to life imprisonment in 1931. Two years later he and Sano Manabu renounced their political faith, asserting that the Japan Communist Party had become nothing more than a "running dog" of the Soviet Union.

[17] Swearingen and Langer, *op.cit.*, p. 38. As a result of the mass arrests on April 16, 1929, three hundred thirty-four defendants were finally brought to trial. Many more were obviously arrested but released without being prosecuted. See Nihon Kōgyō Kurabu, *op.cit.*, pp. 41-42.

representative of the Japan Communist Party, as had been customary in the past, he was now assigned a seat as a member-at-large. The Communist masters in the Kremlin had concluded, and quite correctly, that he could be depended upon to lend unqualified approval to whatever policies they sought to foist upon their instrument of international revolution. Taking under more direct cognizance the major issues and problems confronting the Comintern, he now surrendered his place as representative of the Japan Communist Party to the young but hardened veterans, Nozaka Sanzō, Watanabe Masanosuke, and Sano Manabu.[18]

It may be somewhat fanciful but yet not entirely inaccurate to consider that Katayama had been promoted to the rank of "elder statesman," or *genro*, of the Comintern, a status he continued to enjoy for the remaining years of his life.[19] While keeping a close eye upon the affairs of the embattled, if enfeebled, Japan Communist Party and participating actively in the periodic reshaping of its tactics, he devoted the greater part of his time to the fulfillment of important assignments and politically delicate missions in the international movement. Not only did he represent the Comintern on notable ceremonial occasions within the Soviet Union but he was also frequently despatched abroad to attend international gatherings in which the Communist forces had a heavy stake. Thus, during the depression years his voice was commonly heard at the various anti-imperialist and pacifist congresses staged in the great cities of western Europe.

Busy as his travels kept him, Katayama was not at a loss for time to carry his weight in the unending proceedings of the many revolutionary organizations based in Soviet Russia. Apart from his work with the Comintern and its numerous committees and subcommittees, he continued to attend the

[18] See above, n. 2.

[19] According to Swearingen and Langer, *op.cit.*, p. 44, Katayama "officially ranked with Lenin, Trotsky, and Stalin."

regular meetings of the All-Russian Communist Party and of the Profintern. In this last organization, concerned with the Communist international labor movement, he maintained close liaison with the Japanese representatives. And, as ever, he continued to prepare reports and analyses of the situation in Japan and the Far East for publication in the international Communist press, particularly the journals *International Press Correspondence* and the *Communist International.* His final articles show constant concern over the rise of military fascism in Japan and alarm over her program of aggression in Manchuria.

December 7, 1929, was a red-letter day in Katayama's life. On the occasion of his seventieth birthday, according to the Old-Style Japanese calendar, the event was officially celebrated in the Communist world. Not only were flattering testimonials to his long revolutionary career carried in the Russian press but congratulatory messages were delivered from leaders of the Communist movement in many foreign lands. As a special tribute arrangements were made to republish his Autobiography in one of the foremost revolutionary journals in the Soviet Union. And as a crowning act of appreciation for his ceaseless efforts on behalf of Communism he was nominated for membership in the "Old Bolshevik Club," one of the few foreigners ever so honored.[20]

One aspect of the celebrations unquestionably gave the aged Japanese exile unsurpassed pleasure. His second daughter and youngest child, Chiyoko, had been on hand to greet him in the preceding August upon his return from an anti-imperialist congress in Frankfort. Having completed her studies at the

[20] Kishimoto Eitarō *et al.*, *op.cit.*, II, 316-317. Two photographs of Katayama, taken on the occasion of his seventieth birthday, serve as the frontispiece of Shakai Keizai Rōdō Kenkyū-jo, ed. *Katayama Sen Shū: Nihon ni okeru Kaikyū Tōsō,* Tokyo, 1948. See also the first photograph in *Katayama Sen; Seitan Hyakunen wo Kinen shite, Zen'ei* (Special Issue), no. 161 (November 1959).

Aoyama Jō-Gakuin (Aoyama School for Women) in Tokyo, she had set out for Russia to see the father she scarcely knew. The reunion was all the more precious to him, since he had taken action to secure a divorce from his second wife in 1923; his second-born, his son, Kan'ichi, had died and had been buried in the same plot as his mother, Fude, in the Aoyama Cemetery in Tokyo. His oldest child Yasuko, who had joined him in California shortly after his flight from Japan and had remained with him on and off until 1920, did not meet her father again until January 1931. But with Chiyoko present at his seventieth-birthday festivities the old man was able for the first time in years to feel that he was not completely alone in the world.

Photographs taken of Katayama during the last few years of his life are apt to be extremely deceptive. At the age of seventy and perhaps for the next two years his outward appearance is that of a hale, robust, but perceptibly elderly man. His broad and heavy face, topped by close-cropped hair and marked by bushy eyebrows, flecked, to be sure, by spots of gray, and his strong and flaring nose portray resistance to the toll of time. But picture after picture reveals a hardness of the eye and a grim set of the lips which are almost frightening. More so than any other evidence they betray the evolution of a man of rugged and stubborn will into an uncompromising fanatic.

Actually Katayama's physical appearance belied his seriously deteriorating state of health. Since at least 1925 he had suffered from periodic bouts of illness which required prolonged medical attention and rest cures in spas and sanatoria in the Soviet Union and abroad. Once he had passed his seventieth birthday, however, his ailments occurred with disturbing frequency, so much so that he was often compelled to interrupt his work and retire for treatment and recuperation in the hospital. His trips to the hot-spring resorts of the

Crimea became a fairly regular routine, possibly because in his advanced years he could not cope with the bitterly cold winters in Moscow. Afflicted by a heart condition, by attacks of the grippe, and by spells of fatigue, his health declined sharply from about the middle of 1932.

Though he probably realized that his remaining days of life were numbered, Katayama remained in good spirits. Politically active when he could be and ever alert to the critical tide of affairs in his homeland and throughout the world, he could not break completely with the busy routines that were as vital to him as breathing itself. More and more often hints of nostalgia may be detected in his ways and behavior. Always delighted to be called upon by visitors from Japan, especially friends from the old days, he began to take to reminiscing. And in place of the Western garb which he had worn for years he showed a renewed fondness for the *yukata, obi,* and sandals which have proverbially become more dear, even to the most modern of Japanese, in their later years. To the very end, however, he refused to part with his flat, brimmed cap of the worker, which was as much the mark of the old revolutionary Bolshevik as the hammer and sickle were the symbol of the Bolshevik Revolution.

On November 4, 1933, Katayama's condition took a sudden and critical turn for the worse. Taken in great haste to the Kremlin hospital, his recovery was anxiously awaited by his two daughters and an assembly of close friends. On the verge of his seventy-fourth year, the stricken revolutionary struggled desperately for the rest of the day to keep alive the dim spark of life. Shortly after midnight, on November 5, Sen Katayama was dead.[21]

There is an old story about the demise of Katayama which has continued to circulate in Japan for a long time. Lying on

[21] Kishimoto *et al., op.cit.,* pp. 331ff., give a detailed account of the last hours of Katayama.

his death bed in Moscow, his home for almost twelve years, it is said that he sighed, "Oh! If I could only die on the straw mats of my native country." Whether the tale is true or not is immaterial. Yet it is certain that, though he was in his final moments an internationalist, a Communist, and a revolutionary, he had never really forgotten the land where he was born.

EPILOGUE

The death of Sen Katayama, sudden yet expected, plunged the entire world of Communism into deep mourning. In deference to his lofty status in the hierarchy of the Communist International, arrangements for his funeral were made with fastidious care. Nothing less than a full-fledged state ceremony was considered worthy of the Japanese revolutionary who had lived out his final years as an expatriate in the Soviet Union.

On November 8, three days after he had passed away, a a crowd numbering about one hundred and fifty thousand people poured into the famed Red Square in Moscow to pay their last respects to Katayama. The vast cobblestoned expanse was covered with a hard-packed mat of fresh white snow. In front of the ultra-modern pyramidal tomb of Lenin, overshadowed by the medieval crenelated walls of the Kremlin, was Katayama's bier. Standing close by, bare-headed in the cold wintry air, were the pallbearers, chief among them Stalin, and other dignitaries of the Russian Communist Party and the Communist International.[1] All wore the black brassard of the mourner on the left sleeves of their heavy overcoats. And surrounding this assembly of top officials and intimate friends was a single-lined square of Red Army soldiers standing at rigid attention. It was, *mutatis mutandis*, a funeral pageant in the style of the tsars.

Lying in his open coffin, completely enclosed by banks of

[1] For an eyewitness description of Katayama's funeral see Nozaka Sanzō, *Bōmei Jūroku-nen*, Tokyo, 1946, pp. 22-24. Nozaka, who became Katayama's successor as leader of Japanese Communism, was imprisoned in 1928 but secured his release in 1930. He made his way to Soviet Russia shortly thereafter, not returning to Japan until after the end of World War II. Rodger Swearingen and Paul Langer, *Red Flag in Japan*, Cambridge, Mass., 1952, pp. 113-114, have called into question Nozaka's explanation of how he got out of prison. Rejecting his claim that he obtained permission to leave jail in order to undergo major surgery (Nozaka, *op.cit.*, pp. 11-12), they present evidence indicating that he successfully feigned conversion to anti-Communism.

gayly colored flowers, lay the body of Katayama. Looking far older in death than he ever had in life, the toll of his lifelong exactions and privations was sharply revealed upon his shrunken face. A wisp of hair, blown by the wind, lay carelessly upon his forehead. This was the last view his friends had of Katayama.

After the appropriate orations had been delivered by the mighty men of Communism, Katayama's coffin was closed and he was borne to the crematorium. His ashes were soon interred in a crypt in the Kremlin Wall, alongside the final remains of the great heroes of the Bolshevik movement. The Japanese revolutionary was the first, perhaps the only, Asian ever accorded this distinctive honor.

Katayama's death was officially observed not only in the Soviet Union. For more than a decade his international revolutionary work had brought him into close relations with leaders of Communist parties and movements in all the continents of the globe. Glowing tributes to the "grand old man," interspersed occasionally with personal notes of condolence by revolutionaries who had known him well, were thus published in Communist journals and newspapers throughout the world. The "bourgeois" press in Europe, Asia, and America generally passed over his death in silence.

With his demise Katayama soon slipped from the minds of busy Communist officialdom. The stirrings of the movement in Japan were far too faint during the next twelve years to evoke memories or to necessitate the fabrication of political myths. And as Japan rapidly drifted into the tight grip of military fascism, his successors to revolutionary leadership found it utterly impossible either to act or breathe in the stiflingly repressive atmosphere. Languishing in prison, hibernating in the political underground, or seeking refuge in Soviet Russia or the Chinese Communist "liberated areas," they had no alternative but to wait patiently for the day.[2]

[2] The classic types are Nozaka Sanzō, Tokuda Kyūichi, and Shiga

On August 15, 1945, World War II in the Pacific came to a close. Pulverized by a merciless aerial bombardment, Katayama's homeland lay prostrate and helpless. Within the next few weeks American troops began to land in Japan, inaugurating a military occupation that lasted for almost seven years. In keeping with the basic policy of the United States to reconstruct defeated Japan in a democratic and peaceful mold, all political prisoners were quickly released and free political activity was strongly encouraged. In these circumstances the long dormant Japan Communist Party was given a new lease of life. Within a matter of a few months the prewar veterans regrouped their ranks and prepared to resume the discontinued revolutionary struggle.

In its search for political myths and symbols to link their prewar struggle against authoritarianism with the movement for democracy during the Occupation era the Japan Communist Party, like the Communist International in earlier years, moved quickly to exploit the name and reputation of Katayama. Its very first act had a human touch which could not help but arouse popular sympathy for the old revolutionary leader. Mindful of the fact that Katayama, almost alone among the pioneers of the Japanese social movement, had died and lay buried outside the homeland, steps were rapidly taken to remedy the situation. The family plot in Aoyama Cemetery in Tokyo, was carefully refurbished. The rough stone markers, which had for years denoted the graves of Fude and Kan'ichi, were now topped by a huge marble stone inscribed with the name of Katayama. A simple legend, incised in the monument, set forth, but not with complete accuracy, a sketch of his life. Legal responsibility for the care of the plot was assumed by the Central Headquarters of the Japan Communist Party.

Today, as a result of the work of scholars, polemicists, and revolutionaries, Katayama's name is far more familiar than

---

Yoshio, the triumvirate who guided the Japan Communist Party after the close of World War II.

ever before to millions of his countrymen. To many of them he continues to be a source of rich inspiration as well as the embodiment of their own hopes for the social future of Japan. To others he is the symbol and epitome of the leftist political instability which has perennially plagued modern Japan. But, however he be viewed by his many admirers and critics, it is certain that Sen Katayama has won a permanent position in the history of modern Japan.

⁂ BIBLIOGRAPHY (SEN KATAYAMA)

BOOKS BY KATAYAMA

Katayama, Sen. *The Labor Movement in Japan*. Chicago, 1918.

———. *Sakushu Naki Shakai e no Netsujō*. Tokyo, 1948.

———. *Toshi Shakai Shugi . . . Waga Shakai Shugi*. Ed. by Kishimoto Eitarō. Tokyo, 1949.

———. *Nihon no Rōdō Undō*. Tokyo, 1952.

———. *Jiden*. Tokyo, 1954.

———. *Hansen Heiwa no Tame ni*. Tokyo, 1954.

———, and Nishikawa, Kōjirō. *Nihon no Rōdō Undō*. Tokyo, 1955.

———. *Waga Shakai Shugi* (and Tazoe Tetsuji. *Keizai Shinka Ron*). Ed. with Introduction by Kishimoto Eitarō. Tokyo, 1955.

ARTICLES BY KATAYAMA

Katayama, Sen. "Why We Are Coming to America," *News Letter* [Iowa College], XVII, no. 3 (October 12, 1889), 30-31.

———. "The Origin of the Japanese," *News Letter* [Iowa College], XVII, no. 4 (October 26, 1889), 41-42.

———. "The Art of Japan," *News Letter* [Iowa College], XVII, no. 5 (November 9, 1889), 53.

———. "The H'yakusho's Summer Pleasures," *Harper's Monthly*, XC, no. 537 (February 1895), 403-406.

———. "Labour Problem Old and New," *Far East*, II, no. 10 (October 1897), 477-490.

———. "A Study in Socialism," *Asylum Record*, II, no. 2 (December 1897), 9-10.

———. "Katayama's Thanks," *Commons*, II, no. 12 (April 1898), 5.

Katayama, Sen Joseph. "The Labor Movement and Socialism

in Japan," *International Socialist Review*, II, no. 3 (September 1901), 188-191.

Katayama, Sen. "La situation politique et sociale au Japon," *Mouvement Socialiste*, VI, no. 66 (September 15, 1901), 338-344.

———. "Attitude of Japanese Socialists toward Present War," *International Socialist Review*, IV, no. 9 (March 1904), 513-514.

———. "La guerre russo-japonaise et le socialisme international," *Mouvement Socialiste*, XII, no. 134 (March 15, 1904), 337-343.

———. "Les socialistes japonais et la guerre," *Mouvement Socialiste*, XII, no. 135 (April 15, 1904), 456-458.

———. "Le socialisme au Japon," in Secrétariat Socialiste Internationale, *L'organisation socialiste et ouvrière en Europe Amérique et Asie* (Brussels, 1904), pp. 454-461.

———. "California and the Japanese," *International Socialist Review*, XIV, no. 1 (July 1913), 31-32.

———. "What It Means to Be a Socialist in Japan," *International Socialist Review*, XIV, no. 8 (February 1914), 467-468.

———. "The War and the Japanese," *International Socialist Review*, XV, no. 5 (November 1914), 287.

———. "Japanese Socialists in America," *American Labor Year Book* (New York, 1916), pp. 137-138.

———. "Armed Peace on the Pacific," *Class Struggle*, II (September–October 1918), 388-404.

———. "A Japanese Interpretation of the Recent Food Riots," *Class Struggle*, II, no. 5 (December 1918), 600-606.

———. "Morris Hillquit and the Left Wing," *Revolutionary Age*, II, no. 4 (July 26, 1919), 6.

———. "Radicalism in Japan," *Gale's Magazine*, III, no. 3 (October 1919), 4.

———. "Japan und Sowjetrussland," *Kommunistische Internationale*, II, no. 9 (1920), 49-51.

———. "Japanese Women," *Gale's Magazine*, III, no. 7 (February 1920), 12-13.

———. "Real Siberian Policy of Japan," *Gale's Magazine*, IV, no. 5 (December 1920), 14-15; 28.

———. "The First Congress of Communist and Revolutionary Organizations of the Far East," *International Press Correspondence*, II, no. 15 (February 24, 1922), 105-106.

———. "Present-day Japan," *Labour Monthly*, II, no. 3 (March 1922), 251-255.

———. "To the Soldiers of the Japanese Army in Siberia," *International Press Correspondence*, II, no. 45 (June 7, 1922), 338.

———. "Report and Resolution on the Egyptian S.P.," *International Press Correspondence*, III, no. 2 (January 5, 1923), 21.

———. "Die kommunistische internationale und der Ferne Osten," *Kommunistische Internationale*, V, nos. 31-32 (1924), 99-101.

———. "Der Kampf des koreanische Volkes gegen Japan," *Das Flammenzeichen vom Palais Egmont* (Berlin, 1927), pp. 146-148.

———. "Der antiimperialistische Kongress in Brüssel," *Rote Gewerkschafts-Internationale*, VII, no. 3 (March 1927), 142-145.

———. "The General Election in Japan," *International Press Correspondence*, VIII, no. 6 (February 2, 1928), 129-130.

———. "Die japanische auswanderung und die imperialistischen gegensätze," *Rote Aufbau*, II, no. 4 (August 1929), 161-166.

———. "Japan in bannkreis der weltwirtschaftskrise," *Kommunistische Internationale*, XI, no. 8 (February 26, 1930), 441-454.

———. "Der drohende interventionskrieg gegen die sowjetunion," *Rote Aufbau*, V, no. 6 (March 15, 1932), 255-257.

Katayama, Sen. "The Fight of the Japanese Toilers against War and Intervention," *International Press Correspondence*, XII, no. 33 (July 28, 1932), 689-691.

———. "My Appeal to the Proletarians of the World," *International Press Correspondence*, XIII, no. 26 (June 16, 1933), 570.

———. "With Comrade Lenin," in Clara Zetkin *et al.*, *We Have Met Lenin* (Moscow, 1939), pp. 11-15.

———. "Waga Kuni Shōrai no Shūkyō," *Nihon Shūkyō*, II, no. 6 (December 20, 1896), 291-296.

———. "Raishin," *Tobei Zasshi*, IX, no. 5 (May 3, 1905), 36.

———. "Beikoku Tayori," *Tobei Zasshi*, IX, no. 1 (January 3, 1905), 18-19.

———. "Beikoku Tayori," *Tobei Zasshi*, IX, no. 2 (February 3, 1905), 15-17.

———. "Rōdō-sha Shokun ni Tsugu," *Tobei Zasshi*, IX, no. 3 (March 3, 1905), 2-4.

———. "Taibei Mondai no Nanjū to Nihon Kirisutokyō-to no Sekinin," *Tōyō Keizai Shimpō*, no. 500 (October 5, 1909), 14-16.

———. "Beikoku Minshu-tō no Bokkō to Kokujō no Henka," *Tōyō Keizai Shimpō*, XXXIV, no. 569 (August 15, 1911), 11-13.

———. "Shina Ryokō Zakkan," *Kaizō*, VII, no. 6 (June 1925), 190-197.

———. "Nihon Kaikyū Undō no Hihan-teki Sōkan," *Chūō Kōron*, XLVI, no. 4 (April 1931), 107-125.

———, "Byōchū no Kansō," *Kaizō*, XIII, no. 10 (October 1931), 146-152.

SPECIAL COLLECTIONS OF WRITINGS OF KATAYAMA

Katayama Sen Seitan Hyakunen Kinen-kai. *Katayama Sen Chosaku-shu*. 3 vols. Tokyo, 1959-1960.

Kishimoto, Eitarō, "Katayama Sen to Meiji Rōdō Undō-shi,"

Keizai Ronsō, LXI, no. 3 (September 1947), 35-60; LXII, no. 3 (September 1948), 24-70.

Kishimoto, Eitarō (ed.). *Katayama Sen/Tazoe Tetsuji Ni-Shu*. Tokyo, 1955.

Kishimoto, Eitarō (ed.). *Katayama Sen Ha no Shakai Shugi to Sono Undō*. Tokyo, 1956.

Nihon Kyōsan-tō Tōshi Shiryō Iin-kai. *Katayama Sen Senshū*. Vol. 1 (vols. 2 and 3 apparently never published). Tokyo, 1949.

Shakai Keizai Rōdō Kenkyū-jo. *Katayama Sen-shū: Nihon ni okeru Kaikyū Tōsō*. Tokyo, 1948.

PRIMARY SOURCES

Books in Western Languages

American Board of Commissioners for Foreign Missions. *Annual Survey of the Work of the American Board, 1895-1896*. Boston, 1896.

Andover Theological Seminary. *General Catalogue of the Theological Seminary, Andover, Massachusetts, 1808-1908*. Boston, 1909.

De Bary, William T. *et al. Sources of the Japanese Tradition*. New York, 1958.

Degras, Jane (ed.). *The Communist International, 1919-1943: Documents*. 2 vols. London, 1956-1960.

De Leon, Daniel. *Flashlights of the Amsterdam Congress*. New York, 1929.

Eudin, Xenia J. and North, Robert C. *Soviet Russia and the East, 1920-1927*. Stanford, 1957.

Fukuzawa, Yukichi. *The Autobiography of Fukuzawa Yukichi*. Trans. by Kiyooka Eiichi. Tokyo, 1947.

Hopkins Academy. *Catalogue of Hopkins Academy, Oakland, Cal.* [sic], *1882-1883*. No date or place of publication. [1882?]

Hopkins Academy. *Catalogue of Hopkins Academy, Oakland, Cal., 1887-1888.* San Francisco, 1888.

Hopkins Academy, *Catalogue of Hopkins Academy, Oakland, Alameda County, California for the Year Ending May, 1892.* San Francisco [1891?].

Joint Legislative Committee Investigating Seditious Activities, State of New York. *Revolutionary Radicalism; Its History, Purpose and Tactics.* 4 vols. Albany, 1920.

Kommunistische Internationale. *Der Erste Kongress der Kommunistischen und Revolutionären Organisationen des Fernen Ostens, Moskau, Januar, 1922.* Hamburg, 1922.

Lenin, Bukharin, and Rutgers. *The New Policies of Soviet Russia.* Chicago [1921].

Murphy, John. *New Horizons.* London, 1941.

National Committee of the Socialist Party. *Proceedings of the National Convention of the Socialist Party Held at Chicago, Illinois, May 1 to 6, 1904.* Chicago, 1904.

Ozaki, Yukio. *The Voice of Japanese Democracy.* Yokohama, 1918.

Secrétariat Socialiste International. *L'organisation socialiste et ouvrière en Europe, Amérique et Asie.* Brussels, 1904.

Secrétariat Socialiste International. *Sixième Congres socialiste international tenu à Amsterdam du 14 au 20 âout 1904; compte-rendu analytique.* Brussels, 1904.

Socialist Publication Society, Brooklyn. *One Year of Revolution Celebrating the First Anniversary of the Founding of the Russian Soviet Republic.* Brooklyn, 1918.

Stead, Alfred. *Japan by the Japanese.* New York, 1904.

Trotsky, Leon. *My Life; an Attempt at an Autobiography.* New York, 1929.

Uchimura Kanzo. *The Diary of a Japanese Convert.* New York, 1895.

PRIMARY SOURCES

Articles in Western Languages

Abe, Iso. "Social Problems and Their Solution," *Far East*, I, no. 6 (July 20, 1896), 14-18.

Abe, Isoh [Isoo]. "Socialism in Japan," in Shigenobu Okuma (ed.), *Fifty Years of New Japan*, 2 vols. (London 1909), pp. 494-512.

Abe, Iso-o. "Socialism in Japan," in Naoichi Masaoka (ed.), *Japan to America* (New York, 1914), pp. 109-116.

Abe, Isoh. "Problems of Labor and Some Needed Legislation in Japan," *International Molders' Journal*, LIV, no. 4 (April 1918), 265-268.

Eckstein, Gustave. "Le premier congrès socialiste japonais," *Mouvement Socialiste*, X, no. 121 (June 1, 1903), 207-211.

Havel, H. (ed.). "Kotoku's Correspondence with Albert Johnson," *Mother Earth*, VI, no. 6 (August 1911), 180-184; no. 7 (September 1911), 207-209; no. 9 (November 1911), 282-287.

Kawakami, Karl Kiyoshi. "Socialism in Japan," *International Socialist Review*, II, no. 8 (February 1902), 561-569.

Lore, Ludwig. "Leon Trotsky," in *One Year of Revolution* (New York, 1918), pp. 7-8.

Murai, Tomoyoshi. "Japanese Settlements," *Commons*, I, no. 13 (April–May 1897), 1-2.

Roy, Manabendra Nath. "Memoirs," *Radical Humanist*, XVII, no. 5 (February 1, 1953), . . . XVIII, no. 4 (January 24, 1954). (Roy's stay in Mexico is recounted in nos. 10-13; 16-35).

Rutgers, S. J. "An Introduction to the History of the Labor Movement in Japan," *International Socialist Review*, XVIII (July 1917), 37-38.

Rutgers, S. J. "Vstrechi s Leninym," *Istorik Marksist*, nos. 2-3 (42-43) (1935), 85-98.

Sakai, Toshihiko. "Uberblick über die sozialistische Bewegung in Japan bis 1917," *Kommunistische Internationale*, II, no. 16 (1921), 144-151.

Tekano [Takano], Fusataro. "Labor Movement in Japan," *American Federationist*, I, no. 8 (October 1894), 163-166.

Takano, Fusataro. "Our Organizer in Japan," *American Federationist*, IV, no. 4 (June 1897), 77-78.

Takano, Fusataro. "Prospects of the Japanese Labor Movement," *American Federationist*, IV, no. 9 (November 1897), 210-211.

Takano Fusataro. "Proposed Factory Act in Japan," *American Federationist*, IV, no. 11 (January 1898), 250-252.

Takano, Fusataro. "A New Trade Union in Japan," *American Federationist*, IV, no. 12 (February 1898), 272-273.

Takano, Fusataro. "Labor Notes from Japan," *American Federationist*, V, no. 6 (August 1898), 118-119.

Takano, Fusataro. "Factory Legislation in Japan," *American Federationist*, V, no. 10 (December 1898), 200-201.

Takano, Fusataro. "Japanese Factory Legislation," *American Federationist*, V, no. 11 (January 1899), 216.

BOOKS IN JAPANESE LANGUAGE

Abe, Isoo. *Shakai Shugi-sha to Naru made*. Tokyo, 1932.

Hattori, Shisō, and Konishi, Shirō (eds.). *Heimin Shimbun*. 4 vols. Tokyo, 1953-1958.

Hioki, Norio *et al. Nihon Hanrei Taisei*. 24 vols. Tokyo, 1935-1937.

Ishikawa, Sanshirō. *Jijo-den*. 2 vols. Tokyo, 1956.

Kinoshita, Naoe. *Hi no Hashira*, in Yamamoto, Mitsuo (ed.), *Shakai Bungaku-shu*, vol. XXXIX of *Gendai Nihon Bungaku Zenshu*. Tokyo, 1930.

Kinoshita, Naoe. *Hi no Hashira*. Tokyo, 1959.

Kishimoto, Eitarō (ed.). *Meiji Shakai Shugi Shiron*. Tokyo, 1955.

Kishimoto, Eitarō (ed.). *Meiji Shakai Undō Shisō*. 2 vols. Tokyo, 1955.

Kondō, Eizō. *Kominterun no Misshi.* Tokyo, 1949.

Kōtoku, Shūsui. *Shūsui San Meicho.* Tokyo, 1947.

Kōtoku, Shūsui. *Teikoku Shugi.* (Iwanami Bunko). Tokyo, 1959.

Kōtoku, Shūsui. *Shakai Shugi Shinzui.* (Atene Bunko). Tokyo, 1949.

Nabeyama, Sadachika. *Watakushi wa Kyōsan-tō wo Suteta.* Tokyo, 1950.

Nihon Kyōsan-tō Shi Shiryō Iin-kai. *Kominterun Nihon Mondai ni Kan-suru Hōshin-sho Ketsugi-shū.* Tokyo, 1955.

Nozaka, Sanzō. *Bōmei Jūroku-nen.* Tokyo, 1946.

Riron-sha Henshū-bu (ed.). *Tokuda Kyūichi Den.* Tokyo, 1955.

Rōdō Sekai, 1897-1901. 5 vols. (incomplete). Microfilm copy in possession of author.

Sakai, Toshihiko. *Sakai Toshihiko Den.* Tokyo, 1926.

———. *Nihon Shakai Shugi Undō-shi.* Tokyo, 1954.

———. *Sakai Toshihiko Zenshū.* vol. 3. Tokyo, 1933.

Shioda, Shōbei (ed.). *Kōtoku Shūsui no Nikki to Shokan.* Tokyo, 1954.

Suzuki, Bunji. *Nihon Rōdō Undō Hattatsu-shi.* [Tokyo?], *ca.* 1926-1927.

Suzuki, Mosaburō. *Aru Shakai Shugi-sha no Hansei.* Tokyo, 1958.

Tokuda, Kyūichi, and Shiga, Yoshio. *Gokuchū Jūhachi-nen.* Tokyo, 1947.

Watanabe, Haruo. *Katayama Sen to Tomo ni.* Tokyo, 1955.

Yamagiwa, Keiji. *Kakumei no Jomaku: Kinoshita Naoe Genron-shū.* Tokyo, 1955.

Articles in Japanese Language

Ishigaki, Eitarō. "Amerika Hōryō Yonjū-nen," *Chūō Kōron,* LXVII, no. 7 (June 1952), 198-212; no. 8 (July 1952), 218-225; no. 9 (August 1952), 224-232; no. 10 (September

1952), 209-217; no. 12 (November 1952), 246-254; no. 14 (December 1952), 232-241.

Kinoshita, Naoe, "Katayama Sen Kun to Boku," *Chūō Kōron,* XLVIII, no. 12 (December 1933), 298-303.

Kublin, Hyman. "Kōtoku Shūsui no Ichi-Beijin Anakisuto e no Shokan-shū," *Shakai Kagaku Kenkyū,* IX, no. 1 (June 1957), 103-129.

Oka, Shigeki. "Katayama Sen to Amerika," *Kaizō,* XXXII, no. 8 (July 1951), 77-83.

Suzuki, Bunji. "Meiji Taishō Rōdō Undō-shi," in Shibusawa, Eiichi, *et al.* (ed.), *Meiji Taishō-shi.* 15 vols. Tokyo (1929-1930), III, 361-393.

Yamakawa, Hitoshi. "Katayama Sen Shi no Omoidashi," *Kaizō,* XV, no. 12 (December 1933), 92-102.

Yoshimura, Taishirō. "Tekisasu Nihon-jin," *Tobei Zasshi,* IX, no. 1 (January 3, 1905), 8-10.

SECONDARY SOURCES

Books in Western Languages

Abegglen, James C. *Japanese Factory: Aspects of the Social Organization.* Glencoe, Illinois, 1958.

Alexander, Robert J. *Communism in Latin America.* New Brunswick, 1957.

Allen, G. C. *Modern Japan and Its Problems.* London, 1928.

———. *A Short Economic History of Japan, 1867-1937.* London, 1946.

American Sociologist [A. Morgan Young]. *The Socialist and Labour Movement in Japan.* Kobe, 1921.

Anderson, Ronald S. *Japan, Three Epochs of Modern Education.* (U.S. Dept. of Health, Education, and Welfare, Bulletin 1959, No. 11). Washington, D.C., 1959.

Bainton, Roland H. *Yale and the Ministry; a History of Education for the Christian Ministry at Yale from the Founding in 1701.* New York, 1957.

Beals, Carleton. *Glass Houses, Ten Years of Free-Lancing.* Philadelphia, 1938.

Beardsley, Richard K., Hall, John W., and Ward, Robert E. *Village Japan.* Chicago, 1959.

Bellah, Robert N. *Tokugawa Religion; the Values of Pre-Industrial Japan.* Glencoe, Illinois, 1957.

Bennett, John W., Passin, Herbert, and McKnight, Robert K. *In Search of Identity; the Japanese Overseas Scholar in America and Japan.* Minneapolis, 1958.

Borkenau, Franz. *European Communism.* New York, 1953.

Borton, Hugh. *Japan's Modern Century.* New York, 1955.

Brown, Delmer M. *Nationalism in Japan; an Introductory Historical Analysis.* Berkeley, 1955.

Bryan, J. Ingram. *Japan from Within.* New York, 1924.

Colbert, Evelyn S. *The Left Wing in Japanese Politics.* New York, 1952.

Douglass, Truman O. *The Pilgrims of Iowa.* Boston, 1911.

Draper, Theodore. *The Roots of American Communism.* New York, 1957.

———. *American Communism and Soviet Russia.* New York, 1960.

Ebon, Martin. *World Communism Today.* New York, 1948.

Freeman, Joseph. *An American Testament; a Narrative of Rebels and Romantics.* New York, 1936.

Gankin, Olga, and Fisher, H. H. *The Bolsheviks and the World War; the Origins of the Third International.* Stanford, 1940.

Hall, John Whitney. *Tanuma Okitsugu, 1719-1788; Forerunner of Modern Japan.* Cambridge, Mass., 1955.

Harada, Shuichi. *Labor Conditions in Japan.* New York, 1928.

Hyndman, H. M. *The Awakening of Asia.* London, 1919.

Ichihashi, Yamato. *Japanese in the United States; a Critical Study of the Problems of the Japanese Immigrants and Their Children.* Stanford, 1932.

Iglehart, Charles W. *A Century of Protestant Christianity in Japan.* Tokyo, 1959.

Ike, Nobutaka. *The Beginnings of Political Democracy in Japan.* Baltimore, 1950.

Ishii, Ryosuke (ed.). *Japanese Legislation in the Meiji Era.* Translated by William J. Chambliss. Tokyo, 1958.

Kai, Miwa, and Yampolsky, Philip B. *Political Chronology of Japan, 1885-1957.* (Columbia University East Asian Institute Studies No. 5.) New York, 1957.

Kawakami, Karl Kiyoshi. *The Political Ideas of Modern Japan.* Iowa City, 1903.

Keene, Donald. *Living Japan; the Land, the People and Their Changing World.* Garden City, New York, 1959.

Kennedy, M. D. *The Changing Fabric of Japan.* London, 1930.

Kimura, Ki (ed.). *Japanese Literature; Manners and Customs in the Meiji-Taisho Era.* Translated and adapted by Philip Yampolsky. Tokyo, 1957.

Kishimoto, Hideo (ed.). *Japanese Religion in the Meiji Era.* Translated and adapted by John F. Howes. Tokyo, 1956.

Kosaka, Masaaki (ed.). *Japanese Thought in the Meiji Era.* Translated and adapted by David Abosch. Tokyo, 1958.

Kurzman, Dan. *Kishi and Japan: the Search for the Sun.* New York, 1960.

Levine, Solomon B. *Industrial Relations in Postwar Japan.* Urbana, Illinois, 1958.

Linebarger, Paul M. A., Chu, Djang, and Burks, Ardath W. *Far Eastern Government and Politics: China and Japan.* New York, 1954.

Lockwood, William W. *The Economic Development of Japan: Growth and Structural Change, 1868-1938.* Princeton, 1954.

Lyons, Eugene. *The Red Decade, the Stalinist Penetration of America.* Indianapolis, 1941.

Murray, Robert K. *Red Scare; a Study in National Hysteria, 1919-1920.* Minneapolis, 1955.

Nomad, Max. *Aspects of Revolt.* New York, 1959.

Norman, E. Herbert. *Japan's Emergence as a Modern State; Political and Economic Problems of the Meiji Period.* New York, 1940.

Omura, Bunji. *The Last Genro; the Statesman Who Westernized Japan.* Philadelphia, 1938.

Parsons, Herbert Collins. *A Puritan Outpost; a History of the Town and People of Northfield, Massachusetts.* New York, 1937.

Pooley, A. M. *Japan at the Crossroads.* New York, 1917.

Ransome, Stafford. *Japan in Transition.* New York, 1899.

Reischauer, Edwin O. *The United States and Japan.* Rev. ed. Cambridge, Mass., 1957.

Sansom, Sir George B. *Japan; a Short Cultural History.* Rev. ed. New York, 1943.

Scalapino, Robert. *Democracy and the Party Movement in Prewar Japan, the Failure of the First Attempt.* Berkeley, 1953.

Sheldon, Charles D. *The Rise of the Merchant Class in Tokugawa Japan, 1600-1868; an Introductory Survey.* Locust Valley, New York, 1958.

Smith, Thomas C. *Political Change and Industrial Development in Japan: Government Enterprise, 1868-1880.* Stanford, 1955.

———. *The Agrarian Origins of Modern Japan.* Stanford, 1959.

Smith, Warren W., Jr. *Confucianism in Modern Japan; a Study of Conservatism in Japanese Intellectual History.* Tokyo, 1959.

Stead, Alfred, *Great Japan.* New York, 1906.

Swearingen, Rodger, and Langer, Paul. *Red Flag in Japan; International Communism in Action, 1919-1951.* Cambridge, Mass., 1952.

Swisher, Jacob Armstrong. *Leonard Fletcher Parker.* Iowa City, 1927.

Takekoshi, Yosaburo. *Prince Saionji*. Kyoto, 1929.

Thomas, Winburn T. *Protestant Beginnings in Japan, the First Three Decades, 1859-1889*. Tokyo, 1959.

Uyehara, Cecil H. *Leftwing Social Movements in Japan; an Annotated Bibliography*. Tokyo, 1959.

Uyehara, George E. *The Political Development of Japan, 1867-1909*. New York, 1910.

Williams, Daniel Day. *The Andover Liberals; a Study in American Theology*. New York, 1941.

Wilson, Samuel T. *Chronicles of Maryville College; a Story of Altruism*. Maryville, Tenn., 1935.

Wolfe, Bertram D. *Three Who Made a Revolution*. New York, 1948.

Yanaga, Chitoshi. *Japan since Perry*. New York, 1949.

Young, A. Morgan. *Japan under Taisho Tenno, 1912-1926*. London, 1928.

ARTICLES IN WESTERN LANGUAGES

"Help Needed for Work in Japan," *International Socialist Review*, XVIII (March 1917), 569.

"Kingsley Kwan Opened," *Asylum Record*, I, no. 4 (April–May 1897), 9.

"Social Christianity—The Andover House Association," *Andover Review*, XVII, no. 97 (January 1892), 82-88.

"Social Settlements in Japan," *Outlook*, LVI, no. 9 (June 26, 1897), 511.

"Socialist Work among American Japanese," *International Socialist Review*, XVII (October 1916), 250.

"The Socialists of Japan and the War," *Comrade*, III, no. 11 (August 1904), 239.

"The Socialists of Japan to the Socialists of Russia," *Arena*, XXXII, no. 178 (September 1904), 322.

Apter, David A. "Lewis Corey: a Portrait of an American Radical," *Columbia Library Columns*, VIII, no. 2 (February 1959), 4-11.

Asari, Junshiro. "The Development of the Social Movement and Social Legislation in Japan," in Inazo Nitobe, *et al.*, *Western Influences in Modern Japan* (Chicago, 1931), pp. 307-341.

Bailey, Jackson H. "Prince Saionji and the Popular Rights Movement of the 1880's," *Journal of Asian Studies*, XXI, no. 1 (November 1961), 49-63.

Bell, Daniel. "The Background and Development of Marxian Socialism in the United States," in D. D. Egbert and S. Persons (eds.), *Socialism and American Life*, 2 vols., Princeton, 1952, pp. 215-405.

Burks, Ardath W. "Administrative Transition from *Han* to *Ken*: the Example of Okayama," *Far Eastern Quarterly*, XV, no. 3 (May 1956), 371-382.

Carter, J. "Factories of Osaka," *Economic Review*, XVIII, no. 2 (April 1908), 146-153.

Conroy, Hilary. "*Chōsen Mondai*: the Korean Problem in Meiji Japan," *American Philosophical Society, Proceedings*, C (October 1956), 443-454.

Dore, Ronald P. "The Meiji Landlord: Good or Bad?", *Journal of Asian Studies*, XVIII, no. 3 (May 1959), 343-355.

Feldman, Horace Z. "The Meiji Political Novel; a Brief Survey," *Far Eastern Quarterly*, IX, no. 3 (May 1950), 245-255.

Foxwell, E. "The Protection of Labour in Japan," *Economic Journal*, XI, no. 41 (March 1901), 106-124.

Gruliow, Leo. "Lenin and Lewis Corey (Louis Fraina)," *Columbia Library Columns*, VIII, no. 2 (February 1959), 12-15.

Harootunian, Harry D. "The Progress of Japan and the Samurai Class, 1868-1882," *Pacific Historical Review*, XXXVIII, no. 3 (August 1959), 255-266.

Hayakawa, Tetsuya. "The Necessity of Enacting a Law for Labourers," *Far East*, II, no. 12 (December 1897), 657-662.

Howland, A. H. "A Japanese Socialist Paper," New York *Call* (December 10, 1916), 8.

Humphreys, M. G. "Trade-unions in Japan," *Century Magazine*, LXI (April 1901), 892-897.

Ike, Nobutaka. "Triumph of the Peace Party in Japan in 1873," *Far Eastern Quarterly*, II, no. 3 (May 1942), 286-295.

———. "Kōtoku: Advocate of Direct Action," *Far Eastern Quarterly*, III, no. 3 (May 1944), 222-236.

Ishimoto, K. "Order Reigns in Soviet Russia," *Gale's Magazine*, II, no. 12 (July 1919), 5.

Jansen, Marius B. "Ōi Kentarō: Radicalism and Chauvinism," *Far Eastern Quarterly*, XI, no. 3 (May 1952), 305-316.

Johnson, Oakley C. "In Memoriam: Sen Katayama," *Political Affairs*, XXXVIII, no. 12 (December 1959), 42-48.

Kakehi, Mitsuaki. "Protestantism and Socialist Movement in Japan," *Contemporary Japan*, XVI, nos. 7-9 (July–September 1947), 285-291.

Kawakami, K. K. "Japanese on American Farms," *Independent*, LIX (October 26, 1905), 961-967.

Kellogg, D. O. "Ferdinand Lassalle, the Socialist," *Atlantic Monthly*, LXI, no. 4 (April 1888), 483-496.

Kublin, Hyman. "The Japanese Socialists and the Russo-Japanese War," *Journal of Modern History*, XXII, no. 4 (December 1950), 322-339.

———. "A Bibliography of the Writings of Sen Katayama in Western Languages," *Far Eastern Quarterly*, XI, no. 1 (November 1951), 71-77.

———. "The Origins of Japanese Socialist Tradition," *Journal of Politics*, XIV, no. 2 (May 1952), 257-280.

———. "Katayama Sen: the Birth of a Bolshevik," *Shakai Kagaku Tōkyū*, I, no. 2 (June 1956), 369-398.

———. "Takano Fusatarō: a Study in Early Japanese Trades-unionism," *American Philosophical Society, Proceedings*, CIII, no. 4 (August 15, 1959), 571-583.

Lebra, Joyce C. "Ōkuma Shigenobu and the 1881 Political

Crisis," *Journal of Asian Studies*, XVIII, no. 4 (August 1959), 475-487.

Lewis, Austin. "The 'Japanese Problem,'" *New Review*, III, no. 16 (November 1, 1915), 273-275.

Longuet, Jean. "Le socialisme au Japon," *La Revue*, L (May–June 1904), 281-299; 442-457.

McAlpine, E. W., "Russian and Japanese Socialists Join Hands despite Looming Clash," *The World* [Oakland, Calif.] (March 22, 1918), 1, 5.

Matsubara, I. *Darkest Tokyo*. Translated by Kimura Keinosuke. Yokohama, 1897. Originally published serially in the *Japan Evangelist*, I, no. 4 (April 1894) to III, no. 3 (February 1896).

Maybon, Albert. "Le socialisme au Japon," *Grande Revue*, CXIII (February 1924), 569-597.

Peterson, Burke C. "The Japan Communist Party, 1922-1945," *University of Michigan, Center for Japanese Studies, Occasional Papers*, I (1951), 7-25.

Powles, Cyril H. "Abe Isoo and the Role of Christians in the Founding of the Japanese Socialist Movement (1895-1905)," *Papers on Japan* (East Asian Research Center, Harvard University), I (1961), 89-129.

Pringle, J. C. "Labour in Japan," *Economic Review*, XX, no. 4 (October 1910), 387-405.

Redman, H. Vere. "Sen Katayama," *Contemporary Japan*, II, no. 4 (March 1934), 668-680.

Ronin, H. "Religious Indifference and Anarchism in Japan," *Westminster Review*, CLXXVI, no. 2 (August 1911), 154-163.

Shannon, David A. "The Socialist Party before the First World War: an Analysis," *Mississippi Valley Historical Review*, XXXVIII, no. 2 (September 1951), 279-288.

Silberman, B. L. "The Political Theory and Program of Yoshino Sakuzō," *Journal of Modern History*, XXXI, no. 4 (December 1959), 310-324.

Stead, Alfred. "Socialism in Japan," *Independent Review*, IV, no. 14 (November 1904), 244-259.

———. "Le socialisme au Japon," *Avenir Social*, x, no. 1 (January 1905), 14-20.

Takagi, Masayoshi. "Conditions of the Japanese Laborers," *Far East*, III, no. 4 (April 20, 1898), 290-297.

Watkins, Gordon S. "The Present Status of Socialism in the United States," *Atlantic Monthly*, CXXIV (December 1919), 821-830.

———. "Revolutionary Communism in the United States," *American Political Science Review*, XIV, no. 1 (February 1920), 14-33.

Weatherly, Arthur L. "Kingsley Hall, Tokyo, and Its Founder," *Commons*, II, no. 8 (December 1897), 1-3.

BOOKS IN JAPANESE LANGUAGE

Katayama Sen: Seitan Hyakunen wo Kinen shite, Zen'ei (Special Issue), no. 161 (November 1959).

Akamatsu, Katsumaro. *Nihon Rōdō Undō Hattatsu-shi*. Tokyo, 1925.

———. *Nihon Shakai Undō-shi*. Tokyo, 1955.

Arahata, Kanson. *Nihon Shakai Shugi Undō-shi*. Tokyo, 1948.

———. *Kyōsan-tō wo Meguru Hito-bito*. Tokyo, 1950.

Arakawa, Jitsuzō. *Katayama Sen; Sekai ni okeru Kare ga Chii to Taiken*. Tokyo, 1930.

Asahi, Shimbun-sha. *Meiji Taishō-shi*. 6 vols. Tokyo, 1930.

Hattori, Shisō. *Monogatari Nihon no Rōdō Undō*. Tokyo, 1953.

Hosokawa, Karoku, Watanabe Yoshimichi, and Shioda, Shōbei (eds.). *Nihon Shakai Shugi Bunken Kaisetsu*. Tokyo, 1958.

Hosotani, Matsuta. *Nihon Rōdō Undō-shi*. 2 vols. Tokyo, 1948-1949.

Ichikawa, Masaichi. *Nihon Kyōsan-tō Tōsō Shōshi*. Tokyo, 1955.

Ichinose, Masayuki. *Nihon Kyōsan-tō*. Tokyo, 1955.

Irimajiri, Yoshinaga. *Meiji Ishin-shi Kenkyū no Hatten.* Tokyo, 1949.

Itoya, Hisao. *Kōtoku Shūsui Den.* Kyoto, 1950.

Kada, Tetsuji. *Nihon Shoki Shakai Shisō no Kenkyū.* Tokyo, 1933.

Kaizō-sha. *Nihon Shakai Shugi Undō-shi. Shakai Kagaku,* IV, no. 1, Special Issue (February 1928). Tokyo, 1928.

Kaji, Ryūichi. *Meiji no Shakai Mondai.* Tokyo, 1955.

Katayama Sen Zenshū Henshū Iin-kai. *Katayama Sen Chosho Rombun Mokuroku.* Tokyo [1955?].

Kawai, Eijirō. *Meiji Shisō-shi no Ichi-Dammen: Kanai En wo Chūshin to Shite.* Tokyo, 1949.

Kishimoto, Eitarō. *Nihon Rōdō Undō-shi.* Tokyo, 1953.

Kishimoto, Eitarō. Watanabe, Haruo, and Koyama, Hirotake. *Katayama Sen.* 2 vols. Tokyo, 1959-1960.

Koyama, Hirotake. *Nihon Marukusu Shugi-shi.* Tokyo, 1956.

Kublin, Hyman. *Meiji Rōdō Undō-shi no Hito-koma; Takano Fusatarō no Shōgai to Shisō.* Tokyo, 1959.

Kyōchō-kai. *Saikin no Shakai Undō.* Tokyo, 1929.

Machida, Tatsujirō. *Nihon Shakai Hendō Shikan.* Tokyo, 1924.

Maruyama, Yugehei. *Yuge-machi Shi.* Yuge-machi, Okayama, 1954.

Matsumoto, Jin. *Meiji Taishō Showa Jijū-jin no Hatten.* 2 vols. Osaka, 1946.

Matsushita, Yoshio. *Hansen Undō-shi.* Tokyo, 1954.

Morito, Tatsuo. *Nihon ni okeru Kirisuto-kyō to Shakai Shugi Undō.* Tokyo, 1950.

Murayama, Shigetada. *Nihon Rōdō Sōgi-shi.* Tokyo, 1947.

Nakamura, Kikuo. *Kindai Nihon to Fukuzawa Yukichi.* Tokyo, 1953.

Nihon Kōgyō Kurabu, Chōsa-ka. *Nihon Kyōsan-tō Jiken Tem-matsu.* [Tokyo?], *ca.* 1930.

Noguchi, Yoshiaki. *Musan Undō So-tōshi Den.* Tokyo, 1931.

Ōhara Shakai Mondai Kenkyū-jo. *Nihon Shakai Shugi Bunken.* Tokyo, 1929.

Okayama-shi Kyōiku Iin-kai. *Okayama no Ayumi.* Okayama City, 1956.

Ōkōchi, Kazuo. *Reimei-ki no Nihon Rōdō Undō.* Tokyo, 1955.

———. *Sengo Nihon no Rōdō Undō.* Tokyo, 1955.

Sakisaka, Itsurō. *Kindai Nihon no Shisō-ka.* Tokyo, 1954.

Sanshō-dō Henshū-jo. *Nihon Rekishi Chizu.* Tokyo, 1939.

Sekine, Etsurō. *Rōdō Undō Musan Seitō-shi.* Tokyo, 1954.

Shirayanagi, Shūko. *Saionji Kimmochi Den.* Tokyo, 1929.

Sumiya, Etsuji. *Nihon Keizai-gaku Shi no Hito-koma: Shakai Seisaku Gakkai wo Chūshin to Shite.* Tokyo, 1948.

Sumiya, Mikio. *Katayama Sen.* Tokyo, 1960.

Tanaka, Sōgorō. *Kōtoku Shūsui; Ichi Kakumei-ka no Shisō to Shōgai.* Tokyo, 1955.

Taniguchi, Zentarō. *Nihon Rōdō Kumiai Hyōgi-kai Shi.* 2 vols. Tokyo, 1953-1954.

Watanabe, Haruo. *Nihon Marukusu Shugi Undō no Reimei.* Tokyo, 1957.

Watanabe, Kango. *Nihon Shakai Undō-shi.* Tokyo, 1955.

Watanabe, Yoshimichi, and Shioda, Shōbei. *Nihon Shakai Shugi Bunken Kaisetsu.* Tokyo, 1958.

Yamagiwa, Keiji. *Kinoshita Naoe; Ichi Senkaku-sha no Tatakai to Nayami.* Tokyo, 1955.

Yasuda Shin'ei and Ishigura Toshio (eds.). *Saikin Jūnen-kan ni okeru Shisō Kankei Shuppan-butsu Sōran.* Tokyo, 1933.

Yasuda, Tokutarō. *Hikari wo Ageta Hito-bito; Minshu Shugi-sha no Shisō to Shōgai.* Tokyo, 1956.

Yokomizo, Mitsuteru. *Nihon Shakai Shugi Undō-shi Kōwa.* Rev. ed., Tokyo, 1932.

Yokoyama, Gennosuke. *Nihon no Kasō Shakai.* Tokyo, 1955.

Articles in Japanese Language

Abe, Kozō. "Meiji Kōki ni okeru Kirisuto-kyō to Shakai Shugi," *Riron*, IV, no. 1 (January 1950), 1-13.

Asō, Hisashi. "Meiji Taishō Shakai Undō Shōshi," in Shibusawa, Eiichi *et al.*, *Meiji Taishō-shi*, 15 vols. Tokyo, 1929-1930, III, 328-360.

Amaha, Eiji. "Matsukata-San to Katayama Sen," *Soren Kenkyū*, II, no. 9 (December 1953), 2.

Doi, Takuji. "Katayama Sen no Tegami," *Okayama Shunjū*, VII, no. 6 (July 20, 1957), 4, 24-28.

Hayashi, Shigeru. "Nihon ni okeru Shakai Shugi Kenkyū Sōshiki no Shotai," *Shakai Kagaku Kenkyū*, I, no. 1 (February 1948), 58-100.

Kimura, Tsuyoshi. "Nihon Shakai Shugi-shi," *Shakai Mondai Kōza*, VII (1926), 1-26; VIII (1926), 27-50; IX (1926), 51-78; X (1926), 79-96; XI (1927), 97-116.

Kondō, Kenji. "Chinsen-ki Igo; Shakai Shugi Domei no Kaisan made," in *Nihon Shakai Shugi Undō-shi, Shakai Kagaku* (Special Issue), IV, no. 1 (February 1928), 162-174.

Miyakawa, Torao. "Katayama Sen to Tobari Kogan," *Rekishi Hyōron*, no. 102 (February 1959), 66-69.

Nakamura, Katsunori. "Ōsugi Sakae to Shakai Shugi," in *Keiō Gijuku Sōritsu Hyakunen Kinen Rombun-shū, Hōgaku-bu.* 3 vols. Tokyo, 1958, II, 387-411.

———. "Chokusetsu Kōdō-ron no Taitō; Kōtoku Shūsui no Riron wo Megutte," *Hōgaku Kenkyū*, XXXI, no. 10 (October 1958), 35-58.

———. "Suzuki Bunji to Taishō Rōdō Undō," *Hōgaku Kenkyū*, XXXII, no. 1 (January 1959), 43-67; XXXII, nos. 2-3 (March 1959), 139-163; XXXII, no. 6 (June 1959), 481-509.

———. "Shukan Shimbun *Chokugen* Sō-mokuji to Kaisetsu," *Hōgaku Kenkyū*, XXXII, no. 8 (August 1959), 46-66.

———. "Heimin-sha to Sono Zaisei Jijo" *Hōgaku Kenkyū*, XXXII, no. 12 (December 1958), 20-56.

———. "Heimin-sha no Kaisan to Dan'atsu," *Hōgaku Kenkyū*, XXXIII, no. 2 (February 1960), 521-541.

———. "*Hikari* Sō-mokuji to Kaisetsu," *Hōgaku Kenkyū*, XXXIII, no. 6 (June 1960), 39-60.

Ōkōchi, Kazuo. "Rōdō," in Yanaihara Tadao, *Gendai Nihon Shōshi.* 2 vols. Tokyo, 1952, II, 111-214.

Sugiyama, Sakae. "Kyōri ni okeru Katayama Sen Shi," *Meiji Bunka Kenkyū,* I (February 1934), 132-134.

Susuki, Shigeto. "Seiji Kenkyū-kai no Rekishi-teki Nimmu," in *Nihon Shakai Shugi Undō-shi, Shakai Kagaku* (Special Issue), IV, no. 1 (February 1928), 316-324.

Yamanabe, Kentarō. "Nihon no Marukusu Shugi: Sono Hatten no Rekishi to Bunken," *Shisō,* no. 7 (July 1956), 75-101.

———. "Katayama Sen," *Nihon Jimbutsu-shi Taikei,* VI, no. 2 (Modern Series). Tokyo, 1960, 293-324.

INDEX

Abe, Isoo, 132n, 133n, 144-145, 178n, 198, 209
"adopted husband," *see yoshi*
Airin-sha, 97
Alameda, 50-52
All-Russian Communist Party, 333
American Bureau, *see* Third International
American Communist Party, 269
American Federation of Labor, 109, 111, 115
American Socialist Party, 163, 222, 242, 266-267; national convention (1904), 165
Amerika, 186n, 187n
Amsterdam Congress, *see* Second International, Sixth Congress
Andover House, 82
Andover Review, 79
Andover Theological Seminary, 52-53
Ankoku Jidai, 139
antiprostitution campaign in Japan, 135
Aono, Suekichi, 303
Aoyama-jō Gakuin, 334
"April Raids" (1929), 331
Arahata, Kanson, 273, 301; helps found Japan Communist Party, 293-294; in prison, 312; and Shanghai Thesis, 303
Association for Universal Suffrage, 143
Atlantic Monthly, publishes article by Katayama, 71
August "Rice Riots" in Japan, 252-253, 272
Autobiography, *see Jiden*

Bankoku Shakai-tō, 187
Barbers' Union, 143
Bebel, August, 179
"Bethink Yourselves," 172
Bismarck, Otto von, 71, 72
Bitchū, 5
Bizen, 5
Blatchford, Robert, 179-180n
Borodin, Michael, 280, 284, 306
Boudin, Louis, 240
Bukharin, Nikolai, 239n, 240, 243, 320-321

California, discrimination against Japanese, 216ff
Cary, Otis, 78
Charter Oath, 47
Cherry Blossom Picnic Affair, 121-122
Chiang Kai-shek, 305, 323-324
Chiba Prison, Katayama jailed in, 211
Chokugen, publication launched, 180-181; discontinued, 198
Chōsen Mondai, 158
Chou En-lai, 306
Christian missionaries in Japan, 30, 44
Christian Socialism, of Katayama, Sen, 133-134; of Richard T. Ely, 70-71
Class Struggle, 244
Comintern, *see* Third International
Communist International, *see* Third International
Communist Manifesto, 145; Japanese translation of, 179
Concord Reformatory School, 84
Confucian classics, 25, 37
Congregational Church, 51-52, 53
Congregational Mission in Japan, 96
Corey, Lewis, *see* Fraina, Louis

Dai Nihon Rōdō Sōdōmei, 308
Day Laborers' Union, 228n
Debs, Eugene V., 222
De Leon, Daniel, 174n, 263
Denton, Florence, 98
Department of International Propaganda, *see* Third International
Deutsch, L. G., 179-180n
Diaz, Porfirio, 283-284
Doshi-kai, 201
Doshisha University, 78, 92n
Draper, Theodore, 283
Dutch Communist Party, 236
Dutch Socialist Party, 232

Edo, in Tokugawa period, 33

Eikoku Konnichi no Shakai, 94
Ely, Richard T., 70, 145
Engels, Frederick, 145, 179, 179-180n

Fabian Society, 133, 145
Factory Law in Japan (1911), 128
Farmer-Labor Party, organization and suppression, 310
Farmers' Union, *see Nihon Nōmin Kumiai*
First Congress of Communist Organizations of the East, 276
First Congress of the Toilers of the Far East, planning for, 274; proceedings, 290ff
Fraina, Louis, 7, 34n, 240, 244, 280-281; early years, 262ff; anarcho-syndicalist tendencies, 264-265; efforts to found Communist Party in U.S., 268ff, 271; publishes writings of Lenin, 265; in Mexico, 281ff; leaves Communist movement, 285
Friends of Labor, *see Shokkō Giyū-kai*
Fujioka, 45-46
Fukao, Shō, 191
Fukumoto, Kazuo, rise to prominence, 311ff; recantation, 313
"Fukumotoism," *see* Fukumoto, Kazuo
Fukuzawa, Yukichi, 43
Fuyu no Jidai, 225-226n

General Federation of Labor, *see Dai Nihon Rōdō Sōdōmei*
"Gentlemen's Agreement," 216
Glasgow, 84
Gompers, Samuel, 109, 112
Gordon, Marquis L., 78, 97
Goshiki, meeting of Japan Communist Party, 312-313, 315
Greene, Daniel C., 78, 96
Greene, Mrs. Daniel C., 98
Grinnell College, 59, 62ff

Hadeki, 6, 30, 32, 90; history of, 8; during Katayama's childhood, 16; impact of early Meiji reforms, 23
Hara, Nobuko, 219, 281
Hara, Tama, *see* Katayama, Tama
Harper's Monthly, 84, 94
Hartt, Rollin Lynde, 83
Hashimoto, Junzō, 185-186
Hatzfeld, Countess von, 71
Hechima no Hana, 225-226n
Heimin, 230ff
Heimin-sha, 162, 171-172, 177-178, 181
Heimin Shimbun, founding of, 162: antiwar program, 163ff; attacks war policies of state, 167ff; closed by police, 179-180; discontinued, 180
Heller, 303
Hi no Hashira, 168, 169n
"High Treason Case," *see Taigyaku Jiken*
Higuchi, Den, 191
Hikari, 198
Hillquit, Morris, 268
Hirotsu, Tomonobu, 78n
Hokubei Shimbun, 230-231
Hoover, J. Edgar, 272
Hopkins Academy, 53-54, 58
Hotel Luxe, 289-290
Hotel Northfield, 76, 77
Hoyt, 51-52, 55
Humbert-Droz, Jules, 319n
Hyndman, H. M., 215-216
Hyōgi-kai, see Nihon Rōdō Kumiai Hyōgi-kai

Ichikawa, *Shōichi*, 327
Imperial rescript on constitutional government, 44
Imperial Restoration, *see* Meiji Restoration
industrialism in Japan, 108
Inomata, Tsunao, 250
International Press Correspondence, 333
International Socialist Review, 209, 222, 229, 237, 244-245
Internationalist, 237
i-ro-ha, 24
Ishigaki, Eitarō, 250, 257n
Ishikawa, Sanshirō, 198
Iskra, 171

Itagaki, Taisuke, 44
Itō, Hirobumi, 68
Iwasaki, Seishichi, 41, 43ff, 89, 104, 193; financial aid to Katayama, 66; as match-maker for Katayama, 103; cares for Katayama's children, 189
Iwasaki, Yatarō, 41

Japan Communist Party, 254; preparation for founding of, 274ff; discussed at First Congress of the Toilers of the Far East, 292-293; founded, 293-294; initial program, 295ff; attacked by police, 299ff; disbandment, 301ff; Third Congress, 312-313; tactics in 1927 Shanghai Thesis, 313ff; in national elections of 1927, 325-326; assault upon in "March Raids," 326ff; tactics after "March Raids," 328ff; driven underground, 330ff; revival after World War II, 339
Japan Farmers' Union, *see Nihon Nōmin Kumiai*
Japan Railway Company, 120
Japanese emigrants to United States, 47-48
Jaurès, Jean, 175n
Jiden, begun by Katayama, 211; completion of, 256ff; as source for Yabuki family history, 10n; for image of Katayama as child, 18; Katayama's account of *Keikoku Bidan*, 40; description of Katayama's work at San Raphael, 50; discrepancies in, 7-8, 54n; inaccuracies in Chronology, 75n, 76n, 184-185n, 187n, 194n
Jimmu, 4
Jō, Tsunetarō, 105, 109, 110-111, 114-115
Johnson, Carl, 280, 284-285

Kaben, 198
Kalinin, Mikhail, 286, 291
Kamenev, Lev, 320-321
Kanai, En, 136, 137-138
Kanda, Saichirō, 51-52
Kanda YMCA, 58
Katayama, Chiyoko, 61n; birth, 197; joins father in Moscow, 333-334
Katayama, Fude, 103, 104, 184
Katayama, Ikutarō, 29
Katayama, Kan'ichi, 197; birth, 104; death, 221
Katayama, Sen, *see* also Yabuki family,
Yabuki, Sugatarō, and Katayama Ikutarō
life: birth, 5, 6, 12-13; name by adoption, 7, 29; date of birth, 7n; childhood rivalries, 19; feminine influences, 18-19; as peasant boy, 22, 26-27; relations with natal father, 18, 25; grievances with Yabuki, 13; views on Meiji Restoration, 16, 38; illnesses, 30-31, 45-46, 96, 334ff; decision to leave home, 31; printer's apprentice, 35ff; cook, 50; physical description, 60-62; personality, 42-43; convert to Christianity, 51ff, 66, 75-76; first marriage, 103-104; second marriage, 197; writing of *Jiden*, 211, 256ff; theorist, 73; death, 335; funeral, 337ff; monuments to, 9, 39
education: beginning of schooling, 24-25, 26; studies Confucian classics, 27-28, 37, 50; at *Oka Juku*, 36ff; at *Kodama-sha*, 38ff; Hopkins Academy, 53-54; Maryville College, 55ff; Grinnell College, 62ff; Andover Theological Seminary, 74, 77ff; Yale Divinity School, 85ff
teaching career: at Yuge, 28; at Uetsuki, 28; Fujioka, 45; Waseda Preparatory School, 95ff; Kingsley Hall, 99ff
travels: leaves Okayama, 34; first journey to United States, 46ff, 49; visit to England, 83ff; home-coming, 88ff; at Hayama, 93; second trip

to United States, 163ff; third trip to United States, 194; in Texas, 165, 178, 185ff; in Amsterdam, 173ff; fourth trip to United States, 213-214; World War I years in California, 218ff; in Mexico, 281ff; tour of China, 305ff

socialism and trade-unionism: Christian Socialism, 133-134; early interest in socialism, 69-70; promotion of socialism, 151-152; joins trade-union movement, 113ff; trade-union organizer, 116ff; editor of *Rōdō Sekai*, 119ff; antiwar views, 161, 165ff, 177ff, 238-239n; shift to Marxism, 154-155; at Second International, Sixth Congress, 173-174, 184; break with Nishikawa Kōjirō, 201-203; involvement in Tokyo Streetcar Strike, 209ff; position on California Alien Land Laws, 217ff; publisher of *Heimin*, 230-231

Communism: encounters with Bolshevism, 241-242, 265-267; attack against Morris Hillquit, 269-270; organizes Japanese in New York, 249ff; plans to found Japan Communist Party, 274-275; flight to Atlantic City, 261-264; version of Lenin's *State and Revolution*, 265-266; leaves Mexico for Russia, 286-287; relations with Lenin, 321; as propagandist for Third International, 294ff; member of American Bureau, 280ff; at First Congress of the Toilers of the Far East, 290-292; place in Third International, 275ff, 317ff; member of Executive Committee of Third International, 318ff; at Third International, Fourth Congress, 295ff; at Fifth Congress, 302; at Sixth Congress, 331-332; member of "Old Bolshevik Club," 333

Katayama, Tama, 197; abandons Sen, 221

Katayama, Yasuko, 197, 281; birth, 104; trip to United States, 218-219; joins father in Moscow, 334

Katō, Hiroyuki, 130

Katō, Takaaki, 310

Katō, Tokijirō, 191

Katsura, Tarō, 147, 169, 175n, 183, 189ff, 204ff

Kawakami, Kiyoshi, 133n, 135, 144, 164, 176

Keikoku Bidan, 40

Keio University, 43, 44

Kelsey, Carl, 84

Kerr, Charles H., 222, 229, 233n, 245

Kibi no Kuni, 4

Kienthal Conference, 238n

kindergartens in Japan, 99ff

Kingsley Hall, 82, 96ff, 116, 135n

Kinoshita, Naoe, 135, 144, 152-153; joins *Heimin Shimbun*, 168; as political candidate, 181

Kinyō-kai, 203

Kishi, Nobusuke, 31

Kiyota family, 10n

Kiyota, Jakusen, *see* Koyō, Kunizō

Kodama-sha, 38ff, 43

Kokumin no Tomo, 102

Kol, Henri Van, 173-174

Kollontai, Alexandra, 239-240, 243

Kondō, Eizō, 250, 302, 305; return to Japan after World War I, 254, 272; efforts to found Communist Party in Japan, 273ff; arrest, 293

Koreans in Japan, 300

Kōtoku, Shūsui, 133n, 147; joins socialist movement, 143-144; anti-Christian views, 152-153; resigns from *Yorozu Chōhō*, 162; writer for *Heimin Shimbun*, 168ff; rejoinder to Tolstoi, 172; release from prison, 182; meets Katayama in San Francisco, 188; shift to anarchism, 188; at first annual meeting of *Nihon Shakai-tō*, 194ff; involvement in *Tai-*

gyaku Jiken, 207ff; execution, 208
Koyō, Kunihei, *see* Koyō, Kunizō
Koyō, Kunizō, family village, 10-11; first marriage, 12; divorce from Yabuki, Kichi, 13-14; becomes priest, 14; second marriage, 14
Kozaki, Hiromichi, 130
Kropotkin, Peter A., 179, 179-180n
Kumiai Church, 91, 92, 95, 116
Kun, Bela, 253
Kuomintang, 306, 322-324
Kuroiwa, Ruikō, 159-160
Kuusinen, Ottomar, 319n
Kuwata Kumazō, 136, 138
Kyōsei-kai, 120

labor agitation in Japan, 119ff
labor conditions in Japan, 124
Labor-Farmer Party, 325-326, 327, 329
labor legislation in Japan, 124ff
The Labor Movement in Japan, 244ff
labor unrest in Japan, 107-108, 109
Labor World, see Rōdō Sekai
Lassalle, Ferdinand, 71-72, 95, 145
Learned, Dwight W., 131n
Lenin, N., 236, 238-239n, 289
Liebknecht, Karl, 253
Lore, Ludwig, 239ff
Lunarcharski, A. V., 286
Luxemburg, Rosa, 253

Macaulay, Clay, 233
Mamiya, Sueyoshi, 250
Manchuria, 158
Mao Tse-tung, 306
"March Raids," 326-327
Martens, Ludwig, 277
Maryville College, 52, 55ff
Maryville College YMCA, 58
Marx, Karl, 72, 145, 177, 179, 179-180n
Matsumura, Kaisuke, 114
Meiji Constitution, 68
Meiji Emperor, 23, 47
Meiji oligarchs, 23, 44, 68, 130, 160
Meiji reforms, 33-34, 37, 106
Meiji Restoration, 23
Methodist Episcopal Chinese Mission, 49, 51
Mexico, revolutionary movement, 283ff
Millerand, Alexander, 150
Mimisaka, 16
Minseitō, 326
missionary work in Japan, 91-92, 97
Mitsubishi holding company, 41
Mizuno family, 14
Mizuno, 233n
momiji, 21
Moody, Dwight L., 75
Mori Ōson, 45, 89
Morichika Umpei, 199n, 203
Mount Hermon School, 75
Mukyō-kai, 136

Nabeyama, Sadachika, 330-331n
Naigai Shimpō, 150
Naitō, Kansaburō, 261
Nakae, Chōmin, 143n
national elections in Japan (1927), 325ff
National Readers, 50
Neue Rheinische Zeitung, 180
Die Neue Zeit, 209
New Economic Program, 289
New International, 244, 248
New Review, 237
Nihon Heimin-tō, 191
Nihon Nōmin Kumiai, 310
Nihon Rōdō Kumiai Hyōgi-kai, 308-309, 327, 329
Nihon Shakai-tō, 191ff; first annual meeting, 194ff; suppression by state, 196-197
Niijima, Jō, 78
Nikaidō, Umekichi, 232
Nikkan Heimin, 197, 198-199
"1927 Thesis," 313-314
Nippon Railroad Workers' Union, 143
Nishikawa, Kōjirō, 179n; joins *Heimin Shimbun*, 168; jailed, 180; organizer of *Nihon Heimin-tō*, 191; writer for *Hikari*, 198; helps found *Shakai Shimbun*, 199; break with Katayama, 201ff

Nomad, Max, 199
Nonaka, Masayuki, 230, 232, 233n, 250
Northfield, Mass., 75-76
Northfield Seminary for Young Ladies, 75
Nozaka, Sanzō, 332; in prison, 312; arrested in "March Raids," 327; successor of Katayama, 337n

Ō-Bei no Tōshi Mondai, see "Urban Problems in Europe and America"
Ojii-san, 43
Oka Juku, 36, 37, 41, 43, 45
Oka, Shigeki, 187-188, 230
Oka, Shikamon, 38, 41, 45
Okayama City, 4, 29, 30
Okayama Normal School, 29-30, 31, 34, 46n
Okayama Prefecture, 3, 4, 5-6
Okazaki Tsuneyoshi, 187ff, 193ff
Okuma Shigenobu, 44, 68, 125
"Old Bolshevik Club," 333
Ōsaka Heimin, 200
Ōsugi, Sakae, 273; murdered, 301
"Ota Incident," 220-221n
Outlook, 70
Oxford House, 83
Ōyama Ikuo, 325-326

Palmer Raids, 260, 261ff, 271ff, 278
Parker, Leonard, 63, 87
Parker, Mrs. Leonard, 67
peasant uprisings in Japan, 16
Perry, Commodore Matthew C., 47
Plekhanov, Georgii, 173-174
police regulations, 45
Profintern, *see* Red International of Trade Unions
Proudhon, Pierre, 145
Public Peace Preservation Law, 1887, 140; 1900, 138ff, 142; socialist opposition, 195; 1925, 304; 1928 revisions, 327

Radek, Karl, 286
Radical Review, 244
"Red Flag Affair," 203-204, 206
Red International of Trade-Unions, 284, 333
"Red Scare," *see* Palmer Raids
Reed, John, 246, 268; helps found Communist Labor Party, 271
Revolutionary Age, 244
rice planting in Japan, 19-20
Rikugo Zasshi, 95, 101, 102
Robbins, H. H., 63, 66
Rōdō Kumiai Kisei-kai, 115ff, 119ff, 124ff, 127-128
Rōdō Sekai, 119, 124, 127, 139, 142, 146; discontinuance, 150; resumption of publication, 150
Roy, M. N., 280, 284, 275, 318n, 319n
Rutgers, S. J., 262, 275-276, 278-279; invites Katayama to New York, 232-233; employer of Katayama, 235ff; revolutionary background, 236-237; leaves New York for Russia, 248
Ruthenberg, Charles E., 268

Saionji, Prince Kimmochi, 183, 204; policy toward radicals, 190ff
Sakai, Toshihiko, 178, 273; joins socialist movement, 143-144, 147; editor of *Heimin Shimbun*, 162; attacks war program of state, 168ff; sentenced to jail, 169; helps organize *Nihon Shakai-tō*, 191; at first annual meeting of *Nihon Shakai-tō*, 195-196; imprisonment after "Red Flag Affair," 204; visited by S. J. Rutgers, 276; helps found Japan Communist Party, 293-294; urges liquidation of Japan Communist Party, 301-302; leaves Japan Communist Party, 303
Sakai, Yusaburō, 130, 173n
Sakuma, Teiichi, 113-114
Salvation Army, 83
San Francisco Labor Council, 224
San Raphael, *see Jiden*
Sano, Fumio, 303-304
Sano, Manabu, 302, 319n, 327, 332; leaves Japan Communist Party, 330-331n

Sankey, Ira D., 76
Satsuma Rebellion, 44
Sawada, Hannosuke, 105, 109, 110-111, 115
Second International, Sixth Congress, 163-164
Seiji Kenkyū-kai, 309-310
Seiyū-kai, 191, 326
Sekibun-sha, 35-36, 37-38
Shakai Minshu-tō, founding, 144; program, 145; suppression, 146-147
Shakai Seisaku Gakkai, 136-137, 138
Shakai Shimbun, 199ff
Shakai Shugi, 151
Shakai Shugi Kenkyū-kai, 129, 132ff, 135, 143
Shakai Shugi Kyōkai, 148ff, 162, 197
Shakai Shugi Shinzui, 152-154
Shakai Zasshi, 102
Shanghai textile workers' strike, 306
Shanghai Thesis, 303, 307
Shimada Saburō, 113, 115, 121
Shimo-Kamime, 29
Shiga, Yoshio, 327, 338-339n
Shin Kigen, 198
Shin Shakai, 225-226n, 230
Shin Shakai, by Yano Fumio, 40n
Shokkō Giyū-kai, 109-110, 112-113, 114
Shokkō Shokun ni Yokosu, 105, 111-112, 120
Sino-Japanese War, 157
The Social Aspects of Christianity, 70
social Christianity, 81
socialism in early Meiji Japan, 130ff
Socialist Association, *see Shakai Shugi Kyōkai*
Socialist League, 273
Socialist Propaganda League, 237, 244
Society for the Promotion of Trade-Unions, *see Rōdō Kumiai Kisei-kai*
Sōdōmei, *see Dai Nihon Rōdō Sōdōmei*
Sombart, Werner, 179-180n
South End Settlement House, 82, 97
Special Higher Police in Japan, 330
Stalin, Joseph, 320-321
State and Revolution, Spanish edition, 286
streetcar fares in Tokyo, 193
strikes in Meiji Japan, 140
strikes in Taishō Japan, 227, 254, 296-297
Stratnievas, 88-89
Suematsu, Baron, 146
Suga-chan, *see* Yabuki Sugatarō
Sugita Kinnosuke, 87-88, 92
A Summons to the Worker, *see Shokkō Shokun ni Yokosu*
Sun-Joffe Agreement, 306
Sun Yat-sen, 228, 306, 323
Suzuki, Bunji, 223ff, 308
Suzuki, Junichirō, 113

Tacoma, 88
Taguchi, Unzō, 250, 261n, 281, 290
Taigyaku Jiken, 207ff
Taiyō, 95, 102
Takahashi, Kamekichi, 251
Takahashi, Ken, 57-58
Takano, Fusatarō, 105, 109-110; writes *A Summons to the Worker*, 111-112; efforts to establish trade-unions, 113; officer of *Rōdō Kumiai Kisei-kai*, 115-116; organizes cooperative store, 128; retires from trade-union movement, 141
Takase, Kiyoshi, 293, 295
Tanaka, Giichi, 326-327, 328
Tazoe, Tetsuji, 195-196, 202
Teikoku Shugi, 152, 161
Tekkō Kumiai, 119-120, 121, 123, 150
terakoya, 24-25
Tetsudō Shinron, 94
Texas, Japanese emigrants in, 185ff
Third International, founding, 267, 272, 333; First Congress, 276-277; Department of International Propaganda, 276; Second Congress, 278, 288; American Bu-

reau, 280, 282; Third Congress, 281, 284; Fourth Congress, 295ff; Fifth Congress, 302; Sixth Congress, 329ff
To-bei Annai, 99
Tobei Zasshi, 184-185n, 186-187
Tokuda, Kyūichi, 293; and Shanghai Thesis, 303; in prison, 312; arrested in "March Raids," 327
Tokugawa, Ieyasu, 5
Tokugawa Shogunate, founding, 5; decline and fall, 15-16
Tokutomi, Sohō, 130
Tokyo, riots after Russo-Japanese War, 182
Tokyo Earthquake, 300
Tokyo Shakai Shimbun, 201
Tokyo Streetcar Strike, 210-211
Tolstoi, Leon, 172, 179, 179-180n
Toynbee Hall, 82-83
Tōyō Keizai Shimbun, 251
Tōyō Keizai Shimpō, 209, 212
"Tribunists," 236
Treaty of Portsmouth, 176n, 182
Trotsky, Leon, 239n, 320-321; meets Katayama, 240; leaves United States, 243; greets Katayama in Moscow, 286
Tsuyama, 8, 90
Tucker, William Jewett, 81-82

Uchimura, Kanzō, 136, 161-162, 162n
"unequal treaties," 68
Unitarian Church, 101, 104
Universal Suffrage Law, 304-305; effect on political parties, 309ff
"Urban Problems in Europe and America," 86

Vandervelde, 150-151
Victoria, 88
village headmen, 9-10
Voitinski, Grigorii, 302-303
Volkszeitung, 171

Waga Shakai Shugi, 153-155
Waseda Preparatory School, 92-93
Watanabe, Haruo, 250
Watanabe, Masanosuke, 319n, 332
Weatherly, Arthur L., 75n, 80, 81, 100
winter in Japan, 22
Woods, Robert Archey, 82-83
Woodstock Convention, 285

Yabuki family, 7; homestead, 8-9; graves, 9; descent, 8, 10ff; "lost generation," 10n; decline in fortunes, 26
Yabuki, Kichi, birth, 11; marriage, 12; influence upon Sen, 17; death, 73
Yabuki, Kichiyo, *see* Yabuki, Kichi
Yabuki, Kichizaemon, 10-11; wife of, 10
Yabuki, Mansaburō, birth, 11; legal heir of Yabuki family, 14; cares for Sen, 17
Yabuki, Matsu, 11, 12, 17
Yabuki, Mokutarō, 11, 12, 17
Yabuki, Noe, 10
Yabuki, Sugatarō, *see* Katayama, Sen
Yabuki, Yoshitarō, 11
Yale Divinity School, 84, 85ff
Yale University, 48, 59
Yamaguchi, Yoshizō, 198
Yamaji, Aizan, 138
Yamakawa, Hitoshi, 99n, 204, 273, 291ff, 303; urges liquidation of Japan Communist Party, 301-302; tradeunion activities, 311
Yamamoto, Kenzō, 327
Yano, Fumio, 40
Yokodzuka, Fude, *see* Katayama, Fude
Yokohama, 34, 46
Yokohama *Advertiser*, 105, 109, 141
Yorozu Chōhō, 152, 159, 161
yoshi, 11, 12
Yuai-kai, 223-224, 308
Yuge, 8, 90

Zetkin, Clara, 319n
Zimmerwald Conference, 236-237
Zinoviev, Grigorii, 286, 291-292, 320-321
Zola, Emile, 150, 179-180n